T0100520

Haptic Interaction: Science, Engineering and Design

Haptic Interaction: Science, Engineering and Design

Edited by Natalia Roberts

www.clanryeinternational.com

Clanrye International,
750 Third Avenue, 9th Floor,
New York, NY 10017, USA

ISBN: 978-1-64726-589-2

Cataloging-in-publication Data

Haptic interaction : science, engineering and design / edited by Natalia Roberts.
p. cm.
Includes bibliographical references and index.
ISBN 978-1-64726-589-2
1. Haptic devices. 2. User interfaces (Computer systems). 3. Human-computer interaction.
4. Engineering. 5. Computer science. 6. Computer input-output equipment. I. Roberts, Natalia.
QA76.9.H85 H37 2023
004.019--dc23

For information on all Clanrye International publications
visit our website at www.clanryeinternational.com

Contents

Preface

Haptics is a kind of human-computer interaction technology that uses tactile feedback or other physiological sensations to guide activities or processes in a computer. A haptic interface refers to a type of system that enables human beings to interact with computers using movements and bodily sensations. It is most commonly used in virtual reality settings, where people can interact with virtual items and elements. It uses specially designed sensors to transmit an electrical signal to the computer in response to various sensory movements or interactions. The computer interprets each electrical signal in order to carry out an action or process. The haptic interface, in turn, transmits a signal to the human body or organ in the form of rapid movement and vibration. This book explores the science, engineering and design aspects of haptic interaction in the present day scenario. It is appropriate for students seeking detailed information in this area as well as for experts.

All of the data presented henceforth, was collaborated in the wake of recent advancements in the field. The aim of this book is to present the diversified developments from across the globe in a comprehensible manner. The opinions expressed in each chapter belong solely to the contributing authors. Their interpretations of the topics are the integral part of this book, which I have carefully compiled for a better understanding of the readers.

At the end, I would like to thank all those who dedicated their time and efforts for the successful completion of this book. I also wish to convey my gratitude towards my friends and family who supported me at every step.

Editor

1

A Proposal and Investigation of Displaying Method by Passive Touch with Electrostatic Tactile Display

Hirobumi Tomita[1(✉)], Satoshi Saga[2], Shin Takahashi[1], and Hiroyuki Kajimoto[3]

[1] University of Tsukuba, 1-1-1 Tennodai, Tsukuba, Ibaraki, Japan
tomita@iplab.cs.tsukuba.ac.jp, shin@cs.tsukuba.ac.jp
[2] Kumamoto University, 2-39-1, Kurokami, Chuo-ku, Kumamoto, Japan
saga@saga-lab.org
[3] The University of Electro-Communications, 1-5-1, Chofugaoka, Chofu, Tokyo, Japan
kajimoto@kaji-lab.jp

Abstract. In the field of tactile displays, electrostatic force displays have been developed for presenting tactile stimulation on a screen. However, with the conventional electrostatic force displays, the user cannot feel the stimulation without rubbing on the display. In this paper, to solve this problem, we propose a new method to present a tactile sensation without moving a finger by creating a small space between an electrode and an insulating surface. Moreover, we evaluate the perceived threshold of the proposed display through the experiment.

Keywords: Electrostatic tactile display · Passive touch · Conductive thread

1 Introduction

In the field of tactile displays, electrostatic force displays have been developed for presenting tactile stimulation on a screen. The electrostatic tactile display consists of a high-voltage generator, an electrode, and an insulator. In this method, the user touches the insulating film on the electrode. If high voltage is applied to the electrode, he/she feels the tactile stimulation by rubbing on the film. In the 1950s, Mallinckrodt et al. discovered that a phenomenon such as vibration-like friction was generated through an insulating film by electrostatic force [5]. Related surveys, dealing with parameters like the effect of input frequencies, waveforms, or amplitude modulations were conducted by many researchers [1,3,4,7,9].

However, in this method, the tactile stimulation is not presented when the user stops moving the finger, and there is little research on displaying the method by passive touch with an electrostatic tactile display. Pyo et al. developed the tactile display, which generates electrovibration and mechanical vibration by using the electrostatic parallel plate actuator [6]. This device enables passive touch with electrostatic force, however, it requires a voltage higher than 1 kV.

In this paper, we propose a new method to present tactile sensation without moving a finger; we also implement and evaluate a device applying the proposed method. If passive tactile presentation becomes possible by this technique, the range of applications of tactile presentation using electrostatic force will be widely expanded.

2 Implementation of Device for Passive Touch with Electrostatic Tactile Display

The electrostatic tactile display consists of a high-voltage generator, an electrode, and an insulator. In the conventional method, an insulating film covers a flat electrode shown in Fig. 1 (a), and a user moves his/her finger on the insulator. When a high voltage is applied to the electrode, the dielectric polarization is generated in the finger. In this state, the electrode applies an attractive static force to the finger. When the user slides his/her finger on the display, s/he feels a tactile stimulation. However, when the user does not slide his/her finger on the display, s/he cannot perceive the tactile sensation.

Here, we proposed a method that employs a parallel-plate electrostatic actuator mechanism [2,6] for displaying tactile stimulation to a stationary finger without significantly changing the configuration of the electrostatic tactile display. Figure 1 (b) shows the schematic sketch of the parallel-plate electrostatic actuator to generate mechanical vibration. The stationary electrode and non-stationary electrode are set in parallel. When high-voltage is applied to the stationary electrode, the attractive electrostatic force occurs on the non-stationary electrode. We considered that a passive tactile presentation was possible by adopting Pyo et al.'s method [6]. The finger is considered as the non-stationary electrode. We created a small space by using cylindrical electrodes, which have a small diameter, such as a conductive thread or wire, as shown in Fig. 1 (c, d). In this paper, we used 120 μm diameter stainless steel fiber as a conductive thread. These threads were arranged lengthwise without any gaps between them on PET resin (Fig. 2 (b)). The width of these threads arranged is 25 mm to allow enough space for one finger. All of these threads are conductive. They are connected to the high voltage generator. Then, we covered them with a polyvinylidene chloride insulation film. This insulating film is inexpensive and easy to replace. The thickness of this insulating film is 11 μm.

We considered that the slight vibration of the insulating film and finger surface became possible by applying periodic high-voltage from the high-voltage generator to the cylindrical electrode, and the vibration could be perceived by the finger. The high-voltage generator shown in Fig. 2 (c) is developed by Kajimoto laboratory (The University of Electro-Communications, Tokyo). The device includes an mbed LPC1768 microcontroller, which controls the output voltage at a maximum of 600 V by modifying the firmware.

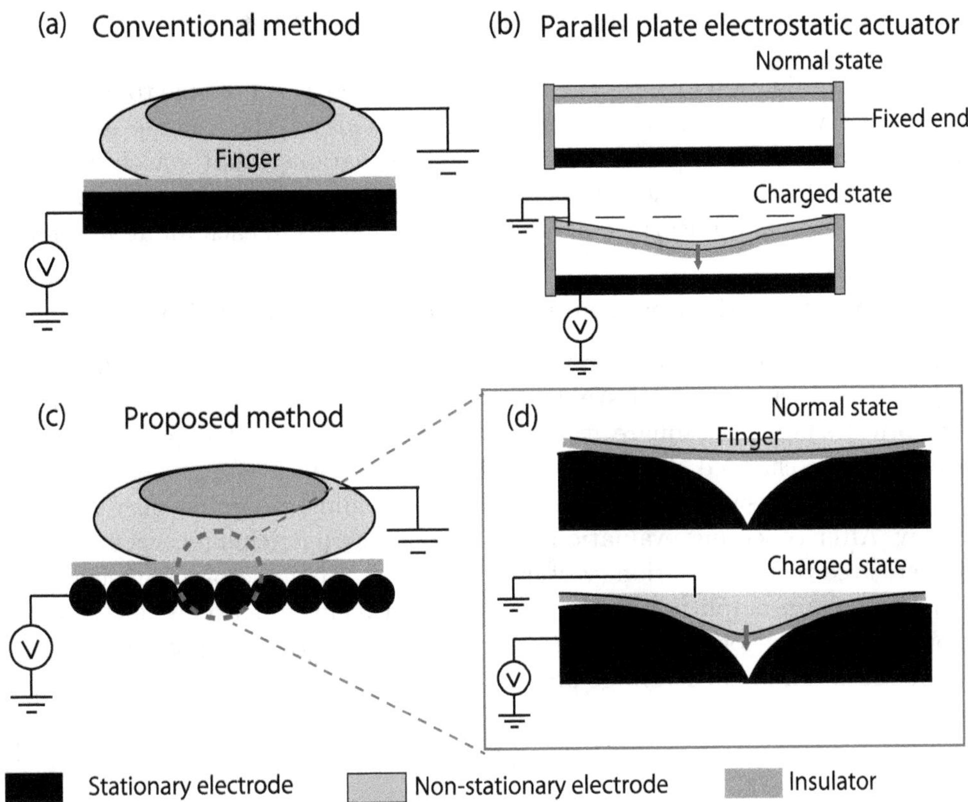

Fig. 1. (a) Conventional electrostatic tactile display: An insulating film is placed on a flat electrode. (b) Schematic sketch of the parallel plate electrostatic actuator [2,6]. (c) Proposed method: A soft insulating film is placed on a nonplanar electrode, such as a conductive thread or wire. (d) Enlarged view of finger surface with the proposed method.

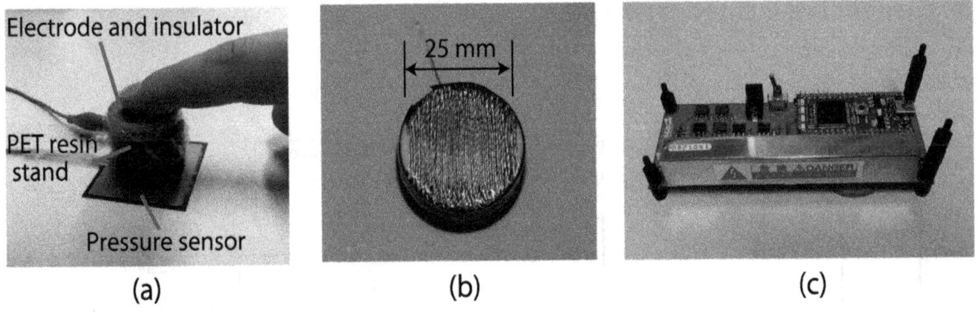

Fig. 2. (a) Overview of our display device, (b) a conductive thread arranged lengthwise and (c) the high-voltage generator.

3 Evaluation Experiment of Proposed Method

We held an evaluation experiment to explore whether it is possible to feel tactile stimulation with the proposed method. Thresholds of the voltage amplitude at which the user feels the tactile sensation for various input waveforms were investigated. In this manner, we can confirm the input waveform that displays tactile sensation and how the voltage threshold changes in each input waveform.

3.1 Evaluation Method Using Method of Constant Stimuli

In this experiment, we investigated the perception thresholds of each voltage amplitude by using constant stimuli. As shown in Fig. 3 (a), we prepared three waveforms: sine wave, square wave, and a delta function that occurs periodically. Then we changed the voltage amplitude of these waveforms and asked the participants to answer whether they felt the stimulus presented on the tactile display. After collecting evaluation results from the participants, we calculated the perceived tactile sensation (vertical axis of Fig. 3 (b)) and psychometric function with voltage amplitude on the horizontal axis. This function is calculated by approximating the logistic curve shown in the following equation to the perceived tactile sensation in each voltage amplitude.

$$R = \frac{1}{1 + ae^{-bv}} \tag{1}$$

R shows the perceived tactile sensation, v shows a voltage amplitude, a and b show constant parameters. By using this function, we estimate the threshold voltage at which the user feels the tactile sensation. In this experiment, a voltage where the psychometric function went across 50% of the perception rate was set as a threshold. An example of a psychometric function obtained from the averaged results of all participants was shown in Fig. 3 (b). By calculating the thresholds of every waveform and frequency of the input waves, we can estimate the trend of the voltage thresholds.

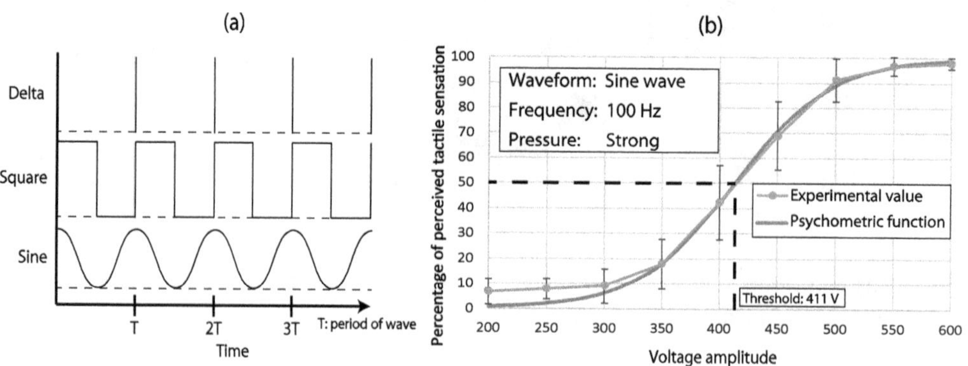

Fig. 3. (a) Three prepared waveforms and (b) an example of a psychometric function.

3.2 Outline of Evaluation Experiment

We conducted an evaluation experiment of constant stimuli with 9 university students (2 female), 22 to 25 years old.

We prepared the display device, a personal computer, a polyethylene terephthalate (PET) resin stand, and a pressure sensor (FSR406) for the experiment. The display device is put on the PET resin stand to isolate it from the floor and to make it easier to place the finger. The pressure sensor is installed under the PET resin stand (Fig. 2 (a)) to measure the pressing force of the finger. We fed back the value of the pressure sensor to the participants via an LCD monitor and instructed them to keep it constant.

We prepared three waveforms and 10 types of dominant frequencies from 10 Hz to 630 Hz of each waveform. Furthermore, we prepared 9 voltage amplitudes from 200 V to 600 V for calculating the voltage threshold, and each condition was displayed ten times. These conditions were selected in random order. In addition, we investigated whether the voltage threshold changes by the difference of the pressing force of the finger. The participants were requested to perform the experiments under the conditions of a weaker pressing force (between 35 gf and 44 gf) and a stronger one (between 75 gf and 84 gf). From these conditions, participants conducted 5400 trials evaluation (3 waveforms $\times$ 10 frequencies $\times$ 9 amplitudes $\times$ 2 pressure $\times$ 10 trials for each condition).

First of all, we explained the outline of the experiment and obtained written informed consent for participation in the study (based on ethical guidelines of University of Tsukuba) from all participants. For masking the external sound, white noise was applied to participants using a headphone during the experiment. We instructed them to place their right index finger on the display device and to keep the pressure condition during the experiment. After a waveform was inputted to the display device, participants were instructed to select either "feel something" or "feel nothing" by using the installed keyboard. After participants finished the evaluation with all the waveforms, we instructed them to keep the other pressure condition and repeat the evaluation. 5-minute breaks were taken three times during the experiment. After the experiment, we collected the participants' answers and calculated a voltage threshold for each input waveform.

3.3 Results and Discussion

The results of the evaluation experiment are shown in Fig. 4 and Fig. 5. The horizontal axis of these graphs shows the frequency of the input waveform. The blue line indicates the condition of a weaker pressure, and the orange line indicates the condition of a stronger pressure in these graphs. Figure 4 shows the number of participants who perceived some tactile sensation for each input waveform. Figure 5 shows the result of the voltage thresholds in each input waveform. These thresholds are derived from the intersection of the 50% line and the logistic curve. From Fig. 4 and Fig. 5, we observed that most of the participants could perceive the displayed tactile sensation in all conditions of square waves and limited frequency conditions of sine waves or delta functions. From the result, the

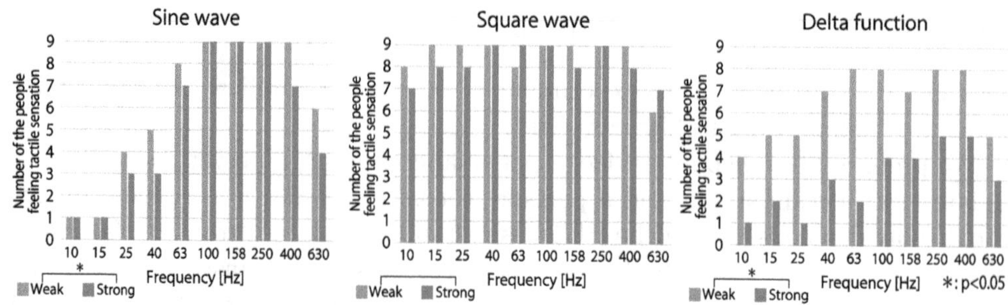

Fig. 4. Results of the number of participants who feel tactile sensation for each input waveform. (Color figure online)

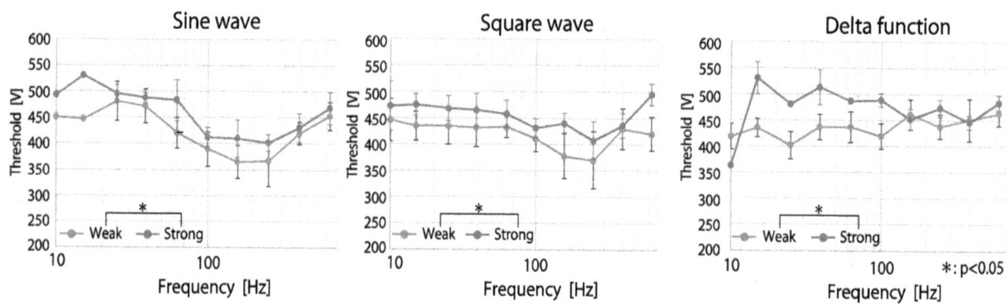

Fig. 5. Results of the threshold of voltage amplitude for each input waveform.

availability of the tactile display without moving a finger is confirmed by using our proposed method. Furthermore, the voltage thresholds are observed to be less than 500 V in most waveforms. In addition, we found the following two characteristics; the evaluation results differed according to the pressing force, and the outline of the graph differed according to the waveform.

Regarding the voltage thresholds, the results of 350 V to 500 V are very high compared to general tactile display devices. However, it is possible to reduce the voltage thresholds by making the insulation film thinner, and the advantage of this method is that there is almost no current flow and power at the display side. Then, it is possible to install many tactile displays or large area tactile displays. Therefore, even if a high voltage is required, we consider that this method of tactile presentation is effective for some specified applications.

Regarding the pressing force, we confirmed that the evaluation result differs depending on the pressing force. In Fig. 4, there is a significant difference in the number of participants who perceived the tactile sensation between the two pressing conditions in the sine waves and delta function. From Fig. 4, we observe that the number of participants who perceived the tactile sensation is larger under the weak pressure condition than that of under the strong pressure condition in most sine waves and delta functions. Most participants perceived the tactile sensation under both conditions in the square waves. In Fig. 5, there was a significant difference between the two pressure conditions at all waveforms. Furthermore, the averaged voltage threshold appeared to be smaller under the weak pressure condition than that under the strong pressure condition in all of the square waves, some sine waves and some delta function. We considered that the factor of this result is based on the ratio between the pressing force of the finger and a just noticeable difference. We focused on Weber's law and showed it in the following equation.

$$\frac{\Delta R}{R} = \text{Const} \tag{2}$$

where ΔR is a just noticeable difference in the tactile sensation, and R is a pressing force in this evaluation experiment. From Eq. (2), the more pressing force, the more a difference of perceived amount is needed. Therefore, we considered that the threshold of input voltage amplitude had to be high for decreasing a just noticeable difference when the pressing force was strong.

Regarding the trend difference of graphs between waveforms (Fig. 4), when square waves were displayed, most of the participants could perceive the displayed tactile sensation. However, the participants could not perceive the tactile sensation in some frequencies of sine waves and delta functions. As seen in Fig. 5, the graphs in the case of sine and square waves are downward convex with the minimum value around 200 Hz. The graph in the case of the delta function is gentle and upward right. The reason for the shapes is considered to be related to the frequency components of each input waveform and the frequency responses of human mechanoreceptors. Vardar et al. investigated how displayed waveforms affect haptic perceptions of vibration under electrostatic tactile display [8]. Then they observed that the participants were more sensitive to square wave stimuli than sine-wave stimuli for a dominant frequency lower than 60 Hz. Furthermore, they discussed that a low dominant frequency square wave still contains high-frequency components that stimulate the Pacinian channel. Our experimental results were similar to the results of theirs; voltage thresholds are higher in the case of sine wave stimuli than in the case of square one under 40 Hz frequencies. In the case of the delta function, these waves have many frequency components, however, they are smaller in amplitude than the other two waveforms. This could be because the waveforms did not have sufficient amplitude to stimulate mechanoreceptors at low dominant frequencies.

4 Conclusions

In this paper, we proposed a method that can display tactile stimulation without moving a finger with an electrostatic tactile display, and we conducted an evaluation experiment. The proposed method is based on the vibration of a thin insulating film, which is realized by creating a small space between the electrode and the insulator. We use a conductive thread as an electrode and place a plastic film on the conductive thread. We explored whether the user can feel tactile stimulations under several conditions. We collected the evaluation results of the participants under the conditions of waveforms, frequencies and pressing forces, and calculated the voltage threshold. From the results, the possibility of a tactile display without moving a finger is confirmed by using our proposed method.

Besides, we also revealed the following fact: the evaluation results differed according to the pressing force and the outline of the graph differed according to the waveform. Regarding the pressing force of the finger, we considered that the ratio between the pressing force and the suction force induce the difference of perceptibility. Regarding the difference in the shapes of the graphs, we considered that the frequency components of the input waveform and the frequency responses of mechanoreceptors is the reason.

In the near future, we plan to clarify the modeling of tactile perception using our proposed method and the difference in the width of tactile expression compared with the conventional method. Further, we will perform more precise experiments to observe the physical phenomenon between the surface of the finger and the display.

References

1. Bau, O., Poupyrev, I., Israr, A., Harrison, C.: Teslatouch: electrovibration for touch surfaces. In: Proceedings of the 23Nd Annual ACM Symposium on User Interface Software and Technology, UIST 2010, pp. 283–292. ACM, New York (2010). https://doi.org/10.1145/1866029.1866074
2. Burugupally, S.P., Perera, W.R.: Dynamics of a parallel-plate electrostatic actuator in viscous dielectric media. Sens. Actuators A: Phys. **295**, 366–373 (2019)
3. Jiao, J., et al.: Detection and discrimination thresholds for haptic gratings on electrostatic tactile displays. IEEE Trans. Haptics **12**(1), 34–42 (2018)
4. Kang, J., Kim, H., Choi, S., Kim, K.D., Ryu, J.: Investigation on low voltage operation of electrovibration display. IEEE Trans. Haptics **10**(3), 371–381 (2016)
5. Mallinckrodt, E., Hughes, A., Sleator Jr., W.: Perception by the skin of electrically induced vibrations. Science (1953)
6. Pyo, D., Ryu, S., Kim, S.-C., Kwon, D.-S.: A new surface display for 3D haptic rendering. In: Auvray, M., Duriez, C. (eds.) EUROHAPTICS 2014. LNCS, vol. 8618, pp. 487–495. Springer, Heidelberg (2014). https://doi.org/10.1007/978-3-662-44193-0_61
7. Strong, R.M., Troxel, D.E.: An electrotactile display. IEEE Trans. Man-Mach. Syst. **11**(1), 72–79 (1970)
8. Vardar, Y., Güçlü, B., Basdogan, C.: Effect of waveform on tactile perception by electrovibration displayed on touch screens. IEEE Trans. Haptics **10**(4), 488–499 (2017)
9. Vezzoli, E., Amberg, M., Giraud, F., Lemaire-Semail, B.: Electrovibration modeling analysis. In: Auvray, M., Duriez, C. (eds.) EUROHAPTICS 2014. LNCS, vol. 8619, pp. 369–376. Springer, Heidelberg (2014). https://doi.org/10.1007/978-3-662-44196-1_45

2

Midair Tactile Reproduction of Real Objects

Emiri Sakiyama[1(✉)], Atsushi Matsubayashi[1], Daichi Matsumoto[2], Masahiro Fujiwara[2], Yasutoshi Makino[2], and Hiroyuki Shinoda[2]

[1] The University of Tokyo, 7-3-1 Hongo, Bunkyo-ku, Tokyo, Japan
sakiyama@hapis.k.u-tokyo.ac.jp

[2] The University of Tokyo, 5-1-5 Kashiwanoha, Kashiwa-shi, Chiba-ken, Japan

Abstract. Midair tactile display using ultrasound radiation pressure is suitable for tactile reproduction because of its reproducibility and controllability. This paper is the first report that compares the tactile feelings of real objects with those associated with artificial stimuli reproduced through a sequence of sensing, processing, and reproduction. We previously proposed the concept of a midair tactile reproduction system and examined the basic properties of the sensing part, but had not achieved the tactile display to the human skin. In this paper, we report a practical method for the pressure reproduction from the measured data and examine the accuracy of the reproduced stimulation. The psychophysical experiments evaluate the fidelity of the tactile reproduction for some objects such as brushes, sponges, and towels.

Keywords: Midair haptics · Tactile reproduction · Tactile sensor

1 Introduction

An airborne ultrasound tactile display (AUTD) [1,2] can present tactile sensations with high spatio-temporal controllability in a non-contact manner. This advantage is suitable for tactile reproduction of real objects. However, the fidelity of tactile reproduction performance has not been studied in detail since the development of the device in 2008 [1]. In this study, we achieve a midair tactile reproduction system which consists of the AUTD and a tactile array sensor.

The concept behind the system was first introduced in our previous work-in-progress paper [3]. Further, we examined the design of the sensor and the reproduction scheme in [4]; however, the reproduced pressure distribution was strongly distorted owing to problems in the reproduction algorithm.

This paper is the first report that compares the tactile feelings of real objects to those associated with artificial stimuli reproduced through a sequence of sensing, processing, and reproduction. As a key part of the system, we report a practical method of the pressure reproduction. Conventional methods [4,5] have no constraints on the upper limit of the output amplitude, and sometimes, it is impossible for devices to output the optimization results. In this study, we acquire a feasible solution by executing the Levenberg–Marquardt algorithm (LMA) [6,7] with the constraint that the amplitudes of the transducers must all be equal. After confirming the basic physical performance of pressure reproduction, the fidelity of the reproduced sensation was evaluated in comparison with that of real objects by psychophysical experiments.

2 Tactile Presentation by Ultrasound Phased Array

2.1 Acoustic Radiation Pressure

Midair tactile stimulation using ultrasound is based on the acoustic radiation pressure. This pressure is a non-linear acoustic phenomenon which generates DC positive pressure on the boundary between the two types of media with different acoustic impedances. The acoustic radiation pressure P for plane ultrasound wave is described as $P = \alpha\frac{p_0^2}{\rho c^2}(> 0)$, where ρ is the density of the medium on the incident side; c is the speed of sound in the medium; p_0 is the RMS sound pressure of the ultrasound; and α is a constant that is dependent on the power reflection coefficient R such that $\alpha \equiv 1 + R$, and $1 \leq \alpha \leq 2$. In this study, we consider acoustic radiation pressure on solid surfaces in standard air; hence, $\rho = 1.25$ kg/m^3, $c = 340$ m/s, and $\alpha = 2$.

2.2 Sound Field Generated by Phased Array

In this study, a desired pressure distribution is reproduced by the radiation pressure. We control the radiation pressure field by controlling the sound field.

Assuming a steady sinusoidal wave, a complex sound amplitude vector $\boldsymbol{p}$ generated by a phased array is expressed as follows [5]:

$$\boldsymbol{p} = \boldsymbol{G}\boldsymbol{q}, \tag{1}$$

$$\boldsymbol{p} = [p_1, p_2, \ldots, p_M]^\top, \; p_m = p(\boldsymbol{r}_m) = p_{\mathrm{amp},m}e^{j\psi_m}, \tag{2}$$

$$G_{mn} = C\frac{D(\theta_{mn})}{|\boldsymbol{r}_m - \boldsymbol{r}_n|}e^{-\beta|\boldsymbol{r}_m - \boldsymbol{r}_n|}e^{jk|\boldsymbol{r}_m - \boldsymbol{r}_n|}, \tag{3}$$

$$\boldsymbol{q} = [q_1, q_2, \ldots, q_N]^\top, \; q_n = A_n e^{j\phi_n}. \tag{4}$$

Here, $p_m (m = 1, \ldots, M)$ is a complex sound amplitude at the m-th control point $\boldsymbol{r}_m$, and $q_n (n = 1, \ldots, N)$ is a complex amplitude of the surface vibration velocity of the n-th transducer at $\boldsymbol{r}_n$. $\boldsymbol{G}$ is the transfer matrix, where C is a constant, $D(\theta)$ is the directivity function of a transducer, θ_{mn} is the angle between the transducer normal and $\boldsymbol{r}_m - \boldsymbol{r}_n$, β is the attenuation coefficient and k is the wave number.

2.3 Controlling Pressure Field by Phased Array

In the case of tactile presentation, the driving signal of the phased array $\boldsymbol{q}$ is decided based on the sound pressure amplitude distribution $\boldsymbol{p}_{\mathrm{amp}}$ converted from the desired instantaneous pressure distribution $\boldsymbol{P}$. The proposed method solves the following problem; find $\boldsymbol{q}$ s.t. $\boldsymbol{p}_{\mathrm{amp}} = |\boldsymbol{G}\boldsymbol{q}|$ at each time. The tactile presentation is performed by outputting the time series of $\boldsymbol{q}$ in a quasi-stationary manner. The phases of the complex sound distribution $\boldsymbol{p}$ are unconstrained. A more efficient output can essentially be achieved by modifying these phases [8].

3 Tactile Sensing

In order to measure a slight contact force of around 0.01 N/cm^2($\simeq$the maximum presentation force per 1 AUTD) at sufficient sampling rate, we adopted the new tactile sensor that we had designed previously [4] using high-sensitivity microphones for use in this study. The sensor is composed of a 4×4 channels microphone array (Fig. 1a). The contact pressure of the sensor surface causes pressure change in the sensor cavity and the microphone detects the change (Fig. 1b). Using this sensor, we can acquire a pressure distribution of 4×4 channels at 11 mm intervals by a sampling frequency of 1 kHz. The frequency characteristics are compensated for components with $20 - 470$ Hz in this study. The components under 20 Hz and over 470 Hz are removed because of the low sensitivity of the microphones.

In order to achieve high fidelity of tactile sensation by this system, the vibrations produced on the tactile sensor must be similar to the actual vibrations on the human skin. Therefore, the mechanical characteristics of the sensor surface are required to be similar to those of the human skin. HITOHADA® gel sheet (hardness: Askar C0, thickness: 1 mm) of EXSEAL Co., Ltd., Japan is used as the contact surface. This is a super-soft urethane sheet comparable to human skin. Moreover, human fingerprints affect the generation and detection of slip. In this study, we compared the reproduction fidelity of tactile sensation between two conditions of the contact surface shape: non-treated condition and concentric circle groove pattern imitating fingerprints, as shown in Fig. 2.

4 Tactile Reproduction

4.1 Data Preprocessing

Before the optimization of the driving signal of AUTD, four preprocesses are performed on the measured data. First, half-wave rectification of the measured data is performed because the radiation pressure is always positive. Though this process generates unnecessary harmonics, we adopt it for the easiness and clearness of the process. Second, the pressure distribution data P is converted to sound pressure amplitude distribution p_{amp} by $p_{\mathrm{amp}} = \sqrt{2}p_0 = c\sqrt{\frac{2\rho P}{\alpha}}$.

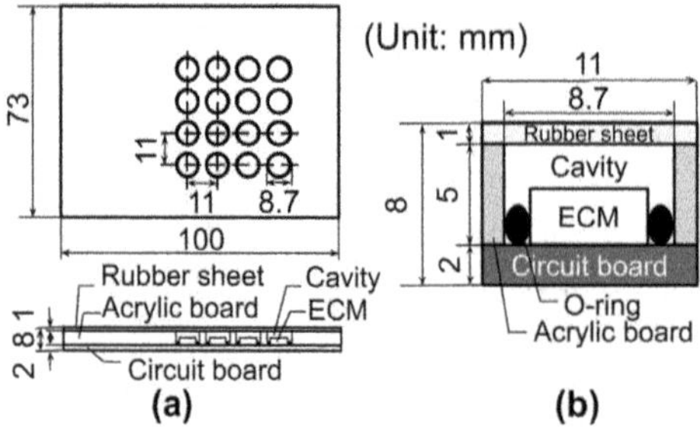

Fig. 1. Structure of (a) all the 4 × 4 elements and (b) the single element of the sensor [4].

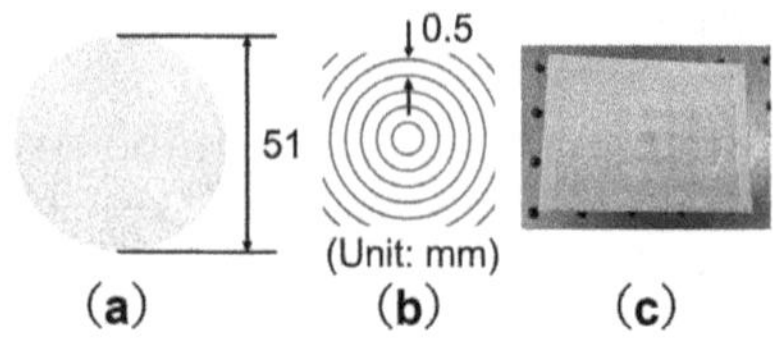

Fig. 2. The concentric circle pattern of the sensor surface. (a) The whole pattern. (b) The enlarged view. (c) The appearance of the sensor.

In order to limit the effects of pressures outside the region of interest, 20 control points are added around the region at 11-mm intervals ($4 \times 4 \rightarrow 6 \times 6$ points), and the sound pressure amplitudes are set to zero at the peripheral points. Subsequently, the 36-point data with 11 mm intervals are converted into 256-point data with 11/3 mm intervals by linear interpolation of the original data on the assumption that the pattern is smooth.

4.2 Optimization of Driving Signal of AUTD

In this study, the LMA [6,7] was used to optimize the driving signal of AUTD. LMA is an iterative algorithm for solving non-linear least squares problems. In general, to solve a problem $\min_{\boldsymbol{\theta}} \|\boldsymbol{f}(\boldsymbol{\theta})\|_2^2$ by LMA, the parameter $\boldsymbol{\theta}$ is updated to $\boldsymbol{\theta}^{k+1} = \boldsymbol{\theta}^k - [(\boldsymbol{J}^k)^\top \boldsymbol{J}^k + \lambda^k \boldsymbol{I}]^{-1} \boldsymbol{f}(\boldsymbol{\theta}^k)$, where λ is the damping parameter and $\boldsymbol{J}$ is the Jacobian matrix of $\boldsymbol{f}(\boldsymbol{\theta})$.

We solved the problem using the LMA with the constraint that the amplitudes of the transducers $A_1, \ldots, A_N$ must all be equal. In this case, the optimization problem is described as follows:

$$\min_{\boldsymbol{\theta}} \left\| \begin{matrix} \mathrm{Re}(G\boldsymbol{q} - \mathrm{diag}(\boldsymbol{p}_{\mathrm{amp}})\boldsymbol{u}) \\ \mathrm{Im}(G\boldsymbol{q} - \mathrm{diag}(\boldsymbol{p}_{\mathrm{amp}})\boldsymbol{u}) \end{matrix} \right\|_2^2 \tag{5}$$

$$\boldsymbol{q} = A \times \left[e^{j\theta_1}, e^{j\theta_2}, \ldots, e^{j\theta_N}\right]^\top, \boldsymbol{u} = \left[e^{j\theta_{N+1}}, e^{j\theta_{N+2}}, \ldots, e^{j\theta_{N+M}}\right]^\top \tag{6}$$

where Re and Im are the real and imaginary parts of the complex vector, respectively. The results of the LMA depend on the initial value of $\boldsymbol{\theta}_0$ because the algorithm determines only a local minimum. In this study, we use a zero vector or a final value of a previous time frame as the initial value.

5 Experiments

5.1 Numerical Simulation

First, the reproduction performance of arbitrary static pressure distribution was evaluated via numerical simulation. We generated binary distributions on the

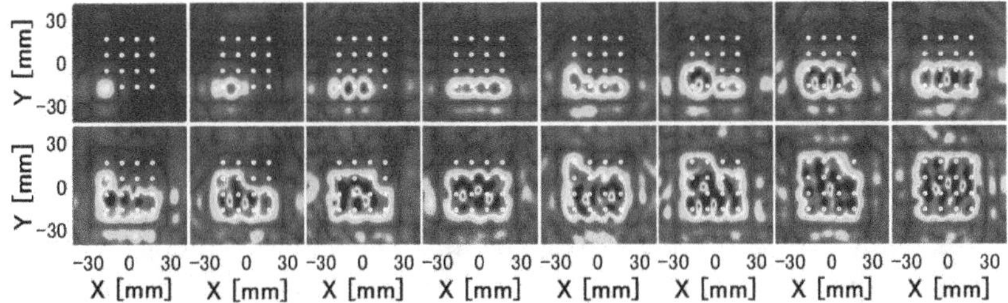

Fig. 3. An example of the simulated optimization results: The white circle indicates the position of each channel. They were optimized with 996 transducers (4 AUTDs), 256 control points at 50 iterations.

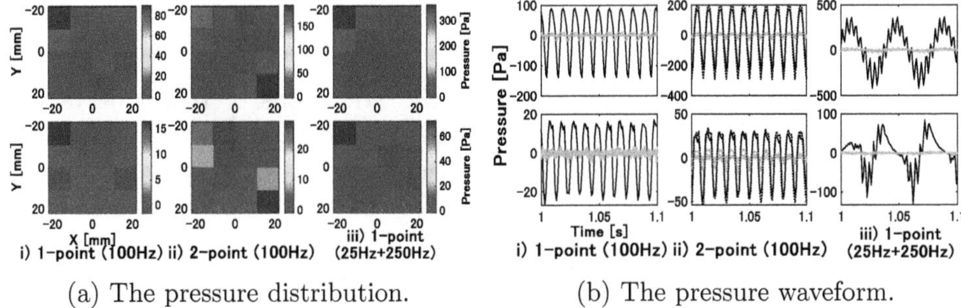

(a) The pressure distribution. (b) The pressure waveform.

Fig. 4. The results of the reproduction of AUTD stimuli recorded by the sensor. **Top:** Original data. **Bottom:** Reproduction data. In (a), the top-left corner: 0 ch, bottom-right corner: 15 ch. In (b), Black solid line: 0 ch, black dotted line: 15 ch, and gray line: other channels.

control points such that the sound pressure amplitude of each channel was 0 or 1. The number of distributions was $2^{16}-1$ in total for 16 control points, with the exception of a distribution in which all the amplitudes were zero. Subsequently, we reproduced these distributions based on the point source model using MATLAB software. The examples of the simulated optimization results are shown in Fig. 3. The average error $\frac{1}{M}\sqrt{\|\boldsymbol{Gq}-\boldsymbol{p}\|_2^2/\|\boldsymbol{p}\|_2^2}$ was approximately $5-15\%$.

5.2 Reproduction of Dynamic Radiation Pressure Distribution

Due to half-wave rectification and optimization errors in the reproduction algorithm, the waveform may change to some extent in the actual reproduction. Therefore, in the preliminary experiment, the dynamic pressure distribution generated by AUTD was reproduced by the system and again recorded by the sensor. Thus, the degree of distortion was examined and the distortion was corrected.

The presented stimuli were i) 1-point amplitude modulation (AM) stimulus to the 0 channel position of the sensor, ii) 2-point AM stimulus to the 0 and 15 channel positions, and iii) 1-point AM containing multiple frequency components to the 0 channel position. The AM frequency of i) and ii) was 100 Hz. As for iii), the AM 25 Hz waveform and the AM 250 Hz waveforms were added together, where the amplitude ratio was 3:2. Except for the first-time frame, 20 iterations of the LMA were performed using a final value of a previous time frame as an initial value each time. The other settings of equipment layout and optimization were the same as those of the numerical simulation.

As a result, the system reproduced some features of the original distributions, such as the peak position, the waveform and the AM frequency (Fig. 4a, 4b). Though there were some distortions caused by half-wave rectification, especially in iii), we left these distortions as they were. The amplification factor between the AUTD-driving voltage and the observed sensor output voltage is determined experimentally. We determined it so that the focused beam to the sensor just below the AUTD center produces an expected output amplitude.

5.3 Psychophysical Experiment

In the psychophysical experiment, the tactile sensations of real objects were reproduced and evaluated. This system can reproduce weak pressure of temporal frequency components over 20 Hz, so it is assumed that soft, light, and unsmooth objects are suitable. Therefore, the three types of objects, namely, soft brush, sponge and towel were selected. First, the waveform generated when tracing the sensor by each object was recorded for five times using an automatic stage as shown in Fig. 5a. The speed is approximately 5 cm/s and the contact surface is of circular shape, approximately 2 cm in diameter. This measurement was performed in each condition of the sensor surface with and without concentric circle grooving treatment. The reproduction stimulation was then generated on a palm according to the proposed method. Simultaneously, amplitude correction was carried out based on the result of the preliminary experiment.

The experiment was carried out in two stages. First, the ability of the real object to discriminate tactile sensation was confirmed. The tactile sensation of the real object was randomly presented 12 times to the blindfolded participants by a human hand. They answered which object was presented each time. Next, the reproduction stimulation was evaluated. In practice, each type of reproduced stimulation was once presented without the prior information of what object was reproduced. Subsequently, the remaining three types of stimulation were randomly presented four times. The number of trials was minimized considering the fatigue of the participants. For each stimulus, participants were asked to answer two types of questions, i.e., A) how much they were similar to the tactile sensation of the brush/sponge/towel (1: totally different $\sim$ 7: very similar), and B) which object they felt it was closest to. This experiment was carried out twice by changing the surface treatment conditions. The participants were 10 people in their 20's, two of whom were females, and all stimuli were presented on the palm of the dominant hand (one male was left-handed). While presenting the reproduction stimulus, the participants were listening to white noise by a headphone, and were allowed to touch the real objects freely.

As shown in Fig. 6a, the real objects could be discriminated with a correct answer rate of over 95%. In contrast, the correct answer rate of the reproduction stimulus was lower(Fig. 6b, 6c). In Fig. 7, the F-measure was calculated from

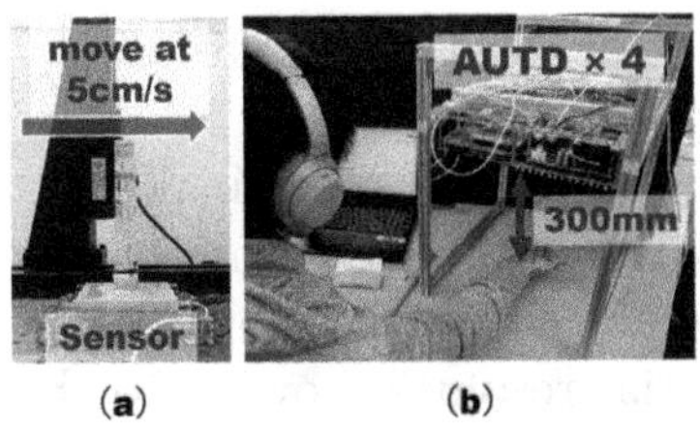

Fig. 5. (a) The measurement of the tactile sensations of the real objects. (b) The presentation of the reproduction stimulation.

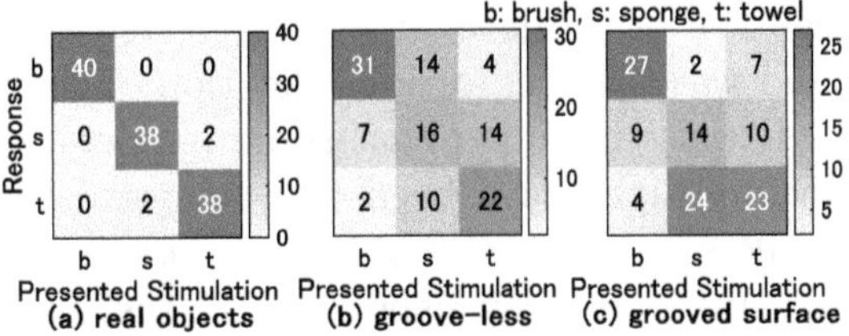

Fig. 6. The responses to the question "which object they felt it was closest to." The number indicates the number of responses.(b)/(c) is the result of the groove-less/grooved sensor surface condition.

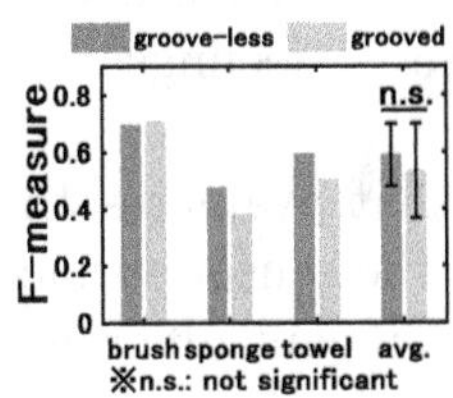

Fig. 7. The F-measure calculated from the responses to the question B.

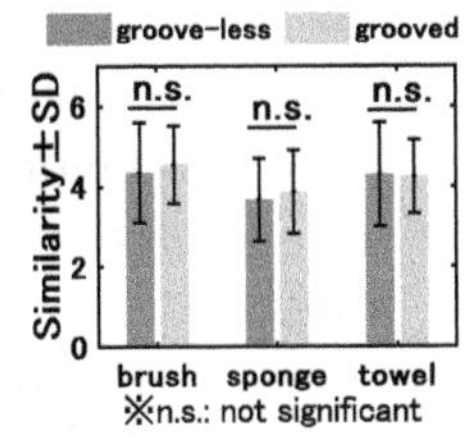

Fig. 8. The similarity to the tactile sensation of real objects that the participants answered.

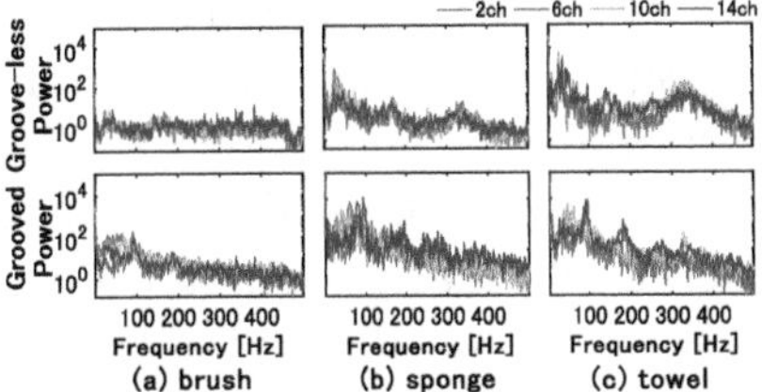

Fig. 9. The power spectrum of the original tactile sensation data at the four major channels that the objects passed through (2, 6, 10, 14 ch). These are all after calibration and half-wave rectification.

the answer to question B) shown in Fig. 6b, 6c. As the result indicates, the F-measure exceeds 0.33, which is the chance rate. Moreover, a paired t-test did not show a significant difference between non-treated condition and concentric circle treated condition($t(2) = 1.60, p = .25$). In addition, a three-way repeated measures ANOVA was carried out on the answers to question A). As shown in Fig. 8, there is also no significant difference in the subjective similarity evaluation by the surface treatment condition.

Based on these results, it was confirmed that three types of tactile sensation could be discriminated to some extent by this system without prior information. However, there were no significant differences of subjective evaluation and discrimination results between two surface conditions. Therefore, it is assumed that the reproduced stimulation contains some important tactile features, regardless of the surface treatment, for identification of the three types of objects. As shown in Fig. 9, the intensity increased by the surface groove, especially in the components under 300 Hz. In both surface conditions, the intensity of high-frequency band over 300 Hz was largest in the towel data, followed by the sponge data, and then the brush data. It was suggested that the intensity of the high-frequency band was the clue for identification of the three types of objects.

It must be noted that some important tactile features in the original stimulation might have been lost owing to the spatial resolution of 11 mm of the tactile sensor. The other possible issues include the acoustic streaming, lack of tangential force, and shortness of the displayed spatial resolution owing to the limitation of the ultrasound wavelength.

6 Conclusion

In this study, we proposed an accurate tactile reproduction system by introducing the LMA for determining the driving signals of transducers on the AUTD. We evaluated the fidelity of the reproduced sensations of three typical elastic objects. As a result, the system could reproduce similar tactile feelings to a certain degree and display significant differences among them.

A crucial physical problem is the surface of the sensor that evaluates the tactile information of real objects. We evaluated the effect of the sensor surface characteristics. Regarding the tested objects, there was no significant difference between the two types of surfaces, i.e., the one with a concentric circle groove pattern and the other with no groove pattern.

The most demanding future work is to improve the spatial resolution of the sensor. The system can be used as a useful tool to clarify the human tactile sensation and as a practical system that records and reproduces the tactile feelings associated with various products.

References

1. Iwamoto, T., Tatezono, M., Shinoda, H.: Non-contact method for producing tactile sensation using airborne ultrasound. In: Ferre, M. (ed.) EuroHaptics 2008. LNCS, vol. 5024, pp. 504–513. Springer, Heidelberg (2008). https://doi.org/10.1007/978-3-540-69057-3_64
2. Hoshi, T., Takahashi, M., Iwamoto, T., Shinoda, H.: Noncontact tactile display based on radiation pressure of airborne ultrasound. IEEE Trans. Haptics **3**(3), 155–165 (2010)
3. Sakiyama, E., Matsumoto, D., Fujiwara, M., Makino, Y., Shinoda, H.: Midair tactile reproduction of real objects using microphone-based tactile sensor array. In: IEEE World Haptics Conference, WPI.35(Work-in-Progress Papers), 9–12 July, Tokyo, Japan (2019)
4. Sakiyama, E., Matsumoto, D., Fujiwara, M., Makino, Y., Shinoda, H.: Evaluation of multi-point dynamic pressure reproduction using microphone-based tactile sensor array. In: IEEE International Symposium on Haptic Audio-Visual Environments and Games, Sunway, Malaysia, 3–4 October 2019
5. Inoue, S., Makino, Y., Shinoda, H.: Active touch perception produced by airborne ultrasonic haptic hologram. In: 2015 IEEE World Haptics Conference, pp. 362–367 (2015)
6. Levenberg, K.: A method for the solution of certain non-linear problems in least squares. Q. J. Appl. Math. II (2), 164–168 (1944)

7. Marquardt, D.W.: An algorithm for least-squares estimation of non-linear parameters. J. Soc. Ind. Appl. Math. **11**(2), 431–441 (1963)
8. Long, B., Seah, S.A., Carter, T., Subramanian, S.: Rendering volumetric haptic shapes in mid-air using ultrasound. ACM Trans. Graph. **33**(6), Article 181 (2014)

3

Midair Haptic Presentation Using Concave Reflector

Kentaro Ariga[1(✉)], Masahiro Fujiwara[1,2], Yasutoshi Makino[1,2], and Hiroyuki Shinoda[1,2]

[1] Graduate School of Information Science and Technology, The University of Tokyo, Tokyo, Japan
ariga@hapis.k.u-tokyo.ac.jp
[2] Graduate School of Frontier Sciences, The University of Tokyo, Chiba, Japan
Masahiro_Fujiwara@ipc.i.u-tokyo.ac.jp,
{yasutoshi_makino,hiroyuki_shinoda}@k.u-tokyo.ac.jp

Abstract. An airborne ultrasound tactile display (AUTD) can focus on an arbitrary position by controlling the phase shift and amplitude of each transducer, and provide a tactile stimulus on the human body without direct contact. However, beyond a distance from the phased array, it cannot secure a focal size comparable to the wavelength and the displayed pressure pattern blurs. In this study, we propose a method with a concave reflector to focus at a farther position and present a tactile sensation without enlarging the array. By appropriately designing the focal length of the concave reflector, the focal point can be formed at a distant position using a mirror formula while keeping the focus size non-extended. We conducted two experiments, the results of which show that the proposed method is valid and that a workspace of several square centimeters can be achieved.

Keywords: Airborne ultrasound haptics · Concave reflector · Mirror formula

1 Introduction

An airborne ultrasound tactile display (AUTD) [4,9] can present a tactile stimulus on the surface of a human body without direct contact. An AUTD creates an ultrasound focus at an arbitrary position within the workspace by controlling the phase shift and amplitude of the output emission of each ultrasonic transducer. However, it has difficulty forming a focus far from the phased array and presenting a tactile sensation [10]. Only up to a distance comparable to the aperture of the phased array can an AUTD secure a focal size comparable to the wavelength, and the focus diameter increases as the focus moves farther from the phased array. To tackle this problem, multiple AUTDs were used in previous studies to enlarge the aperture of the phased array or place them near the focus [6,13].

We propose a method for forming a focus and providing a tactile sensation farther from an AUTD without enlarging the phased array or placing the devices near the focal point. There are several approaches which provide comparable workspace extension without enlarging the phased array [1,5]. In the proposed method, ultrasound waves emitted from an AUTD are reflected and focused using a concave reflector. A technique of reflecting ultrasound waves in order to focus them, has been applied in other studies [7,8]. The technique has also been applied in a previous study in haptics [11], through which the phased array can present a tactile stimulus at an arbitrary position within the workspace, but a focus-formable distance has not been extended owing to the planar reflections. In the proposed method, it is possible to generate a focus farther from the AUTD and provide a tactile sensation while maintaining the ability to steer the focus electrically, by applying a mirror formula [3]. A mirror formula has been applied in another study so as to reconstruct the geometry of arbitrary reflectors using ultrasound phased arrays [12].

The theory supporting the proposed method and its advantages are described in Sect. 2. In Sect. 3, two experiments conducted in this area are described. First, we investigated whether a focus is formed when applying the proposed method and if a sufficient sound pressure that can provide a tactile sensation is obtained. Next, we experimentally confirmed the range of the workspace by focusing at certain points.

2 Proposed Method

2.1 Mirror Formula

The procedure to create a focal point at an arbitrary position using a concave reflector is illustrated in Fig. 1. To simplify the following equation, let us define the z-axis as shown in Fig. 1, where f is the focal length of the concave reflector. We assumed a paraxial approximation system and ignored any aberrations. When an acoustic source is placed at $A = (a_x, a_y, a_z)$, the reflected wave is concentrated and forms a focus at $B = (b_x, b_y, b_z)$ using the following mirror formula,

$$\frac{1}{a_z} + \frac{1}{b_z} = \frac{1}{f}, \tag{1}$$

as well as the magnification formulae,

$$b_x = -\frac{b_z}{a_z} a_x, \tag{2}$$

$$b_y = -\frac{b_z}{a_z} a_y. \tag{3}$$

Therefore, a focus can be created at (b_x, b_y, b_z) by driving the AUTD to reproduce the sound wave emitted from the image sound source placed at (a_x, a_y, a_z), as derived from Eqs. (1)–(3).

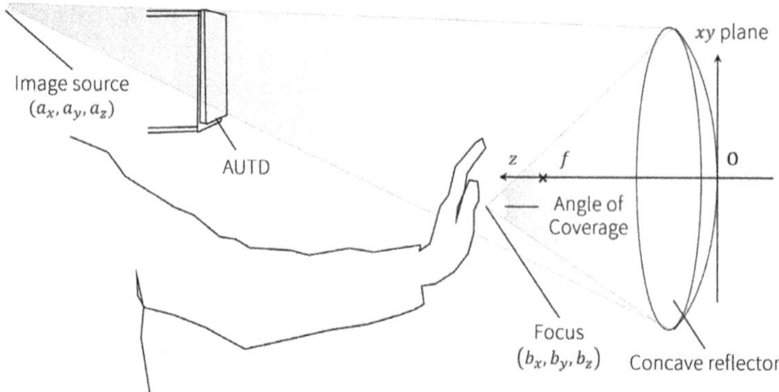

Fig. 1. The process to form a focal point using a concave reflector. AUTD reproduces the propagating waves as if they were emitted from the image sound source, which are reflected by the reflector and concentrated at the focal point.

2.2 Contributions by Concave Reflector

The focus can be formed farther away from the phased array because the angle of coverage can be changed arbitrarily through an appropriate design of the concave reflector. In the case where focal points are formed by direct incident waves or reflected waves from a planar reflector, the angle of coverage is uniquely determined for each focal position, and becomes narrower as the distance from the AUTD increases. As a result, the focal diameter lengthens and a tactile sensation cannot be obtained; in addition, the phased array has to be enlarged to increase the angle of coverage. By contrast, concave reflectors can have various focal lengths. If we appropriately design the focal length and use the mirror formula, the angle of coverage can be increased even at a position far from the AUTD. Therefore, the diameter of the focal point can be smaller, which produces a tactile stimulus, without enlarging the phased array.

3 Experiment

3.1 Implementation

Figure 2 shows the experiment setup. An AUTD is composed of 249 transducers. A T4010A1 (developed by Nippon Ceramic Co., Ltd.) was employed as the transducer. The T4010A1 emits a 40-kHz ultrasound at 121.5 dB in sound pressure level (SPL) at a distance of 30 cm. Each ultrasonic transducer was driven by the full power of the AUTD. The phase shift of each transducer was calculated and driven using the wavelength $\lambda = 8.5$ mm at a sound speed of $c = 340$ m. The concave mirror is a symmetrical parabolic dish shape, the diameter of which is 400 mm and the focal length is 180 mm. The distance between the AUTD and the reflector is 669 mm. A standard microphone (Brüel & Kjær 4138-A-015) was moved using a 1-axis motorized stage. The sound pressure was estimated by calculating the absolute value of the 40 kHz component of DFT.

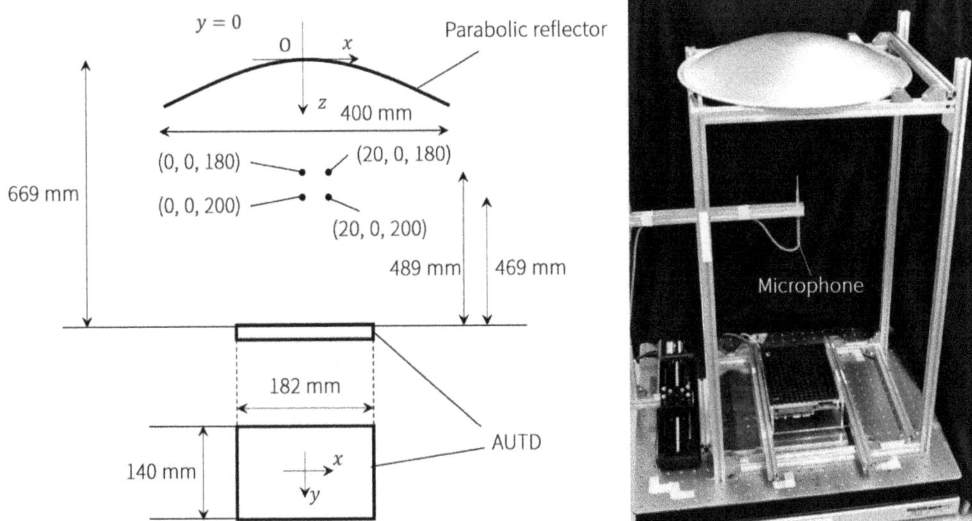

Fig. 2. Geometry of the proposed system. The position $(0, 0, 180\,\text{mm})$ is the focus of the reflector.

3.2 Experiment 1: Validation of Mirror Formula

In Experiment 1, the sound pressure distribution around the focus was measured along the x-axis at the depth of designed focal position, and it was confirmed whether the focal point was formed by the mirror formula. The focal points were formed at $(0, 0, 180\,\text{mm})$, $(20, 0, 180\,\text{mm})$, and $(20, 0, 200\,\text{mm})$, where the distances from the AUTD were 489 and 469 mm. As a reference experiment, the sound pressure distribution was also measured, where a focal point was directly formed at $(0, 0, 200\,\text{mm})$ without using a reflector. The microphone was moved within the range of $-100\,\text{mm} \leqq x \leqq 100\,\text{mm}$, where it was fixed vertically upward when using the reflector and vertically downward when not using it, in order to steer the microphone toward the direction of sound wave arrival.

The results of Experiment 1 are shown in Fig. 3. As shown in this figure, it can be confirmed that each designed focus can be presented by the concave mirror. The maximum sound pressure at each focal position with the reflector is 6.34×10^3, 5.43×10^3, and 5.69×10^3 Pa, or 170.0, 168.7, and 169.1 dB SPL, respectively, which is sufficient to provide a tactile stimulus [2].

By contrast, the maximum sound pressure at $(0, 0, 200\,\text{mm})$, without the reflector is 1.49×10^3 Pa, or 157.4 dB SPL. Furthermore, the focal diameter without the concave reflector is more than twice that with the reflector. Figure 3 shows that proposed method achieves a higher focal sound pressure and a smaller focal diameter than the conventional method, and that the proposed method can present tactile stimuli.

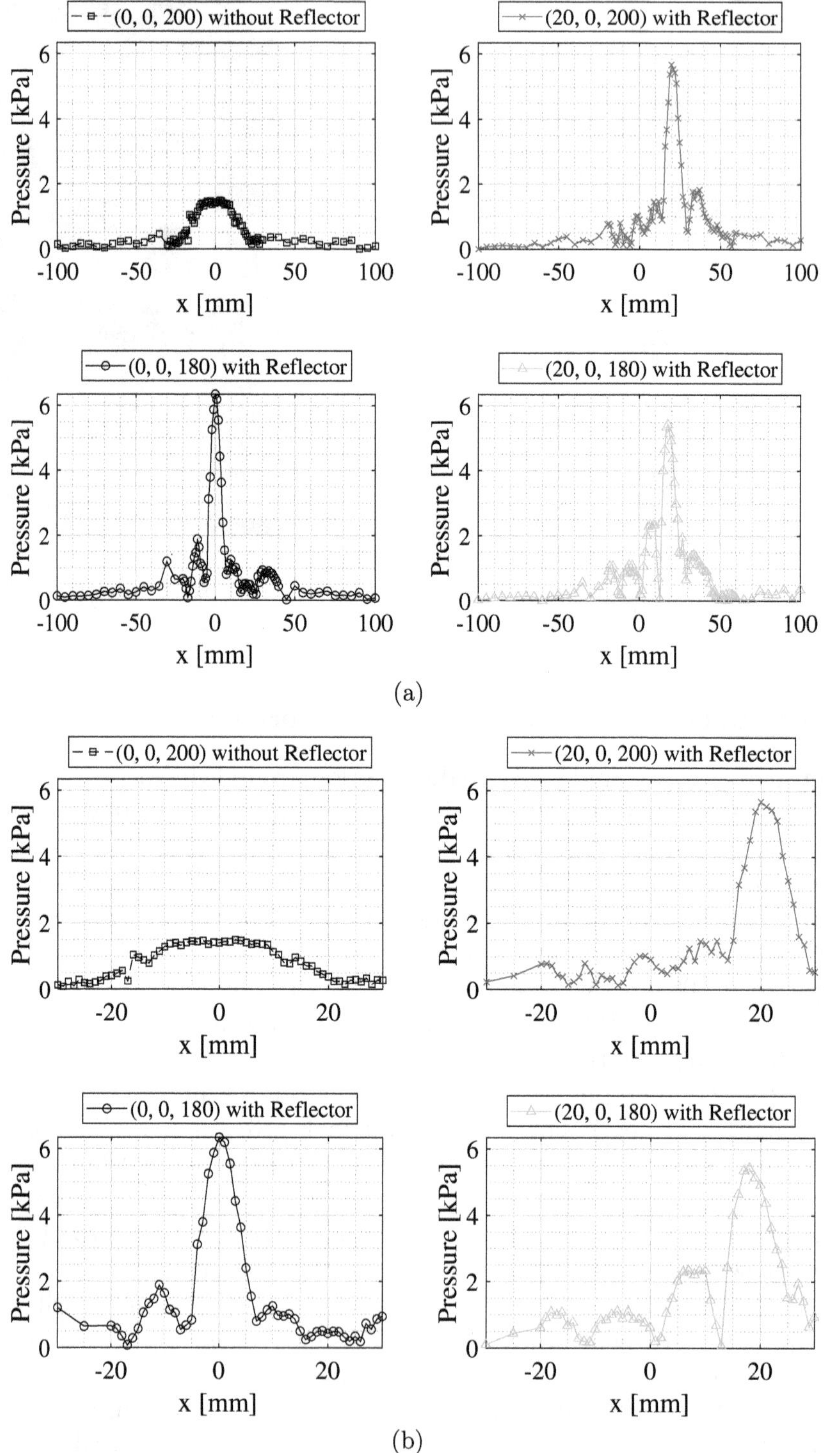

Fig. 3. Measured acoustic pressure distribution in the x-axis direction around each focal point. The position of the focus is at $(x, y, z) = (0, 0, 180\,\text{mm})$, $(20, 0, 180\,\text{mm})$, and $(20, 0, 200\,\text{mm})$ using the reflector, and at $(0, 0, 200\,\text{mm})$ without the reflector. (b) shows an enlarged view of (a).

3.3 Experiment 2: Range of the Workspace

The sound pressure at the focal point when the focus was moved was measured in order to confirm the range of the workspace. The focal position was set at $y = 0\,\text{mm}$ and $z = 160$, 180, and 200 mm, where the distance from the AUTD was 509, 489, and 469 mm, respectively, and moved in the x-axis direction. The microphone was fixed vertically upward and was moved within the range of $-100\,\text{mm} \leqq x \leqq 100\,\text{mm}$.

The results of Experiment 2 is shown in Fig. 4. As indicated in this figure, the focal sound pressure under each condition is sufficiently high around $x = 0\,\text{mm}$, which enables to present a tactile stimulus, and decreases as the focus moves away from the z-axis.

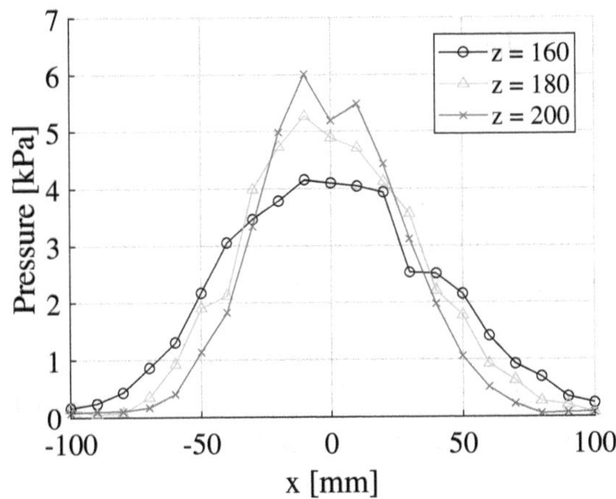

Fig. 4. Measured focal acoustic pressure at each position when the focal point was moved in the x-axis direction. The y coordinate of the focal point is 0 mm.

4 Discussion

As the authors' comment, we were able to perceive a tactile stimulus at the focal points when entering the hands between the reflector and the AUTD. The hand is an obstacle shielding the incident wave, but the focus remains because the aperture of the reflector is sufficiently larger than the obstacle.

In Experiment 1, when the focal point was formed at $(20, 0, 180\,\text{mm})$, the position where the sound pressure became the highest in the x-axis direction was $x = 18\,\text{mm}$, which was shifted from the set position of $x = 20\,\text{mm}$. This is thought to be because of aberrations and displacement of the device. In this study, we did not consider the difference in the acoustic path length, which causes a decrease in the focal sound pressure. Therefore, the focal sound pressure can be increased if we optimize the phase shift of each transducer.

The results of Experiment 1 showed that a focal point can be formed at an arbitrary point through the proposed method. Figure 5 shows an example

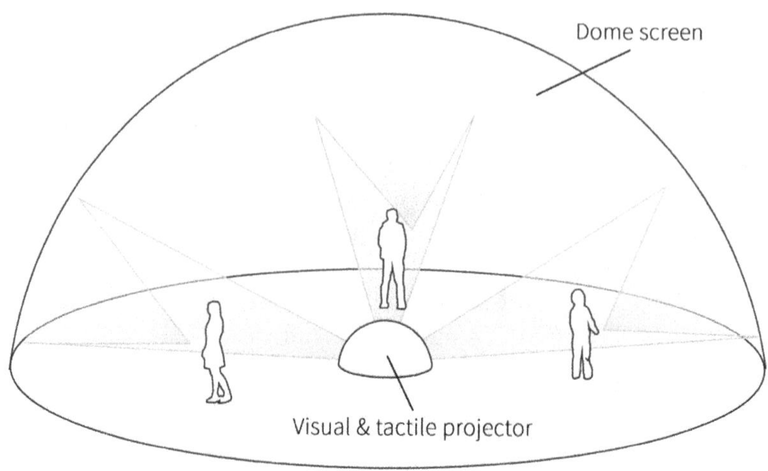

Fig. 5. Application example of the proposed method.

application of this system, in which an image and a tactile sensation are simultaneously presented in a large dome screen by a visual and tactile projector.

Although the proposed method theoretically forms a focal point at an arbitrary position, there are cases where a focal point cannot be formed depending on the position of the phased array and the concave reflector, as well as the aperture of the reflector. For example, in Experiment 2, when the focal point was set to $(0, 0, 240\,\text{mm})$, the position of the image sound source formed by the AUTD was $(0, 0, 720\,\text{mm})$ according to the mirror formula, which is only 51 mm below the AUTD. However, most of the emitted sound waves are not reflected in this case because when simply considering the geometric acoustic model, a concave reflector of approximately 2.57×10^3 mm in diameter is required if the position and focal length of the reflector are fixed. In fact, the focal sound pressure at $(0, 0, 240\,\text{mm})$ was 1.20×10^3 Pa. Moreover, when the irradiation direction of the incident wave is sufficiently shifted from the direction toward the concave mirror, a focal point can be formed at an unexpected position. This is because the grating lobe generated focuses at unintended positions accompanying with the main focus. In fact, in Experiment 2, when the focal point was set at a position sufficiently far from the z-axis, the focus formed by the grating lobe was confirmed. In addition, in this paper we did not consider the attenuation during propagation, by which the amplitude of sound waves exponentially decreases with distance. Therefore, if the propagation distance is too long, the focal sound pressure can be attenuated significantly [2,4].

5 Conclusion

We proposed a method for focusing on an arbitrary point farther from the AUTD using a concave mirror. Our experiments showed that the proposed method can form a focus whose diameter is approximately the wavelength of ultrasound at a point 49 cm away from the phased array with an $18 \times 14\,\text{cm}^2$ aperture and present a tactile stimulus. The focus was electrically steerable within several centimeters in the lateral direction.

References

1. Brice, D., McRoberts, T., Rafferty, K.: A proof of concept integrated multi-systems approach for large scale tactile feedback in VR. In: De Paolis, L.T., Bourdot, P. (eds.) AVR 2019. LNCS, vol. 11613, pp. 120–137. Springer, Cham (2019). https://doi.org/10.1007/978-3-030-25965-5_10
2. Hasegawa, K., Shinoda, H.: Aerial vibrotactile display based on multiunit ultrasound phased array. IEEE Trans. Haptics **11**(3), 367–377 (2018)
3. Hecht, E.: Optics, 4th edn. Addison-Wesley, San Francisco (2002)
4. Hoshi, T., Takahashi, M., Iwamoto, T., Shinoda, H.: Noncontact tactile display based on radiation pressure of airborne ultrasound. IEEE Trans. Haptics **3**(3), 155–165 (2010)
5. Howard, T., Marchal, M., Lécuyer, A., Pacchierotti, C.: PUMAH: pan-tilt ultrasound mid-air haptics for larger interaction workspace in virtual reality. IEEE Trans. Haptics **13**, 38–44 (2019)
6. Inoue, S., Makino, Y., Shinoda, H.: Active touch perception produced by airborne ultrasonic haptic hologram. In: 2015 IEEE World Haptics Conference (WHC), pp. 362–367. IEEE (2015)
7. Ito, Y.: Linearly convergent aerial ultrasonic source providing a variable incident angle and acoustic radiation force by standing-wave ultrasonic field. Jpn. J. Appl. Phys. **48**(7S), 07GM11 (2009)
8. Ito, Y.: High-intensity aerial ultrasonic source with a stripe-mode vibrating plate for improving convergence capability. Acoust. Sci. Technol. **36**(3), 216–224 (2015)
9. Iwamoto, T., Tatezono, M., Shinoda, H.: Non-contact method for producing tactile sensation using airborne ultrasound. In: Ferre, M. (ed.) EuroHaptics 2008. LNCS, vol. 5024, pp. 504–513. Springer, Heidelberg (2008). https://doi.org/10.1007/978-3-540-69057-3_64
10. Korres, G., Eid, M.: Haptogram: ultrasonic point-cloud tactile stimulation. IEEE Access **4**, 7758–7769 (2016)
11. Monnai, Y., Hasegawa, K., Fujiwara, M., Yoshino, K., Inoue, S., Shinoda, H.: HaptoMime: mid-air haptic interaction with a floating virtual screen. In: Proceedings of the 27th Annual ACM Symposium on User Interface Software and Technology, pp. 663–667 (2014)
12. Rodriguez-Molares, A., Løvstakken, L., Ekroll, I.K., Torp, H.: Reconstruction of specular reflectors by iterative image source localization. J. Acoust. Soc. Am. **138**(3), 1365–1378 (2015)
13. Suzuki, S., Takahashi, R., Nakajima, M., Hasegawa, K., Makino, Y., Shinoda, H.: Midair haptic display to human upper body. In: 2018 57th Annual Conference of the Society of Instrument and Control Engineers of Japan (SICE), pp. 848–853. IEEE (2018)

4

Switching Between Objects Improves Precision in Haptic Perception of Softness

Anna Metzger(✉) and Knut Drewing

Justus-Liebig University of Giessen, Giessen, Germany
anna.metzger@psychol.uni-giessen.de

Abstract. Haptic perception involves active exploration usually consisting of repeated stereotypical movements. The choice of such exploratory movements and their parameters are tuned to achieve high perceptual precision. Information obtained from repeated exploratory movements (e.g. repeated indentations of an object to perceive its softness) is integrated but improvement of discrimination performance is limited by memory if the two objects are explored one after the other in order to compare them. In natural haptic exploration humans tend to switch between the objects multiple times when comparing them. Using the example of softness perception here we test the hypothesis that given the same amount of information, discrimination improves if memory demands are lower. In our experiment participants explored two softness stimuli by indenting each of the stimuli four times. They were allowed to switch between the stimuli after every single indentation (7 switches), after every second indentation (3 switches) or only once after four indentations (1 switch). We found better discrimination performance with seven switches as compared to one switch, indicating that humans naturally apply an exploratory strategy which might reduce memory demands and thus leads to improved performance.

Keywords: Softness · Haptic · Perception · Psychophysics

1 Introduction

We usually have to actively move our sensory organs to obtain relevant information about the world around us. Such exploratory movements are often tuned to maximize the gain of information [1–4]. In active touch perception tuning of exploratory movements is very prominent. Humans use different highly stereotypical movements to judge different object properties [2]. For instance, they move the hand laterally over the object's surface to judge its roughness, in contrast, the hand is held statically on the object to judge its temperature. For each haptic property precision is best with the habitually used *Exploratory Procedure* as opposed to others [2]. Also motor parameters of *Exploratory Procedures*, such as finger force in perception of softness and shape [5,6], are tuned to optimize performance. This fine tuning is based on available predictive signals as well as on progressively gathered sensory information [3,7]. However, it could also reflect a compensation for limitations of the perceptual system. For instance it is believed that most eye movements are not designated to gain novel information for building up an internal representation of the scene, but to obtain momentary necessary information using the world as an external memory given limited capacity of short-term working memory [8,9]. Here we study whether natural haptic exploration is tuned to compensate for memory limitations.

Integration of accumulated sensory information was in many cases shown to be consistent with Bayesian inference [10]. In this framework available sensory information and assumptions based on prior knowledge are integrated by weighted averaging, with weights being proportional to the reliability of single estimates. This integration is considered statistically optimal because overall reliability is maximized. This framework was successfully applied to describe the integration of sensory and prior information (e.g. [11]), simultaneously available information (e.g. [12]) as well as information gathered over time (e.g. [13]). For the later purpose usually a Kalman filter [14] is used: A recursive Bayesian optimal combination of new sensory information with previously obtained information, which can also account for changes of the world over time.

In haptic perception it was shown that prior information is integrated into the percept of an object's softness [15]. It was also shown that sequentially gathered information from every indentation contributes to the overall perception of an object's softness [16] and information from every stroke over the object's surface contributes to the perception of its roughness [17]. However, the contribution of these single exploratory movements to the overall percept seems to be not equal, as would be predicted if there was no loss of information and integration was statistically optimal. When two objects are explored one after the other in a two-interval forced-choice task, information from later exploratory movements on the second object contributes less to the comparison of the two objects [16,17]. These results are consistent with the idea that perceptual weights decay with progressing exploration of the second object due to a fading memory representation of the first object. Indeed it could be shown that when a stronger representation of the first object's softness is built up by longer exploration, information from later indentations contributes more than with a weaker representation [18]. Also, consistent with memory characteristics [19] mere temporal delay of 5s after the exploration of the first object does not affect the memory representation of the first object [20]. A model for serial integration of information using a Kalman filter could explain the decrease of perceptual weights in the exploration of the second object by including memory decay of the first object's representation [17]. In the modelled experimental conditions people had to discriminate between two objects that are explored strictly one after the other, i.e. in their exploration people switched only once between the two stimuli. In this case memory decay of the first object's representation should have had particularly pronounced negative effects on discrimination. However, in free explorations participants usually switch more often between the objects in order to compare them (in softness discrimination on average 4 times, given 6–14 indentations in total and an achieved performance of 85–90% correct [7,21]). This might be a strategy to cope with memory decay and improve discrimination performance.

Using the example of softness perception here we test the hypothesis that discrimination improves when participants switch more than once between the two objects given the same number of indentations of each of them, i.e. the same sensory input. In our experiment participants were instructed to indent each test object four times. There were three switch conditions: Participants switched between the two objects after every single indentation (7 switches), after every second indentation (3 switches) or only once after four indentations (1 switch).

2 Methods

2.1 Participants

Eleven volunteers (6 female, right-handed) participated in the experiment. Written informed consent was obtained from each participant and they were reimbursed with 8€/h for their time. The study was approved by the local ethics committee at Justus-Liebig University Giessen LEK FB06 (SFB-TPA5, 22/08/13) and was in line with the declaration of Helsinki from 2008.

2.2 Apparatus

The experiment was conducted at a visuo-haptic workbench (Fig. 1A) consisting of a force-sensor (bending beam load cell LCB 130 and a measuring amplifier GSV-2AS, resolution .05 N, temporal resolution 682 Hz, ME-Messsysteme GmbH), a PHANToM 1.5A haptic force feedback device, a 22"-computer screen (120 Hz, 1280 × 1024 pixel), stereo glasses and a mirror. Participants sat at a table with the head resting in a chin rest. Two softness stimuli were placed side-by-side (distance in between 2 cm) in front of them on the force sensor. To prevent direct sight of the stimuli and of the exploring hand but in the same time indicating their position, a schematic 3D representation of the stimuli and the finger spatially aligned with the real ones was shown via monitor and mirror. The finger was represented as a 8 mm diameter sphere only when not in contact with the stimuli (force < 1N). Participants touched the stimuli with the right index finger. The finger's position was detected with the PHANToM. For this purpose it was attached to the PHANToM arm with a custom-made adapter (Fig. 1B) consisting of magnetically interconnected metallic pin with a round end and a plastic fingernail. We used adhesive deformable glue pads to affix the plastic fingernail to the fingernail of the participant. Connected to the PHANToM the finger pad was left uncovered and the finger could be moved with all six degrees of freedom within a workspace of 38 × 27 × 20 cm. Custom-made software (C++) controlled the experiment, collected responses, and recorded finger positions and reaction forces every 3 ms. Signal sounds were presented via headphones.

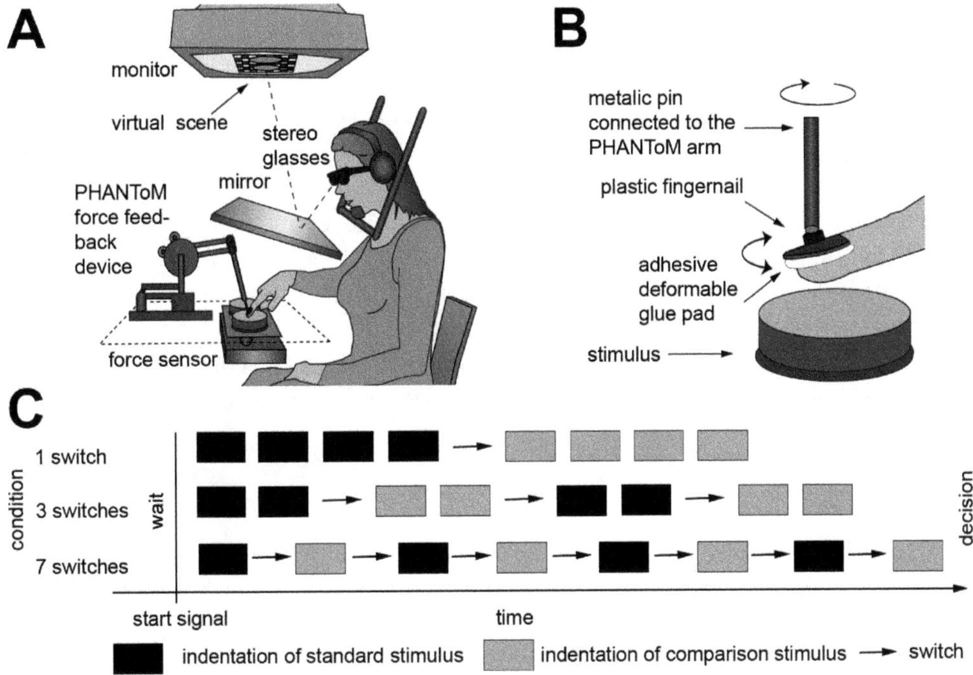

Fig. 1. A. Visuo-haptic workbench. **B.** Custom made finger PHANToM to finger connection. **C.** Experimental procedure. Timing of single trial phases was not restricted. Either the comparison or the standard stimulus could have been explored first.

2.3 Softness Stimuli

We produced softness stimuli with different elasticity by mixing a two-component silicon rubber solution (AlpaSil EH 10:1) with different amounts of silicon oil (polydimethylsiloxane, viscosity 50 mPa/s) and pouring it into cylindrical plastic dishes (75 mm diameter × 38 mm height). We produced in total 10 stimuli: 1 standard (Young's modulus of 59.16 kPa) and 9 comparison stimuli (Young's moduli of 31.23, 42.84, 49.37, 55.14, 57.04, 69.62, 72.15, 73.29 and 88.18 kPa). To characterize the elasticity of the stimuli we adopted the standard methodology proposed by [22]. From the solution mixed for every stimulus a portion was poured into a small cylinder (10 mm thick, 10 mm diameter) to obtain standardized substrates of the same material for the measurement. We used the experimental apparatus to measure elasticity. They were placed onto the force sensor and were indented by the PHANToM force feedback device. For this purpose we attached an aluminium plate of 24 mm diameter instead of the fingertip adapter. The force was increased by 0.005 N every 3 ms until a minimum force of 1 N and a minimum displacement of 1 mm were detected. Measures in which the force increased quicker than it should were considered as artefacts and removed before analysis. From the cleaned force and displacement data we calculated stress and strain. A linear Young's modulus was fitted to each stress-strain curve (only for 0–0.1 strain) in MATLAB R2017.

2.4 Design

There were three *Nr of switches* conditions: 1, 3 and 7 switches. The dependent variable was the just noticeable difference (JND), which we measured using a two-alternative-force-choice task combined with a method of constant stimuli. For each condition the standard stimulus was presented 12 times with each of the 9 comparison stimuli (overall 324 trials). The experiment was organized in 3 blocks of 108 trials, comprising 4 repetitions of each standard-comparison pairing, to balance for fatigue effects. Trials of different conditions were presented in random order. The position of the standard (right or left) and its presentation as first or second stimulus was balanced for every standard-comparison pairing. Differences between the conditions were analysed with paired two-sample t-tests.

2.5 Procedure

In every trial, participants sequentially explored the standard and a comparison and decided which one felt softer. A schematic of the procedure is outlined in Fig. 1C. Before a trial, participants rested the finger in the left corner of the workspace and waited until the experimenter changed the stimuli. The beginning of a trial was signaled by a tone and by the appearance of the schematic representation of the first stimulus. The number of indentations allowed to explore the stimulus (1, 2 or 4) was indicated above it. To detect and count stimulus' indentations we used the algorithm from [16]. After the necessary number of indentations the visual representation of the first stimulus disappeared and the representation of the second stimulus appeared. Participants switched to the other stimulus, and again the number of sequential indentations was indicated. Participants continued to switch between the stimuli until every stimulus was indented 4 times in total. Following this, participants indicated their decision on softness by pressing one of two virtual buttons using the PHANToM. A trial in which the stimuli were indented more then 8 times was repeated later in the block. Before the experiment participants were acquainted to the task and the setup in a training session of 12 trials. They did not receive any feedback on their performance to avoid explicit learning. Each participant completed the experiment on the same day within on average 2.5 h.

2.6 Analysis

We calculated for each participant, each condition, and each comparison stimulus the percentage of trials in which it was perceived to be softer than the standard. Combined for all comparisons these values composed individual psychometric data, to which we fitted cumulative Gaussian functions using the psignifit 4 toolbox [23]. Only the means and the standard deviations of the functions were fitted, lapse rates were set to 0. From the fitted psychometric functions, we estimated the JNDs as the 84% discrimination thresholds.

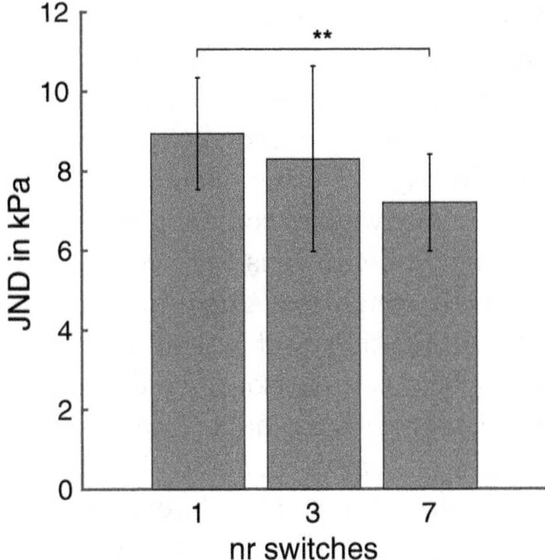

Fig. 2. Average discrimination thresholds for softness of two silicon stimuli each indented 4 times with the bare finger. Participants switched between the stimuli once after 4 indentations, after every 2. indentation (3 switches) or after every indentation (7 switches). Error bars represent within-subject standard error [24]. $**p < 0.005$

3 Results

Figure 2 depicts the average JNDs in the three different *Nr of switches* conditions (1, 3 and 7). The average Weber fractions were 15.08%, 14.01% and 12.14% for 1, 3, and 7 switches respectively. The JNDs decreased with increasing number of switches between the stimuli. Pairwise comparisons revealed that performance was significantly better, when participants switched after every indentation of the stimulus as compared to switching only once after 4 indentations, $t(10) = 4.64$, $p = 0.001$. The performance in the intermediate condition (switching after every second indentation) was numerically in between the other ones. However, we did not find significant differences in the comparisons with this condition (1 vs. 3 switches: $t(10) = 0.57$, $p = 0.578$; 3 vs. 7 switches: $t(10) = 1.07$, $p = 0.311$). We observed higher variance in this condition, possibly due to a more complicated task than in the other two conditions (Fig. 2).

4 Discussion

In the present study, we investigated whether more frequent switching between the stimuli improves discrimination performance in active touch perception of objects' softness. Participants explored two softness stimuli with the same number of indentations (4 per stimulus) but switched between the stimuli either only once after four indentations, after every second indentation or after every indentation. We showed that if participants could switch after every indentation discrimination performance was significantly better than if they could switch only once. We argue that this is due to greater memory demands, because the first stimulus' has to be remembered longer to compare it to every indentation of the second stimulus, than when switching after every indentation. It could also be argued that integration across more indentations of the first stimulus demands greater attention, leading to worse performance, especially because here we did not manipulate factors directly affecting memory i.e. inter-stimulus delay or masking. However, we previously observed that in the exploration of the first stimulus the weights of single indentations were equal, as would be predicted for optimal integration [12] while weights of single indentations of the second stimulus decreased with time, indicating that not all information about the second stimulus could be used for the comparison. We could also show that observed decay in weights was consistent with memory decay in tactile perception [17,25], suggesting that a difference in memory demands is a more likely explanation for the observed difference in performance in different switch conditions.

The Kalman model of serial integration proposed by [17], assumes that when switching only once between the stimuli, differences between each sequentially gathered estimate of the second stimulus and the overall estimate of the first stimulus are integrated in a statistically optimal way given memory decay, modelled as increasing variance of the first stimulus' estimate over time. Thus, given the same amount of information, this model predicts that precision should be higher the shorter the first stimulus needs to be remembered, which is consistent with our results. However, to apply this model to our data, we would need to extend it by the variable containing the result of one comparison. To test the predictions of this extended model we would need additional data (e.g. precision based on one indentation per stimulus).

Overall our results suggest that in active touch perception where integration of information is limited by memory [16–18,20], the naturally applied strategy of switching between the stimuli [21] can be more beneficial for performance than prolonged accumulation of information about each stimulus.

References

1. Najemnik, J., Geisler, W.S.: Optimal eye movement strategies in visual search. Nature **434**(7031), 387–391 (2005)
2. Lederman, S.J., Klatzky, R.L.: Hand movement: a window into haptic object recognition. Cogn. Psychol. **19**, 342–368 (1987)
3. Saig, A., Gordon, G., Assa, E., Arieli, A., Ahissar, E.: Motor-sensory confluence in tactile perception. J. Neurosci. **32**(40), 14022–14032 (2012)
4. Toscani, M., Valsecchi, M., Gegenfurtner, K.R.: Optimal sampling of visual information for lightness judgments. Proc. Natl. Acad. Sci. **110**(27), 11163–11168 (2013)
5. Drewing, K.: After experience with the task humans actively optimize shape discrimination in touch by utilizing effects of exploratory movement direction. Acta Psychologica **141**(3), 295–303 (2012)
6. Kaim, L., Drewing, K.: Exploratory strategies in haptic softness discrimination are tuned to achieve high levels of task performance. IEEE Trans. Haptics **4**(4), 242–252 (2011)

7. Lezkan, A., Metzger, A., Drewing, K.: Active haptic exploration of softness: indentation force is systematically related to prediction, sensation and motivation. Front. Integrative Neurosci. **12**, 59 (2018)
8. O'Regan, J.K.: Solving the "real" mysteries of visual perception: the world as an outside memory. Can. J. Psychol. **46**, 461–488 (1992)
9. Ballard, D.H., Hayhoe, M.M., Pelz, J.B.: Memory representations in natural tasks. J. Cogn. Neurosci. **7**(1), 66–80 (1995)
10. Kersten, D., Mamassian, P., Yuille, A.: Object perception as Bayesian inference. Ann. Rev. Psychol. **55**, 271–304 (2004)
11. Körding, K.P., Wolpert, D.M.: Bayesian integration in sensorimotor learning. Nature **427**(6971), 244–247 (2004)
12. Ernst, M.O., Banks, M.S.: Humans integrate visual and haptic information in a statistically optimal fashion. Nature **415**(6870), 429–433 (2002)
13. Kwon, O.S., Tadin, D., Knill, D.C.: Unifying account of visual motion and position perception. Proc. Natl. Acad. Sci. **112**(26), 8142–8147 (2015)
14. Kalman, R.E.: A new approach to linear filtering and prediction problems. J. Basic Eng. **82**(1), 35–45 (1960)
15. Metzger, A., Drewing, K.: Memory influences haptic perception of softness. Sci. Rep. **9**, 14383 (2019)
16. Metzger, A., Lezkan, A., Drewing, K.: Integration of serial sensory information in haptic perception of softness. J. Exp. Psychol.: Hum. Perception Perform. **44**(4), 551–565 (2018)
17. Lezkan, A., Drewing, K.: Processing of haptic texture information over sequential exploration movements. Attention Percept. Psychophys. **80**(1), 177–192 (2017)
18. Metzger, A., Drewing, K.: The longer the first stimulus is explored in softness discrimination the longer it can be compared to the second one. In: 2017 IEEE World Haptics Conference, WHC 2017 (2017)
19. Lewandowsky, S., Oberauer, K.: No evidence for temporal decay in working memory. J. Exp. Psychol.: Learn. Memory Cogn. **35**(6), 1545–1551 (2009)
20. Metzger, A., Drewing, K.: Effects of stimulus exploration length and time on the integration of information in haptic softness discrimination. IEEE Trans. Haptics **12**(4), 451–460 (2019)
21. Zoeller, A.C., Lezkan, A., Paulun, V.C., Fleming, R.W., Drewing, K.: Integration of prior knowledge during haptic exploration depends on information type. J. Vis. **19**(4), 1–15 (2019)
22. Gerling, G.J., Hauser, S.C., Soltis, B.R., Bowen, A.K., Fanta, K.D., Wang, Y.: A standard methodology to characterize the intrinsic material properties of compliant test stimuli. IEEE Trans. Haptics **11**(4), 498–508 (2018)
23. Schuett, H.H., Harmeling, S., Macke, J.H., Wichmann, F.A.: Painfree and accurate Bayesian estimation of psychometric functions for (potentially) overdispersed data. Vis. Res. **122**, 105–123 (2016)
24. Cousineau, D.: Confidence intervals in within-subject designs: a simpler solution to Loftus and Masson's method. Tutorial Quant. Methods Psychol. **1**(1), 42–45 (2005)
25. Murray, D.J., Ward, R., Hockley, W.E.: Tactile short-term memory in relation to the two-point threshold. Q. J. Exp. Psychol. **27**(2), 303–312 (1975)

5

LinkRing: A Wearable Haptic Display for Delivering Multi-Contact and Multi-Modal Stimuli at the Finger Pads

Aysien Ivanov(✉), Daria Trinitatova(✉), and Dzmitry Tsetserukou(✉)

Skolkovo Institute of Science and Technology (Skoltech), Moscow 121205, Russia
{aysien.ivanov,daria.trinitatova,d.tsetserukou}@skoltech.ru

Abstract. LinkRing is a novel wearable tactile display for providing multi-contact and multi-modal stimuli at the finger. The system of two five-bar linkage mechanisms is designed to operate with two independent contact points, which combined can provide such stimulation as shear force and twist stimuli, slippage, and pressure. The proposed display has a lightweight and easy to wear structure. Two experiments were carried out in order to determine the sensitivity of the finger surface, the first one aimed to determine the location of the contact points, and the other for discrimination the slippage with varying rates. The results of the experiments showed a high level of pattern recognition.

Keywords: Haptic display · Wearable tactile devices · Multi-contact stimuli · Five-bar linkage

1 Introduction

Recent developments in computer graphics and head-mounted displays contributed to the appearance of different applications and games that implement VR technologies. Nevertheless, there is still a lack of providing haptic feedback, which is a crucial component to accomplish the full user immersion in a virtual environment.

Tactile information obtained from the fingers is one of the most important tools for interacting with the environment as fingertips have a rich set of mechanoreceptors. Thereby, the finger area plays an essential role in haptic perception. Nowadays, there are many research projects aimed at the design and application of fingertip haptic devices. One of the common methods for providing cutaneous feedback to the fingertips is by a moving platform shifting on the finger pad [2,4]. Several works are focused on delivering mechanical stimulations and can reliably generate normal forces to the fingertip [8], as well as shear deformation of the skin [9]. The most general method to simulate the object texture is using vibration [7,12], and the friction sensation is usually generated by electrostatic force [5]. A number of studies investigate the perception of object softness [3,15]. Villa Salazar et al. [11] examined the impact of combining simple passive tangible VR objects and wearable haptic display on haptic sensation by modifying the stiffness, friction, and shape perception of tangible objects in VR. Some research works explore multimodal tactile stimulation. In [13], Yem et al. presented FinGAR haptic device, which combines electrical and mechanical stimulation for generating skin deformation, high/low-frequency vibration, and pressure. Similarly, the work [14] presents the fingertip haptic interface for providing electrical, thermal, and vibrotactile stimulation. Still, there is a need for a device that allows users to interact with virtual objects in a more realistic way. The interaction can be improved by the physical perception of the objects and their dimensions. Our approach suggests the use of a wearable haptic device, which can provide a multi-contact interaction on the finger pad that a person can experience when interacting with a real object.

In this paper, we propose LinkRing, a novel wearable haptic device with 4-DoF, which provides multi-contact and multi-modal cutaneous feedback on the finger pad (Fig. 1(a)). The haptic display is designed as the system of two five-bar linkage mechanisms which operate with two independent contact points. The proposed device can deliver a wide range of tactile sensations, such as contact, pressure, twist stimuli, and slippage.

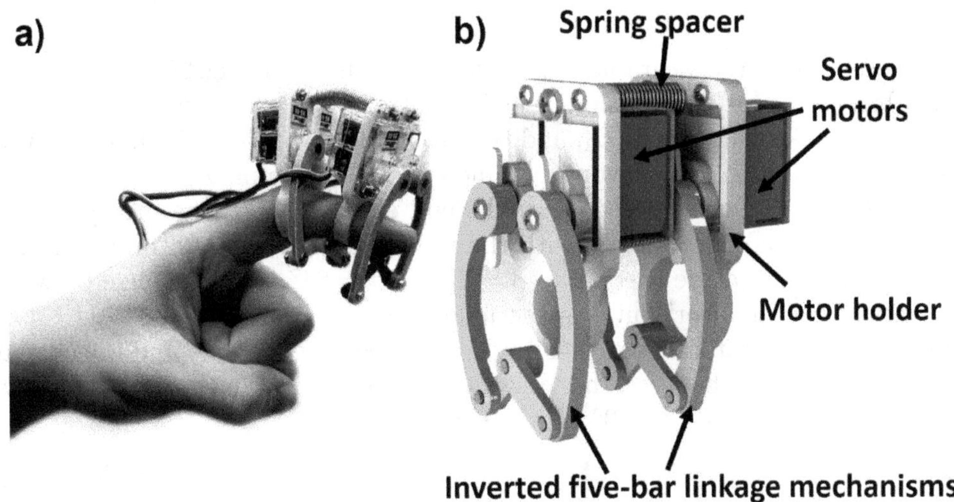

Fig. 1. a) A wearable haptic display LinkRing. b) A CAD model of wearable tactile display LinkRing.

2 Design of Haptic Display LinkRing

LinkRing is designed to deliver multi-modal and multi-contact stimuli at the finger pads. The proposed device is based on the planar parallel mechanism, which was previously applied in several works [1,6,10]. Two parallel inverted five-bar mechanisms with 2-DoF each deliver tactile feedback in two independent points on the finger pads. Each of them can generate normal and shear forces at the contact point. And in combination, they can simulate different sizes of grasped objects, the feeling of spinning objects, and the sense of sliding a finger on the surface to the left, to the right, and around the axis perpendicular to the finger pad plane. The prototype consists of 3D-printed parts, namely, motor holders fastened to the finger and links made of flexible PLA and PLA, respectively, and metal spring spacers with diameter 6 mm connecting the system of inverted five-bar linkages (Fig. 1(b)). The distance between the end-effectors is 26 mm, and it can vary by choosing the different lengths of the spacers. The fastening for the finger was designed as a snap ring to be suitable for different sizes. The specification of the device is shown in Table 1.

Table 1. Technical specification of LinkRing.

Motors	Hitec HS-40
Material of the motor holders	Soft PLA
Material of the links	PLA
Weight [g]	33
Link length L1, L2 [mm]	35, 17
Max. normal force at each contact point [N]	1.5 ± 0.15

The scheme of the wearable haptic display is shown in Fig. 2(a). The mechanism has two input links with length L_1 controlled by the input angles θ_1, θ_2, two output links with length L_2, and the ground link with length D. The developed prototype has the following parameters: $L_1 = 35$ mm, $L_2 = 17$ mm, and $D = 15$ mm. The initial position for the end effector, when the mechanism is symmetric and in contact state with the user's finger, is $H = 22$ mm. For this position, the input angle is equal to $\alpha = 180 - \theta_1 = 84°$, and the angle between the output link and horizontal is the following $\beta = arcsin(\frac{L_1 sin\alpha - H}{L_2}) = 49°$. From Fig. 2(b) we can calculate the angle γ between the force F_1 and the output link and the angle φ between the force F_2 and the vertical in the following way: $\varphi = 90° - \beta = 41°$ and $\gamma = 90° - \alpha + \beta = 55°$.

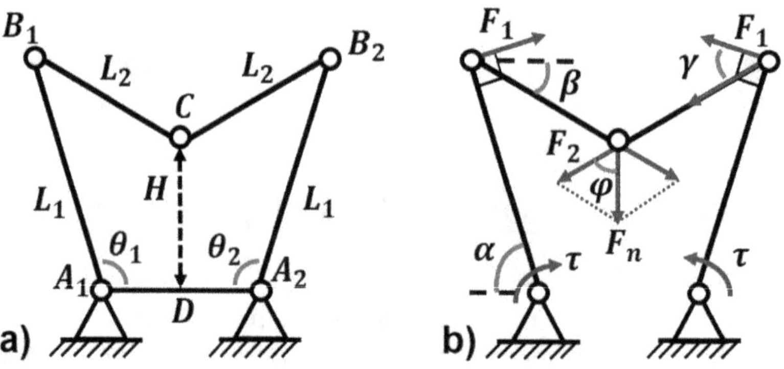

Fig. 2. a) Device kinematic scheme. b) Static force diagram.

The device is actuated by Hitec HS-40 servo motors with a low mass and rather high output torque (Weight is 4.8 g, dimensions are $20 \times 8.6 \times 17$ mm, maximum torque is 0.6 kg-cm). The maximum force is achieved with the symmetric case when the resulting force applied to the finger is a normal force (directed vertically). In this case: $F_1 = \tau/L_1$; $F_2 = F_1 \cdot cos(\gamma)$; $F_n = 2 \cdot F_2 \cdot cos(\varphi)$. The maximum value of the normal force is $F_n = 1.46$ N. To verify this result, we experimentally measured the force with a calibrated force sensing resistor (FSR 400). The experiment showed that the maximum generated force is $F = 1.5\,\text{N} \pm 0.15\,\text{N}$.

3 User Study

We evaluated the performance of the developed haptic display in two user studies. Firstly, we estimated the distinction in the perception of different static contact patterns simulated on the user's finger. Secondly, we tested the ability of users to distinguish the sliding speed of end effectors at the contact area. For the two experiments, the user was asked to sit in front of a desk, and to wear the LinkRing display on the left index finger. To increase the purity of the experiment, we asked the users to use headphones and fenced off the hand with a device from the user by a barrier (Fig. 3 (a)).

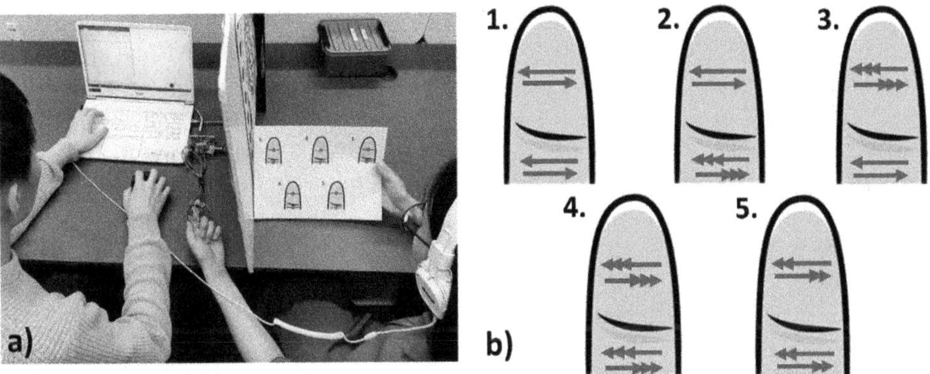

Fig. 3. a) Overview of the experiment. b) Slippage patterns for the experiment. Single arrows indicate the slow speed in the contact point, double arrows mean middle rate, and triple arrows represent fast speed. The direction of the arrow indicates the side of the contact point motion.

3.1 Static Pattern Experiment

The purpose of the experiment was to study the recognition of various patterns on the user's finger differing in the location of the contact points. Nine patterns with different positions of static points were designed (Fig. 4). In total, ten subjects took part in the experiment, two women and eight men, from 21 to 30 years old.

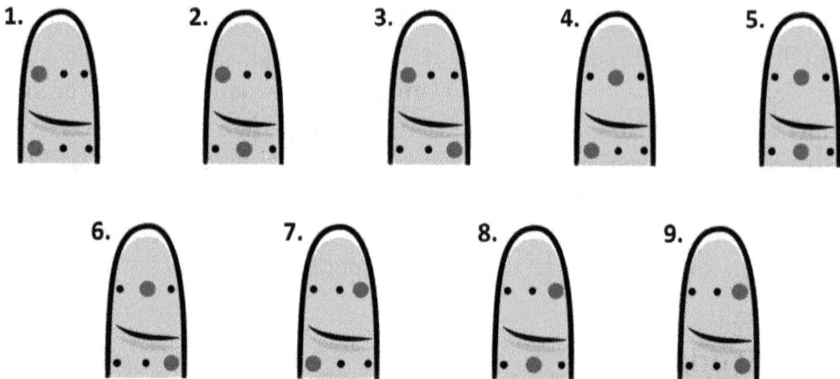

Fig. 4. Patterns for the experiment with static points. Blue dots represent pressed point, and back dots show the possible contact locations. (Color figure online)

Before the experiment, the calibration was conducted for each participant to provide all the contact points on the finger. The calibration was based on two parameters: the thickness and width of the finger. During the training session, each pattern was delivered two times to the user.

During the experiment, the participant was provided with a visual guide of the designed patterns. For each trial, end effectors reached a specified location in a non-contact position. After that, one pattern was delivered to the finger for three seconds, and they returned to the non-contact position. After the delivery of the static pattern on the user's finger, the subject was asked to specify the number that corresponds to the provided contact pattern. Each pattern was delivered five times in random order. In total, 45 patterns were presented to each subject.

Experimental Results

Table 2 shows a confusion matrix for actual and perceived static patterns. Every row in the confusion matrix represents all 50 times a contact pattern was provided.

The results of the experiment revealed that the mean percent of correct answers for each pattern averaged over all the participants ranged from 68% to 100%. The mean percentage of the correct answers is 90%. The most recognizable contact positions were 1st, 4th, and 5th, with a recognition rate of 98%, 98%, and 100%. And the least distinct pattern was 9th with a rate of 68%. It can be observed that a high number of participants confused pattern 9 with 8, which are very close.

In order to understand if there is a real difference between pattern perception, the experimental results were analyzed using one-factor ANOVA without replication with a chosen significance level of $p < 0.05$. According to the test findings, there is a statistically significant difference in the recognition rates for the different contact patterns ($F(8, 81) = 2.43,\ p = 0.02 < 0.05$). It was significantly more difficult for participants to recognize pattern $9th$ than $5th(F(1, 18) = 16,\ p = 8.4 \cdot 10^{-4} < 0.05)$, $1st$ and $4th(F(1, 18) = 13.2,\ p = 1.88 \cdot 10^{-3} < 0.05)$, and $2nd$, $6th$ and $7th(F(1, 18) = 6.23,\ p = 0.022 < 0.05)$.

Table 2. Confusion matrix for actual and perceived static patterns across all the subjects

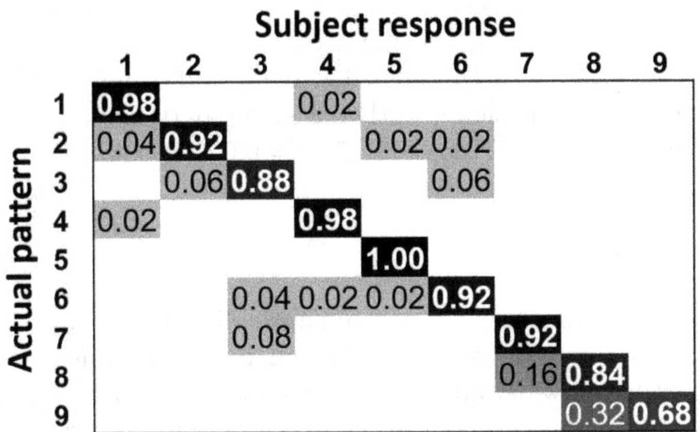

Actual pattern \ Subject response	1	2	3	4	5	6	7	8	9
1	0.98			0.02					
2	0.04	0.92			0.02	0.02			
3		0.06	0.88			0.06			
4	0.02			0.98					
5					1.00				
6			0.04	0.02	0.02	0.92			
7			0.08				0.92		
8							0.16	0.84	
9								0.32	0.68

3.2 Experiment of the Recognition of Moving Patterns

The objective of the experiment was to study the user recognition of end effector slippage with various speeds which were delivered to the finger at the same time by both contact points. Eleven participants volunteered into the experiments, two females and nine males, from 21 to 31 years old.

Three different speeds for slippage on the finger were used: slow (43 mm/s), middle (60 mm/s), and fast (86 mm/s). The five slippage patterns were designed to study the sensing of the end effectors velocity. Second and third patterns transmit different speeds on contact points, and other patterns deliver equal rates (Fig. 3 (b)). Each pattern was presented five times in random order, thus, 25 patters were provided to each subject.

Experimental Results

The results of the experiment are summarized in a confusion matrix (Table 3). The mean percentage of the correct answers is 81%. The most distinctive speed patterns are 2nd and 3rd, with a recognition rate of 94% and 89%. They have represented patterns with different velocities of the end effector in two contact points. And the most confusing pattern is 5th with a recognition rate of 65%.

Table 3. Confusion matrix for actual and perceived slippage patterns across all the subjects

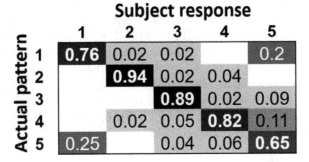

Actual pattern \ Subject response	1	2	3	4	5
1	0.76	0.02	0.02		0.2
2		0.94	0.02	0.04	
3			0.89	0.02	0.09
4		0.02	0.05	0.82	0.11
5	0.25		0.04	0.06	0.65

Using the one-factor ANOVA without replications, with a chosen significance level of $p < 0.05$, we found a statistically significant difference among the different dynamic patterns ($F(5, 50) = 3.28,\ p = 1.83 \cdot 10^{-2} < 0.05$). According to ANOVA results, $2nd$ pattern has a significantly higher recognition rate than the patterns $1st(F(1, 20) = 5.75,\ p = 0.026 < 0.05)$ and $5th(F(1, 20) = 11.4,\ p = 2.97 \cdot 10^{-3} < 0.05)$. It was significantly easier for participants to recognize the $3rd$ pattern than the $5th(F(1, 20) = 6.17,\ p = 0.022 < 0.05)$.

4 Conclusion

We have developed LinkRing, a wearable haptic display that can provide multi-contact stimuli in two independent points of the user's finger. The device is capable of generating a wide range of tactile sensations such as contact, slippage, twist stimuli, and pressure. The structure of the device is lightweight and easy to wear. The user study revealed high recognition rates in discrimination of static and dynamic patterns delivered to the finger pads. The obtained results allow us to determine the most suitable patterns for further presenting the static and moving object for the finger perception with the proposed display.

The future work will be aimed at expending multi-modal stimuli by adding vibration motors to the end effectors as well as improving the design of the device by reducing its dimensions and increasing its ergonomics. Various virtual applications are going to be developed to study virtual immersion quality and fidelity of multi-modal tactile stimuli. The developed haptic display can potentially bring a highly immersive VR experience in the guiding blind navigation systems, teleoperation, and medical VR simulators.

References

1. Cabrera, M.A., Tsetserukou, D.: LinkGlide: a wearable haptic display with inverted five-bar linkages for delivering multi-contact and multi-modal tactile stimuli. In: Kajimoto, H., Lee, D., Kim, S.-Y., Konyo, M., Kyung, K.-U. (eds.) AsiaHaptics 2018. LNEE, vol. 535, pp. 149–154. Springer, Singapore (2019). https://doi.org/10.1007/978-981-13-3194-7_33
2. Chinello, F., Malvezzi, M., Pacchierotti, C., Prattichizzo, D.: Design and development of a 3RRS wearable fingertip cutaneous device. In: 2015 IEEE International Conference on Advanced Intelligent Mechatronics (AIM), pp. 293–298. IEEE (2015)
3. Frediani, G., Mazzei, D., De Rossi, D.E., Carpi, F.: Wearable wireless tactile display for virtual interactions with soft bodies. Front. Bioeng. Biotechnol. **2**, 31 (2014)
4. Gabardi, M., Solazzi, M., Leonardis, D., Frisoli, A.: A new wearable fingertip haptic interface for the rendering of virtual shapes and surface features. In: 2016 IEEE Haptics Symposium (HAPTICS), pp. 140–146. IEEE (2016)
5. Meyer, D.J., Wiertlewski, M., Peshkin, M.A., Colgate, J.E.: Dynamics of ultrasonic and electrostatic friction modulation for rendering texture on haptic surfaces. In: 2014 IEEE Haptics Symposium (HAPTICS), pp. 63–67, February 2014. https://doi.org/10.1109/HAPTICS.2014.6775434

6. Moriyama, T.K., Nishi, A., Sakuragi, R., Nakamura, T., Kajimoto, H.: Development of a wearable haptic device that presents haptics sensation of the finger pad to the forearm. In: 2018 IEEE Haptics Symposium (HAPTICS), pp. 180–185. IEEE (2018)
7. Romano, J.M., Yoshioka, T., Kuchenbecker, K.J.: Automatic filter design for synthesis of haptic textures from recorded acceleration data. In: 2010 IEEE International Conference on Robotics and Automation, pp. 1815–1821, May 2010. https://doi.org/10.1109/ROBOT.2010.5509853
8. Scheggi, S., Meli, L., Pacchierotti, C., Prattichizzo, D.: Touch the virtual reality: using the leap motion controller for hand tracking and wearable tactile devices for immersive haptic rendering. In: ACM SIGGRAPH 2015 Posters. Association for Computing Machinery (2015)
9. Schorr, S.B., Okamura, A.M.: Three-dimensional skin deformation as force substitution: wearable device design and performance during haptic exploration of virtual environments. IEEE Trans. Haptics **10**(3), 418–430 (2017)
10. Tsetserukou, D., Hosokawa, S., Terashima, K.: LinkTouch: a wearable haptic device with five-bar linkage mechanism for presentation of two-DOF force feedback at the fingerpad. In: 2014 IEEE Haptics Symposium (HAPTICS), pp. 307–312, February 2014. https://doi.org/10.1109/HAPTICS.2014.6775473
11. Villa Salazar, D.S., Pacchierotti, C., De Tinguy De La Girouliere, X., Maciel, A., Marchal, M.: Altering the stiffness, friction, and shape perception of tangible objects in virtual reality using wearable haptics. IEEE Trans. Haptics **13**(1), 167–174 (2020). https://doi.org/10.1109/TOH.2020.2967389
12. Yatani, K., Truong, K.N.: SemFeel: a user interface with semantic tactile feedback for mobile touch-screen devices. In: Proceedings of the 22nd Annual ACM Symposium on User Interface Software and Technology, UIST 2009, pp. 111–120 (2009). https://doi.org/10.1145/1622176.1622198
13. Yem, V., Kajimoto, H.: Wearable tactile device using mechanical and electrical stimulation for fingertip interaction with virtual world. In: Proceedings - IEEE Virtual Reality, pp. 99–104 (2017). https://doi.org/10.1109/VR.2017.7892236
14. Yamamoto, S., Mori, H. (eds.): HCII 2019. LNCS, vol. 11570. Springer, Cham (2019). https://doi.org/10.1007/978-3-030-22649-7
15. Yem, V., Vu, K., Kon, Y., Kajimoto, H.: Softness-hardness and stickiness feedback using electrical stimulation while touching a virtual object. In: 25th IEEE Conference on Virtual Reality and 3D User Interfaces, VR 2018 - Proceedings (2018). https://doi.org/10.1109/VR.2018.8446516

6

Sensing Ultrasonic Mid-Air Haptics with a Biomimetic Tactile Fingertip

Noor Alakhawand[1,2](✉), William Frier[3], Kipp McAdam Freud[1,2], Orestis Georgiou[3], and Nathan F. Lepora[1,2]

[1] Department of Engineering Mathematics, University of Bristol, Bristol, UK
noor.alakhawand@bristol.ac.uk
[2] Bristol Robotics Laboratory, Bristol, UK
[3] Ultraleap Ltd., Bristol, UK

Abstract. Ultrasonic phased arrays are used to generate mid-air haptic feedback, allowing users to feel sensations in mid-air. In this work, we present a method for testing mid-air haptics with a biomimetic tactile sensor that is inspired by the human fingertip. Our experiments with point, line, and circular test stimuli provide insights on how the acoustic radiation pressure produced by the ultrasonic array deforms the skin-like material of the sensor. This allows us to produce detailed visualizations of the sensations in two-dimensional and three-dimensional space. This approach provides a detailed quantification of mid-air haptic stimuli of use as an investigative tool for improving the performance of haptic displays and for understanding the transduction of mid-air haptics by the human sense of touch.

Keywords: Tactile sensors · Biomimetic · Mid-air haptics

1 Introduction

Ultrasonic phased arrays can generate haptic sensations in mid-air. They focus acoustic radiation pressure in space, which deflects the skin to induce tactile sensation [1]. To evaluate whether the array is producing the desired haptic sensations, we need to understand how focal points of pressure interact with compliant skin to cause it to deform. In this paper, we propose a method for sensing mid-air haptics with a biomimetic tactile fingertip inspired by the human sense of touch. Using the data obtained from the sensor, we are able to visualize the different patterns produced by the haptic array.

Efforts to measure the haptic output from a phased ultrasonic array range from quantitative to qualitative. Quantitative methods include microphones to measure the sound pressure level of the generated focal points [1,8], directly measuring the ultrasonic output of the system without considering its interaction with other material. On the other hand, to quantitatively consider the interaction of the sensations with skin-like materials, Laser Doppler Vibrometry (LDV), a tool commonly used for non-contact vibration measurement, can give insight on how the haptic stimuli would interact with human skin at high frequencies [2]. Alternatively, qualitative methods include pulsed schlieren imaging, which was used to visualize the pressure field produced by a focal point as it interacts with external materials [5]. Additionally, by projecting the focal points onto the surface of an oil bath, it can be used to visualize the patterns generated by the haptic array [6]. New research has used a microphone-based tactile sensor array to evaluate the vibrations of its surface due to ultrasonic haptic sensations [9], highlighting the potential of tactile sensors for testing the output of a haptic system.

In this work, we propose a method to sense and evaluate mid-air haptics using the TacTip, a biomimetic tactile fingertip. The TacTip is biologically inspired by glabrous (hairless) human skin, which has an intricate morphology of layers, microstructures, and sensory receptors that contribute to its functions [3,10]. We present a method for analyzing mid-air haptic sensations with a tactile sensor, allowing us to quantitatively test ultrasonic arrays with a method inspired by the human sense of touch.

2 Experimental Setup and Method

This work aims to develop a method for testing mid-air haptics with a biomimetic tactile sensor. We carried out experiments with the tactile fingertip mounted on a robot arm and an ultrasonic array (Fig. 1).

Fig. 1. The TacTip, a biomimetic tactile sensor (left): the flat-tipped model used in this study; the skin of the TacTip with 127 inner nodular pins (middle); and the experimental setup with the tactile sensor mounted on a robot arm to collect data over the ultrasonic phased array (right).

2.1 Biomimetic Tactile Sensor

The TacTip (Fig. 1, left panel) is a biomimetic tactile sensor developed at the Bristol Robotics Laboratory [3,10], based on the structure of glabrous skin. The human fingertip has *dermal papillae* where the dermis interdigitates with *intermediate ridges* in the epidermis. These ridges and papillae focus strain from the skin surface down to mechanoreceptors within the dermis. The TacTip mimics this structure with an outer rubber-like skin which connects to inner nodular pins (Fig. 1, middle panel). As the soft sensor interacts with objects, its skin deforms and the nodular pins transmit surface strain into inner mechanical movements, similar to human skin. An internal camera tracks the movement of its artificial papillae, making it possible to detect the shear deformation of the skin. The sensor has been used in many tasks in robot touch such as object exploration and slip detection [10]. The TacTip is manufactured using dual-material 3D printing, which prints both the sensor's plastic base and the soft rubber-like material for the skin. This allows for low-cost and rapid prototyping of different designs as well as its integration with robotic grippers and hands. Additionally, the design of the TacTip is modular, allowing for different tips to be used, such as varying the shape or texture of the skin or varying the layout of the nodular pins [10]. The tip of the sensor can be filled with gel to affect its compliance or be left unfilled. Since this is the first time the TacTip has been used to detect small forces on the order of millinewtons, we needed a more compliant tip; after testing tips with these variations, we found the flat-tipped TacTip without gel (Fig. 1, left panel) to be more sensitive, and thus suitable for this work.

2.2 Ultrasound Phased Array

To generate the mid-air haptic stimuli for the experiments, we used the Ultrahaptics Evaluation Kit (UHEV1) from Ultraleap. The array has a 16 by 16 grid of ultrasonic transducers which operate at 40 kHz to generate focal points in mid-air, with an update rate of 16 kHz. The device is accompanied by software which allows us to modulate these focal points so that they can be felt by users [1] and to generate various shapes and textures [6].

2.3 Experiment

We used a 6-DOF robotic arm (ABB IRB120) to move the tactile sensor over the haptic array. The robot arm moved the sensor in 10 mm increments over an 80 mm by 80 mm grid at a height of 200 mm above the haptic array. At each position, 30 frames were captured from the camera to image the TacTip's inner nodular pins at 30 fps. This was done for a focal point generated by the array, as well as two shapes (a line and a circle). The shapes were generated by the array using Amplitude Modulation (AM) and Spatiotemporal Modulation (STM), to see whether the sensor distinguishes between these two standard modulation techniques. AM generates focal points in the path of the desired pattern and modulates their intensity over time, while STM generates one focal point and moves it rapidly along the path.

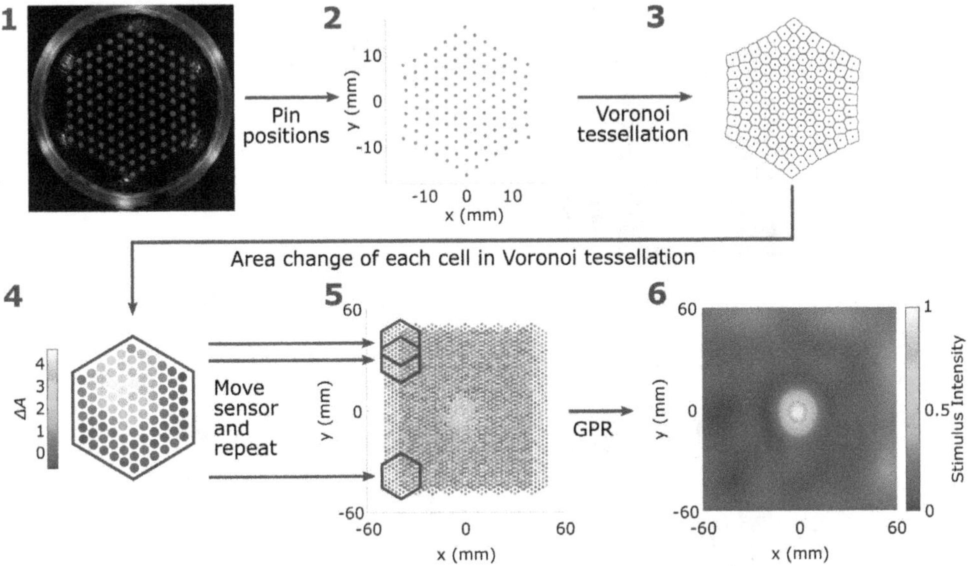

Fig. 2. Analysis method. We capture an image from the tactile sensor as it interacts with the mid-air haptic stimulus (1) and extract each pin position (2). Voronoi tessellation is generated with pin positions as the center point for each cell (3); the change of area of each cell compared to an unstimulated sensor, ΔA, is used as a measure of the stimulus intensity (4). This is repeated for readings over a grid (5). Gaussian Process Regression combines the data sets to produce detailed visualizations (6).

2.4 Analysis

In this work, we developed an analysis method to sense mid-air haptics with a biomimetic tactile fingertip (Fig. 2). The images captured from the tactile sensor as it interacts with the mid-air haptic stimulus were processed to find the positions of the nodular pins at each time step. Then we used the pin positions to generate a bounded Voronoi tessellation, shown by Cramphorn et al. to transduce a third dimension to the sensor data [4]. Voronoi tessellation partitions a plane based on the distance between points on that plane; each point along an edge is equidistant from two points, and each vertex is equidistant from at least three points. The areas of the cells give us information for tactile perception; increasing areas indicate a compression of the skin. Thus, the areas of each cell in the Voronoi tessellation were compared with a data set in which the sensor was not stimulated, and the difference between the two areas, ΔA, was used as a measure of the intensity of the stimulus as felt by the sensor. This was done for every time step, and then averaged over the 30 frames of data. The process was repeated for readings in a grid over the haptic display to populate a two-dimensional plane. Then we trained a Gaussian process regression (GPR) model for the measured intensity, represented by ΔA (using the MATLAB function *fitrgp* with the default squared exponential covariance function). The output values were then scaled between zero and one, to represent the relative intensity of the stimulus as felt by the tactile sensor.

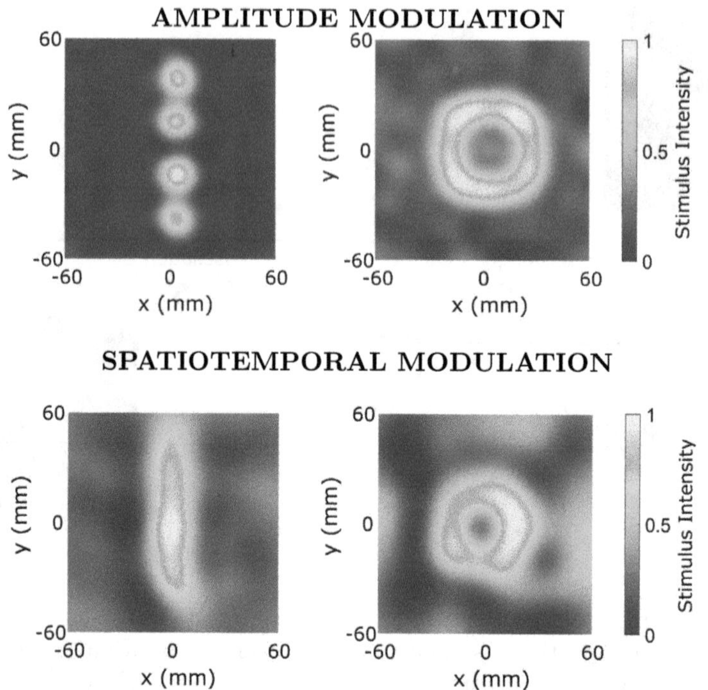

Fig. 3. The mid-air haptic shapes, line and circle, as felt by the biomimetic tactile sensor. The Amplitude Modulation (AM) cases use four focal points modulated with a 200 Hz sine wave. The Spatiotemporal Modulation (STM) cases use one focal point moving at a repeat frequency of 100 Hz along the path of the shape.

3 Results

In this work, we used a biomimetic tactile fingertip to sense mid-air haptics, to develop a method for testing the output of a haptic display. We measured the response of the tactile sensor to a focal point of pressure generated by an ultrasonic haptic array as well as two haptic shapes, each generated by Amplitude Modulation (AM) and Spatiotemporal Modulation (STM).

3.1 Sensing Mid-Air Haptics on a Two-Dimensional Grid

The experiments showed that the biomimetic tactile fingertip used in this study, the TacTip, is able to sense the mid-air haptic stimuli produced by the ultrasonic phased array using our developed method (Fig. 2). The focal points of pressure generated by the ultrasound caused the skin-like surface to deform, expanding the areas of the cells in the Voronoi tessellation, allowing us to identify the location and intensity of contact. Voronoi tessellation was a valuable tool in transducing a third dimension in the data, which allowed us to visualize the sensations produced by the ultrasonic array.

Our analysis methods enables us to produce detailed visualizations of the mid-air haptic sensations (Fig. 3), allowing us to distinguish between different patterns produced by the ultrasonic array. Additionally, the variation in the strength of the focal point can be clearly seen. The visual representation of the focal point shows that it creates a localized region of increased displacement (Fig. 2, lower right panel). The point is much stronger in the center, and then decreases in intensity as you move radially outwards. This is similar for the other shapes; the center path of the shape has increased intensity, which decreases as you move away (Fig. 3).

The visualizations produced by our method allow us to compare the shapes generated by the ultrasonic array using different modulation techniques. We see that the tactile sensor is able to distinguish the four focal points that make up the amplitude modulated line (Fig. 3, top left panel). A user of the ultrasonic array would not distinguish the points as the distance between them is small [1], and so it creates the illusion of a continuous line. The sensor can discriminate between the points because our analysis method is measuring the deformation of the tactile sensor's surface, which would correspond to the deformation of the user's skin rather than their perception of the sensation. On the other hand, the spatiotemporally modulated line (Fig. 3, lower left panel) is felt as a continuous line by the sensor. The focal point used to generate the line is moved along its path at very small increments. The distance between the points in this case is too small to be distinguished by the sensor, making the output more similar to how a user would sense the stimulus.

3.2 Sensing a Focal Point in Three-Dimensional Space

In the previous section, we presented our results when sensing various shapes over a two-dimensional grid. In this section, we extend our method to sense mid-air haptic stimuli in three dimensions. When a person interacts with the haptic array to sense the shapes it generates, they naturally move their hand around the display surface, which includes moving their hands up and down as they process the sensations they feel. Thus, understanding how the generated sensations vary with height is important to determine whether the desired effect is being produced and to check that there are no undesired artefacts. We repeated the data collection process described earlier for the point stimulus at different heights over the array, at 10 mm increments. This results in a three-dimensional grid on which we applied our presented analysis method.

This experiment allows us to see how the shape is sensed over a three-dimensional surface, looking at how the shape varies by height. The focal point is generated by the array at a specific height in space; however, there are still sensations at other points due to the interaction of the ultrasonic waves [8]. The point stimulus is sensed by the tactile fingertip as an elongated spheroid, with a localized region of increased intensity (Fig. 4). It appears the lower the intensity of the stimulus felt, the more elongated it is. As the sensor moves away from the center height, the stimulus becomes fainter.

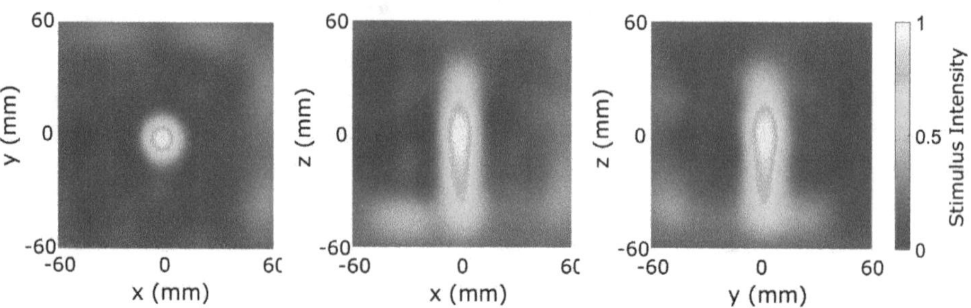

Fig. 4. The three-dimensional view of a focal point as felt by the biomimetic tactile sensor presented as cross sections at $z = 0$ (left), which corresponds to 200 mm above the array; $y = 0$ (middle); and $x = 0$ (right).

4 Discussion and Conclusion

Tactile sensors can further our understanding of the human sense of touch. Our experiments have shown that we can use a biomimetic tactile fingertip to sense the mid-air haptic stimuli produced by an ultrasonic phased array, providing insights on the deformation of the skin-like material of the TacTip due to ultrasonic mid-air haptic sensations. This allows us to produce detailed visualizations of the sensations produced by the device. Using our analysis methods, we were able to see the difference between shapes that are amplitude modulated versus spatiotemporally modulated by the ultrasonic array. Additionally, we were able to sense and visualize a focal point in three-dimensional space, providing insights on how the focal point varies by height.

The visualizations of the stimuli produced in our study are similar to those in other works which use alternative methods. For example, Laser Doppler Vibrometry was used to measure the deformation of skin-like material due to ultrasonic mid-air haptics [2]; it measured the high frequency vibrations (50 Hz and above) of the skin surface, and the root mean square (RMS) of the deformation was used to visualize the sensations. While we do not measure the high frequency vibrations, we get similar results. This could indicate that the data we collect is similar to the RMS of the skin deformation. Additionally, our three-dimensional measurements of the focal point look very similar to simulations of the same stimulus [8]. The elongated spheroid felt by the sensor looks like the higher values of acoustic field pressure in the simulation, suggesting that the tactile fingertip is able to sense the ultrasound when it crosses a threshold pressure.

This work has provided insights into the measurement of haptic stimuli, but it has areas for improvement. At this point, we have measured the intensity of the stimulus without relating it to a specific physical value. Further work is planned to determine the relationship of the measured stimulus intensity to the skin deformation, which would allow us to compare our results with other quantitative experiments. Additionally, we do not measure the skin deformation at high frequencies. While the results we get are similar to those which use vibrometry, studying the vibrations of the artificial skin could determine whether the sensor does behave similarly to human skin. One approach is to modify the sensor with a higher frame rate camera which could allow us to see the high-frequency deformations of the skin; another approach would be to add another high-frequency tactile sensing modality to the TacTip [7].

Our work has shown promising results for sensing mid-air haptics with a biomimetic tactile fingertip. The developed approach could be used as an investigative tool for evaluating and improving the capabilities of haptic displays. The insights gained from this work could also be used to investigate human perception. In the future, we could apply our methods to intelligent exploration of the haptic stimuli. This could allow us to develop an autonomous robotic system that is able to feel and interact with the sensations similar to how a person would explore mid-air haptic stimuli.

Acknowledgements. We thank A. Stinchcombe, K. Aquilina, and J. Lloyd for their help. N. Alakhawand was supported by an EPSRC CASE award with Ultraleap. N. Lepora was supported by an award from the Leverhulme Trust on 'A biomimetic forebrain for robot touch' (RL-2016-39).

References

1. Carter, T., Seah, S.A., Long, B., Drinkwater, B., Subramanian, S.: UltraHaptics: multi-point mid-air haptic feedback for touch surfaces. In: Proceedings of the 26th Annual ACM Symposium on User Interface Software and Technology, pp. 505–514 (2013)
2. Chilles, J., Frier, W., Abdouni, A., Giordano, M., Georgiou, O.: Laser doppler vibrometry and FEM simulations of ultrasonic mid-air haptics. In: 2019 IEEE World Haptics Conference, pp. 259–264 (2019)
3. Chorley, C., Melhuish, C., Pipe, T., Rossiter, J.: Development of a tactile sensor based on biologically inspired edge encoding. In: International Conference on Advanced Robotics (2009)
4. Cramphorn, L., Lloyd, J., Lepora, N.: Voronoi features for tactile sensing: direct inference of pressure, shear, and contact locations. In: 2018 IEEE International Conference on Robotics and Automation, pp. 2752–2757 (2018)
5. Iodice, M., Frier, W., Wilcox, J., Long, B., Georgiou, O.: Pulsed schlieren imaging of ultrasonic haptics and levitation using phased arrays. In: 25th International Congress on Sound and Vibration 2018, ICSV 2018 Hiroshima Call, pp. 1736–1743 (2018)
6. Long, B., Seah, S.A., Carter, T., Subramanian, S.: Rendering volumetric haptic shapes in mid-air using ultrasound. ACM Trans. Graph. **33**(6), 1–10 (2014)
7. Pestell, N., Lloyd, J., Rossiter, J., Lepora, N.: Dual-modal tactile perception and exploration. IEEE Robot. Autom. Lett. **3**(2), 1033–1040 (2018)
8. Price, A., Long, B.: Fibonacci spiral arranged ultrasound phased array for mid-air haptics. In: 2018 IEEE International Ultrasonics Symposium, pp. 1–4 (2018)
9. Sakiyama, E., Matsumoto, D., Fujiwara, M., Makino, Y., Shinoda, H.: Evaluation of multi-point dynamic pressure reproduction using microphone-based tactile sensor array. In: 2019 IEEE International Symposium on Haptic, Audio and Visual Environments Games (2019)
10. Ward-Cherrier, B., Pestell, N., Cramphorn, L., Winstone, B., Giannaccini, M.E., Rossiter, J., Lepora, N.: The TacTip family: soft optical tactile sensors with 3D-printed biomimetic morphologies. Soft Robot. **5**(2), 216–227 (2018)

7

ElectroAR: Distributed Electro-Tactile Stimulation for Tactile Transfer

Jonathan Tirado[1(✉)], Vladislav Panov[1(✉)], Vibol Yem[2(✉)], Dzmitry Tsetserukou[1(✉)], and Hiroyuki Kajimoto[3(✉)]

[1] Skolkovo Institute of Science and Technology (Skoltech), Moscow 121205, Russia
{jonathan.tirado,vladislav.panov,D.tsetserukou}@skoltech.ru
[2] Tokyo Metropolitan University, Tokyo, Japan
yemvibol@tmu.ac.jp
[3] The University of Electro-Communications, 1-5-1 Chofugaoka, Chofu, Tokyo 182-8585, Japan
kajimoto@kaji-lab.jp

Abstract. We present ElectroAR, a visual and tactile sharing system for hand skills training. This system comprises a head-mounted display (HMD), two cameras, a tactile sensing glove, and an electro-tactile stimulation glove. The trainee wears the tactile sensing glove that gets pressure data from touching different objects. His/her movements are recorded by two cameras, which are located in front and top side of the workspace. In the remote site, the trainer wears the electro-tactile stimulation glove. This glove transforms the remotely collected pressure data to electro-tactile stimuli. Additionally, the trainer wears an HMD to see and guide the movements of the trainee. The key part of this project is to combine distributed tactile sensor and electro-tactile display to let the trainer understand what the trainee is doing. Results show our system supports a higher user's recognition performance.

Keywords: Tactile display · Tactile sensor · Tactile transmission · Virtual reality

1 Introduction

There are several tasks that incorporate hand-skill training, such as surgery, palpation, handwriting, etc. We are developing an environment where a skilled person (trainer), who actually works at a different place, can collaborate with a non-skilled person (trainee) in high precision activities. The trainer needs to feel as if he/she exists at the place and work there. The trainee can improve his/her performance with the trainer's help. This can be regarded as one type of telexistence [1], in which remote robot is replaced by trainee.

We especially focus on the situation that incorporates finger contact. This requires a tactile sensor on the trainee's side and tactile display on the trainer's side. The trainee handles real objects, and the tactile sensor-display pair enables the trainer to feel the same tactile experience as the trainee; thus, he/she can command or show what the trainee should do next.

For tactile sensors, a wide variety of these pads have been developed in the past for robotics and medical applications, using resistive, capacitive, piezoelectric, or optical elements. These pads have often been placed in gloves to monitor hand manipulation. While some of them are bulky and inevitably deteriorate the human haptic sense, recently, several researches are focused on reducing this problem by using thinner and more flexible force-sensing pads [3]. In this study, we use a similar tactile sensor array with high spatio-temporal resolution.

For tactile display, there were also several researches on wearable tactile displays [4]. They are simple, yet cannot present distributed tactile information that our sensor can detect. As we believe that distributed tactile information is important, especially when we recognize shapes, we need some way to present distributed tactile information to fingertips. There were also several works on pin-array type tactile display [2,5]. We employ electro-tactile display [6,7], since it is durable, light-weight, and easy to be made small and extends to several fingers.

This paper is an initial report of our system, especially focuses on how well the shape information can be transmitted through our system.

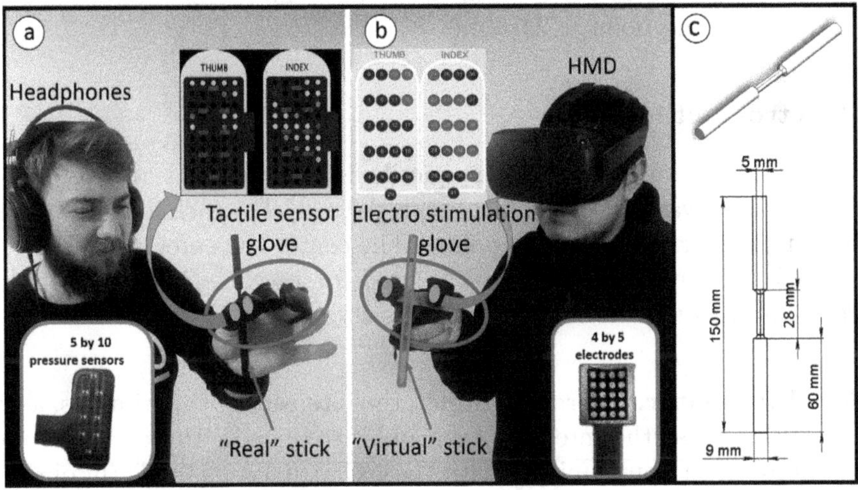

Fig. 1. ElectroAR. (a) Follower side. (b) Leader side. (c) Cylindrical stick with regular prismatic shape

2 System Overview

As shown in Fig. 1, the system consists of three main components. On the follower (trainee's) side, the user wears a tactile sensing glove. The glove gets the pressure data from touching objects. The data of pressure sensors were spatially filtered by using Eq. (1),

$$p'_{i,j} = \frac{p_{i,j} + p_{i+1,j} + p_{i,j+1} + p_{i+1,j+1}}{4} \tag{1}$$

where p is a pressure value and p' is a filtered pressure value, i and j are order number on the axis of width and height of the sensor array [9].

The leader's glove transforms the filtered pressure data to electro-tactile stimuli at fingertips. They are linked not only with haptic feedback but also with visual and audio feedback. Visual feedback gives for the leader side full information of the movement on the follower side, and audio feedback provides for the follower side commands from the leader.

2.1 Tactile Sensor Glove

We are using a glove that contains three tactile sensor arrays [9]. These sensor arrays are located on the three fingers of the right hand (thumb, index and middle). Figure 1 (a) shows the internal distribution of the pressure sensors in the array of 5 by 10 for each finger. The force range of sensing element was not accurately measured, but it can discriminate edge shapes by natural pressing force, as will be shown in the experiment section. The center-to-center distance between each sensing point is 2.0 mm.

2.2 Electro-Tactile Glove

Figure 1 (b) shows the glove of electro-tactile display for the leader user [9]. The module controller was embedded inside the glove [8]. For each finger, the electro-tactile stimulator array has 4 by 5 points. The center-to-center distance between each point is 2.0 mm. This module was used for tactile stimulation of thumb, index and middle finger. The pulse width is set to 100 *us*.

Random Modulator. In order to adjust the intensity of the stimulus, a typical method is to express the intensity by a pulse frequency. However, in practice, the stimulator must communicate with the PC at fixed intervals (in our case at 120 Hz). Therefore, although it is relatively easy to set the pulse frequency to, for example, 30 Hz, 60 Hz, or 120 Hz, it is a little difficult to perform electrical stimulation of an arbitrary frequency.

Here, we propose a method to change the probability of stimulation as a substitute for setting pulse frequency. For each time interval (in our case 1/120 *second*), the system gives the probability of stimulating each electrode. The higher the probability, the higher the average stimulus frequency. The algorithm is expressed as follows.

$$\textbf{if} \ \ rand\,() \leq p \ \ \textbf{then} \ \ stimulate\,() \tag{2}$$

Where $rand\,()$ is a uniformly distributed random variable from 0 to 1. If it is less than or equal to a value p, the electrode is stimulated. Otherwise, it is not stimulated. The probability that the electrode is stimulated is hence p. This calculation is performed for the electrode every cycle, resulting in an average stimulation cycle of $120 * p\,\mathrm{Hz}$.

The value p represents the probability of stimulation, and a function representing the relationship between p and the subjective stimulus intensity S is required. In general, higher stimulus frequency gives stronger subjective stimulus, so this function is considered to be a monotonically increasing function.

$$S = F(p) \tag{3}$$

If F is obtained, the inverse function can be used to determine how the stimulus probability p should be set for the intensity S to be expressed as follows.

$$p = F^{-1}(s) \tag{4}$$

2.3 View Sharing System

Ideally, the view sharing system should be bi-directional. However, as the scope of this paper is to examine the ability of our tactile sensor-display pair, we used a simplified visual system only for the trainer.

As shown in Fig. 1 (b), the trainer wears an HMD. At the remote side, two cameras are installed for having full view information for the trainer, both from the top and from the side. This information is presented in virtual screens which are located in front and the horizontal view. Although the view is not three-dimensional, it can provide sufficient information of the trainee's hand movement, and the trainer can mimic the movement while perceiving the tactile sensation by the electro-tactile display glove.

3 Experiment

3.1 Preliminary Experiment : Random Modulator's Function

The proposed random modulation method needs a function F, which can represent the relationship between strength perception and the probability of stimulating each electrode. This preliminary experiment has the objective of collect data for fitting function F. In the whole experiment, the base stimulation frequency was 120 Hz. For example, if the probability is 1, the stimulation is done at 120 *pps* (pulses per second).

Experimental Method. The strength of stimulation was evaluated by the magnitude estimation method. First, the user's right index fingertip was put on the electrodes' array, and exposed to a pulsatory stimulation, provided by electrodes. The user was asked to find a comfortable and recognizable level (absolute stimulation level), which was set as 100.

In the second part, we prepared six probability levels: 0.1, 0.2, 0.4, 0.6, 0.8, 1.0. There were five trials for each level, 30 trials in total in random order. Each trial was composed of an initial one-second impulse with the 100 intensity level, followed by a one-second randomly modulated stimulation with assigned probability. After each trial, the user must determine how lower or higher was the second stimulus presented. We recruited seven participants, five males and two females aged 21–27; all right-handed and all without previous training.

Result. The result in Fig. 2 (a) shows a sigmoid function tendency. Thus, the data were fitted using Matlab, as shown in Fig. 2 (b).

Once we know the function, we calculated the inverse function that determines the stimulation probability from desired strength, which is the function F^{-1}, described in the Eq. (5), where a, b and k are coefficients of the sigmoid function, p is the probability of the electrode being stimulated and S is the subjective stimulus intensity.

$$p = \frac{a - log(\frac{k}{S} - 1)}{b} \tag{5}$$

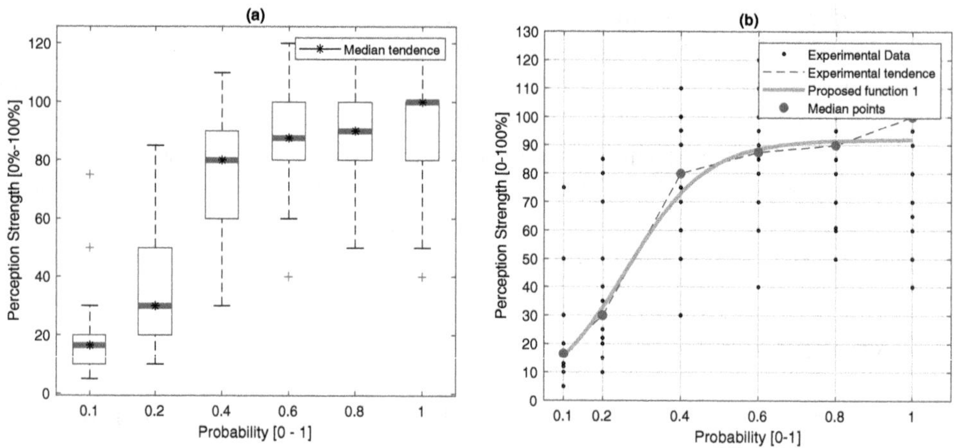

Fig. 2. Random Modulation. (a) Experimental results. The quantitative relation between cumulative probability distribution and the strength perception percentage estimated for the volunteers. (b) Sigmoid function regression. Experimental data were fitted to sigmoid function by logistic regression

3.2 Experiment 1: Static Shapes Recognition

The following two experiments try to validate that our system is capable of transmitting tactile information necessary for tactile skill transfer. In many haptic related tasks, we typically use a pen-type device that we pinch by our index finger and thumb. These can be a scalpel, a driver, a tweezer, or a pencil. In such situations, we identify the orientation of the device with tactile sense.

Our series of experiments try to reproduce part of these situations. Experiment 1 was carried out to assess the electro-tactile display's capacity for presenting bar-shape in different orientations.

Experimental Method. Four patterns, which are line with inclinations of 0, 45, 90 and 135° were presented on the right index finger. The experiment was divided into three steps. The first step was to identify a suitable stimulus level. The second step was the training phase, in which each pattern was presented twice to the volunteers.

After a two minutes break, the evaluation stage was performed. They were asked to try randomly chosen pattern and chose from the four candidates. The recognition time was also recorded. We recruited ten volunteers, nine males and one female, aged 21–27; all right-handed. There were seven trials per pattern, 28 in total.

Result. Figure 3 (a) shows a numerical comparison of the effective recognition level for each proposed pattern. The four patterns have a similar range of recognition, being the 90° pattern pointed the lowest (73% accuracy) and the 0° pattern the highest (87% accuracy). The result also indicates that the 90° pattern is often confused with the 135° (10% error), and in the same way the 45° is confused with 90° pattern (10% error).

Figure 3 (b) shows that the recognition time for the majority of the volunteers ranges between 4 and 10 s for all of the patterns. The median time is close to 6 s.

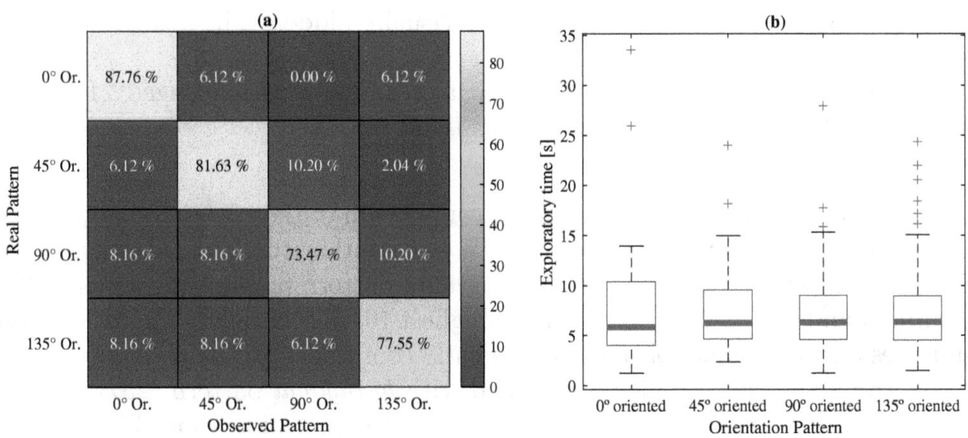

Fig. 3. Experiment 1. (a) Confusion Matrix Pattern recognition rate. (b) Exploratory time comparative evaluation

3.3 Experiment 2: Dynamic Pattern Perception

Experiment 2 was carried out to assess our system's capacity to convey dynamic tactile information. As mentioned before, we focused on the situation of handling a bar-shaped device. We confirmed if we can identify different "devices" that we handle with our index finger and thumb.

Data Set Acquisition. Four cylindrical sticks with regular prismatic shape in their middle section were designed for the experiment (Fig. 1 (c)). The total length of each stick is 150 mm, and 28 mm for their middle section. Every prism has a different cross-section: circle, triangle, square, and hexagon. The radius of the sticks was 9 mm and the circumradius of the prisms 5 mm. This special design visually covers the middle section for avoiding the possibility of answering only by observation. On this way, we provide only the motion of the hand as visual feedback.

Using the tactile sensing glove, one of the authors grasped the stick in a 90° orientation, and he slowly scrolled the bar back and force between two fingers, repeating for ten times. The pressure patterns were recorded, and the video was taken by two cameras that we described in the previous section.

Experimental Method. In the main experiment, the recorded videos were replayed so that the user can mimic the hand motion. Simultaneously, the tactile feedback was delivered to two fingertips (right index finger and thumb) using the recorded pressure patterns.

A set of twenty randomly ordered samples was presented, and the user must associate this visual and tactile sensation with one of the previously indicated shapes. Visual feedback was provided to show the motion of the hand, but at the same time, the shape of the prism was visually hidden. The recognition time was also recorded.

We recruited eight participants, six males and two females aged 21–27; all right-handed and all without previous training.

Result. Figure 4 (a) shows a numerical comparison of the effective shape recognition level for each proposed pattern. We observe that the four patterns have a different range of recognition, being the *square* pattern pointed the lowest (40% accuracy) and the *cylinder* pattern the highest (65% accuracy). The result also indicates that the *square* pattern is frequently confused with the *triangle* pattern (37% error), and the *cylinder* is confused with *hexagonal* pattern (25% error).

The experiment also includes an analysis of exploration time. Figure 4 (b) shows that the recognition time for the majority of the volunteers ranges between 8 and 18 s. The median time is close to 13 s also for all of the cases, except for the *triangle* pattern which median exploratory time is 16 s.

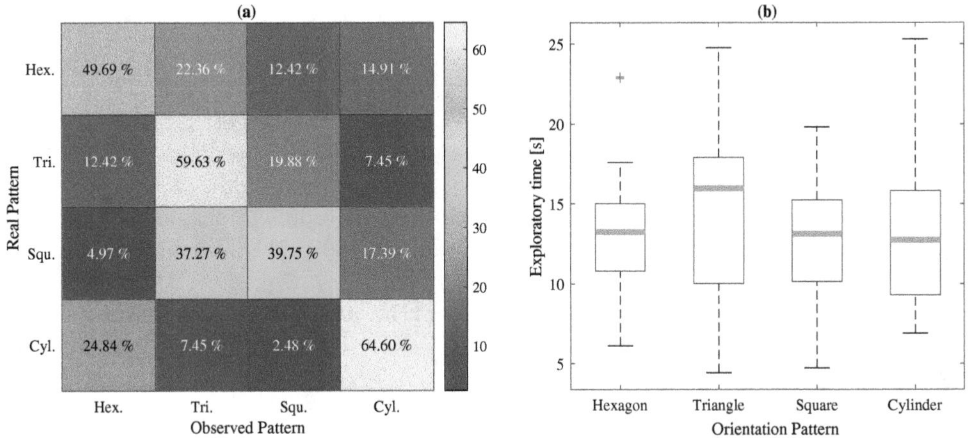

Fig. 4. Experiment 2. (a) Confusion Matrix about 3D Shape recognition rate. (b) Exploratory time comparative evaluation for 3D shape recognition

4 Conclusion

In this paper, we mainly developed a haptic feedback component of the virtual reality system for remote training. We implemented a simple tactile communication capable of transmitting shape sensations produced at the moment of manipulating 3D objects with two fingers: thumb and index fingers. The follower side comprises a tactile-sensor glove and the leader side comprises an electro-tactile display glove.

We tested our system with two experiments: static shape perception and dynamic pattern perception, both assuming the situation of grasping a bar-like object. The results confirmed our expectations, that this system has the ability to deliver information of 3D bar-like object.

There are several limitations to the current work. The visual part of the system is incomplete; the follower side should see the hand gesture of the trainer, and the leader side should see 3D visual information of the follower by the use of 3D display technologies. Tactile display and sensor are slightly small, and it must be enlarged to cover the whole fingertips. Roughness and temperature sensations must be considered for providing material sense. All these will be handled in our future work.

References

1. Tachi, S.: Tele-existence - toward virtual existence in real and/or virtual worlds. In: Proceedings of ICAT 1991, pp. 85–94 (1991)
2. Kim, S.-C., et al.: Small and lightweight tactile display (SaLT) and its application. In: Proceedings WorldHaptics, pp. 69–74 (2009)
3. Beebe, D., Denton, D., Radwin, R., Webster, J.: A silicon-based tactile sensor for finger-mounted applications. IEEE Trans. Biomed. Eng. **45**, 151–159 (1998)

4. Choi, I., Hawkes, E.W., Christensen, D.L., Ploch, C.J., Follmer, S.: Wolverine: a wearable haptic interface for grasping in virtual reality. In. Proceedings of IROS, pp. 986–993 (2016)
5. Sarakoglou, I., Tsagarakis, N., Caldwell, D.G.: A portable fingertip tactile feedback array - transmission system reliability and modelling. In: Proceedings of WHC 2005, pp. 547–548 (2008)
6. Saunders, F.A.: In functional electrical stimulation: applications. In: Hambrecht, F.T., Reswick, J.B. (eds.) Neural Prostheses, pp. 303–309. Marcel Dekker, New York (1977)
7. Bach-y-Rita, P., Kaczmarek, K.A., Tyler, M.E., Garcia-Lara, J.: Form perception with a 49-point electrotactile stimulus array on the tongue. J. Rehab. Res. Dev. **35**, 427–430 (1998)
8. Kajimoto, H.: Electro-tactile display: principle and hardware. In: Kajimoto, H., Saga, S., Konyo, M. (eds.) Pervasive Haptics, pp. 79–96. Springer, Tokyo (2016). https://doi.org/10.1007/978-4-431-55772-2_5
9. Yem, V., Kajimoto, H., Sato, K., Yoshihara, H.: A system of tactile transmission on the fingertips with electrical-thermal and vibration stimulation. In: Yamamoto, S., Mori, H. (eds.) HCII 2019. LNCS, vol. 11570, pp. 101–113. Springer, Cham (2019). https://doi.org/10.1007/978-3-030-22649-7_9

8

Stiffness Discrimination by Two Fingers with Stochastic Resonance

Komi Chamnongthai(✉), Takahiro Endo, Shohei Ikemura, and Fumitoshi Matsuno

Kyoto University, Kyoto 615-8540, Japan
chamnongthai.komi.46m@st.kyoto-u.ac.jp

Abstract. This paper focuses on Stochastic Resonance (SR) for stiffness discrimination by two fingers. In particular, we show that the subthreshold vibrotactile noise applied on a remote position can improve tactile sensations of both index finger and thumb for a task requiring multiple fingers. We evaluate the user performances in a virtual environment (VE) by Weber fraction for stiffness perception under one of three different vibration source positions: on the index finger, on the thumb, and between the index finger and thumb. The results show that the stiffness discrimination ability increase under all three vibration source positions with the best performance obtained for the source location between index finger and thumb. The finding indicates the potential of using a single vibration source to enhance sensation of multiple fingers by the effect of SR.

Keywords: Stiffness discrimination · Stochastic Resonance · Haptic interface · Multiple fingers

1 Introduction

In clinical field, palpation is one process to identify properties such as size, texture, location, etc., of an organ by a physical examination with multiple fingers. The ability to address the abnormality of the organ stiffness is one vital skill before operating other processes. However, to achieve the expert level performance to distinguish the difference accurately, the medical students must be trained strenuously with various models and difficulties. Furthermore, training with traditional methods consume a lot of time to obtain new skills. In addition, it also costs a large amount of money to prepare the instruction equipment for covering the various difficulties of training. To solve this problem, a haptic training system which combines a virtual environment (VE) and haptic interface is one interesting solution.

The common approach followed to communicate with haptic training system is to design a finger holder into which the user will insert his or her finger. However, the use of a finger holder decreases the force-detection ability at the finger [1] and therefore it is necessary to enhance the force-detection capability of the finger through other mechanisms in the presence of finger holder.

There are several techniques to enhance tactile sensation: transcutaneous electrical nerve stimulation [2], temporary deafferentation [3], and passive sensory stimulation [4]. One effective solution is the addition of sensory noise which provides vibrotactile noise through the human skin in order to boost the sensitivity in several body parts such as the feet [5] and fingers [6]. This phenomena, which boosts the weak signal to be detectable by adding white noise, is called Stochastic Resonance (SR).

There are numerous studies that show the increase of haptic sensitivity by the effect of SR. According to Kurita *et al.* [8], the effect of SR is applied directly to the tip of the index finger, which shows the improvement of the user performance in grasping task. Furthermore, the effect of SR does not only occur when the vibration source is close to the tip of the index finger, but also happen while the vibration is generated from remote positions, which is away from the tip of the finger [9]. The study shows that the haptic sensation of the user is enhanced when a subthreshold vibration with a remote position is applied to the stroke patients. The fingertip perception is also shown to improve using SR when the finger is enclosed in the finger holder [10]. Therefore, the effect of SR has a potential to raise the haptic sensation at the user fingertip. However, there is no study that investigates the effects of SR on the fingertip when multiple fingers are enclosed within finger holders while doing the motor task.

The goal of this study is to determine the effect of SR in stiffness discrimination task using two fingers in VE. For this, we propose a novel method which consists of haptic feedback generated by haptic devices and the effect of SR provided by a piezoelectric actuator, in a stiffness discrimination task which is manipulated by multi-fingers through VE. The user performances are evaluated with three different vibration source positions (on the index finger (Position 1), between the index finger and thumb (Position 2), on the thumb (Position 3)) in order to find the possibility of the enhancement of the sensitivities at the fingertips. Many papers address that the haptic sensation of one finger is increased by one vibration source, but in this paper, we newly reveal that even one vibration source can improve the sensations of the two fingers via the effect of SR.

2 Proposed Method

We propose a method which integrates haptic feedback and the effect of SR for a better haptic sensitivity in the stiffness discrimination task. To provide the effect of SR, the mechanical vibration is applied to one of the three positions shown in Fig. 1 with varying vibration intensities. We would like to investigate the possibility that one vibration source can enhance the sensation of both fingers via the effect of SR. Two haptic devices, both being Geomagic Touch haptic devices, are used in this study. The original end-effectors of the haptic devices are customized for the task to operate with a finger as shown in Fig. 2(b). The modified end-effector consists of the finger holder, made from polyoxymethylene, and a force sensor (Leptrino, CFS018CA101U). On the other hand, the VE is programmed by using the CHAI3D library [11].

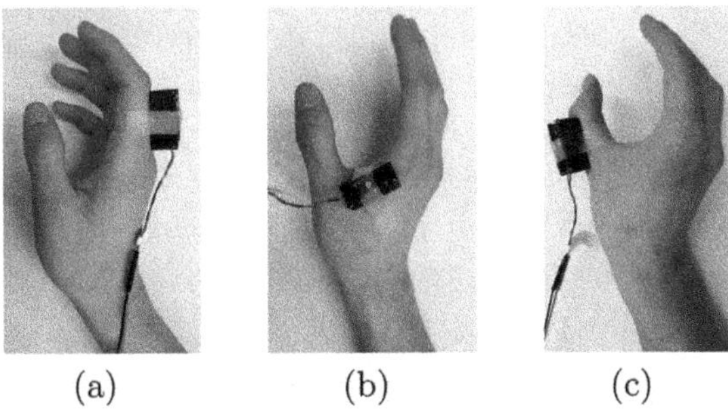

(a) (b) (c)

Fig. 1. The vibration source position in this study (a) on the index finger (Position 1), (b) between the index finger and the thumb (Position 2), (c) on the thumb (Position 3).

A piezoelectric actuator (Cedrat Technology Inc.: APA120S) is placed at the one of the three positions of the user hands to generate additive white Gaussian noise and gain the effect of SR. Additionally, the piezoelectric actuator can control the amplitude and the frequency of displacement freely, thus, the complicated signal is possible to generate. The generated vibration frequency is low-pass filtered at 400 Hz in order to activate all mechanoreceptors, as Pacinian corpuscles are active at frequencies between 0.5 and 400 Hz [12]. The Box–Muller method [13] is used to generate the white gaussian noise vibration $x(t)$ through the piezoelectric actuator:

$$x(t) = \sigma\sqrt{-2\ln\alpha(t)}\sin(2\pi\beta(t)), \tag{1}$$

where t is time, σ is the noise intensity, and α and β are independent random variables in the interval (0,1), and $x(t)$ corresponded to the voltage.

3 Evaluation Method

3.1 Subjects

Six healthy participants (mean age ± SD: 24.5 ± 1.88 years, all male) participated in the study. Before doing the experiment, all participants understood and consented to the experimental protocol approved by the Institutional Review Board of the Graduate School of Engineering, Kyoto University (No. 201707). The Weber Fraction (WF) value of stiffness perception was used to compare the user performance to detect the fingertip force. The participants inserted their index finger and thumb in the finger holders which are attached to the haptic devices, while VE in the computer monitor displayed two virtual objects to the participants.

3.2 Experimental Procedure

In this experiment, the sensory threshold (T) of each participant was measured using the *the staircase-method* [7] as the lowest vibration intensity that could be felt by the participants. Then participants performed the task with each of seven different vibration intensities; i.e., no vibration ($0T$), 40% ($0.4T$), 50% ($0.5T$), 60% ($0.6T$), 70% ($0.7T$), 80% ($0.8T$), and 100% ($1.0T$) of the sensory threshold with three different positions. The vibration intensities were provided randomly to participants to avoid learning effects. Furthermore, participants wore passive noise-cancelling headset to avoid hearing the vibration sound.

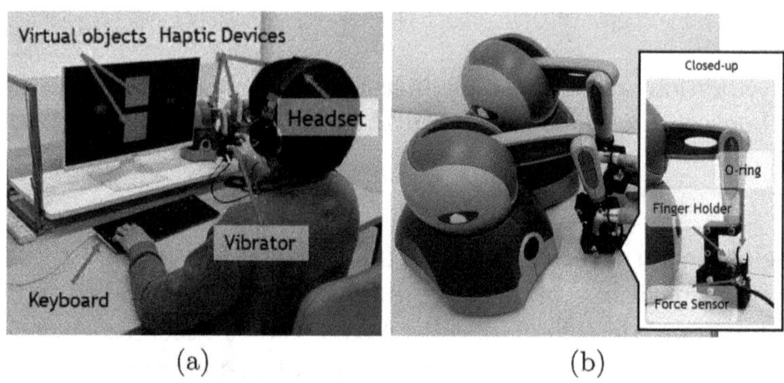

Fig. 2. Overview of experimental setup. (a) experimental setup when the participant was performing the task. The participants gets a force feedback through the haptic devices when he or she touches a virtual object through the red cursors which represent the finger positions on the screen, (b) the modified haptic devices were used in the study. The finger holder is attached to the device arm.

In VE, two virtual objects were presented as shown in Fig. 2(a). The objects were displayed as non-deformable in order to avoid the effect of visual feedback. The reference stiffness values were selected to be close to that of body fat of breast tissue (35 N/m [14]) as one of 25, 35 and 55 N/m. One virtual object had one of four reference stiffness value whereas the other object started with corresponding difference of 10 N/m and changed afterward as described later. The participants could touch the virtual objects for as long as they wanted. The force feedback was calculated using Hook's law; i.e., by multiplying the depth of the penetration of the finger into the virtual object and the stiffness of the touched object. The participants touched the two virtual objects and then chose the stiffer object by pressing a designated key on the keyboard, before starting the next trial. The task was completed by the white objects turning red. Average time spent on the experiment was around 2.5 h for one participant, including rest time.

For each reference value if the first object, Wald rule [15] was used to decide when to change the comparison stiffness for altering the stiffness of the second object. Furthermore, the change of the stiffness amount was decided by PEST rule [15], because the fixed step size takes longer time to complete the task, which lead the participant frustrated. A reversal point is defined as the turning point after which change in stiffness goes to the opposite direction of the previous direction. The average of the last four reversal values is used to determine the just noticeable difference (JND) of stiffness perception. Then we calculated WF of the subject in each condition as the average value between JND and reference stiffness:

$$WF = \frac{JND}{Reference\ Stiffness}. \quad (2)$$

4 Experimental Results and Discussion

The average WF values of each vibration intensity and stiffness difference are shown in three sub-figures of Fig. 3. The vertical axes show the WF value while the horizontal axes show the reference stiffness in each session. For example, a 35 N/m of reference stiffness with $0.6T$ is a point at 35 N/m. A lower WF value implies a higher haptic sensitivity of the user.

The results show that the WF values in all vibration-existed conditions tend to be less than the WF in no-vibration condition. As shown in Fig. 3, there are significant differences ($p < 0.05$) in the average WF values at $0T$ and $0.6T$ in all three sub-figures, confirmed by a two-tailed paired t-test. Moreover, the average of performance at $0.6T$ has the lowest WF values among other vibration levels.

Table 1. Results of Anova (Single Factor) in each vibration level

ANOVA (Single Factor)				
Vibration Intensity	Reference Stiffness (N/m)			
	25	35	45	55
$0T$	$F<F_{crit}$	$F<F_{crit}$	$F<F_{crit}$	$F<F_{crit}$
$0.4T$	$F<F_{crit}$	$F<F_{crit}$	$F<F_{crit}$	$F<F_{crit}$
$0.5T$	$F<F_{crit}$	$F>F_{crit}$	$F<F_{crit}$	$F<F_{crit}$
$0.6T$	$F>F_{crit}$	$F>F_{crit}$	$F>F_{crit}$	$F>F_{crit}$
$0.7T$	$F<F_{crit}$	$F<F_{crit}$	$F<F_{crit}$	$F<F_{crit}$
$0.8T$	$F<F_{crit}$	$F<F_{crit}$	$F<F_{crit}$	$F<F_{crit}$
$1.0T$	$F<F_{crit}$	$F<F_{crit}$	$F<F_{crit}$	$F<F_{crit}$

To compare the performances between the three positions, Analysis of Variance (ANOVA) was used to confirm a significant difference, shown in Table 1. In this table, $F-$value is calculated by the ANOVA test to examine whether the means between two conditions are significantly different or not, where the threshold is taken as $F_{crit(0.05,3,15)} = 3.28$. According to Table 1, $F > F_{crit}$ indicates a significant difference is observed for this comparison. Furthermore, Tukey's range test is used to find a pair of difference after the ANOVA test. $q-$value is calculated by the differences between means of two conditions to compare with $q_{crit(0.05,3,15)} = 3.67$. In Table 2, $q > q_{crit}$ shows the significant difference in each pair. Darker-color blocks in both tables show the significant difference in each comparison with $p < 0.05$. The ANOVA test reveals a significant difference from

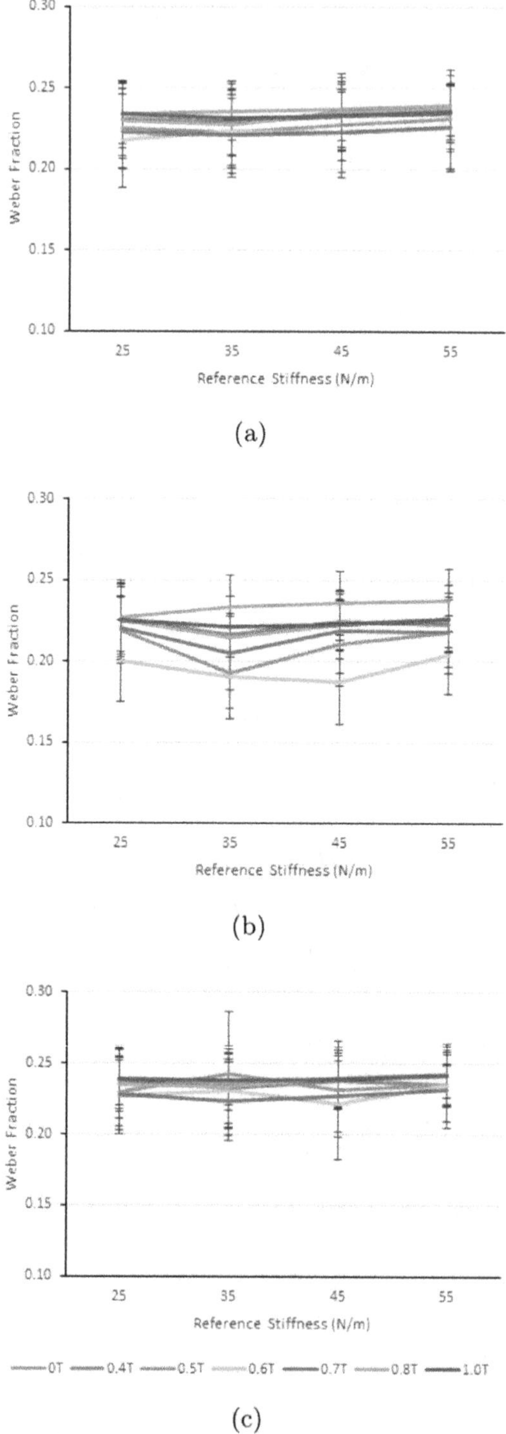

Fig. 3. User performance in each position of the vibration source (a) on the index finger, (b) between index finger and the thumb, (c) on the thumb.

Table 2. Results of Tukey's range test in the comparison of the position of vibration source

Tukey's Range Test				
Vibration Intensity	Reference Stiffness (N/m)	Pos.1 - Pos.2	Pos.1 - Pos.3	Pos.2 - Pos.3
$0.5T$	35	$q<q_{crit}$	$q<q_{crit}$	$q>q_{crit}$
$0.6T$	25	$q<q_{crit}$	$q<q_{crit}$	$q>q_{crit}$
	35	$q>q_{crit}$	$q<q_{crit}$	$q>q_{crit}$
	45	$q>q_{crit}$	$q<q_{crit}$	$q>q_{crit}$
	55	$q<q_{crit}$	$q<q_{crit}$	$q>q_{crit}$

Pos.1, Pos.2, and Pos.3 are Position 1, Position 2, and Position 3, respectively.

the position when the intensity is at $0.5T$ in 35 N/m and $0.6T$ in all reference stiffnesses. Then the results of the Tukey's test in Table 2 also show significant differences against Position 2 for Position 1 ($q > q_{crit}$) when the vibration is at $0.6T$ in all reference stiffnesses and $0.5T$ at 35 N/m. Furthermore, in comparison between Position 1 and Position 2, significant differences ($q > q_{crit}$) are also observed when the intensity is at $0.6T$ in both 35, and 45 N/m.

The present study showed the SR improves the fingertip sensation of both fingers even when the fingers are within the holders. It is hypothesized that when the vibration source is on Position 2, the vibration propagates to both fingers and not only a single finger as the other two conditions. Furthermore, the results indicated the potential of one vibration source at a remote position being able to improve the sensations of the two fingers. In addition, the limitation of this study is that the test subjects are still small in number and there is no variety of gender and age of the participants. Moreover, the subject in other conditions, such as stroke and other disability in haptic sensation, are not examined. Further investigations would be necessary, including the possibility of the improvement of the haptic performance through stochastic resonance.

5 Conclusion

We proposed a novel method for emphasizing the stiffness discrimination ability with multiple fingers in VE. The proposed method combined haptic feedback and the effect of SR in order to enhance the haptic performance while carrying out the task. The experimental results show the increase of the performance while applying a subthreshold vibration. Therefore, the proposed method is believed to enhance the sensation of two fingers in stiffness discrimination task with one vibration source when the fingers are inserted in the holders by the effect of SR. In future work, we will investigate the potential of this application and other possibilities in order to enhance haptic performances.

Acknowledgment. This work was supported in part by KAKENHI Grant No. 17K00270 and 20H04227.

References

1. Lederman, S.J., Klatzky, R.L.: Sensing and displaying spatially distributed fingertip forces in haptic interfaces for teleoperator and virtual environment systems. Presence Teleoperators Virtual Environ. **8**(1), 86–103 (1999)
2. Karol, S., Koh, K., Kwon, H.J., Park, Y.S., Kwon, Y.H., Shim, J.K.: The effect of Frequency of Transcutaneous Electrical Nerve Stimulation (TENS) on maximum multi-finger force production. Korean J. Sport Biomech. **26**(1), 93–99 (2016)
3. E, Sens., et al.: Effects of temporary functional deafferentation on the brain, sensation, and behavior of stroke patients. J. Neurosci. **32**(34), 11773–11779 (2012)
4. Smith, A.: Effects of caffeine in chewing gum on mood and attention. Hum. Psychopharmacol. Clin. Exp. **24**(3), 239–247 (2009)
5. Dettmer, M., Pourmoghaddam, A., Lee, B.C., Layne, C.S.: Effects of aging and tactile stochastic resonance on postural performance and postural control in a sensory conflict task. Somatosens. Motor Res. **32**(2), 128–135 (2015)
6. Collins, J.J., Imhoff, T.T., Grigg, P.: Noise-mediated enhancements and decrements in human tactile sensation. Phys. Rev. E **56**(1), 923 (1997)
7. Cornsweet, T.N.: The staircase-method in psychophysics. Am. J. Psychol. **75**(3), 485–491 (1962)
8. Kurita, Y., Shinohara, M., Ueda, J.: Wearable sensorimotor enhancer for fingertip based on stochastic resonance effect. IEEE Trans. Hum. Mach. Syst. **43**(3), 333–337 (2013)
9. Enders, L.R., Hur, P., Johnson, M.J., Seo, N.J.: Remote vibrotactile noise improves light touch sensation in stroke survivors' fingertips via stochastic resonance. J. Neuroengineering. Rehabil. **10**(1), 105 (2013)
10. Chamnongthai, K., Endo, T., Nisar, S., Matsuno, F., Fujimoto, K., Kosaka, M.: Fingertip force learning with enhanced haptic sensation using stochastic resonance. In: Proceedings of the IEEE World Haptics Conference, pp. 539–544 (2019)
11. Conti, F., et al.: The CHAI libraries. In: Proceedings of the Eurohaptics, pp. 496–500, (2003)
12. Johansson, R.S., Landstro, U., Lundstro, R.: Responses of mechanoreceptive afferent units in the glabrous skin of the human hand to sinusoidal skin displacements. Brain Res. **244**(1), 17–25 (1982)
13. Box, G.E.P.: A note on the generation of random normal deviates. Ann. Math. Stat. **29**, 610–611 (1958)
14. Samani, A., Zubovits, J., Plewes, D.: Elastic moduli of normal and pathological human breast tissues: an inversion-technique-based investigation of 169 samples. Phys. Med. Biol. **52**(6), 1565 (2007)
15. Taylor, M., Creelman, C.D.: PEST: efficient estimates on probability functions. J. Acoust. Soc. Am. **41**(4A), 782–787 (1967)

9

Two-Point Haptic Pattern Recognition with the Inverse Filter Method

Lucie Pantera(✉), Charles Hudin, and Sabrina Panëels

CEA, LIST, Sensory and Ambient Interfaces Laboratory, Palaiseau, France
{lucie.pantera,charles.hudin,sabrina.paneels}@cea.fr

Abstract. Touchscreens are widely used nowadays, yet still crucially lack haptic feedback for a rich interaction. Haptic feedback presents several benefits for touch interactions but can be difficult to achieve on a surface, due to issues of vibration propagation. The Inverse Filter Method enables to achieve localised multitouch haptic feedback on a glass surface by controlling the vibrations field over the entire surface. This recent method could enable a wide range of novel interactions. Yet, it has not been tested with users. This paper presents an initial study evaluating 2-point based pattern recognition using IFM with two fingers from each hand and with different timing difference in presentation, varying from 0 ms to 300 ms. The results are promising as participants could discriminate rather well the different patterns with averaged rates of 83% for simultaneous stimuli and up to 92% for stimuli separated by 300 ms.

Keywords: Surface haptics · Localised feedback · Pattern recognition

1 Introduction

Touchscreens have become a new standard for mobile devices as they enable a natural user interaction by directly touching and interacting with the items of interest, rather than using an external peripheral to map the gestures to the display and possible actions (e.g. a mouse). Unfortunately, current touchscreens are still devoid of rich haptic feedback, such as being able to render different textures and localised multitouch haptic feedback. Yet, rich haptic feedback on a surface presents several benefits. For instance, it is helpful for typing on a virtual keyboard as it increases performance and reduces typing errors [4, 11]. It can also enrich the interaction by providing different sensations to different actions to help differentiate them (e.g. long vs short click, etc.) or to enrich the overall experience (e.g. in a game) [9, 1]. Non-visual interactions could even be envisioned in order to help visually impaired access digital contents [15, 13].

Consequently, rich localised haptic feedback on a surface can open up many new interaction possibilities. However, delivering localised haptic feedback on a surface can be very challenging technically. The work conducted on user interactions often either directly equips the fingers of the users [13] or relies on a single or two actuators at most [15, 4, 11], thus avoiding the issues of vibration propagation when multiple actuators are required, but then with limited feedback possibilities. Few methods are currently available to render localised haptic feedback on a surface [6, 5, 2, 8]. The time reversal approach focuses on bending waves to produce localised impulsive displacements on transparent glass plates [6]. Another method relies on a phased actuator array in a surface, which can focus ultrasounds to create localised mid-air sensations [5]. These two methods work in ultrasonic frequencies, far beyond the tactile sensitivity range. The perception of such stimulation then relies on nonlinear demodulation phenomena that are not easily controlled. Another method uses an array of electromagnets and a magnetorheological fluid [8] but this technique is not very accurate and thus, it cannot isolate the effect to areas as small as a single fingertip and thus is not suitable for multitouch. Another approach investigated the use of the vibration modes of a surface to localise haptic feedback [2] in the tactile sensitivity range. It combines the different vibration modes of the surface to vibrate chosen locations while canceling others. However, this method does not permit to choose the desired frequency of the haptic feedback. The Inverse Filter Method has been proposed [7] that provides such flexibility with a similar idea. This method uses a glass surface equipped with piezoelectric actuators glued on the bottom of the glass and produces a localised haptic feedback at the locations of these actuators while canceling the signals at the other actuator positions. A user study was conducted demonstrating that the stimulus on a finger was better perceived than without the method. However, no studies were conducted evaluating the recognition of multiple simultaneous stimuli. Recently, this method has been improved [14] by permitting localised haptic feedback at any point of a surface without the necessity to put the fingers on top of the actuators. Furthermore, this method provides a good resolution of about 1.5 cm, far below the wavelength $\lambda_{250Hz} = 19$ cm. However, this novel method has not yet been tested with users, which is the contribution presented in this paper.

Therefore, this paper presents a user study of two-point based pattern discrimination using the Inverse Filter Method (IFM) to investigate the effect of varying the temporal difference between stimuli on pattern recognition and subjective evaluation. The setup and results are presented in the following sections.

2 Experimental Setup

2.1 Setup Description

The user study carried out in this paper was conducted on the setup depicted on the left of Fig. 1. Eleven piezoelectric actuators (Murata 7BB-35-3, 35 mm diameter, 0.51 mm thickness) were glued on the bottom of a $96 \times 162 \times 1$ mm touchscreen (7" pingbo PB70DR8272-R1), which can detect up to five fingers. An Arduino receives the finger localisation data through an I2C protocol. After decoding the data with Python, the number of control points can be obtained as well as their X, Y coordinates. Actuators were driven individually with piezo haptic drivers (DRV8662-Texas Instrument) delivering up to 200 Vpp. Surface displacements were measured by a laser vibrometer (Polytec OFV-5000/MLV-100) mounted on a motorised three axis platform. The acquisition device (NI-9264, NI-9205 and cDAQ-9174) allowed for a synchronous emission and acquisition of actuators and vibrometer signals. All signals were sampled at $F_s = 10$ kHz.

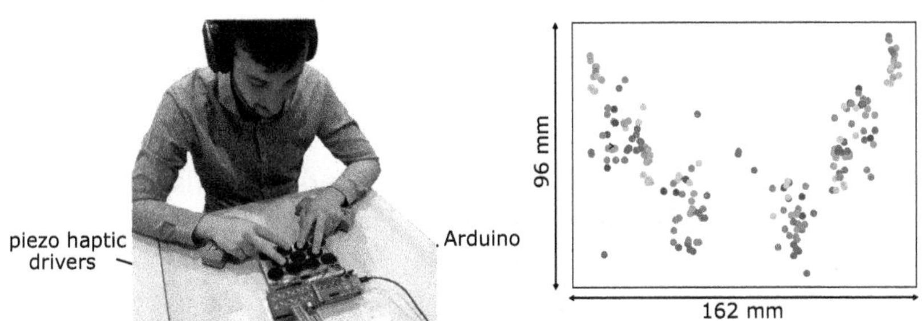

Fig. 1. Left: experimental setup. Right: finger positions of the participants.

2.2 System Calibration

In order to apply the IFM, a matrix of impulse response is needed (more details in [14]). It captures the mechanical transduction of the actuators as well as the propagation, reverberation and attenuation of waves into the touch surface at calibration points spaced at 2 mm. These entries of the matrix of impulse response are calculated as the ratio between the displacement above a calibration point and the driving signal sent to an actuator, in the frequency domain for each actuator on the surface. We chose to acquire experimentally the matrix with the multiple sweep method [12]. Each entry was measured by sending an exponential sweep sine signal sequence of duration $T = 2$ s, with frequency varying linearly from 0 to $F_s/2 = 5$ kHz to all the actuators. All actuators were driven simultaneously with a time shifted version of the same exponential sweep while measuring synchronously the resulting displacement at the calibration point. Then, the matrix is the ratio of the displacement by the sweep signal in the frequency domain. The same procedure was repeated for all the actuators and all the calibration points. When the user places his fingers on the screen, the matrix of impulse response at the current positions of the fingers is computed. Using the initial matrix of impulse response and an interpolation function, we can calculate the matrix of impulse response of the current different fingers (Fig. 2).

When the output signal sent to the different actuators is calculated thanks to the IFM, a rescaling is applied to this signal in order to avoid saturation at the output of the amplifiers, which in turn causes inaccurate localisation rendering. However, this rescaling induces an amplitude variation between 1.5 and 5 μm under the different fingers. As a consequence, this amplitude is not controlled,

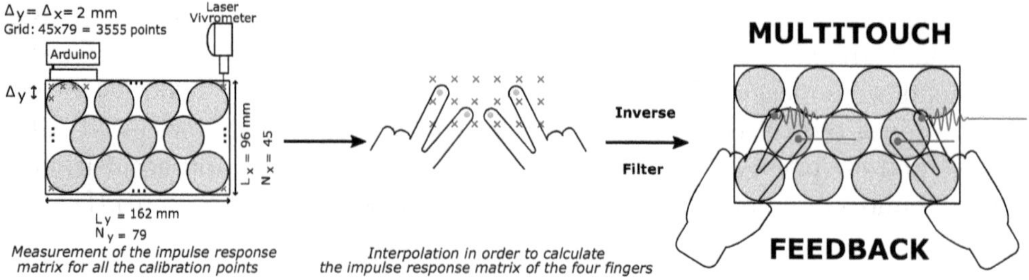

Fig. 2. Calculation of the matrix of impulse responses under the four fingers.

in favour of an optimal localisation rendering, and depends on the position of the fingers on the plate. However, this is not an issue for the user study as the focus was on multitouch pattern recognition with an optimal setup. The haptic signal delivering to the different fingers was a burst at 250 Hz with 25 cycles.

3 User Study

The purpose of this user study was to conduct preliminary investigations of multitouch pattern recognition on a tactile surface using the IFM. Specifically, this study investigated whether users could discriminate vibrotactile stimuli on two different fingers and in particular simultaneous stimuli. To that effect, four different timing differences were chosen, i.e. 0 ms, 100 ms, 200 ms and 300 ms.

3.1 Methodology

Participants. The study was conducted with 12 participants (4f–8m), aged between 14 and 45 ($M = 28.25$, $SD = 7.5$). 11 participants were aged between 25 and 45 and only one minor participated. All but two participants were right-handed. Half of the participants were very familiar with haptic technologies (researchers recruited within the laboratory), while the rest had limited or no knowledge about haptics (a college student, a security coordinator, a project manager in construction project management and three researchers from the vision laboratory). None reported any issues with their fingers or sensitivity.

Technical Settings. The device was placed on a table, in front of the participant (see Fig. 1). The participants were instructed to place their fingers onto the tactile screen for the trials, at the positions that were comfortable to them, as displayed on Fig. 1, with their wrists on resting supports to minimize the fatigue. They wore noise-canceling headphones during the trials with pink noise to cancel any biais due to the noise generated by the setup. The experimenter used a standard Windows laptop both for running the Python application controlling the feedback and for logging the verbal answers.

Procedure. The experiment was a within-subject repeated measures design with four conditions (0, 100, 200, 300 ms), tested in different sessions. The order of the sessions was counterbalanced between participants as well as the direction of the stimuli within a session (i.e. either playing from left-to-right, or from right-to-left). There were 10 trials per stimuli/finger combination (depicted on Fig. 3) with half from each direction, accounting for 60 trials per session. In total, each participant performed 240 trials. The experiment lasted one hour on average.

In each trial, the task was to identify the positions/finger combination that received the haptic stimuli with the fingers numbered from 1 to 4 (e.g. stimuli on the index fingers of each hand corresponded to '2–3', see Fig. 3). The participants were instructed to provide the answer verbally as soon as they recognised the stimuli, which was provided only once, whilst their hands remained on the device. The experimenter logged the answer by first, pressing a button to measure the response time and then, typing the given answer. This was a forced-choice experiment: if participants had doubts, they were asked to answer the most likely option. To accustom participants and reduce the impact of learning effects, prior to each condition, participants were presented with each of the stimuli twice per direction and performed a blind test.

After each session, the participants were asked whether they perceived a difference with the previous condition and to describe it. They were also asked to rate the difficulty of discrimination on a continuous numeric scale from 0 to 10 (10: very difficult). At the end of the last session, the participants were asked which timing difference they preferred and general comments about the perception. As for quantitative measures, the interface collected the responses and the response times. The response time was collected to provide trends, as the experimenter logging the responses induced a bias, in particular in terms of longer hesitations to answer for a condition.

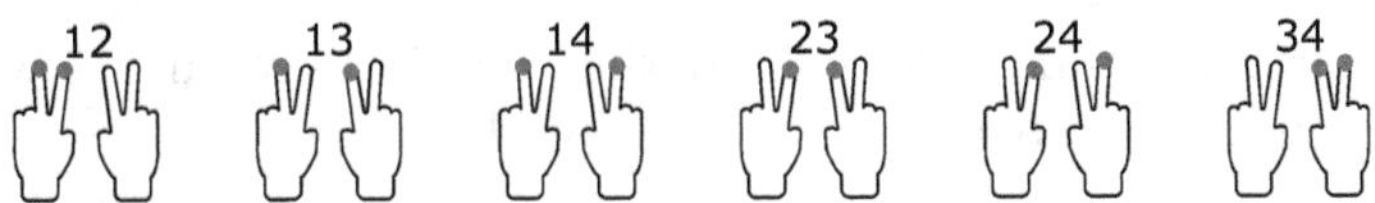

Fig. 3. Stimulation number corresponding to the stimulated fingers.

3.2 Results

Recognition Rates. The average recognition rates are displayed left of Fig. 4. The distribution was normal for all the conditions except for 0 ms. Therefore, a Friedman's ANOVA was conducted and revealed that the recognition rates were significantly different between the timing conditions, $\chi^2(3) = 13.07$, $p < .05$ ($M_0 = 49.58$ or 82.64%, $SE_0 = 6.1$, $M_{100} = 51.83$ or 86.39 %, $SE_{100} = 4.78$, $M_{200} = 54.75$ or 91.25%, $SE_{200} = 3.52$, $M_{300} = 55$ or 91.67%, $SE_{300} = 4.59$). Post hoc tests were conducted based on the following inequality [3]: $|\overline{R_u} - \overline{R_v}| \geq$

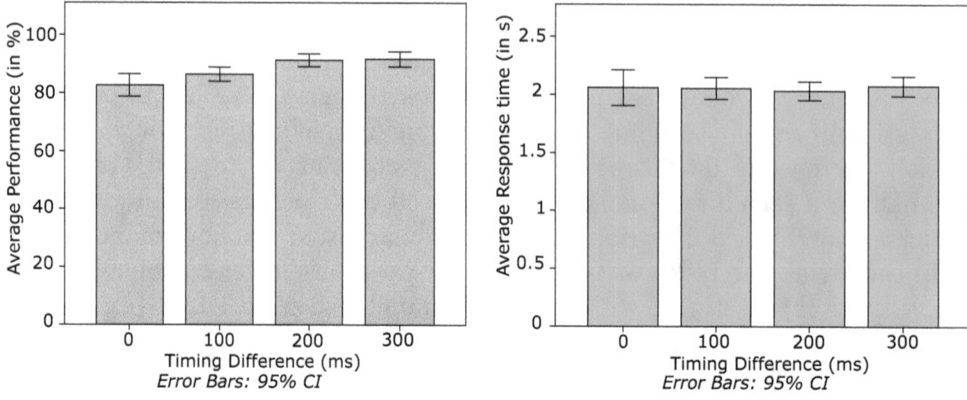

Fig. 4. Left: average performance (in %). Right: average response time (in s).

$z_{\alpha/k(k-1)}\sqrt{k(k+1)/6N}$ (Eq. 1), with $R_{u,v}$ the mean rank of a group, z the statistic from the table of the standard normal distribution, k the number of conditions and N the total sample size. We computed the critical difference (right side of Eq. 1) as being equal to 1.39 with a z value of 2.64. We then calculated the differences between the mean ranks of the groups with the most likely significant differences, i.e. 0–200, 0–300, 100–200 and 100–300. The inequality of Eq. 1 indicates that if the differences between mean ranks is greater than or equal to the critical difference, then that difference is significant. In this case, the pairs 0–200 ($|1.67 - 3.13|$) and 0–300 ($|1.67 - 3.17|$) have values of 1.45 and 1.5, greater than 1.39, thus their difference is significant. Overall, the results indicate that participants recognised well patterns made of two distinct stimuli on the surface using the IFM, even simultaneous ones (82.64% recognition, chance level at 17%). However, to further confirm this hypothesis, studies involving mixed stimuli on one to several fingers need to be conducted as the knowledge of having only two stimuli could have biased the conditions with a lower temporal difference by guessing. There were no major differences between participants judged as haptic experts and non-experts, if anything, non-experts had higher scores than experts. As expected, participants performed better at longer timing differences with a significant difference between 0 and 200 ms onwards.

For further analysis of the participants' performance, we computed confusion matrices for each of the conditions (see Fig. 5). They show that the pairs '12' and '34' are nearly always recognised, no matter the timing difference between stimuli. Most of the confusion happened when involving pairs of fingers from different hands. In particular, for 0 and 100 ms, the pairs with the lowest scores were '13', '14' and '24' and the confusion most often happened with one adjacent finger. Further analysis of the direction of the stimuli could inform us whether it had any effect on the confusions. Preliminary analysis of the results of amplitude differences between patterns did not indicate any notable impact on the perception. For 0 ms, the amplitude varied on average between 2.95 (patterns '13' and '24') and 4.16 μm (pattern '23'), for 100 ms between 2.75 (pattern '24') and 3.72 (pattern '23'), for 200 ms between 2.69 (patterns '13' and '14') and 3.75 (pattern '23') and for 300 ms between 2.78 (patterns '12' and '13') and 3.8 (pattern '23'). There was no clear correlation between this difference in amplitude and the recognition rates, as for instance '23' always had the highest amplitudes, but not the highest recognition rates. For 100 ms the lowest recognition was for '13' and yet had an amplitude of 3.06 μm. Further analysis will be conducted to assess the impact of the different amplitudes.

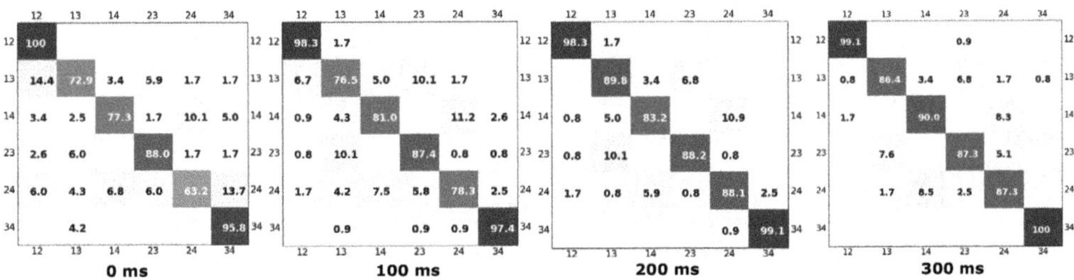

Fig. 5. Confusion matrices. From left to right: 0 ms, 100 ms, 200 ms and 300 ms

Response Times. The average response times are displayed right of Fig. 4. The distribution was normal for all the conditions except for the 300 ms condition. Therefore, a Friedman's ANOVA was conducted and revealed that the response times did not significantly change between the different timing conditions, $\chi^2(3) = 3.6$, $p > .05$ ($M_0 = 2.06$, $SE_0 = 0.57$, $M_{100} = 2.05$, $SE_{100} = 0.37$, $M_{200} = 2.03$, $SE_{200} = 0.41$, $M_{300} = 2.07$, $SE_{300} = 0.37$). This shows that participants had no particular difficulty according to the timing difference, even with simultaneous stimuli, which is confirmed by the relatively high recognition rates.

Qualitative Feedback. During the study, after each session, participants were asked to rate the difficulty of discrimination for each condition. 0 ms obtained an average score of 6.42 out of 10, 100 ms a score of 3.63, 200 ms a score of 3.36 and 300 ms an average score of 2.33. This shows that despite good recognition rates for the 0 ms condition, participants felt less confident, some participants reported feeling a movement rather than two distinct points. This echoes the work on 'out of the body' phantom sensations on a surface [10] and warrants further exploration. On the contrary, the 300 ms condition was deemed the less difficult as participants could clearly feel and distinguish the two stimuli. From a pattern recognition point of view, this is an interesting result as the 0 ms could produce patterns or textures that need to be perceived as continuous movements, whereas timing delays above 200 ms could be used to ensure the discrimination of several points. In concordance with the perceived difficulty ratings, 7 participants preferred the 300 ms condition as they were more confident about the perception, with stimuli well separated, whereas 5 participants preferred the 100 ms where the stimuli were still well perceived and the rhythm was faster. Some participants reported perceiving different intensities on their fingers in a trial, though not consistently. This could be explained by the uncontrolled amplitude of the setup, though the difference in amplitude of the stimuli were constant for a given pattern in a trial, which contradicts user perceptions.

4 Conclusion

This paper reported the results of an initial user study on 2-point based pattern recognition on a surface using the Inverse Filter Method, with different timing differences between stimuli. The results are promising as participants could discriminate rather well the different patterns with averaged rates of 83% for simultaneous stimuli and up to 92% for stimuli separated by 300 ms, without any significant differences in response times. The sensations reported varied between a fast movement to two clearly distinct points depending on the timing difference, thus opening up possibilities for rich patterns. A lot of data remains to be analysed to assess the impact of stimuli direction and uncontrolled amplitudes on the observed confusions. This initial study also opens up many future leads for experiments by evaluating 3 to more actuated fingers at a time, perceptual illusions and for future design of patterns using this method.

References

1. Chen, H.Y., Park, J., Dai, S., Tan, H.Z.: Design and evaluation of identifiable key-click signals for mobile devices. IEEE TOH **4**(4), 229–241 (2011)
2. Emgin, S.E., Aghakhani, A., Sezgin, T.M., Basdogan, C.: Haptable: an interactive tabletop providing online haptic feedback for touch gestures. IEEE TVCG **25**(9), 2749–2762 (2018)
3. Field, A.: Discovering Statistics Using IBM SPSS Statistics, 3rd edn. Sage, Thousand Oaks (2009)
4. Hoggan, E., Brewster, S.A., Johnston, J.: Investigating the effectiveness of tactile feedback for mobile touchscreens. In: CHI 2008, pp. 1573–1582 (2008)
5. Hoshi, T., Takahashi, M., Iwamoto, T., Shinoda, H.: Noncontact tactile display based on radiation pressure of airborne ultrasound. IEEE TOH **3**(3), 155–165 (2010)
6. Hudin, C., Lozada, J., Hayward, V.: Localized tactile feedback on a transparent surface through time-reversal wave focusing. IEEE TOH **8**(2), 188–198 (2015)
7. Hudin, C., Panëels, S.: Localisation of vibrotactile stimuli with spatio-temporal inverse filtering. In: Prattichizzo, D., Shinoda, H., Tan, H.Z., Ruffaldi, E., Frisoli, A. (eds.) EuroHaptics 2018. LNCS, vol. 10894, pp. 338–350. Springer, Cham (2018)
8. Jansen, Y., Karrer, T., Borchers, J.: MudPad: localized tactile feedback on touch surfaces. In: Adjunct proceedings of UIST 2010, pp. 385–386 (2010)
9. Kim, S., Lee, G.: Haptic feedback design for a virtual button along force-displacement curves. In: UIST 2013, pp. 91–96. ACM (2013)
10. Kim, Y., Lee, J., Kim, G.J.: Extending "Out of the Body" tactile phantom sensations to 2D and applying it to mobile interaction. Pers. Ubiquit. Comput. **19**(8), 1295–1311 (2015)

11. Ma, Z., Edge, D., Findlater, L., Tan, H.Z.: Haptic keyclick feedback improves typing speed and reduces typing errors on a flat keyboard. In: WHC 2015, pp. 220–227. IEEE (2015)
12. Majdak, P., Balazs, P., Laback, B.: Multiple exponential sweep method for fast measurement of head-related transfer functions. J. Audio Eng. Soc. **55**(7/8), 623–637 (2007)
13. Nicolau, H., Guerreiro, J., Guerreiro, T., Carriço, L.: Ubibraille: designing and evaluating a vibrotactile braille-reading device. In: ACM SIGACCESS Conference on Computers and Accessibility, pp. 1–8 (2013)
14. Pantera, L., Hudin, C.: Sparse actuator array combined with inverse filter for multitouch vibrotactile stimulation. In: WHC 2019, pp. 19–24. IEEE (2019)
15. Rantala, J., et al.: Methods for presenting braille characters on a mobile device with a touchscreen and tactile feedback. IEEE TOH **2**(1), 28–39 (2009)

10

KATIB: Haptic-Visual Guidance for Handwriting

Georgios Korres and Mohamad Eid(✉)

Engineering Division, New York University Abu Dhabi, Abu Dhabi, United Arab Emirates
{george.korres,mohamad.eid}@nyu.edu

Abstract. Haptic-visual guidance is shown to improve handwriting. This work presents a platform named KATIB (writer in Arabic) to support multi-stroke handwriting using haptic-visual guidance. A rotating neodymium magnet mounted onto a 2 DoF parallel robot underneath the writing surface is proposed to improve the fidelity of haptic guidance and mechanically decouple the stylus. The stylus utilizes stackable magnets to intensify magnetic forces. Full and partial haptic guidance methods are developed and evaluated. The current implementation demonstrates sufficient workspace of $80\,\text{mm} \times 60\,\text{mm}$ and a perceivable (tangential) guidance force of 0.4 N. Magnetostatic analysis is conducted to study the effects of friction and tilting on the rendered force.

1 Introduction

Handwriting requires cognitive, visual-motor, and memory skills to master. Due to the complexity of human perception, a growing trend in the design of handwriting assistive technologies involves using multimodal interfaces [5,10]. Traditional assistive technologies for handwriting acquisition have focused on audio and visual modalities, but recently there has been a trend to exploit the haptic modality to further improve sensorimotor abilities [1,3,8,11].

In order to resemble real-life handwriting experience, haptic-visual feedback in touchscreen with stylus-based interaction are proposed [2]. A vibration motor is attached to the stylus to provide vibrotactile feedback based on the interaction with the touchscreen device [13]. Results showed that users benefit greatly from the vibrotactile feedback. Some combined vibrotactile feedback with visual guidance [9,15], and showed improved performance.

Although promising, existing methods for tactile and/or force feedback guidance are based on using mechanical attachments and do not address ergonomic factors on handwriting performance (such as visual occlusion and flexibility in stylus grip and writing pressure). In this paper, we propose a multimodal system using contactless force feedback guidance based on magnetic forces that overcomes variations in grasping styles and applied pressure forces. Therefore, the contributions of this paper include the following: (1) proposing the hardware and software design of KATIB, a multimodal handwriting system with magnetic-based haptic guidance for improved ergonomics, (2) developing rendering algorithms for full and partial haptic guidance, and (3) characterization and technical evaluation of the proposed platform.

2 Related Work

Magnetically-driven haptic guidance is desirable since magnetic forces can be felt at the tip of the handwriting stylus without having mechanical attachment that may occlude the visual display. A common approach is to utilize an array of electromagnets to guide users to appropriate screen locations [16]. Actuated Workbench [7,12], Proactive Desk II [16], and Fingerflux [12] are tabletop systems that can make physical objects placed on the table move using an array of electromagnets. For instance, Fingerflux provided near-surface haptic feedback to guide the user's finger to appropriate locations on a touchscreen device [12]. However, this approach reported a drifting error of more than 10 mm which makes it unsuitable for handwriting tasks (literature suggests less than 3 mm error for handwriting tasks [4]).

An interesting approach is to attach a magnet or an electromagnet to the end effector of a two DoF motorized linkage mechanism to control the stylus, altogether placed underneath a writing surface (paper) to provide haptic guidance [6,14]. In the dePENd system, a computer controls the xy position of the magnet under the writing surface in order to move the pen and present haptic guidance [14]. As the linkage mechanism moves the magnet along a desired trajectory, it attracts the stylus through magnetic forces to move along the same trajectory. No visual guidance is provided. A recent study demonstrated a system to deliver dynamic guidance in drawing and sketching via an electromagnet placed underneath a pressure sensitive tablet [6]. The system allows the user to move the pen freely and renders pull back forces using a closed-loop time-free approach to minimize the error between the pen position and the desired trajectory.

These systems do not provide synchronized haptic-visual guidance for handwriting. Driven by previous findings that multimodal guidance is more effective for motor learning [10], KATIB provides mechanically decoupled, multimodal feedback system with synchronized haptic-visual guidance to support multi-stroke handwriting. Compared to electromagnetic-based guidance, the permanent magnet provides concentrated magnetic flux and thus higher fidelity of haptic guidance. Furthermore, larger haptic guidance forces are achievable with permanent magnet, compared to electromagnet. Finally, the heating effects of the electromagnet weakens the magnetic flux and thus reduces the haptic guidance force over usage.

3 KATIB System

A schematic diagram of the KATIB system design is shown in Fig. 1(a). The system comprises a 3D printed pen-like stylus that hosts cylindrical 5×5 [mm] (or more) and one cylindrical 2×2 [mm] vertically polarized N42 neodymium magnets that are stacked on top of each other forming the stylus tip, a low-cost 4 mm thick resistive touchscreen 640×480 pixels display to provide visual guidance and capture interactions between the writing surface and the stylus, a N42 neodymium magnet underneath the screen that is attached to the end-effector of a 2 DoF parallel manipulator for moving the magnet along a particular trajectory and provide magnetic haptic guidance, and a board computer that runs an application to provide synchronized audio, visual, and haptic guidance for the learner. A snapshot of the system prototype is shown in Fig. 1(b).

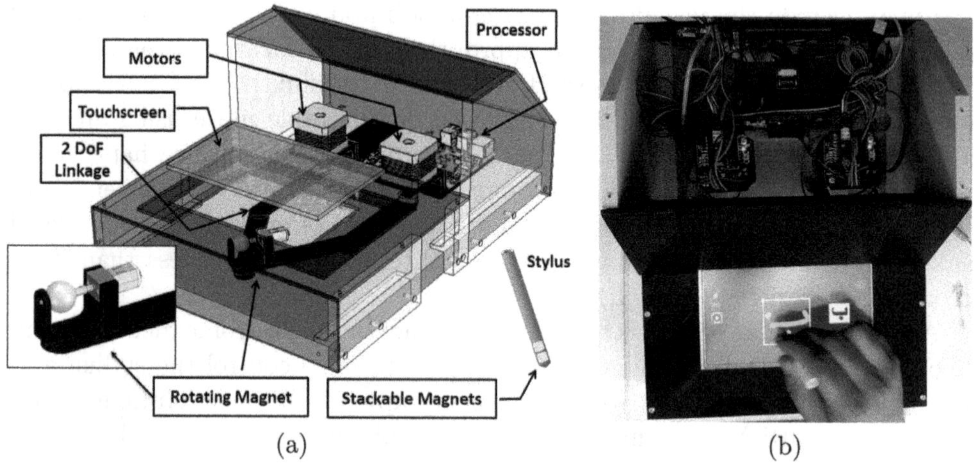

Fig. 1. (a) KATIB system design, (b) KATIB prototype.

3.1 Magnetic Force Acting on the Stylus

The magnetic force due to a non uniform magnetic field can be calculated through the following equation:

$$\mathbf{F} = \nabla (\mathbf{m} \cdot \mathbf{B}), \quad \mathbf{m} = \frac{1}{\mu_0} \mathbf{B}_r V \tag{1}$$

whereas $\mathbf{m}$ is the magnetic moment vector. In case of a permanent magnet the magnetic moment can be expressed through the residual flux density of the magnet B_r. The residual flux density of the magnet is usually provided by the manufacturer and V is the volume of the magnet. The values of the parameters above, as well as the derivation of the magnetic flux distribution $\mathbf{B}$, are discussed in the magnetostatic analysis in Sect. 4.2

3.2 Hardware Implementation

Katib sytem was designed around a Raspberry Pi Model B+ single board computer which is running Linux software. It drives two NEMA17 stepper motors which are equipped with a 5:1 reduction planetary gearbox. The stepper motors are PID controlled through the uStepper driver platform which is based on an ATMEL ATMEGA328 MCU, the Trinamic TMC5130 Motor Driver and the Broadcom AEAT8800-Q24 Hall effect encoder. The motors can operate at a maximum update rate of 1800 Hz. The rotation of the end effector is achieved by the use of a custom solution comprised of a 15k RPM micro DC motor equipped with a 300:1 reduction gearbox and a quadrature hall effect encoder which is driven from a Texas Instruments DRV8838 driver and an ATMEL ATMEGA328. The Rasberry PI is also connected to a 640×480 TFT display which is driven by a generic HDMI-TFT driver. The display is equipped with a resistive touchscreen driven by the MICROCHIP AR1100 touchscreen controller to detect contact with the stylus. The haptic guidance force can be rendered at a frequency of 1800 Hz. A schematic diagram of the hardware implementation is shown in Fig. 2.

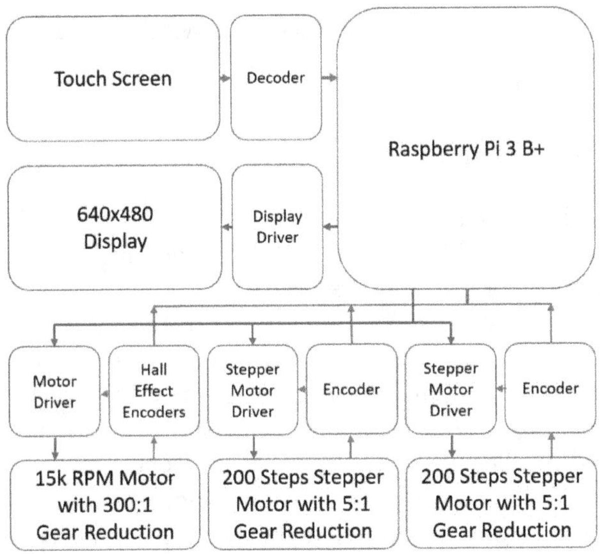

Fig. 2. Hardware implementation.

3.3 Graphical User Interface Design

As shown in Fig. 3, KATIB provides two interfaces: an instructor window and a learner window. The instructor window enables teachers to record a handwriting task, assign it to one or more learners, and examine the learners performance. On the other hand, the learner window provides learners with a list of handwriting

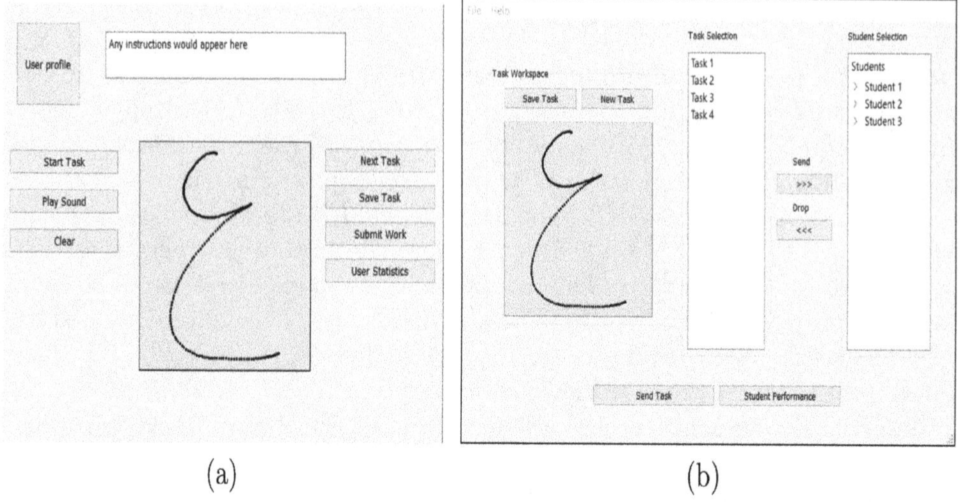

Fig. 3. (a) Learner interface, (b) Instructor interface.

tasks to exercise and record. The recorded handwriting tasks are evaluated and a report about the learner's performance is sent back to the instructor.

3.4 Haptic-Visual Guidance

Visual guidance is implemented by showing a visual trace of the entire handwriting task as well as a highlighted visual target for the immediate next move along the handwriting trajectory. In multi-stroke tasks, a flashing visual dot of different color is displayed to show the starting point of the subsequent stroke. As for haptic guidance, full and partial haptic-visual guidance methods are developed for KATIB system. In the full haptic guidance method, the system leads the movement by providing visual feedback about the next point to move to along the trajectory and applies a maximum force to move the stylus to the desired position. Once the user is at the desired position, the next point is identified and haptic-visual guidance is provided for the next point. The full guidance method is detailed in Algorithm 1. Figure 5 demonstrates high fidelity of full haptic guidance where the average root mean square (RMS) error is 2.73 mm.

Partial haptic-visual guidance is user-led. The KATIB system provides visual feedback for the next point to move the stylus to and provide force guidance only when the user deviates significantly from the desired trajectory. The magnetic force is switched on or off by rotating the magnet by 180° from its original position. If the user completes the entire handwriting task within the trajectory error threshold, no haptic feedback is applied. The partial haptic-visual guidance method is shown in Algorithm 2.

Algorithm 1: Full guidance

```
initialization;
while poitnts#>0 do
    if Stylus_activeAND
    ||Tip_Loc − Point_Loc||L2 < ε then
        points# =points# − 1;
        Move_End_Effector(points#);
        Display_Dot(points#);
    else
        blink_Dot(points#);
    end
end
```

Algorithm 2: Partial guidance

```
while poitnts#>0 do
    if StylusIsActive AND
    ||Tip_Loc − Point_Loc||L2 < ε then
        points# =points# − 1;
        MagnetActive(FALSE);
        Move_End_Effector(points#);
        Display_Dot(points#);
    else
        MagnetActive(TRUE);
        blink_Dot(points#);
    end
end
```

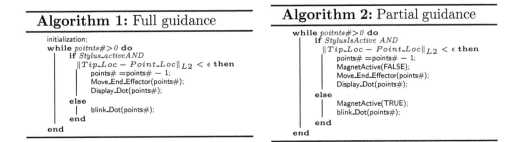

4 System Characterization

4.1 Haptic Guidance Workspace

The work space of the 2DOF parallel manipulator can be calculated by solving the forward kinematics problem. The stepper motors can be driven in up to 16 microsteps and since the planetary gearbox has a 5:1 reduction rate, the final number of steps per motor shaft revolution is 16000 steps. A Matlab scrip was written to solve the kinematic problem for the specified step resolution for a range between −45 to 45° per motor and 100 mm as the length of each parallel manipulator arm. The measured workspace for the device is 80 mm (width) by 60 mm (height), which is sufficient for most handwriting tasks.

4.2 Magnetostatic Analysis

In order to calculate the magnetic force acting on the stylus according to Eq. 1, we need to derive the magnetic field distribution for the specific configuration (magnet, glass screen, stylus magnet) under a steady current, which in this case is equal to zero. The magnetostatic equations are derived from Maxwell's equations under the assumption of either fixed or moving charges with a steady current. In such cases, Maxwell's equations can split into two pairs of equations: two equations describing the electric field (electrostatics) and two equations describing the magnetic field (magnetostatics).

The ANSYS Magnetostatic Analysis module was utilized to solve the magnetic field distribution for the different translational and tilt cases. The geometry consisted of a stack of 2 cylindrical magnets for the stylus(5×5 mm and 2×2 mm respectively) and one cylindrical (5×5 mm) magnet for the end effector, separated by a surface of glass material with 4 mm thickness ($\mu_{r/glass} = 5$). The structure was enclosed in a volume of simulated air ($\mu_{r/air} = 1$). Neodymium N42 (NdFeB) was used to simulate the magnets with a residual induction of 1300 mT and a coercive force of 955 KA/m. The geometry was meshed using a "sphere of influence", a heavily refined spherical mesh volume encapsulating the region whereas the magnets where interacting, to ensure a stable and accurate approximation. The final mesh comprised about 250k elements. Finally, the simulation was repeated for the different translation and tilt configurations of the stylus and end effector. The tilt axis was defined by the tangency between the base of the stylus magnet and the glass surface.

Effects of Stylus Displacement/Tilt on Guidance Force. As the magnet moves to the next position along the trajectory, it attracts the stylus to move into the same direction. The normal and tangential attraction forces are analyzed as function of the horizontal distance between the magnet and the stylus. The effects of displacement is simulated as shown in Fig. 4 (a). The results, shown in Fig. 4 (b), demonstrate a peak tangential force of 0.43 N from 2 mm to 5 mm displacement, which produces a perceivable haptic guidance. Furthermore, the effects of tilting the stylus on the amplitude of the attraction force is also studied. As shown in Fig. 4 (c), tilting the stylus up to 40° from the normal direction would results in a negligible tangential force.

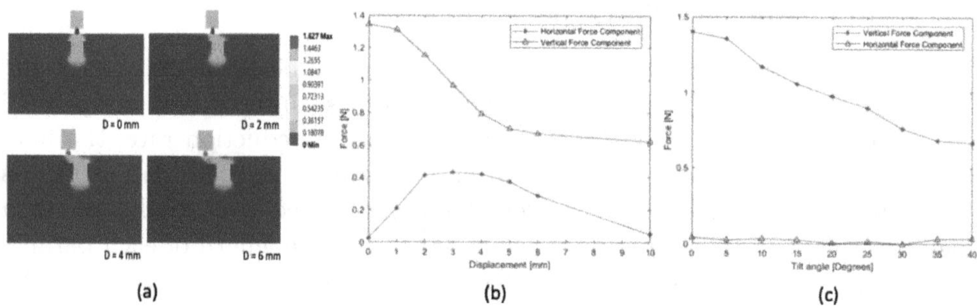

Fig. 4. (a) Magnetic interaction modeling, (b) magnetic forces against displacement, (c) magnetic forces against tilt angle.

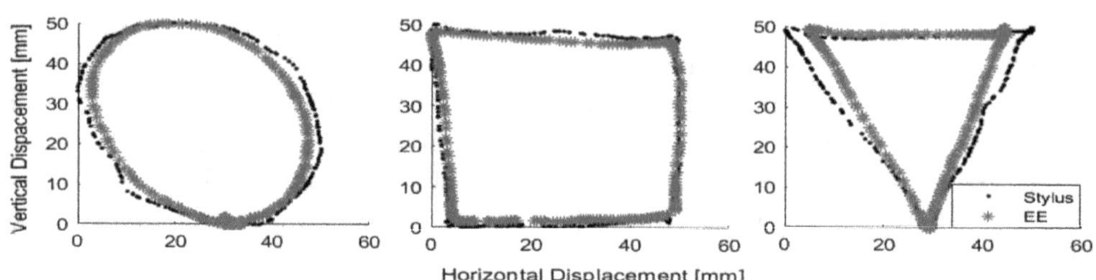

Fig. 5. Sample handwriting tasks with stylus drifting along the writing surface (EE for end-effector).

Friction Effects on Stylus. The effects of friction between the stylus and the handwriting surface is examined. The stylus freely drifts along the handwriting trajectory due to the attraction force by the moving magnet. The magnet and stylus positions are recorded for three different handwriting tasks and plotted in Fig. 5 where differences in traces are mainly due to friction effects. Since the static friction f_s is larger than the dynamic friction f_d, it must be true that the tangential force Fx is larger than the static friction force fs because the stylus is moving. Given the results from Fig. 4(b) showing that the tangential force maximizes at around 0.43 N at 3.5 mm away from the magnet implies that the static friction must be less than 0.43 N to be able to move the stylus (see Fig. 5). It must be noted that this is an extreme case and in reality the user is holding the stylus and applying some forces along the desired trajectory. Also, while the user is grasping the stylus there is always a tilt angle that reduces further the effects of the friction.

5 Conclusion

In this paper, we proposed a haptic-visual guidance system that utilizes magnetic forces for haptic guidance to support handwriting. By using magnetic forces, the system improves the ergonomics of handwriting (support for grasping styles and force profiles) while maintaining a highly fidelity of haptic guidance. As for future work, we will conduct a usability study to thoroughly evaluate the ergonomic benefits for learning as well as augmenting handwriting skills.

References

1. Asselborn, T., et al.: Bringing letters to life: handwriting with haptic-enabled tangible robots. In: Proceedings of the 17th ACM Conference on Interaction Design and Children, pp. 219–230. ACM (2018)
2. Cho, Y., Bianchi, A., Marquardt, N., Bianchi-Berthouze, N.: Realpen: providing realism in handwriting tasks on touch surfaces using auditory-tactile feedback. In: Proceedings of the 29th Annual Symposium on User Interface Software and Technology, pp. 195–205. ACM (2016)
3. Danna, J., Velay, J.L.: Basic and supplementary sensory feedback in handwriting. Front. Psychol. **6**, 169 (2015)
4. Graham, S.: Measurement of handwriting skills: a critical review. vol. 8, pp. 32–42. ERIC (1982)
5. Karpov, A., Ronzhin, A.: A universal assistive technology with multimodal input and multimedia output interfaces. In: Stephanidis, C., Antona, M. (eds.) UAHCI 2014. LNCS, vol. 8513, pp. 369–378. Springer, Cham (2014). https://doi.org/10.1007/978-3-319-07437-5_35
6. Langerak, T., Zarate, J., Vechev, V., Panozzo, D., Hilliges, O.: A demonstration on dynamic drawing guidance via electromagnetic haptic feedback. In: The Adjunct Publication of the 32nd Annual ACM Symposium on User Interface Software and Technology, pp. 110–112. ACM (2019)
7. Pangaro, G., Maynes-Aminzade, D., Ishii, H.: The actuated workbench: computer-controlled actuation in tabletop tangible interfaces. In: Proceedings of the 15th annual ACM symposium on User interface software and technology, pp. 181–190. ACM (2002)
8. Park, W., Korres, G., Moonesinghe, T., Eid, M.: Investigating haptic guidance methods for teaching children handwriting skills. IEEE Trans. Haptics **12**, 461–469 (2019)
9. Portillo, O., Avizzano, C.A., Raspolli, M., Bergamasco, M.: Haptic desktop for assisted handwriting and drawing. In: ROMAN 2005. IEEE International Workshop on Robot and Human Interactive Communication, pp. 512–517. IEEE (2005)

10. Sigrist, R., Rauter, G., Riener, R., Wolf, P.: Augmented visual, auditory, haptic, and multimodal feedback in motor learning: a review. Psychon. Bull. Rev. **20**(1), 21–53 (2013)
11. Teranishi, A., Korres, G., Park, W., Eid, M.: Combining full and partial haptic guidance improves handwriting skills development. IEEE Trans. Haptics **11**(4), 509–517 (2018)
12. Weiss, M., Wacharamanotham, C., Voelker, S., Borchers, J.: Fingerflux: near-surface haptic feedback on tabletops. In: Proceedings of the 24th Annual ACM Symposium on User Interface Software and Technology, pp. 615–620. ACM (2011)
13. Withana, A., Kondo, M., Makino, Y., Kakehi, G., Sugimoto, M., Inami, M.: Impact: immersive haptic stylus to enable direct touch and manipulation for surface computing. Comput. Entertainment (CIE) **8**(2), 9 (2010)
14. Yamaoka, J., Kakehi, Y.: depend: augmented handwriting system using ferromagnetism of a ballpoint pen. In: Proceedings of the 26th Annual ACM Symposium on User Interface Software and Technology, pp. 203–210. ACM (2013)
15. Yang, X.D., Bischof, W.F., Boulanger, P.: Validating the performance of haptic motor skill training. In: 2008 Symposium on Haptic Interfaces for Virtual Environment and Teleoperator Systems, pp. 129–135. IEEE (2008)
16. Yoshida, S., Noma, H., Hosaka, K.: Proactive desk ii: development of a new multi-object haptic display using a linear induction motor. In: IEEE Virtual Reality Conference (VR 2006), pp. 269–272. IEEE (2006)

11

Manipulating the Perceived Directions of Wind by Visuo-Audio-Haptic Cross-Modal Effects

Kenichi Ito(✉), Yuki Ban, and Shin'ichi Warisawa

Graduate School of Frontier Sciences, The University of Tokyo, Chiba 2770882, Japan
itokenichi@lelab.t.u-tokyo.ac.jp,{ban,warisawa}@edu.k.u-tokyo.ac.jp

Abstract. Wind displays, which simulate the sensation of wind, have been known to enhance the immersion of virtual reality content. However, certain wind displays require an excessive number of wind sources to simulate wind from various directions. To realize wind displays with fewer wind sources, a method to manipulate the perceived directions of wind by audio-haptic cross-modal effects was proposed in our previous study. As the visuo-haptic cross-modal effect on perceived wind directions has not yet been quantitatively investigated, this study focuses on the effect of visual stimuli on the perception of wind direction. We present virtual images of flowing particles and three-dimensional sounds of wind as information to indicate wind directions and induce cross-modal effects in users. The user study has demonstrated that adding visual stimuli effectively improved the result corresponding to certain virtual wind directions. Our results suggest that perceived wind directions can be manipulated by both visuo-haptic and audio-haptic cross-modal effects.

Keywords: Wind display · Wind perception · Cross-modal.

1 Introduction

Improving immersion is necessary for most virtual reality (VR) content. An approach to ensure an immersive VR experience involves multisensory presentation. In this context, "wind displays" that simulate the sensation of wind for their users have become a popular topic of study. Heilig used wind along with odors and vibrations in Sensorama [1]. Moon et al. proposed WindCube [9], which simulates wind from several directions using 20 fans.

As many people experience the sensation of wind on their entire body every day, we can easily immerse ourselves in VR presentations with wind displays. The latter can improve immersion by faithfully reproducing the motion of objects in VR environments [5], self-motions [6,12], and climates [11].

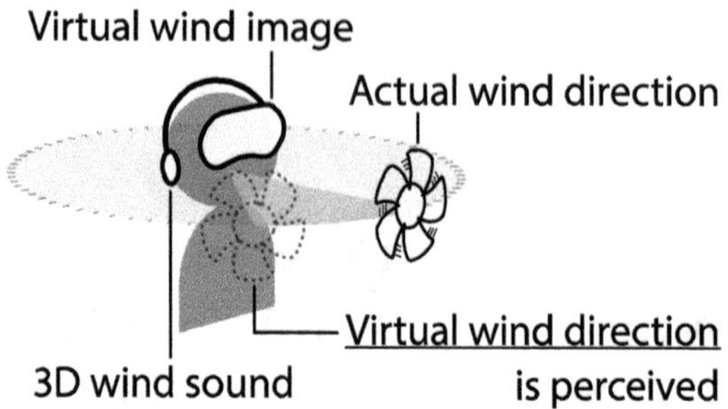

Fig. 1. Manipulation of perceived wind directions by multimodal stimuli

The reproduction of wind blowing from various directions is often crucial to simulate realistic wind. An array of fans [9] is the easiest and most applicable approach to this problem. However, the number of wind sources must match the number of desired directions of simulated wind. Therefore, wind display devices tend to be complicated and large under this implementation. VaiR [12] addresses this problem by implementing two rotatable bow-shaped frames that enable continuous change in wind directions. This approach could reduce the required number of wind sources, but requires actuators and mechanisms to move the device. We propose the presentation method of wind directions without an entire reproduction of physical wind by changing human perception.

Human perception of the directions of wind is investigated to design effective wind displays. Nakano et al. [10] demonstrated that the angles with respect to the human head corresponding to just noticeable differences (JND) in wind directions are approximately 4° in the front and rear regions and approximately 11° in the lateral region. Saito et al. [13] investigated the wind JND angles by presenting users with audio-visual stimuli. They reported that the JND angle values were much higher than those reported by Nakano et al. and suggested that the accuracy of wind perception was lowered by multisensory stimuli.

When we receive multisensory stimuli, different sensations are sometimes integrated with each other and our perception is altered. These phenomena are called cross-modal effects and they can alter the perception of physical stimuli. It has already been established that haptic sensations are altered by the visuo-haptic [7] and audio-haptic integrations [4]. Through cross-modal effects, we can provide rich tactile experiences without reproducing the stimulating physical phenomena completely faithfully.

We proposed a method to manipulate perceived wind directions by audio-haptic cross-modal effect [2] in order to simulate directional winds with simple hardware. We performed experiments that simultaneously presented wind from two fans and three-dimensional (3D) wind sounds, and concluded that the perceived wind directions could be changed by up to 67.12° by this effect.

It is suggested that congruent stimuli from two modalities strengthen the effect of cross-modal illusion on an incongruent stimulus from the other modality in tri-modal perception [14]. Therefore, we designed AlteredWind [3], which combines congruent visual and audio information about the wind direction to more effectively manipulate the perceived wind. We presented the audio-visual information through a head-mounted display (HMD) and headphones, as depicted in Fig. 1. Although we evaluated the perceived wind directions in a user study, there was only qualitative analysis and the sample size was small. In this study, we redesigned the experiment to quantitatively verify the visuo-audio-haptic cross-modal effects on wind direction perception. Our experiment compares the perceived wind directions across the combinations of different sensory modalities and placements of wind sources. Our result suggests new designs of wind displays utilizing cross-modal effects.

2 Implementing Visual, Audio, and Wind Presentation

In this paper, we define "virtual wind direction" as the direction of wind which is presented by multimodal stimuli and is different from the physical one. We implemented software for visual and audio presentations of the virtual wind directions and hardware for actual wind presentation.

2.1 Visual Presentation of Virtual Wind Directions

The virtual wind direction can be visually conveyed to a user by two primary methods—by suggesting the generation of wind or the existence of wind. The former effect can be realized by displaying a virtual image of a rotating fan. However, the wind approaching from behind the user cannot be expressed by this technique because the images would lie outside the field of vision. The latter technique uses images of particles being blown by the wind and images of flags or plants swaying in the wind. This technique can be used to convey wind originating from any direction. In this study, images of particles moving horizontally were used to verify the effects of visual information in a simple environment. We used an HMD (HTC Vive Pro) to display the image three-dimensionally and immersively. We programmed 1000 particles to emerge per second so that they were visible in the HMD along any flowing direction, as depicted in Fig. 2.

2.2 Audio Presentation of Virtual Wind Directions

We manipulated the perceived directions of wind by using 3D sounds recorded by a dummy head [2], which is a life-sized model of the human head with ears. The perception of a sound source can be localized around listeners when recorded sound is played binaurally. We installed a dummy head and a fan in an anechoic room and recorded the sound of the fan blowing wind against the dummy head from directions 30° apart from each other [2]. The sound was presented to users through noise-cancelling headphones (SONY WH-1000XM2). A-weighted sound pressure level (L_A) near the headphones measured with a sound level meter (ONO SOKKI LA-4350) was in the range of 46.8 dB–58.1 dB (it varied depending on the direction of the sound image). The direction of the audio information was always congruent with that of the visual one.

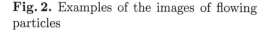

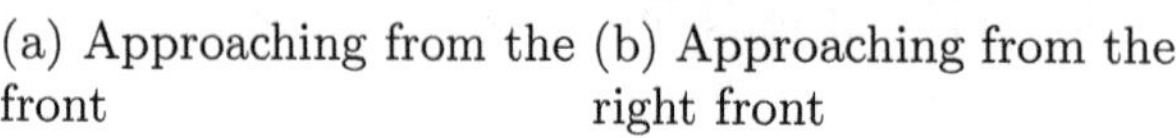

(a) Approaching from the front (b) Approaching from the right front

Fig. 2. Examples of the images of flowing particles

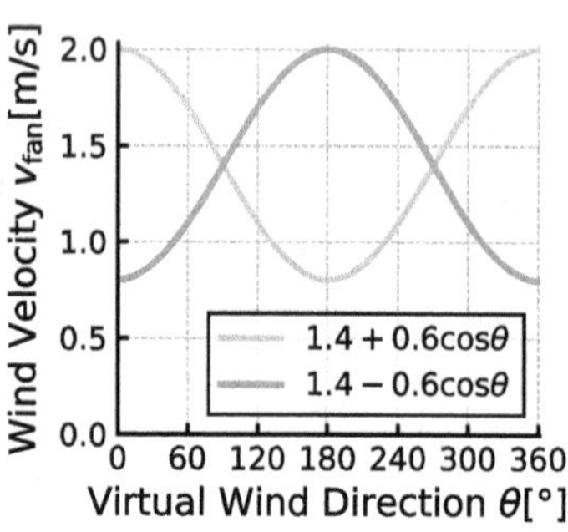

Fig. 3. A Plot of wind velocity

2.3 Proposed Device for Wind Presentation

We had designed a wind display device by placing a fan in front of the users and another behind them in our previous study [2]. In this experiment, we placed four fans (SANYODENKI San ACE 172) around the users' heads at 90-degree intervals. Each fan could be independently controlled by Arduino UNO connected to a computer. During the experiment, wind was generated from the fans at the front and the back or from those to the left and right. The four fans were affixed to camera monopods on a circular rail of 800 mm diameter and directed to the users' heads in about 300 mm ahead. In our previous study, results may have been affected by the participants' prior knowledge of the positions of fans. To ensure that the participants were not aware of the placement of the fans, we made the monopods detachable from the circular rail. The fans and the monopods were removed from the rail and hidden before the experiment and attached to the rail after the participants had worn the HMD.

We had continuously controlled the wind velocities corresponding to the two fans facing each other in the previous research [2] and confirmed that it was effective for manipulation of the perceived wind direction. "Continuously" here means that the wind from a particular fan was weakened as it moved further away from the virtual wind direction. We applied the same method in this study also and changed the wind velocities from 0.8 m/s to 2.0 m/s as shown in Fig. 3.

3 Experiment Regarding Perceived Wind Directions

3.1 Experiment Design

We conducted an experiment to verify the visuo-audio-haptic cross-modal effects on perceived wind directions. We presented the virtual wind directions which are not congruent with the actual wind directions by visual and audio information in this experiment. Six conditions were prepared by varying the existence of multimodal information (visual and audio, visual only, and audio only) and the placements of the fans (front-behind and left-right). Since we confirmed that the actual directions of wind are perceived without multimodal information [2], we omitted that condition in this user study. The experiment had a within-subjects design. For each condition, we presented wind coming from 12 virtual wind directions at intervals of 30° and each direction was repeated twice. Thus, there were a total of 144 presentations for each participant.

The Ethics Committee of the University of Tokyo approved the experiment (No. 19–170). Written informed consent was obtained from every participant. Each participant was instructed to sit in a chair and wear the HMD. As mentioned in Subsect. 2.3, the fans were attached after the participants wore the HMD, preventing them from being aware of the exact location (Fig. 4). To make the wind apparent on the head and neck of the participants, the lower ends of the fans were adjusted to match the height of the participants' shoulders. We asked the participants to stare toward the frontal direction marked in the VR view.

Each presentation consisted of a stimulation time of 12 s and an answering time of a few seconds. Considering the delay in starting and stopping the fans, the timing of wind presentation was advanced by 2 s compared with that of the other stimuli. The order of the presentations was randomized for each participant, and neither the participants nor the experimental staff was aware of the order beforehand. The participants responded with perceived wind direction of wind indicating the direction on the trackpad of a controller as shown in Fig. 5. Finally, they answered questionnaires about their experiences during the experiment.

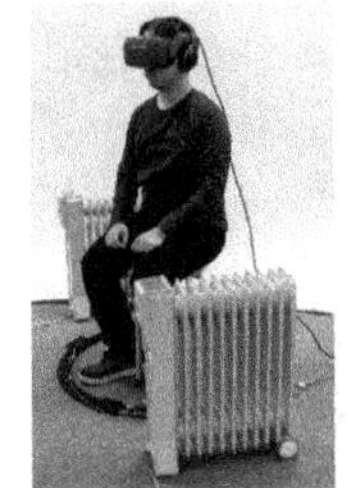

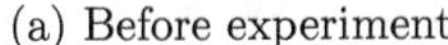

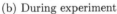

(a) Before experiment

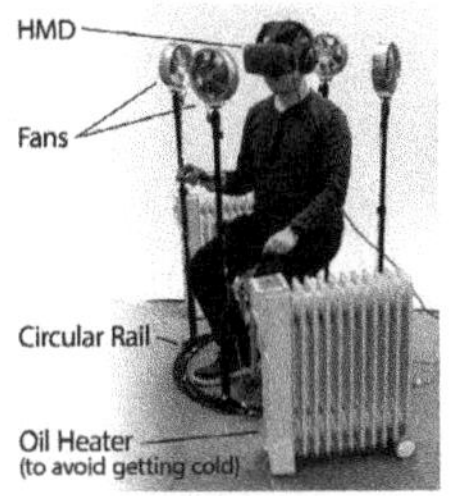

(b) During experiment

Fig. 4. Apparatus for the experiment

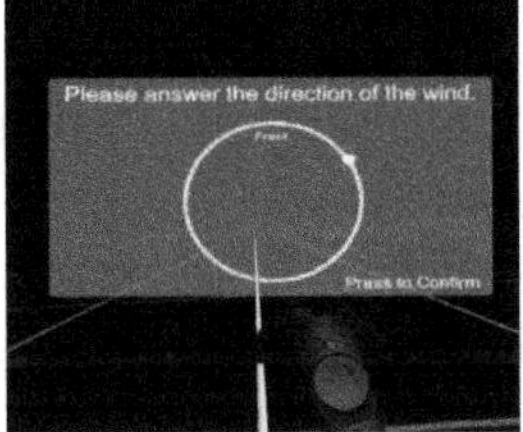

Fig. 5. Interface for answering directions

As the participants wore the HMD and the noise-cancelling headphones, fan operations could not be seen or heard by them. All the windows of the experiment room were closed and the air conditioner was turned off to ensure that there was no wind except the wind from the apparatus. Instead of air conditioning, two oil heaters which produce no airflow were used for warming. The apparatus was at least 1 m away from the walls so that they would not affect the airflow.

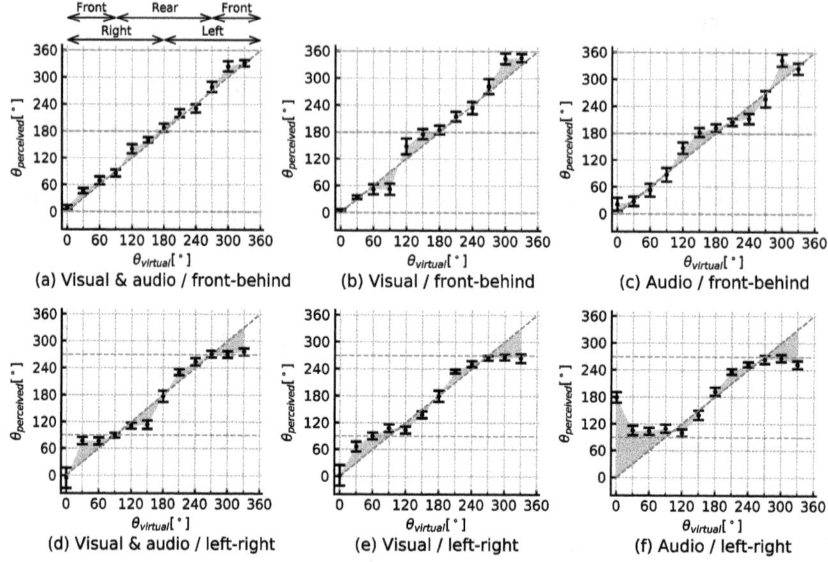

Fig. 6. Plots of the perceived wind directions ($\theta_{\text{perceived}} \pm$ standard error) and the virtual wind directions (θ_{virtual}). Diagonal dashed lines represents $\theta_{\text{virtual}} = \theta_{\text{perceived}}$. Horizontal dashed lines represents the actual directions of the fans.

3.2 Results

Twelve people of ages 22–49 participated in the experiment (7 men 23.9 ± 1.2 years old and 5 women 30.0 ± 11.0 years old). Two of them had ever researched haptics. Ten persons sensed that the perceived wind directions were affected by visual and audio stimuli. Six persons answered that the effect of the auditory stimuli was stronger and four answered that the visual one was stronger.

We calculated the average perceived wind direction ($\theta_{\text{perceived}}$) for every virtual wind direction (θ_{virtual}). The directions represent clockwise angles from the front. If $\theta_{\text{perceived}}$ was close to corresponding θ_{virtual}, we can judge that the perceived wind directions are manipulated effectively to θ_{virtual}. We define such conditions as "good performance" of the manipulation. Figure 6 shows correspondence between $\theta_{\text{perceived}}$ and θ_{virtual}. Data points near diagonal lines mean the good performance. Ones near horizontal lines mean a bad performance because it means that the actual wind directions are perceived instead of θ_{virtual}.

We performed statistical tests following the methods of directional statistics [8] for $\theta_{\text{perceived}}$ under three conditions corresponding to each fan placement. The Mardia–Watson–Wheeler test, which is a non-parametric test for two or more samples, was applied because Watson's U^2 test showed that some of the perceived directions do not arise from von Mises distribution. For directions with significant differences, post-hoc Mardia-Watson-Wheeler tests, with Hommel's improved Bonferroni procedure, were performed. The results have been tabulated in Table 1.

Table 1. Results of statistical tests on $\theta_{perceived}$ for each $\theta_{virtual}$. If there is a significant difference, the condition with $\theta_{perceived}$ closer to $\theta_{virtual}$ is indicated.

Fans	Pair	0°	30°	60°	90°	120°	150°	180°	210°	240°	270°	300°	330°
Front and Behind	All	*	*	*	*	n.s	†	n.s	n.s	*	n.s	n.s	n.s
	VA and V	n.s	n.s	n.s	VA*		n.s			n.s			
	VA and A	n.s	A*	A*	A*		VA†			VA†			
	V and A	V*	A*	n.s	n.s		n.s			n.s			
Left and Right	All	*	*	n.s	*	†	*	n.s	n.s	n.s	n.s	n.s	n.s
	VA and V	n.s	n.s		n.s	n.s	n.s						
	VA and A	n.s	n.s		VA*	VA*	A†						
	V and A	V†	V*		n.s	n.s	n.s						

VA: visual and audio, V: visual, A: audio, *: $p < .05$, †: $p < .1$, n.s.: $p \geq .1$

3.3 Discussion

We abbreviate visual and audio as VA, visual as V, and audio as A in the following discussion. Under the condition of the front-behind fans, the condition VA caused better performance of manipulation than the condition V when $\theta_{virtual}$ was 90°. The condition VA was marginally better than the condition A when ($\theta_{virtual} = 150, 240°$). On the other hand, the performance was better under the condition A than under the condition VA or V for several $\theta_{virtual}$. Under the condition of the left-right fans, the condition VA had a significantly ($\theta_{virtual} = 90°$) or marginally ($\theta_{virtual} = 120°$) better performance than the condition A. It was confirmed that the condition V was significantly ($\theta_{virtual} = 30°$) or marginally ($\theta_{virtual} = 0°$) better than the condition A. From these results, the combination of visual and auditory stimuli and the fans in a front-back position has shown overall better performance in the manipulation of the perceived wind directions.

Still, the performance of manipulation with the condition V or A was better than ones with the condition VA in several virtual wind directions. In these directions, the performance was already sufficient (the differences of $\theta_{perceived}$ and $\theta_{virtual}$ were at most 12°) with the condition V or A. Therefore, we conclude that the manipulation of the perceived wind directions is improved by using visuo-audio-haptic cross-modal effects under the condition that the perception cannot be sufficiently changed by using only visual or auditory stimuli.

For the left-right fan placement, the performance was worse than in front-behind one in condition VA and A, and there were little differences between condition VA and V. The reason may be that the participants did not localize correct sound images due to front-back confusions. Improvement of 3D sounds may enhance the cross-modal effects under left-right placements of fans.

Using more realistic images than the simple flowing particles could increase the effectiveness of visual stimuli. Further, the image of the particles may disturb the contents in practical applications. If the manipulation of the perceived wind can be realized with more diegetic visual information such as flags or swaying trees, it may be effectively used in practical applications using the wind display.

4 Conclusion

In this study, we proposed a method to manipulate the perceived directions of wind through visuo-audio-haptic cross-modal effects. We used virtual images of flowing particles as visual stimuli and 3D sounds of the wind as audio stimuli to make users perceive virtual wind directions. The user study demonstrated that combining visual and audio stimuli exerted significant effects than each stimulus alone corresponding to certain virtual directions. Combining the two modalities are considered to be effective when the perception cannot be sufficiently manipulated by only visual or auditory stimuli.

These results suggest that perceived wind directions can be altered by both visuo-haptic and audio-haptic cross-modal effects. Further improvements of the visual and audio stimuli used for manipulation should be considered in the future. The findings of this study can be applied to wind display technology to present various wind directions with limited equipment.

References

1. Heilig, M.L.: Sensorama simulator. US Patent 3050870, August 1962
2. Ito, K., Ban, Y., Warisawa, S.: Manipulation of the perceived direction of wind by cross-modal effects of wind and three-dimensional sound. In: 2019 IEEE World Haptics Conference (WHC), pp. 622–627, July 2019. https://doi.org/10.1109/WHC.2019.8816111
3. Ito, K., Ban, Y., Warisawa, S.: AlteredWind: manipulating perceived direction of the wind by cross-modal presentation of visual, audio and wind stimuli. In: SIGGRAPH Asia 2019 Emerging Technologies SA 2019, pp. 3–4. ACM, New York (2019). https://doi.org/10.1145/3355049.3360525
4. Jousmäki, V., Hari, R.: Parchment-skin illusion: sound-biased touch. Curr. Biol. **8**(6), R190–R191 (1998). https://doi.org/10.1016/S0960-9822(98)70120-4
5. Kojima, Y., Hashimoto, Y., Kajimoto, H.: A novel wearable device to present localized sensation of wind. In: Proceedings of the International Conference on Advances in Computer Enterntainment Technology ACE 2009, pp. 61–65. ACM, New York (2009). https://doi.org/10.1145/1690388.1690399
6. Kulkarni, S.D., Fisher, C.J., et al.: A full body steerable wind display for a locomotion interface. IEEE Trans. Vis. Comput. Graph. **21**(10), 1146–1159 (2015). https://doi.org/10.1109/TVCG.2015.2424862
7. Lécuyer, A.: Simulating haptic feedback using vision: a survey of research and applications of pseudo-haptic feedback. Presence: Teleoper. Virtual Environ. **18**(1), 39–53 (2009). https://doi.org/10.1162/pres.18.1.39
8. Mardia, K.V., Jupp, P.E.: Directional Statistics. Wiley, Hoboken (2000)
9. Moon, T., Kim, G.J.: Design and evaluation of a wind display for virtual reality. In: Proceedings of the ACM Symposium on Virtual Reality Software and Technology VRST 2004, pp. 122–128 (2004). https://doi.org/10.1145/1077534.1077558
10. Nakano, T., Yanagida, Y.: Conditions influencing perception of wind direction by the head. In: 2017 IEEE Virtual Reality (VR), pp. 229–230, March 2017. https://doi.org/10.1109/VR.2017.7892260

11. Ranasinghe, N., Jain, P., et al.: Ambiotherm: enhancing sense of presence in virtual reality by simulating real-world environmental conditions. In: Proceedings of the 2017 CHI Conference on Human Factors in Computing Systems CHI 2017, pp. 1731–1742 (2017). https://doi.org/10.1145/3025453.3025723
12. Rietzler, M., Plaumann, K., et al.: VaiR: simulating 3D airflows in virtual reality. In: Proceedings of the 2017 CHI Conference on Human Factors in Computing Systems CHI 2017, pp. 5669–5677 (2017). https://doi.org/10.1145/3025453.3026009
13. Saito, Y., Murosaki, Y., et al.: Measurement of wind direction perception characteristics with head mounted display. In: Entertainment Computing (EC2017), vol. 2017, pp. 138–144, September 2017
14. Wozny, D.R., Beierholm, U.R., Shams, L.: Human trimodal perception follows optimal statistical inference. J. Vis. **8**(3), 24–24 (2008). https://doi.org/10.1167/8.3.24

12

Movement-Free Virtual Reality Interface Using Kinesthetic Illusion Induced by Tendon Vibration

Satoshi Tanaka(✉), Keigo Ushiyama, Akifumi Takahashi, and Hiroyuki Kajimoto

The University of Electro-Communications, 1-5-1 Chofugaoka, Chofu, Tokyo, Japan
{tanaka,ushiyama,a.takahashi,kajimoto}@kaji-lab.jp

Abstract. In current virtual reality (VR) systems, the physical movement of the body is required, which creates problems of safety, cost, and accessibility. To solve those problems, we propose a system that fixes a user's body, detects force when a user tries to move, and generates the sensation of movement using kinesthetic illusion caused by tendon vibration. We implemented a system limited to simple motion, and conducted an experiment to evaluate operability, body ownership, and agency. Although we could not statistically verify the effect of kinesthetic illusion, the results suggested that it may be possible that kinesthetic illusion could increase ownership and decrease agency.

Keywords: Kinesthesia · Tendon vibration · Virtual reality

1 Introduction

An interface for manipulating avatars is an essential component of virtual reality (VR). In science fiction works, VR is often described as a system in which users can subjectively move freely while their physical body is lying on a bed. However, present VR systems reflect the movement of the physical body to the avatar using devices such as position tracking controllers.

In VR, the movement of the physical body causes various problems. For example, the risk of collision and injury; the requirement for a large space and equipment; and the problem that people with limited mobility cannot use VR. The development of a VR system that does not require physical movement would lead to the solution of such problems of safety, cost, and accessibility.

A brain-computer interface (BCI) can be used to implement a movement-free VR system. However, BCI has technical difficulties, such as the requirement for expensive devices, and invasive means (e.g., anesthesia) are required to block motor commands.

By contrast, a simpler method may exist. Even if the user's body is physically fixed, by altering user's kinesthesia (sense of body movement), the user may be able to feel moving as if not fixed. Fortunately, our kinesthesia can be modulated relatively easily. For example, the sense of motion can be generated even if the body is not actually moving if vibration stimulus is applied to the tendon [6]. This phenomenon is called kinesthetic illusion.

In this study, we propose a system that detects the force exerted by a user's body fixed on a rigid frame to control an avatar, and presents kinesthetic illusion using tendon vibration. In this paper, We implement a system limited to one degree-of-freedom motion as a proof of concept, and evaluate its operability and effects on body ownership and agency.

2 Related Work

When vibration is applied to the tendon of a muscle, kinesthetic illusion, in which the vibrated muscle is stretched, is generated [6]. This phenomenon is considered to be caused by the activation of the muscle spindle by vibration [6], and it has been reported that the nerve fires at a frequency that agrees with the vibration frequency up to a certain vibration frequency [4,15].

Research has also been conducted on the presentation of complex kinesthetic illusions using this phenomenon. Albert et al. [1] converted recorded nerve firing patterns to vibration and presented kinesthetic illusions that reproduced the movement in the recording. Additionally, Thyrion et al. [16] successfully presented three-dimensional kinesthetic illusion by predicting nerve firing the movement trajectory and converting it into vibration.

This phenomenon has also been applied to VR and human-computer interaction. For example, Hagimori et al. [7] combined tendon vibration with a visual stimulus using a head-mounted display (HMD) to make small physical movements perceived as large movements in VR. Barsotti et al. [3] proposed a system that combined kinesthetic feedback using tendon vibration with a BCI based on motor imagery.

Among the above techniques, in the BCI-based approach, the user does not need to move physically at all. However, in those BCI systems, the user has to perform motor imagery, rather than trying to move physically. This may cause a sense of unnaturalness in VR applications.

Other methods exist to modulate kinesthesia in addition to tendon vibration. Okabe et al. [13] reported that the illusion of finger movement was generated by presenting the flow field of tactile sensation according to the shearing force of the fingertip. Similarly, Heo et al. [8] generated the illusion of bending an object using vibrotactile stimuli according to the force applied to the object.

The modulation of a kinesthetic sensation can also result from visual stimuli alone. Pseudo-haptic feedback proposed by Lecuyer et al. [10] is a technique to present a sense of force only using visual stimuli. However, it was reported that a force-sensing stationary device, similar to our study, was perceived like moving in their experiment [10].

As a method similar to our study, Mochizuki et al. [12] proposed a VR interface that does not require physical movement by measuring the torque exerted by joints of the physically fixed user. However, their current system used visual stimulus only, and techniques that directly alter kinesthesia were not tested.

3 System

3.1 Operating Principle

The operation of the proposed system is shown in Fig. 1. In this system, the user's body (arms, legs, etc.) is fixed to a rigid frame. When the user tries to move the body, a force sensor attached at a fixing position detects the force exerted by the user (Fig. 1a). In response to the detected force, the computer simulates the user's intended motion and renders a virtual arm on the HMD (Fig. 1b). Simultaneously, a vibration stimulus is applied to the user's tendon in response to the simulated motion to present kinesthetic illusion (Fig. 1c). Thus, vision and kinesthesia are presented as if the user is moving the body, despite the user's body being fixed.

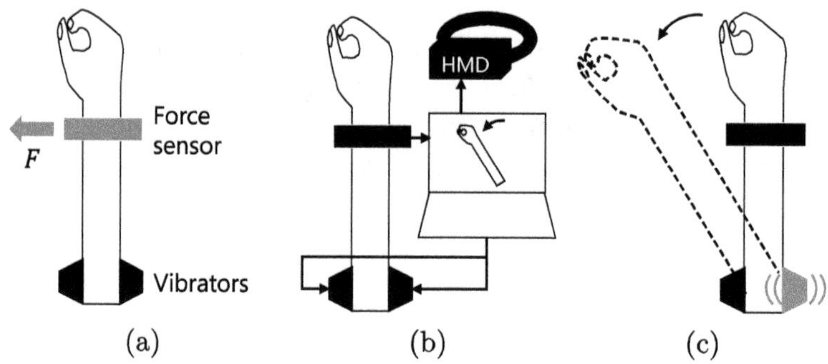

Fig. 1. Operation of the system (a) user tries to move and exerts a force. (b) Computer simulates movement and controls the HMD and vibrators. (c) Vibration induces illusory movement.

3.2 Implementation

As a proof of concept of the proposed method, we implemented a system limited to one degree-of-freedom motion. Although this technique may be applicable to the motion of various joints, we chose the extension and flexion of the forearm following the experiment of Roll et al. [14].

System Configuration. The system detects force using a load cell attached to the wrist fixing component, and connected to the PC through the front-end circuit. The game engine Unity (Unity Technologies) was used for the simulation and rendering, and visual stimuli were presented using an HMD Vive Pro (HTC Corporation) via an external graphics processing unit. The vibration waveform was generated using a waveform generator circuit, amplified using an audio amplifier (MUSE M50), and presented using two vibrators (Vp210, Acouve Laboratory). The vibrators were attached near the right elbow using an elastic fabric supporter, to vibrate distal tendons of the biceps brachii (BB) and triceps brachii (TB) muscles. To make the initial position of the virtual arm coincide with the physical arm, a position tracking device (Vive Tracker, HTC Corporation) was attached to the frame. Additionally, to enhance the ownership of the arm, the actual movement of the user's fingers was captured and reproduced in the display using Leap Motion (Ultraleap).

Algorithms. The angular velocity of the virtual elbow joint was proportional to the force applied to the load cell; that is, when the force applied to the load cell was $F\,[\mathrm{N}]$ (assuming $F = 0$ at system startup), the commanded value of the angular velocity was $\omega_{\mathrm{command}} = 50F\,[\mathrm{deg/s}]$. The angle of the elbow joint $\theta\,[\mathrm{deg}]$ was obtained by integrating the angular velocity, but was limited to -45 to 45°. For the angle and angular velocity, the extension direction was positive. Vibration waveforms were generated by frequency modulating a sine wave between 0 and 100 Hz. Although the amplitude changed according to the frequency because of the frequency response of the system, and kinesthetic illusion is likely to be diminished in lower frequencies, a simple linear mapping was used for the sake of simplicity. This algorithm is based on the knowledge that nerve firing corresponds to the vibration frequency [4,15] and its applications [1,16]. The vibration frequencies $f_{\mathrm{BB}}\,[\mathrm{Hz}]$ (for BB) and $f_{\mathrm{TB}}\,[\mathrm{Hz}]$ (for TB) were

$$f_{\mathrm{BB}} = \begin{cases} 0 & (4\omega < 0) \\ 4\omega & (0 \leq 4\omega < 100) \\ 100 & (\text{otherwise}) \end{cases} \tag{1}$$

$$f_{\mathrm{TB}} = \begin{cases} 0 & (-4\omega < 0) \\ -4\omega & (0 \leq -4\omega < 100) \\ 100 & (\text{otherwise}) \end{cases} \tag{2}$$

where $\omega\,[\mathrm{deg/s}]$ was the angular velocity of the virtual elbow joint ($\omega = 0$ when the angle θ reaches positive or negative limit). However, the coefficients used in the above algorithms were set empirically and not determined theoretically.

4 Experiment

To evaluate the operability, body ownership, and agency of the avatar using the proposed system, we conducted an experiment in which the participants used the system under the following three conditions.

Tendon All elements of the proposed method were incorporated.
None Only visual stimulus was used, without vibration stimulus.
Tactile Only cutaneous cues were presented using high-frequency vibration that was unlikely to cause kinesthetic illusion. Based on the method of Bark et al. [2], an amplitude-modulated sine wave of 250 Hz was used for the vibration waveform, and the amplitudes of the waveform input to the BB and TB vibrators were $A_{\text{BB}} = 0.1 \times 10^{\theta/45}$ and $A_{\text{TB}} = 0.1 \times 10^{-\theta/45}$ (from 0 to 1), where θ [deg] is the virtual elbow angle.

4.1 Methods

Initially, 13 laboratory members that specialize in VR and/or haptics participated in the experiment, but because malfunctions of Leap Motion occurred during experiments involving three of the participants, their data were excluded from subsequent analyses. Finally, data from 10 participants (22 to 25 years old, average 23.6 years old, all right-handed, one female, nine male) were analyzed.

First, the acceleration amplitude of the BB vibrator attached to the participant's arm driven with a 100 Hz sine wave was adjusted to approximately 130 m/s^2 (which was determined to stably evoke kinesthetic illusion), using an accelerometer (LIS331HH, STMicroelectronics). We also presented 100 Hz sine wave stimuli and confirmed orally that the kinesthetic illusion occured in both the extension and flexion directions. When the illusion was not sufficiently obtained, the position of the vibrators was re-adjusted until the illusion occurred.

The participants then performed a task to evaluate the operability of the system based on Fitts' law [5,11] for each condition. The task consisted of 50 trials. In each trial, the participants controlled the virtual forearm and kept the angle aligned with the target for 1 s. The center position of the target was randomly generated from $-30°$ to $30°$ and the width was randomly generated from $5°$ to $15°$. White noise was presented using the built-in headphones of the HMD during task execution.

After the task for each single condition was complete, the participants answered the questions shown in Table 1 using the seven-point Likert scale (-3: totally disagree, $+3$: totally agree), to evaluate body ownership and agency. This questionnaire was a modified version of the questionnaire used in the study on rubber hand illusion by Kalkert et al. [9] and consisted of four categories: Ownership, Ownership Control, Agency, and Agency Control. The questions were translated into Japanese.

To cancel the order effect, the order of the conditions was counterbalanced as much as possible. However, due to the aforementioned malfunctions, among $3! = 6$ permutations, orders of conditions None-Tendon-Tactile and Tactile-Tendon-None was used only once, and the other orders were used twice.

4.2 Results

Operability Evaluation Using Fitts' Law. In the task results for each participant and each condition, the equation of the modified Fitts' law $MT = a +$

Table 1. Questionnaire for evaluating ownership and agency (based on Kalckert et al. [9])

Category	Question
Ownership	I felt as if I was looking at my own hand
	I felt as if the displayed hand was part of my body
	I felt as if the displayed hand was my hand
Ownership control	It seems as if I had more than one right hand
	It felt as if I had no longer a right hand, as if my right hand had disappeared
	I felt as if my real hand was turning like computer-generated image
Agency	I felt as if I could cause movements of the displayed hand
	I felt as if I could control movements of the displayed hand
	The displayed hand was obeying my will and I can make it move just like I want it
Agency control	I felt as if the displayed hand was controlling my will
	It seemed as if the displayed hand had a will of its own
	I felt as if the displayed hand was controlling me

$b \log_2(A/W + 1)$ [11] was fitted, where MT [s] is the time required for the trial, A [deg] is the difference between the angle at the start of the trial and the target angle, and W [deg] is the width of the target. Additionally, the index of performance IP was calculated [11]. Figure 2 compares the average IP for all participants under each condition. The repeated measures analysis of variance showed no significant differences between the conditions ($p = .898$). As a result of multiple comparisons using the Bonferroni correction, no significant differences were found ($p = 1.000$ for all pairs). Additionally, the correlation coefficient r of the fitting ranged from 0.139 to 0.851 with an average of 0.532.

Questionnaires. In the same manner as [9], the answers to questions belonging to the same category were averaged, and four scores (Ownership, Ownership Control, Agency, and Agency Control) were calculated (Fig. 3) and further analyses were done using these scores. The Wilcoxon signed-rank test between Ownership and Ownership Control, Agency and Agency Control was performed in each condition and significant differences in both Ownership-Ownership Control and Agency-Agency Control were found in all conditions ($p < .05$). Also, the Friedman test was performed between conditions for each score, but there was no significant difference ($p = .393$ for Ownership, $p = .087$ for Ownership Control, $p = .607$ for Agency, $p = .098$ for Agency Control).

4.3 Discussion

Operability. There was no significant difference in IP between the conditions, and as shown in Fig. 2, the average IP for the Tactile and Tendon conditions were almost the same or slightly lower than that of the None condition. Hence, we consider that operability was not improved by presenting kinesthetic illusion in the proposed system.

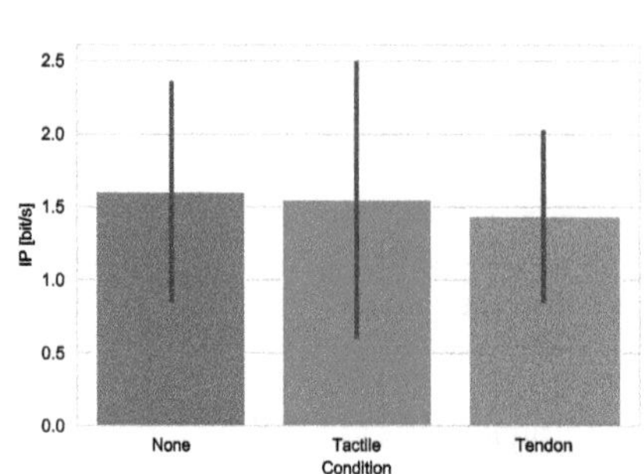

Fig. 2. Comparison of the average IP by condition (error bars indicate the standard deviation)

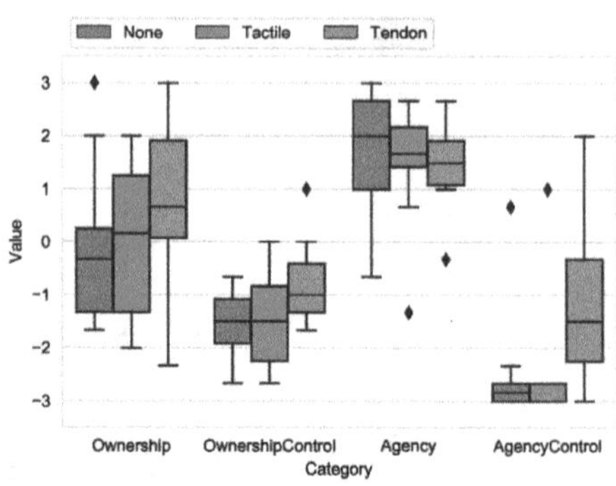

Fig. 3. Comparison of the questionnaire scores by condition

Body Ownership and Agency. For the results of the questionnaire, there was no significant difference in scores between the conditions, possibly due to large variability between participants. However, in Fig. 3, ownership tended to increase in the Tendon condition in comparison with other conditions. Therefore, while we cannot conclude that tendon vibration was effective in the movement-free VR interface, it may contribute to the generation of ownership.

Additionally, in Fig. 3, a small decrease in Agency and an increase in Agency Control in the Tendon condition were observed. In fact, some participants' comments suggested a lack of agency, such as "a feeling of being moved by others" for the Tendon condition. We consider that the loss of agency was because movement simulation and the method for the vibration presentation were imperfect, and the kinesthetic illusion was different from the intended motion of the user.

5 Conclusion

In this paper, we proposed and implemented a VR system that requires no physical body movement by detecting the force exerted by the user's fixed body and presenting kinesthetic illusion. As a result of the experiment, an improvement in operability caused by kinesthetic illusion was not confirmed. Additionally, although not statistically verified, the results suggest that the kinesthetic illusion may lead to an improvement of ownership and decrease of agency. As future work, a more precise verification of usefulness and improvement of the presentation method are required.

Acknowledgements. This research was supported by JSPS KAKENHI Grant Number JP18H04110.

References

1. Albert, F., Bergenheim, M., Ribot-Ciscar, E., Roll, J.P.: The la afferent feedback of a given movement evokes the illusion of the same movement when returned to the subject via muscle tendon vibration. Exp. Brain Res. **172**(2), 163–174 (2006). https://doi.org/10.1007/s00221-005-0325-2
2. Bark, K., Wheeler, J.W., Premakumar, S., Cutkosky, M.R.: Comparison of skin stretch and vibrotactile stimulation for feedback of proprioceptive information. In: 2008 Symposium on Haptic Interfaces for Virtual Environment and Teleoperator Systems, pp. 71–78. IEEE, March 2008. https://doi.org/10.1109/HAPTICS.2008.4479916
3. Barsotti, M., Leonardis, D., Vanello, N., Bergamasco, M., Frisoli, A.: Effects of continuous kinaesthetic feedback based on tendon vibration on motor imagery BCI performance. IEEE Trans. Neural Syst. Rehabil. Eng. **26**(1), 105–114 (2018). https://doi.org/10.1109/TNSRE.2017.2739244
4. Burke, D., Hagbarth, K.E., Löfstedt, L., Wallin, B.G.: The responses of human muscle spindle endings to vibration of non-contracting muscles. J. Physiol. **261**(3), 673–693 (1976). https://doi.org/10.1113/jphysiol.1976.sp011580
5. Fitts, P.M.: The information capacity of the human motor system in controlling the amplitude of movement. J. Exp. Psychol. **47**(6), 381–391 (1954). https://doi.org/10.1037/h0055392
6. Goodwin, G.M., McCloskey, D.I., Matthews, P.B.: The contribution of muscle afferents to kinaesthesia shown by vibration induced illusions of movement and by the effects of paralysing joint afferents. Brain: J. Neurol. **95**(4), 705–748 (1972). https://doi.org/10.1093/brain/95.4.705
7. Hagimori, D., Isoyama, N., Yoshimoto, S., Sakata, N., Kiyokawa, K.: Combining tendon vibration and visual stimulation enhances kinesthetic illusions. In: 2019 International Conference on Cyberworlds (CW), pp. 128–134. IEEE, October 2019. https://doi.org/10.1109/CW.2019.00029
8. Heo, S., Lee, J., Wigdor, D.: PseudoBend: Producing haptic illusions of stretching, bending, and twisting using grain vibrations. In: UIST 2019 - Proceedings of the 32nd Annual ACM Symposium on User Interface Software and Technology, pp. 803–813. ACM Press, New York (2019). https://doi.org/10.1145/3332165.3347941
9. Kalckert, A., Ehrsson, H.H.: The moving rubber hand illusion revisited: comparing movements and visuotactile stimulation to induce illusory ownership. Conscious. Cogn. **26**(1), 117–132 (2014). https://doi.org/10.1016/j.concog.2014.02.003
10. Lecuyer, A., Coquillart, S., Kheddar, A., Richard, P., Coiffet, P.: Pseudo-haptic feedback: can isometric input devices simulate force feedback? In: Proceedings IEEE Virtual Reality 2000 (Cat. No. 00CB37048), pp. 83–90. IEEE Computer Society (2000). https://doi.org/10.1109/VR.2000.840369
11. MacKenzie, I.S.: Fitts' law as a research and design tool in human-computer interaction. Hum.-Comput. Interact. **7**(1), 91–139 (1992). https://doi.org/10.1207/s15327051hci0701_3
12. Mochizuki, N., Nakamura, S.: Motion-Less VR: full-Body immersive VR interface without real body motion. In: The 24th Annual Conference of the Virtual Reality Society of Japan, pp. 6B–09 (2019, in Japanese)
13. Okabe, H., Fukushima, S., Sato, M., Kajimoto, H.: Fingertip Slip Illusion with an Electrocutaneous Display. In: International Conference on Artificial Reality and Telexistence, pp. 10–14 (2011)

14. Roll, J.P., Vedel, J.P.: Kinaesthetic role of muscle afferents in man, studied by tendon vibration and microneurography. Exp. Brain Res. **47**(2), 177–190 (1982). https://doi.org/10.1007/BF00239377
15. Roll, J.P., Vedel, J.P., Ribot, E.: Alteration of proprioceptive messages induced by tendon vibration in man: a microneurographic study. Exp. Brain Res. **76**(1), 213–222 (1989). https://doi.org/10.1007/BF00253639
16. Thyrion, C., Roll, J.P.: Predicting any arm movement feedback to induce three-dimensional illusory movements in humans. J. Neurophysiol. **104**(2), 949–959 (2010). https://doi.org/10.1152/jn.00025.2010

13

Motion Guidance Using Translational Force and Torque Feedback by Induced Pulling Illusion

Takeshi Tanabe[1(✉)], Hiroaki Yano[2], Hiroshi Endo[1], Shuichi Ino[1], and Hiroo Iwata[2]

[1] Human Informatics Research Institute, National Institute of Advanced Industrial Science and Technology (AIST), Central 6, 1-1-1 Higashi, Tsukuba, Ibaraki 305-8566, Japan
{t-tanabe,hiroshi-endou,s-ino}@aist.go.jp

[2] Faculty of Engineering, Information and Systems, University of Tsukuba, 1-1-1 Tennodai, Tsukuba, Ibaraki 305-8577, Japan
yano@iit.tsukuba.ac.jp, iwata@kz.tsukuba.ac.jp
https://unit.aist.go.jp/hiri/hi-fitness/index.html,
http://eva.vrlab.esys.tsukuba.ac.jp

Abstract. It is known that humans experience a kinesthetic illusion similar to a pulling sensation in a particular direction, when subjected to asymmetric vibrations. In our previous study, we developed a device that can apply a translational force and a torque to induce this illusion. The illusory translational force might induce a reaching motion of the upper limb, and the applied torque might induce a flexion–extension motion of the wrist. In the present study, we experimentally verified whether these motions can be induced. The results confirmed that the device could guide the upper limb with a success rate of 94.3% when switching between the application of the translational force and the torque. The results suggested that torque application could be a cue for the user to determine the movement direction intuitively.

Keywords: Illusory force perception · Asymmetric vibration · Non-grounded haptic interface · Motion guidance · Skill transfer

1 Introduction

Conventional methods of motion guidance include a verbal method, in which an expert verbally teaches a motion to a trainee, and a non-verbal method, in which the expert directly touches the trainee's body to induce a targeted motion. In particular, non-verbal methods are used in a wide range of fields, such as rehabilitation, craftsmanship, medical techniques, and sports. These instructions are called extrinsic feedback and are known to be effective in motor learning [1]. In recent years, motion guidance methods using haptic interfaces were proposed for high reproducibility and quantitative training [2,3]. These devices guide the

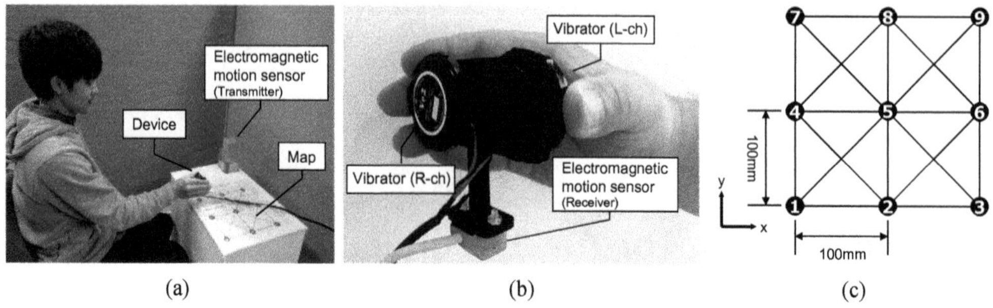

Fig. 1. Upper-limb guidance system: (a) overview, (b) enlarged view of the device, and (c) map of the navigation system.

user in performing the target motion by applying a force or torque to the user's body. However, these haptic interfaces need a large workspace because they must be grounded. Other studies [4,5] proposed a motion guidance method using vibrotactile cues, in which vibrators can be worn on the body because these actuators are smaller. This method has been applied to training for violin playing [5] and snowboarding [6]. Moreover, the application of a vibrotactile cue to an end effector, such as the hand [7] or wrist [4], is more effective than the application to a joint because the motion of the upper limb depends mainly on the hand position. However, the vibration stimuli have no directional cue such as a force or torque. The motions corresponding to vibrotactile cues, such as the movement of an arm in the direction in which vibration was perceived [4], must be mapped in advance. Such mapping of motions is difficult for trainees with a high degree of freedom of motion [8]. Therefore, to achieve efficient motion guidance, the actuator must be able to provide compelling directional information easily to the end effector.

In recent years, haptic interfaces that utilize a kinesthetic sensory illusion have been proposed. It is known that the sensory properties of humans are nonlinear. When strong and weak stimuli are applied sequentially, the user perceives the former but does not clearly perceive the latter. Based on this finding, Amemiya et al. proposed a method of applying vibrations with asymmetric acceleration to induce the perception of force toward a single direction in the user's hand [9]. Furthermore, we previously proposed a method of inducing pulling illusion by using a small voice-coil-type vibrator [10]. In addition, we developed a holdable device that presents an illusory translational force and torque by combining the two force vectors [11]. A new motion guidance method can be developed based on this pulling illusion for applications such as rehabilitation and skill transfer because compelling directional information can be easily provided to the fingertips by only vibration stimuli.

Reaching is a basic motion of the upper limb, in which the hand extends to a target position. Thus, the pulling illusion can be induced to guide the upper-limb motion of reaching. The application of a translational force might be effective for the guidance of reaching because the user's arm can be led by the translational force. However, when applying a translational force in one dimension, only the pushing and pulling motions of the upper limb can be induced. Reaching requires motion guidance in two or three dimensions, which can be achieved by the vector synthesis of translational force. On the other hand, translational force can be applied to guide only large movements of the user's arm to in the forward–backward, upward–downward, and leftward–rightward directions. To guide more complex movements, which are required for applications such as rehabilitation and skill transfer, it is necessary to combine the reaching motion with the motion of an end effector, such as the flexion–extension movement of the wrist. The application of a torque might be effective to induce a rotational motion of the wrist joint. In other words, if the reaching of the upper limb by a translational force and wrist flexion–extension movement by a torque can be combined, a wide range of motions from large to complex movements can be induced. In particular, torque application is important because it can provide a directional cue to perform reaching by changing the angle of the wrist. Therefore, it is hypothesized that torque application can provide intuitive feedback for the direction in which the upper limb should be moved.

In the present study, we experimentally verified whether the motion of upper limb can be induced based on the pulling illusion by using a combination of a translational force and torque. An upper-limb guidance system was developed, and a guidance experiment was performed for a reaching task in two dimensions as a basic study. The characteristics of guidance with and without torque application were investigated.

2 Method

2.1 Participant

Seven right-handed males aged 22–24 years participated in the experiment. The experimental procedure was in accordance with the Declaration of Helsinki. Informed consent was obtained from all participants.

2.2 Upper-Limb Guidance System

Figure 1 shows the upper-limb guidance system, which consists of a device that can apply a translational force and torque to induce the pulling illusion, an electromagnetic motion sensor (Polhemus Inc., 3SPACE FASTRACK), and a printed map. The device consists of two voice-coil-type vibrators (Acouve Lab Inc., Vibration Transducer Vp210). Two vibrators were placed in a side-by-side configuration. When a user holds these between the thumb and index finger, as shown in Fig. 1 (b), the force generated by the adjacent vibrator is primarily perceived by each digit. When the direction of the force exerted by each vibrator is controlled, a user can perceive both a translational force and torque. If forces are applied in the same direction on the participant's thumb and index finger, the participant perceives a translational force in this direction. In contrast, if forces in opposite directions are applied by the vibrator, the participant

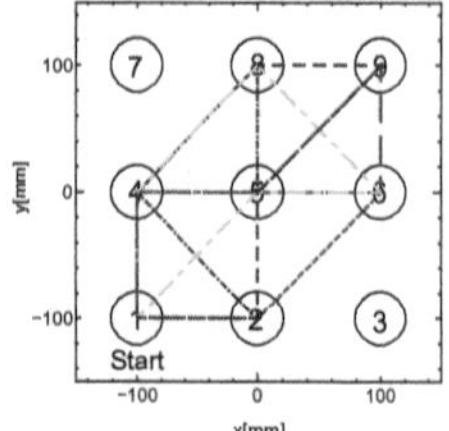

Route1	1→4→5→6→2
Route2	1→2→4→8→5
Route3	1→4→5→9→6
Route4	1→5→6→8→4
Route5	1→2→5→9→8

Fig. 2. Routes used in the experiment.

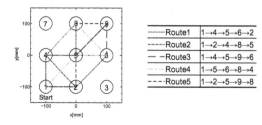

perceives a torque. In other words, this device can apply forces in four directions, in which a forward or backward translational force and a clockwise (CW) or counterclockwise (CCW) torque, by combination of the force vectors. These directions are controlled using an asymmetric-amplitude signal with a two-cycle sine wave that is inverted for a half-cycle [10]. Each signal was amplified with an amplifier circuit using a power amplifier IC (Texas Instruments Inc., LM386) with a maximum output voltage of ±4.5 V. The frequency of the input signal was 75 Hz. More details of this device can be found in Ref. [11].

The transmitter of the motion sensor and map were set on the table in front of the participants (Fig.1 (a)). The receiver of motion sensor is attached to the device (Fig. 1 (b)), and the position and posture of the device on the map were measured. The upper limb of the participant was induced by switching and presenting the translational force and the torque. The map and the device are not fixed, and participants can move the device freely on the map. Numbered circles on the map indicate nodes, and solid lines indicate routes (Fig. 1 (c)). The map has three nodes in the x direction and three nodes in the y direction. A total of nine nodes are arranged at 100 mm intervals. Each node and adjacent nodes in 45° steps were connected by routes. Routes in up to eight directions are connected at one node.

Next, the guidance algorithm is described. In this system, a translational force was applied if the posture of the device faced the direction of the next target node, and a torque was applied to face the target direction otherwise. The target angle θ_P between the position of the device $D(D_x, D_y)$ and the next target node $P(P_x, P_y)$ is

$$\theta_P = \tan^{-1} \frac{P_y - D_y}{P_x - D_x}. \tag{1}$$

The posture around the vertical axis of the device θ_D was measured, and a CW or CCW torque was applied when $\theta_D > \theta_P$ or $\theta_D < \theta_P$, respectively. Considering the range of motion of the wrist and the measurement accuracy, when the difference between the posture of the device and the target angle was less than ±15°, switching from torque to translational force was performed. When the target node was in the positive translational direction from the device, a forward translational force was applied, and when the target node was in the negative direction, a backward translational force was applied. When the device was within a certain distance from the center of the target node (set to

10 mm in this system), the target node was switched to the next node. In this algorithm, even if the position of the device deviates from the predetermined route, the torque and translation force are applied in accordance with the angle and distance to the target node. This system is intended for use with the right hand, and the posture of the device was set to 0° when facing the front (see Fig. 1 (b)), 45°, −45°, and −90° (CW is positive). The upper limb of the participants was guided in eight directions by applying a forward or backward translational force in the above four postures. The angle of the turning motion (difference between the device postures at the start and end of turning, hereinafter referred to as the rotation angle) was 0° at minimum and 135° at maximum.

The route was set to five types, each passing through five out of nine nodes with one stroke (Fig. 2). The start position was fixed at node 1. These routes were selected to make the number of occurrences of each rotation angle approximately equal.

2.3 Procedure

Under the hypothesis that the torque application can provide intuitive feedback for the direction in which the upper limb should be moved, the experiment was conducted with (w.) and without (w/o) torque application. Because the wrist posture could not be guided in the w/o torque condition, the participants performed active exploration for the next target posture by rotating the device. In the w. torque condition, the posture was guided by torque application as explained in Sect. 2.2. Under both conditions, a forward or backward translational force was presented when the device was guiding to the next node.

The experimental tasks are as follows. Participants moved their upper limbs as guided by the device to trace a solid line when traveling along a route and to perform rotation within a node. In total, 30 trials were performed for each participant, with 3 trials for each condition (2 levels) and each route (5 levels), and each condition and each route was randomized. To minimize fatigue during the experiment, the trials were divided into three blocks of 10 trials each, and the participants were given a two-minute break between blocks. In this experiment, audiovisual information was not blocked because actual motion guidance was assumed. Before the trial, the experimenter verbally guided the participant about the condition of torque application. A sound effect was output from the speaker only when the goal was achieved, indicating that the trial was completed. A 5-min practice period was set up so that participants could learn how to operate the device before the experiment.

3 Results

Figure 3 shows typical examples of the device's trajectory. The solid lines show the trajectories in which the device was moved by the participants, and the broken lines show the target routes. The task was determined as successful when the device passed the nodes in the set order.

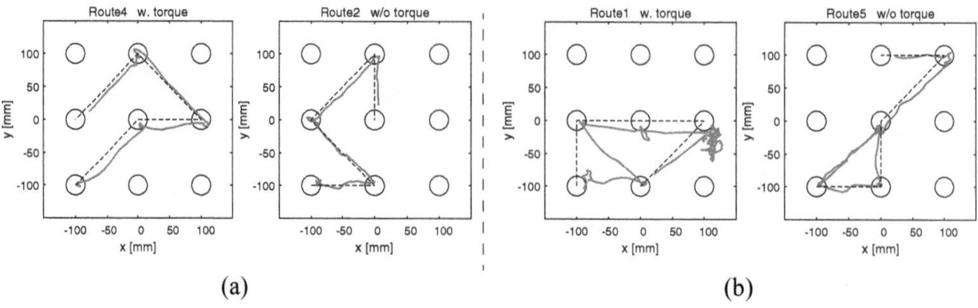

Fig. 3. Typical examples of the device's trajectory: (a) successful task; (b) failed task.

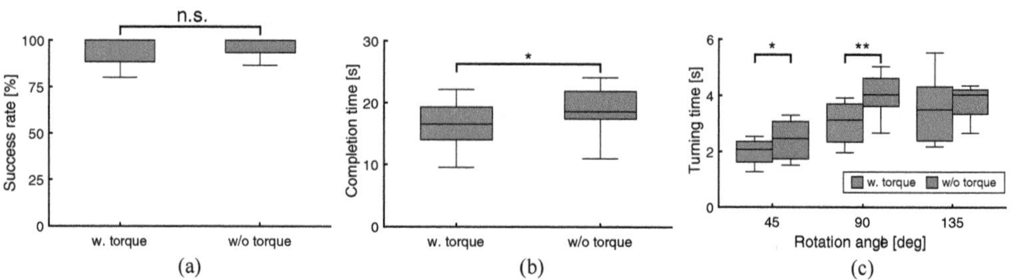

Fig. 4. Experimental results: (a) success rate of guiding along routes, (b) task completion time, and (c) turning time (n.s.: not significant, *: $p < 0.05$, **: $p < 0.01$).

Figure 4 (a) shows the success rate for guiding routes. The average success rate in the w. torque condition was 94.3%, and the rate in the w/o torque condition was 96.2%. In a paired t-test between the conditions, no significant difference was found [$t(6) = 1.00$, $p = 0.37$, $d = 0.28$].

The task completion time and turning time were analyzed for only successful trials. Figure 4 (b) shows the task completion time. The completion time indicates the time from the start signal provided by the experimenter to time at which the fifth node is reached. In a paired t-test between the conditions of torque application, a significant difference was found [$t(6) = 2.49$, $p < 0.05$, $d = 0.53$].

The turning time indicates the time from the moment when a node is reached to the time at which the turn at the node is completed. Figure 4 (c) shows the turning time at each rotation angle. Since the change in turning time was small with respect to the rotation direction, the rotation directions were merged for each rotation angle. Furthermore, the rotation angle was not considered a factor, because the turning time increased as the rotation angle increased. In a t-test between the conditions of torque application, significant differences were found for 45° [$t(6) = 2.67$, $p < 0.05$, $d = 0.68$] and 90° [$t(6) = 3.96$, $p < 0.01$, $d = 1.32$], whereas no significant difference was found for 135° [$t(6) = 0.57$, $p = 0.59$, $d = 0.24$].

4 Discussion

Because the success rates of guidance were high under both conditions, it was shown that the upper-limb motion could be guided by the pulling illusion. This result suggests that the user can be guided to perform large and complex movements by combining the reaching and wrist motions. However, although no significant difference was found between the conditions, the success rate was lower under the w. torque condition. This might have been caused by the adaptation to stimuli induced by the long-term application of asymmetric vibration. We confirmed that the subjective sensitivity of illusory force decreased with the continuous presentation of asymmetric vibration [12]. In the w. torque condition, the asymmetric vibration was always presented, whereas in the w/o torque condition, the stimulus during the turning motion was not presented. The sum of the vibration-stimulation times was larger in the w. torque condition, and the adaptation might be induced earlier. Therefore, an application method that considers adaptation is required.

The completion time and turning time were significantly shortened on applying the torque. Thus, it is considered that the participants intuitively determined the direction in which the wrist must be flexed with the torque application. On the other hand, although the difference in turning time between the torque conditions was remarkable when the turning angle was small, such as 45° or 90°, the effect of the torque application was smaller for a turning angle of 135° ($d = 0.24$). When the turning angle was 135°, either the CW rotation from the −45° posture or the CCW rotation from the 45° posture was performed. Thus, the participant could determine the next direction to rotate to without directional information when the turning angle was 135°. In other words, this result supports the hypothesis that the torque application is effective when it is necessary to determine the direction. Therefore, the illusion may be useful as a trigger of motion.

This method is expected to be effective in an environment where visual information can also be presented because the task is to guide the user along routes on a map. Moreover, it is difficult to induce high-speed motion by using this method because the user needs to move the upper limb by using a force or torque cue. Therefore, guidance for slow motions, such as rehabilitation using a pegboard, welding, and calligraphy, might be feasible. Particularly in the field of rehabilitation, it has been reported that reaching assisted by a robot contributes to the recovery of motor function [13]. Motor learning might be promoted by supporting reaching using our device. However, although this study showed that the pulling illusion could guide reaching and wrist motions, the effects on motor learning were not clarified. In the future, long-term verification of motor learning using our device is required.

5 Conclusion

In this study, we verified whether the motion of upper limb can be induced by using the translational force and torque presentation based on the pulling illusion. As a result, it was confirmed that this device could be guided with a success rate of 94.3% in the condition of switching the presentation of the translational force or the torque. It was also suggested that torque presentation could be a cue to intuitively determine the direction. In the future, we investigate the relationship the pulling illusion and motor learning, and develop the applications, such as rehabilitation or skill transfer.

Acknowledgments. This work was supported by JSPS KAKENHI Grant No. 19K24374.

References

1. Tani, H.: Are Instructions and Feedback by a Therapist Effective in the Motor Learning?. Rigakuryoho Kagaku, vol. 21, no. 1, pp. 67–73, 2006. (in Japanese)
2. Yem, V., Kuzuoka, H., Yamashita, N., Ohta, S., Takeuchi, Y.: Hand-skill learning using outer-covering haptic display. In: Auvray, M., Duriez, C. (eds.) EUROHAPTICS 2014. LNCS, vol. 8618, pp. 201–207. Springer, Heidelberg (2014). https://doi.org/10.1007/978-3-662-44193-0_26
3. Feygin, D., Keehner, M., Tendick, F.: Haptic guidance: experimental evaluation of a haptic training method for a perceptual motor skill. In: Proceedings of 10th Symposium on Haptic Interfaces for Virtual Environment and Teleoperator System (HAPTICS 2002), pp. 40–48 (2002)
4. Salazar, J., Okabe, K., Murao, Y., Hirata, Y.: A phantom-sensation based paradigm for continuous vibrotactile wrist guidance in two-dimensional space. IEEE Robot. Autom. Lett. **3**(1), 163–170 (2018)
5. van der Linden, J., Schoonderwaldt, E., Bird, J., Johnson, R.: MusicJacket-combining motion capture and vibrotactile feedback to teach violin bowing. IEEE Trans. Inst. Meas. **60**(1), 104–113 (2010)
6. Spelmezan, D., Schanowski, A., Borchers, J.: Haptic guidance: experimental evaluation of a haptic training method for a perceptual motor skill. In: Proceedings 4th International ICST Conference Body Area Networks, pp. 1–8 (2009)
7. Basu, S., Tsai, J., Majewicz, A.: Evaluation of tactile guidance cue mappings for emergency percutaneous needle insertion. In: Proceeding of IEEE Haptics Symposium 2016, pp. 106–112 (2016)
8. Bark, K., et al.: Effects of vibrotactile feedback on human learning of arm motions. IEEE Trans. Neural Syst. Rehabil. Eng. **23**(1), 52–63 (2015)
9. Amemiya, T., Ando, H., Maeda, T.: Lead-me interface for a pulling sensation from hand-held devices. ACM Trans. Appl. Percept. **5**(3), art. 15, 1–17 (2008)
10. Tanabe, T., Yano, H., Iwata, H.: Evaluation of the perceptual characteristics of a force induced by asymmetric vibrations. IEEE Trans. Haptics **11**(2), 220–231 (2018)
11. Tanabe, T., Yano, H., Iwata, H.: Proposal and implementation of non-grounded translational force and torque display using two vibration speakers. In: Hasegawa, S., Konyo, M., Kyung, K.-U., Nojima, T., Kajimoto, H. (eds.) AsiaHaptics 2016. LNEE, vol. 432, pp. 187–192. Springer, Singapore (2018). https://doi.org/10.1007/978-981-10-4157-0_32
12. Tanabe, T., Yano, H., Iwata, H.: Temporal characteristics of non-grounded translational force and torque display using asymmetric vibrations. In: Proceedings of IEEE World Haptics Conference, pp. 310–315 (2017)
13. Takahashi, K., et al.: Efficacy of upper extremity robotic therapy in subacute poststroke hemiplegia. Stroke **47**(5), 1385–1388 (2016)

14

Instrumenting Hand-Held Surgical Drills with a Pneumatic Sensing Cover for Haptic Feedback

Chiara Gaudeni[1(✉)], Tommaso Lisini Baldi[1], Gabriele M. Achilli[2], Marco Mandalà[3], and Domenico Prattichizzo[1,4]

[1] Department of Information Engineering and Mathematics, University of Siena, Siena, Italy
{gaudeni,lisini,prattichizzo}@diism.unisi.it
[2] Department of Engineering, University of Perugia, Perugia, Italy
[3] Department of Medicine, Surgery and Neuroscience, University of Siena, Siena, Italy
[4] Department of Advanced Robotics, Istituto Italiano di Tecnologia, Genoa, Italy

Abstract. Despite the recent achievements in the development of open surgery tools, preserving the haptic capabilities during drilling tasks is still an open issue. In this paper, we propose a novel tool for hand-held drills composed of a cover for force sensing and a haptic display for force feedback. A pneumatic device has been developed to estimate the contact force occurring during the interaction between drill bit and bones. A performance comparison with a precise commercial force sensor proved the reliability of the measurements. A haptic ring is in charge of providing cutaneous sensations helping the surgeon in performing the task. The effectiveness of our method has been confirmed by experimental results and supported by statistical analysis.

1 Introduction

Technological advancements in surgical tools have expanded the field of robot-assisted surgery to newer specialties. Even if the achievements in the last years have been impressive, current robotic surgical systems are still limited by the lack of haptic feedback. It has been proved that restoring the haptic capability in robotic surgery contributes to improve accuracy and safety in performing complex and delicate surgical tasks [9]. On the other hand, also open surgery may suffer from a reduction of tactile perception. In fact, even if in these procedures surgeons directly interact with the patient's body, some surgical tools, *e.g.* drills, may limit the haptic perception. As a matter of fact, a common issue in surgical drilling is that vibrations generated by the tool affect the perception of the surgeon, reducing, for instance, the capability in discerning different tissues and detecting the break-through force [5].

In this paper, we focus on otologic procedures, where a precise control of the surgical drill is required because the critical anatomy within the middle ear,

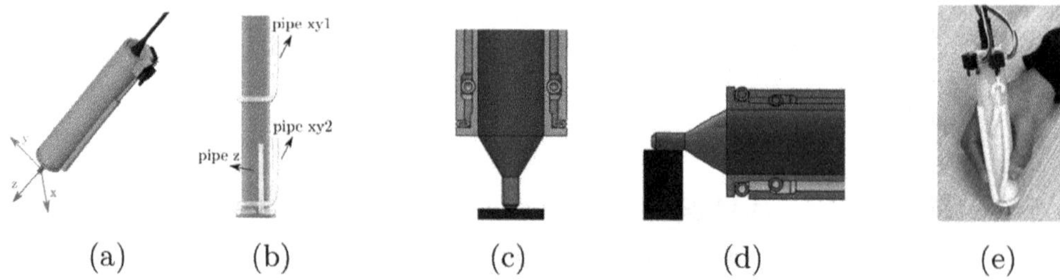

Fig. 1. The developed sensing system: (a) CAD model; (b) attachment of pipes to the inner shell; (c)(d) details of the sensing mechanism measuring perpendicular and tangential forces, respectively; (e) a user holding a surgical drill enriched with the sensing cover. Outer soft silicone pipes are covered by rigid housings to prevent the surgeon from touching them and affecting the measurements.

inner ear, and skull base can be accessed by drilling within the temporal bone for operations which demand high precision and accuracy [8]. Several researchers pointed out benefits of restoring haptic feedback in hand-held drilling procedures. In [1], force sensing has been elected as the appropriate way to obtain controlled penetration in the patient's body and automatic discrimination among layers of different tissues. Hessinger *et al.* integrated a thrust force sensor into the drill to enable high accuracy during pedicle screw positioning [3]. In the aforementioned works, the force measure is obtained integrating sensors into the tool mechanism. In this paper, we propose a pneumatic method to measure the contact force between the drill bit and the bone without modifying the internal structure of the tool. The aim is to create an instrumented cover that can be easily customized and adapted to the off-the-shelf hand-held drills. Moreover, the proposed system is capable of rendering the force feedback to the user by means of a haptic ring. To the best of our knowledge, this represents the first attempt to assist a surgeon with haptic feedback in open surgery without modifying the existing equipment.

2 Design of the Pneumatic Force Sensor

Working Principle

Measuring contact forces between the drill bit and a surface without modifying existing tools encounters several non-trivial challenges. Because of the drilling task, the sensing system has to be placed far from the contact point. Common precise and accurate 3-axis force sensors are bulky and not suitable for small devices. Thus, we developed a pneumatic system capable of estimating forces using pipes and air pressure sensors. The great advantage of using a pneumatic system is that it is lightweight, tiny, and measurement information is transferred by means of a gas to the sensors, which can be located out of the operational workspace. We exploit a sensing structure consisting of two concentric cylindrical shells separated by a gap, as shown in Fig. 1a. The inner shell (Fig. 1b) is rigidly attached to the body of the drill, while the outer shell is the one held by the surgeon. Soft silicone pipes are placed between the two shells to fill the gap, preventing any relative movements when no forces are applied. They represent also the sensing element of the device, as explained below.

The working principle of the developed sensing system relies on the assumption that the drill-hand system is under mechanical equilibrium conditions until an external force is applied to the drill bit. When the drill bit comes into contact with the bone, the inner shell moves towards the outer shell along the direction of the contact (see Figs. 1c and 1d). This displacement generates a compression of soft silicone pipes depending on the external force. In the considered surgical scenarios, torque components are treated as negligible, because the drill bit does not enter deeply into the bone generating significant values of torque. It is worth noting that the grasp squeezing forces applied by the surgeon do not cause any structural deformation of the pipes thanks to the high stiffness of the external shell. Then, the only deformations are due to the forces applied to the drill bit. To estimate the entity of the compression, the increase of pipes internal pressure is measured by means of air pressure sensors placed outside the outer shell. Pipes are not additionally inflated: at the steady state they are at the equilibrium with the external air pressure.

Hardware Implementation

As depicted in Fig. 1e, we present a proof of concept in which the pneumatic force sensor is composed of two 3D-printed parts made of ABSPlus (Stratasys Inc., USA), soft silicone pipes (ID 2.5 mm, OD 3.5 mm), and two 2 kPa differential pressure sensors (MPXV7002DP, NXP Semiconductors, NL) measuring forces along the z-axis and on the xy-plane, respectively (as in the reference system of Fig. 1a). The total weight of the cover is 51 g. Each pipe is ring-shaped and firmly attached to the inner shell as shown in Fig. 1b, with one end leak-proof sealed. The opposite side of the pipe conveys the pneumatic information to the pressure sensors. Forces on the xy-plane are measured by a sensor connected to *pipes xy*. Two pipes spaced along the length of the drill are required to prevent possible relative movements between the two shells when no forces are applied. It is important to notice that each pipe goes out of the outer shell as soon as the loop close, through a small hole. In this way, the measurement resolution is the same in all the directions of the xy-plane. Both the shells contain grooves for enclosing the pipes so as to reduce the width of the device. In this way, the gap between the shells corresponds to the internal diameter of the pipes. In the outer shell, the cavity is vertically extended so as not to detect pressure variations when the only force involved is along the z-axis. Taking advantage of the flange on the lower part of the shell, it is possible to measure with a second pressure sensor the forces exerted on the z-axis by means of *pipe z* (see Fig. 1b). The effect of gravitational force has been considered negligible with respect to the forces at work, due to the lightweight of the drill. Moreover, we supposed that in a such accurate task the surgeon compensates the weight by his hands and the contact force is equivalent to the force exerted by the surgeon. Vibrations generated by the drill are filtered by means of a hardware R-C filter with an experimentally selected cut-off frequency of 144.68 Hz. To further isolate sensors from vibrations, two tiny sponge layers are placed under the sensor housings.

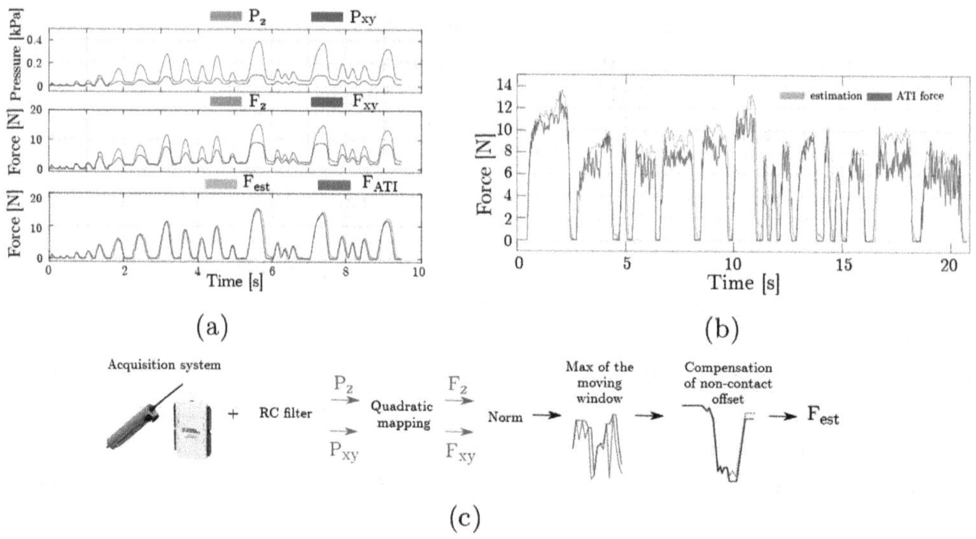

Fig. 2. Force estimation. In (a) raw pressure values, the correspondent forces, and the comparison between the final force estimation and the ground-truth value are reported. Values obtained in a representative trial, affected by vibrational noise, are in (b). In (c), the steps of the force estimation are detailed.

Analog data from the sensors are acquired using a NI USB-6218 DAQ. Finally, a software algorithm, described below, processes the signal.

Software Implementation

A calibration procedure is required to correctly transform data from pressure sensors into forces. The initial calibration and the subsequent validation phase are performed with the drill switched off. A high precision ATI Gamma F/T sensor (ATI Industrial Automation, USA) is used to identify the force-pressure relation. A separate procedure is required for calibrating the two sensors. For what concerns the z-axis calibration, the drill was vertically pushed toward the ATI sensor for a total of 50 contact actions, so that the generated force deforms only *pipe z*, as depicted in Fig. 1c. In accordance with [2], data gathered from the pressure sensor and the ATI were quadratically interpolated using a Matlab© algorithm. The same procedure was repeated for the xy-plane, keeping the drill horizontally (Fig. 1d). For the tool exploited in this work, the two found relations are: $F_z = 5034{\cdot}P_z - 2280{\cdot}P_z^2$ and $F_{xy} = 9542{\cdot}P_{xy} - 1017{\cdot}P_{xy}^2$, being P_{xy} and P_z the pressure values. As a final step, the norm of F_z and F_{xy} is computed. Indeed, from the user point of view, there is no need to distinguish the three components of the force: the surgeon just needs to have a feedback on the total force exerted, which corresponds to the norm of F_z and F_{xy}. As noticeable in Fig. 2a, this value is affected by the relatively slow dynamic of the pneumatic system. After breaking contact, the pressure of the pipes does not immediately reach the initial zero-value. A rapid decrease of the pressure is followed by a slow down-welling. Thus, we introduced a compensation algorithm which brings to zero the *"non-contact offset"*, identified as a flat trend after a significant negative slope.

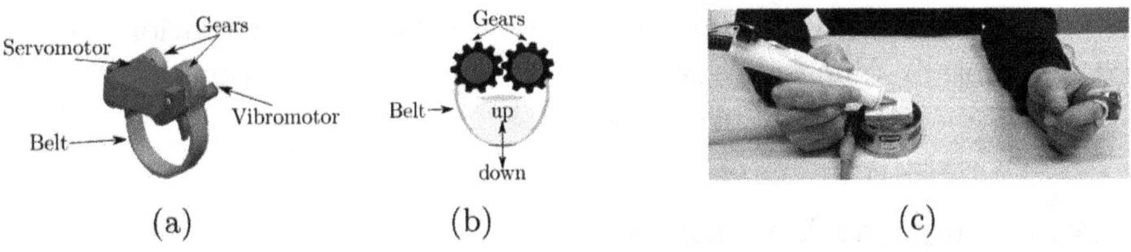

Fig. 3. (a) Rendered 3D model of the device; (b) mechanism for pulling up/down the fabric belt. (c) A user testing the proposed system.

We validated this method comparing the estimated contact force F_{est} to the norm of the forces measured by the ATI in 200 contact actions involving both the z-axis and the xy-plane. The resulting RMSE is 0.967 N, in a force range of $[0-18]$N. Steps from pressure raw data toward force values are depicted in Fig. 2a. Once validated the sensing device in non-vibrating trials, we tested the proposed system switching on the drill. Adding vibrations introduces a significant modification in the force profile, as depicted in Fig. 2b. To compensate this negative effect, a software filter has been implemented. The filtered force value corresponds to the maximum value in a moving window of 33 ms. In this way, the downward peaks are ignored guaranteeing a safer overestimation. This implies that it is not possible to compare the filtered force estimation with the measurements of the ATI in drilling tasks. The duration of the moving window was selected to obtain the best compromise between filter performance and response delay. All the steps of the force estimation are reported in Fig. 2c.

3 Force Feedback

Contextually with the force sensing system, we developed a haptic ring capable of generating cutaneous and vibrotactile force feedback. To have a lightweight device with a limited encumbrance, we employed a single servo-motor (HS-35HD Ultra Nano, HITEC Inc., USA) controlling a flexible belt for generating cutaneous stimuli and an eccentric-mass motor (EMM) to generate vibrotactile stimuli [7]. The device is controlled by the same DAQ board used for sensors data acquisition through an ad-hoc library. The servo motor generates the rotation of a master gear that moves a slave gear. Such mechanism results in opposite spinning directions of the gears, that translate the belt along the vertical axis. The workings are depicted in Figs. 3a and 3b. The maximum range of the belt motion in the vertical direction is 23 mm and it depends on the external diameter of the gears (11 mm), the length of the belt (95 mm), and the maximum rotation range of the servo motor (120°). We selected these values considering that also fingertips bigger than the average should fit. The maximum exploitable displacement range for force generation is 6 mm, so that the device can apply a maximum force of 3 N considering a stiffness of 0.5 N/m as elastic behavior of the finger pulp. Interested readers are referred to [6] and [4] for further details on the force feedback generation. A manual calibration is performed for each participant to adjust the initial position of the belt. The vibrational motor is placed horizontally alongside the device. It generates vibrations (1 g at 3.6 V) to notify the force threshold over-reaching.

4 Experimental Validation

The experimental evaluation was carried out with a twofold aim: *i*) demonstrating the effectiveness of the haptic feedback in the aforementioned surgery and *ii*) identifying the best feedback approach. Ten users (6 males, age 23–56, all right handed) took part in the experiment. One was a surgeon with many years of experience, three were medical students with 5 years of experience, while the remaining six were medical students with lower/no experience in performing open surgical procedures.

The experiment aimed at simulating a cochlear implant surgery. Participants were asked to completely remove a blue colored rectangle (0.6 cm × 2.0 cm) from a piece of plywood using the instrumented drill (rotating at 15.000 rpm). Users wore the haptic ring on the left hand (see Fig. 3c), where a clear perception of the haptic feedback is allowed by the absence of vibrations. Participants were told that the task was considered successfully accomplished when the drilling force was maintained in a specific range, *i.e.* [0–7.5]N, without overreaching the limit time of 13 s. The time limit has been introduced to prevent subjects from being excessively slow in order to completely remove the blue color using low forces. Three feedback conditions were evaluated: *i)* no feedback *(N)*; *ii)* vibratory *(V)* alert in case of exceeding the force threshold; *iii)* vibratory alert and cutaneous feedback proportional to the exerted force *(C)*. A proportional scale factor was used to map the measured maximum force into the admissible range of the ring. Each user performed a set of three trials per each feedback condition (pseudo-randomly selected), resulting in a total of 9 trials. Time to complete the task and impulse (the integral of the force out of the boundaries over the time interval) were considered as metrics for evaluating the task performance. A familiarization period of 2 min was provided to acquaint participants with the system. In this phase, users tested the overreaching of the force limit with and without haptics. In the first case, the exerted force was displayed by the haptic ring, in the latter by a graphical indicator on a LCD screen.

4.1 Results and Discussion

Data collected in the experimental phase were analyzed by means of statistical tests. For each participant completion time and impulse were computed (see Figs. 4b and 4c). All the participants were able to completely remove the blue color in the time limit of 13 s both with and without the haptic feedback. The average completion time among all the trials is 10.85 ± 2.54 s, 10.23 ± 1.72 s, 9.32 ± 1.16 s for N, V, and C feedback conditions, respectively. Statistical analysis revealed that there is no statistically significant difference in the completion time of the task using different feedback. As shown also in Fig. 4a-upper, the

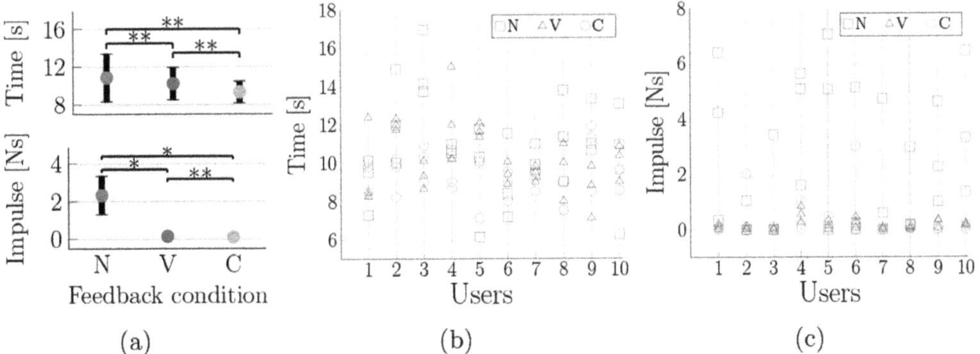

Fig. 4. In (a) mean and 95% CI for all the feedback conditions are reported for time (upper panel) and impulse of the force over the threshold (lower panel). The p-values are reported on top of the error bars, $**$ and $*$ indicate $p > 0.05$ and $p < 0.0005$, respectively. In (b) and (c) users' results for each trial are shown.

task execution is not slowed down by the increasing number of stimuli to be focused on. Concerning the impulse of the force over the threshold, participant exceeded the limit with 2.33 ± 1.25 Ns, 0.15 ± 0.16 Ns, 0.10 ± 0.13 Ns testing the setup with *N*, *V*, and *C* feedback, respectively. Moreover, a one-way repeated measures ANOVA was conducted to determine whether there were statistically significant differences in impulse over the different feedback. There were no outliers. Data were transformed using the squareroot transformation and passed the ShapiroWilk normality test ($p > 0.05$). The assumption of sphericity was violated, as assessed by Mauchly's test ($\chi^2(2) = 7.87$, $p < 0.05$). Therefore, a Greenhouse-Geisser correction was applied. The results of the test (reported in Fig. 4a-lower) assessed that the feedback modality elicited statistically significant changes in over-applied forces ($p < 0.0005$). Post hoc analysis with Bonferroni adjustment revealed that the reduction of impulse was statistically significant. More in detail, the test revealed that there is statistically significant difference in performing the task with or without haptic feedback. In case of feedback, the impulse error had a almost complete reduction, which implies a more controlled penetration in the plywood. For what concerns the difference between the two haptic feedback, the difference is lower, but not statistically significant. Supported by the outcomes of the statistical analysis, we can affirm that haptic feedback can enhance the safety in surgical hand-held drilling tasks, maintaining the drilling force in a specific range. In addition, participants to the experimental campaign reported positive qualitative feedback on the haptic-assisted experience and on the positioning of the ring in the contralateral side. They argued that the cover did not interfere with the task and it would be useful to introduce the device in real surgical procedures, after appropriate refinements.

5 Conclusion and Future Work

In this work, we presented a novel approach to measure the force exerted on bones during drilling tasks in open surgery. A pneumatic sensing cover for drills and a haptic ring to reproduce such forces were developed. We tested our sensing device in a comparison with a high-resolution/accuracy commercial force sensor, demonstrating the robustness of our approach. To properly reconstruct the force profile, we implemented both a hardware and a software filters. The advantage of our sensing system is that it can be easily adapted to any surgical drills, changing only few design parameters in the CAD model (e.g. introducing some shims to modify only the internal profile of the inner shell). The resolution and the range of our sensor are customizable: they can be modified changing the silicone pipes and using pressure sensors with different resolution.

We evaluated the effectiveness of our haptic-assisted hand-held drill with long experience and novice surgeons. Forces and vibrations were exploited to help the users in evaluating the real exerted forces. We compared the performance of the participants with and without haptic feedback, proving that haptic enhancement outperformed the haptic-free technique.

The presented results pave the way for numerous interesting research directions that will be the subject for future works. Different feedback policies and locations will be tested in a future experimental campaign. Additional metrics, such as tissue discrimination, will be considered to evaluate device and feedback. Learning curves in performing the task with and without feedback will be evaluated in a more careful future study, involving a larger sample. In further developments, the cover can be instrumented with additional sensors (e.g. an accelerometer) to measure the inclination of the drill and improve the calibration procedure. Finally, ergonomic studies will be taken into consideration.

References

1. Allotta, B., Giacalone, G., Rinaldi, L.: A hand-held drilling tool for orthopedic surgery. IEEE/ASME Trans. Mech. **2**(4), 218–229 (1997)
2. Gaudeni, C., Meli, L., Prattichizzo, D.: A novel pneumatic force sensor for robot-assisted surgery. In: Prattichizzo, D., Shinoda, H., Tan, H.Z., Ruffaldi, E., Frisoli, A. (eds.) EuroHaptics 2018. LNCS, vol. 10894, pp. 587–599. Springer, Cham (2018)
3. Hessinger, M., Hielscher, J., Pott, P.P., Werthschützky, R.: Handheld surgical drill with integrated thrust force recognition. In: Proceedings of IEEE International Conference on E-Health and Bioengineering, pp. 1–4 (2013)
4. Lisini Baldi, T., Scheggi, S., Meli, L., Mohammadi, M., Prattichizzo, D.: GESTO: a glove for enhanced sensing and touching based on inertial and magnetic sensors for hand tracking and cutaneous feedback. IEEE Trans. Human-Mach. Syst. **47**(6), 1066–1076 (2017)
5. Louredo, M., Diaz, I., Gil, J.J.: DRIBON: a mechatronic bone drilling tool. Mechatronics **22**(8), 1060–1066 (2012)
6. Park, K.H., Kim, B.H., Hirai, S.: Development of a soft-fingertip and its modeling based on force distribution. In: Proceedings of the IEEE International Conference on Robotics and Automation, vol. 3, pp. 3169–3174 (2003)

7. Precision Microdrives: Model No. 304–002 4mm Vibration Motor - 8mm Type Datasheet. https://www.precisionmicrodrives.com/product/datasheet/304-002-4mm-vibration-motor-8mm-type-datasheet.pdf
8. Sang, H., Monfaredi, R., Wilson, E., Fooladi, H., Preciado, D., Cleary, K.: A new surgical drill instrument with force sensing and force feedback forrobotically assisted otologic surgery. J. Med. Dev. **11**(3) (2017)
9. Wagner, C.R., Stylopoulos, N., Howe, R.D.: The role of force feedback in surgery: analysis of blunt dissection. In: Proceedings of the IEEE Haptics Symposium, pp. 68–74 (2002)

15

Perceptually Compressive Communication of Interactive Telehaptic Signal

Suhas Kakade(✉) and Subhasis Chaudhuri

Department of Electrical Engineering, Indian Institute of Technology Bombay, Mumbai, India
{suhaskakade,sc}@ee.iitb.ac.in

Abstract. During telehaptic applications over a shared communication medium, Weber's law of perception based adaptive sampling scheme can be applied to reduce the data rate without degrading the perceptual quality of the haptic signal. However, the perceptual threshold (JND) is often unknown for a user. An experimental design involving bidirectional communication of haptic data over the Internet between the operator and teleoperator is carried out in this paper, which provides a real-time estimate of the Weber threshold for the telehaptic backward channel force signal. Using the proposed data-driven experimental protocol, we are able to reduce the packet rate significantly. We provide a subjective evaluation of the proposed technique to substantiate its usefulness.

Keywords: Adaptive sampling · Telehaptics · Weber threshold

1 Introduction

In recent years, the transmission of haptic data has received the attention of many researchers working in the area of telehaptics. This bidirectional transmission creates a global control loop between the operator and the teleoperator over a communication channel. Contrary to video or audio signal, in order to make the global control loop stable and to maintain the *Quality of Service* (QoS), a maximum communication delay of 30 ms is allowed [8]. Since the haptic signal is typically sampled at 1 kHz, to limit the packet rate while maintaining the QoS, perceptually significant adaptive sampling schemes based on Weber's law of perception [9] or event detection [12] have been applied. Weber's law of perception depicts a logarithmic relation between perceptual stimuli and human perception. Weber threshold is given by $\rho = \frac{\Delta I}{I}$ where ρ represents Weber threshold, ΔI represents just noticeable difference (JND), i.e., the minimum change in signal magnitude required to produce a noticeable variation in signal perception and I is the reference signal magnitude.

In a perceptually significant adaptive sampling scheme, sampling of the kinesthetic force signal will be carried out at instances at which the relative difference exceeds the Weber threshold, i.e., $\frac{|F_i - F_{i-1}|}{|F_{i-1}|} \geq \rho$ where F_i represents force sample at time t_i and F_{i-1} represents the last perceived force sample at time $t_{(i-1)}$. Then these samples are transmitted. This helps in the reduction of packet rate. Hence the study of estimation of Weber threshold is essential. However, the JND depends on perceptual capabilities of an individual as well as the task one is performing.

A lot of research work has been carried out on the estimation of JND and Weber threshold. Though [5] discusses the estimation of JND on off-line data and their application in adaptive sampling, there is little research on the estimation of JND from real-time data. For the multidimensional signal, [5,13] analyzed the variation in Weber threshold due to the change in force direction. Researchers have applied techniques like psychometric function [6,15] mostly on off-line data to determine the Weber threshold of force signal. The work in [9] demonstrated adaptive sampling for telehaptic signal but with a fixed set of Weber threshold values. In this paper, we try to adaptively determine the Weber threshold directly from on-line data acquired in the given environment in real-time and simultaneously use it for adaptive sampling of the data on the backward channel. Haptics over Internet Protocol (HoIP) has been proposed in [7] to carry the haptic signal over the internet. [8] uses HoIP for the propagation of the telehapatic signal and also performs Weber sampling of the velocity signal. The stability of the global control loop is achieved through appropriate approaches, as specified in [10,11,14]. In this work, we assume that our global control loop satisfies the stability criteria, and we did not observe any instability of the global control loop during experimentation.

In this paper, we apply Weber's law of perception based adaptive sampling scheme to the interactive telehaptic force signal under an appropriately simulated environment. The force signal is generated through signed distance field based haptic rendering of different watertight mesh models. This rendering is carried out at the teleoperator end, and the force signal is transmitted from the teleoperator to the operator on the backward channel. The force signal is adaptively sampled based on a real-time data-driven estimate of JND to reduce the packet rate over the Internet. In order to adaptively sample the haptic signal, we need to know the JND for the given task. We use an adaptively updatable probing threshold for sampling the signal on the backward channel while the user provides an intermittent task-nondisruptive feedback to the teleoperator through the forward channel. Our experiment showed that there is a substantial reduction in the haptic packet rate in-spite of not having any prior knowledge of the Weber threshold for the user. It is also well known that the user experience of haptic communication is dependent on network delay. We perform experiments to study this and show how it affects the users.

2 Proposed Method

2.1 Hardware Setup

The experiment is designed in two modes - 1) standalone and 2) networking. In standalone mode, only one haptic device is used with a computer. This mode is used only to study the effect of packetization delay and to serve as the reference (baseline experiment) during user studies. The theme of this paper is to carry out the experimentation in networking mode. Here two phantom omni haptic devices are used, one as an operator and the other as a teleoperator. These haptic devices are connected to two separate computers. These computers acting as end systems are connected through another node computer. A virtual network of these three computers is managed through Wide Area Network Emulator (WaNem) [3]. The unidirectional communication link capacity is set at 1000 Mbps (to avoid any network congestion), and the maximum packet rate is set to 1000 packets per second. The operator device is kept at a distance of 40 cm from the shoulder of the user. Arm and wrist are kept at fixed positions while perceiving the force. To analyze the effect of propagation delay P_d on the estimated Weber threshold, one-way P_d is emulated on the system and is varied between 0–15 ms, increasing in steps of 5 ms. The average packetization delay is observed to be 0.13 ms in the operator side and 0.45 ms in the teleoperator side, which is much lower than the introduced propagation delay P_d.

2.2 Signed Distance Field Based Haptic Rendering

To generate the force signal at the teleoperator, haptic rendering of watertight objects like bunny [1] and teddy [2] are carried out. The bunny model used in the experiment has 4976 faces and 2490 vertices, and it is voxelized into $135 \times 142 \times 90$ grid cells, whereas the teddy model has 3192 faces and 1598 vertices. The teddy model is voxelized into $117 \times 143 \times 97$ voxels. Given a haptic interaction point H_{IP} and the object, the shortest distance between the point and the bounding object surface is obtained. Depending upon the sign of the distance $\phi(H_{IP})$, we can determine whether the interaction point lies inside $(\phi(H_{IP}) > 0)$/outside $(\phi(H_{IP}) < 0)$/on $(\phi(H_{IP}) = 0)$ the surface of an object.

The signed distance field is created for an object as in [4] and stored on a three-dimensional grid. During rendering, the H_{IP} position is first obtained, and depending upon the sign of distance $\phi(H_{IP})$, the presence of H_{IP} inside/outside the object is detected. If H_{IP} lies inside the object, force $F(H_{IP})$ is generated from the gradient using a suitable scaling constant k as follows, $F(H_{IP}) = k\phi(H_{IP})\nabla\phi(H_{IP}) \|\nabla\phi(H_{IP})\|_2^{-1}$.

2.3 Proposed Sampling Scheme

In this section, we discuss the proposed framework for adaptive sampling of force signal along with simultaneous Weber threshold estimation for an individual user.

As shown in Fig. 1, at the teleoperator, haptic and visual renderings of a solid object are carried out to simulate the teleoperation. The operator holds the device stylus and remotely explores the object at the teleoperator's side through the means of video and haptic information transmitted from teleoperator to operator. This interaction is captured and transmitted in the form of position and velocity on the forward channel to the teleoperator. The end-effector running at the teleoperator end generates a force signal which is then adaptively sampled,

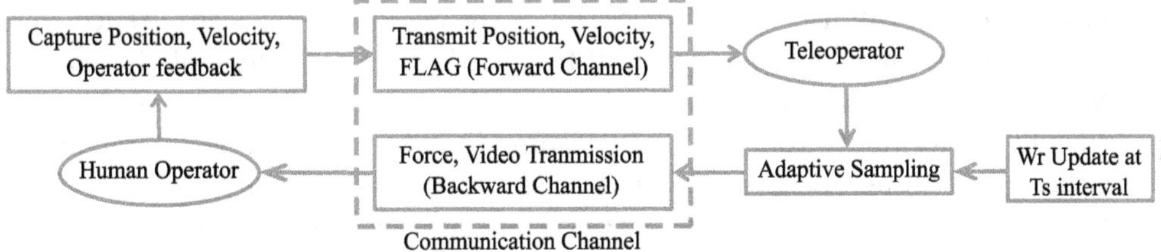

Fig. 1. Proposed scheme for real-time interaction driven adaptive sampling.

and if its relative magnitude is greater than the Weber threshold ρ at that instant, it is transmitted back to the operator on the backward channel. However ρ is not known apriori and needs to be estimated from the interaction itself.

We start with a very small value of ρ (let us call it W_r) at the beginning and use it to adaptively sample the data. Since the user experience at such a small value of W_r will not impede the perception of the user, after Ts interval W_r is incremented by 5% of its previous value, and the adaptive sampler is changed accordingly. This continues until the operator's experience is impaired. At this point, the operator sends a feedback signal (setting the FLAG bit TRUE in Fig. 1) through the forward channel to the teleoperator end. At the teleoperator end, when the FLAG is found to be TRUE, it is understood (see comments later) that the impairment in perception is due to loss of perceptually important samples and hence the threshold value W_r is decremented agressively by 20% of its current value while passing the signal through the adaptive Weber sampler before sending it through the backward channel after packetization. At the operator end, if the user experience is not compromised then the threshold W_r is again raised slowly by 5% else it is further decremented by 20%. The process continues until the teleoperation ends.

A few comments are in order at this point. We implicitly assume that (a) there is no communication delay during teleoperation as it introduces a hysteresis behaviour between exerted and perceived forces, (b) the control loop under which the teleoperation is performed does not suffer from transparency related impairments and (c) any perceptual impairment during teleoperation is due to a higher choice of the Weber threshold W_r when the loss in information received at the operator end becomes perceptually significant.

It is well accepted in the literature that the Weber threshold ρ lies in between $0.04 \leq \rho \leq 0.20$. Hence instead of starting the teleoperator with a value of W_r to be zero, we set $W_{r_{min}} = 0.04$. As the W_r value is slowly incremented, we saturate $W_{r_{max}}$ at 0.20, if required. The choice of an incremental step size of 5% was adhoc, but was found to be a good compromise between being aggressive or sluggish in approaching $W_r \rightarrow \rho$ (true value of the threshold) when the user continues to enjoy the interaction perceptually. A higher choice of increment requires the user to provide feedback more frequently, thus distracting the user away from the assigned task. Similarly, the choice of the decremental step size to be 20% is motivated by the fact that the system should quickly come out of the impaired deadzone of sampling to reduce the scope of continuation of perceptual impairment on overall user experience. Hence the choice of step sizes is such that perceptual impairment happens quite infrequently for the benefit of the user.

Now we address the question on how does the user attend to the problem of perceptual impairment. To start with, assume that the user is always in contact with the object to be operated on, it is expected that there will be always some force feedback and there will be some variation in it due to user interaction. When W_r is small, the user will feel such changes more often and when W_r becomes very high (say, close to 0.20), the user will not be experiencing much changes while still manipulating the object, thus impairing the experience. An immediate reduction in the W_r tries to make the changes in force feedback a lot more perceivable. In the event the end-effector is not in contact with the user, any choice of value for W_r is good as there will be no force feedback and W_r will rapidly approach the value $W_{r_{max}}$.

We now discuss how the FLAG is set to TRUE during the communication over the forward channel. The default value of FLAG is FALSE when W_r is continuously incremented by 5% at the backward channel. We attach a sound detector (a microphone that detects any audio utterance by the user, up to an appropriate choice of threshold to take care of ambient noise) to the user. Whenever the user experience worsens, the user is required to make some utterances which when detected, sets the FLAG to TRUE momentarily before being reset to FALSE. Thus the variable FLAG works on a monostable mode. When the received packet header at the teleoperator end has a FLAG value TRUE, the threshold W_r is decremented by 20%. It may be mentioned that we use HoIP (Haptics over Internet Protocol), as proposed in [7], which has the provision of padding such flags in the packet header for bilateral communication. It may also be noted that one may instead use a call button feedback or a vision based experience impairment detection technique through user specified gesticulation. However, we have found that the audio based technique is less distractive and has comparatively a lower latency without impairing the dexterity of the operator.

The Weber threshold at a given instant depends on the transmission of the FLAG sequence through the forward channel, which in turn, depends on the operator feedback. As is common in any telehaptic communication, we use a sampling rate of 1 kHz, generating up to a maximum of 1000 packets per second when no Weber threshold based adaptive sampler is used. A user can provide her feedback as per her experience on interaction while the Weber threshold W_r is updated every Ts. We select $T = 2\,\text{s}$ or $T = 3\,\text{s}$, and within this interval, the value of W_r is held constant.

3 Experimental Results

Data Collection: The data is collected voluntarily from 16 male users following the standard ethical clearance of the university and the process of acquiring the data through informed consent of the users. The users, all right handed, were in the age-group of 22–34 years, out of which 10 users were unaware of the working of any haptic device before starting the experiment. The users did not have any history of neurophysiological illness. At the beginning of the experiment, every

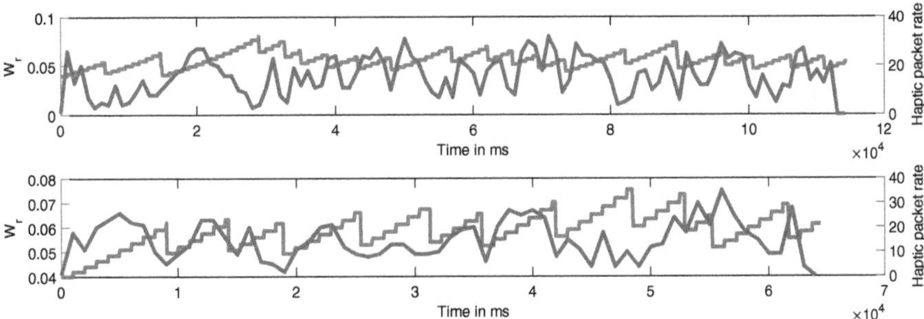

Fig. 2. Computed $W_r(t)$ and haptic packet rate for a given user for the object (top) bunny and (bottom) teddy with $T = 2\,\text{s}$ and $P_d = 0\,\text{ms}$.

user was introduced to the device, and an appropriate training was given to get them familiar with the device to perceive the kinesthetic force signals properly. The experiment was also explained to them in detail.

The experimental protocol was as follows. 3D point cloud data of some solid objects are rendered for haptic interaction using a standard distance field based method. The user is requested to move the interaction stylus in the YZ plane only (Y being the vertical direction), so that the rendered force is along the Z (away from the body) direction only. This allows us to avoid user sensitivity to directional change in force, if any [5]. The rendered force is maintained within the range [0, 3N]. At the emulator level, the propagation delay P_d is set at one of the following four values - 0, 5, 10 and 15 ms (see Sect. 2.1). While sending the force on the backward channel, the Weber threshold based sampling was done. The user orally gives the feedback whenever his interaction is perceived to be poor, as explained earlier. The Weber threshold W_r is updated at 2 s and 3 s interval (T) in two different experiments.

The total time required for the experiment is approximately 1 h per user per rendered object. To avoid physical or device fatigue, users were asked to perform the experiment in multiple sittings with each sitting not exceeding 20 min. During experimentation, users were asked to listen to music using headphone to avoid distractions in the laboratory, if any. Users were also asked to evaluate the experiment on a 5 point scale, with 5 being excellent and 1 being very poor, for different values of P_d and T based on the perceptual parameters: smoothness and experience [8]. The users were asked to rate the experiment relative to the baseline experiment (Sect. 2.1) on the standalone system with zero propagation and packetization delay and with no Weber sampling.

Results: For a given user, the computed W_r as a function of time is plotted for two different objects (bunny and teddy) in Fig. 2 for a propagation delay $P_d = 0\,\text{ms}$ and backward channel update time $T = 2\,\text{s}$. We observe that in both cases, the estimated Weber threshold ρ is quite reasonable (about 7%) and follows a similarly repetitive pattern. The saving in packet rate is quite substantial (about 20 packets per second are being transmitted) to warrant the use of the proposed method. The corresponding SNR of the received force signal is above 30 dB, possibly good enough for most haptic interactions.

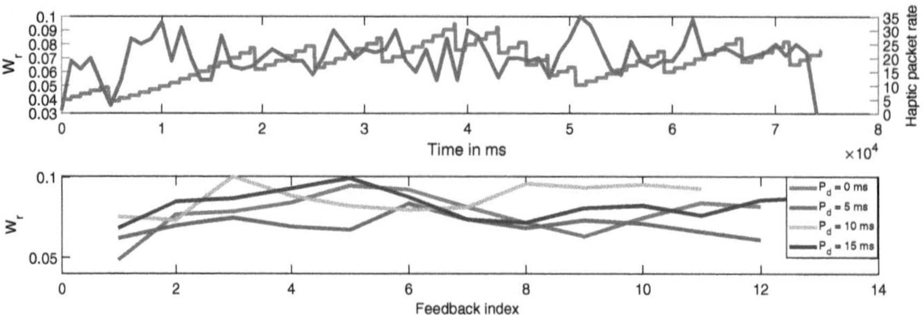

Fig. 3. (top) Computed $W_r(t)$ and haptic packet rate for the object teddy with $T = 3$ s and $P_d = 0$ ms. (bottom) Effect of varying propagation delay P_d on estimated Weber threshold $W_r(t)$ for the object teddy with $T = 3$ s for the same subject.

Table 1. Mean opinion score (MoS) and standard deviation (SD) on user study.

Parameters	$T = 2$ s								$T = 3$ s							
	$Pd = 0$ ms		$Pd = 5$ ms		$Pd = 10$ ms		$Pd = 15$ ms		$Pd = 0$ ms		$Pd = 5$ ms		$Pd = 10$ ms		$Pd = 15$ ms	
	MoS	SD	MoS	SD	MoS	SD	MoS	SD	MoS	SD	MoS	SD	MoS	SD	MoS	SD
Smoothness	4.75	0.45	4.06	0.77	3.00	0.63	2.19	1.05	4.56	0.51	4.00	0.52	3.06	0.68	2.19	0.91
Experience	4.75	0.45	4.38	0.62	3.31	0.60	2.56	0.89	4.75	0.45	4.25	0.45	3.31	0.60	2.48	0.96

As we slow down the backward channel update time T to 3 s, we notice from Fig. 3 (top) that the nature of the corresponding plot of $W_r(t)$ remains more or less the same. However, the updating being slow, as expected, there is a marginal increase in packet rate. Ideally the values of Weber threshold (ρ) will be slightly less than the $W_r(t)$ value at which the user provides a negative feedback. In Fig. 3 (bottom), we plot only the local peaks of $W_r(t)$ function against feedback index (at which the user responded). We repeat the experiment for the same user and for the same object for different values of P_d to study the effect of propagation delay. It may be observed that even though the haptic interaction becomes poorer as P_d increases (see Table 1), the computed value of ρ remains fairly unchanged, substantiating the appropriateness of the proposed method.

We present the result of subjective analysis of user experience for all 16 users for various values of propagation delay P_d and update interval T on two specific perceptual parameters, namely interaction smoothness and user experience, in Table 1. It can be seen that the user experience gets quite impaired if the propagation delay increases to 10 ms and beyond, suggesting that the proposed technique should work under the upcoming 5G communication, but not on the current 4G technology. We also note that both the suggested update intervals $T = 2$ s or $T = 3$ s are acceptable to the user.

4 Conclusions

In this paper, we demonstrated an experimental protocol on how to reduce the interactive haptic signal packet rate over the Internet between the operator and teleoperator when the Weber threshold is not known. However, it is observed that as the propagation delay increases, the immersiveness of the virtual system decreases. However, within the specified QoS of 5 ms delay of 5G technology, the proposed method will work well. Hence the method has the potential for application in telehaptic application over a short-haul communication. However, the stability of the proposed telehaptic loop under the quantization error and delay jitter requires further investigation. One also needs to study the suitability of the proposed method for two handed interactions when the Weber threshold may be different for each hand.

References

1. https://cs.uwaterloo.ca/~c2batty/bunny_watertight.obj
2. https://groups.csail.mit.edu/graphics/classes/6.837/F03/models/teddy.obj
3. WaNem. http://wanem.sourceforge.net/
4. Bridson, R.: Fluid Simulation for Computer Graphics. AK Peters/CRC Press (2015)
5. Chaudhuri, S., Bhardwaj, A.: Kinesthetic Perception: A Machine Learning Approach. Springer, Heidelberg (2017). https://doi.org/10.1007/978-981-10-6692-4
6. García-Pérez, M.A., Alcalá-Quintana, R., Woods, R.L., Peli, E.: Psychometric functions for detection and discrimination with and without flankers. Attention Percept. Psychophys. **73**(3), 829–853 (2011)
7. Gokhale, V., Dabeer, O., Chaudhuri, S.: HoIP: haptics over internet protocol. In: IEEE Haptic Audio Visual Environments and Games (HAVE), pp. 45–50. IEEE (2013)
8. Gokhale, V., Nair, J., Chaudhuri, S., Kakade, S.: Network-aware adaptive sampling for low bitrate telehaptic communication. In: Prattichizzo, D., Shinoda, H., Tan, H.Z., Ruffaldi, E., Frisoli, A. (eds.) EuroHaptics 2018. LNCS, vol. 10894, pp. 660–672. Springer, Cham (2018). https://doi.org/10.1007/978-3-319-93399-3_56
9. Hinterseer, P., Hirche, S., Chaudhuri, S., Steinbach, E., Buss, M.: Perception-based data reduction and transmission of haptic data in telepresence and teleaction systems. IEEE Trans. Sig. Process. **56**(2), 588–597 (2008)
10. Hirche, S., Buss, M.: Transparent data reduction in networked telepresence and teleaction systems. Part II: time-delayed communication. Presence: Teleoper. Virt. Environ. **16**(5), 532–542 (2007)
11. Jafari, A., Nabeel, M., Singh, H., Ryu, J.: Stable and transparent teleoperation over communication time-delay: observer-based input-to-state stable approach. In: IEEE Haptics Symposium, pp. 235–240 (2016)
12. Nadjarbashi, O.F., Najdovski, Z., Nahavandi, S.: Event-driven data transmission in variable-delay network. In: IEEE International Conference on Systems, Man, and Cybernetics, pp. 1681–1686 (2017)
13. Pongrac, H., et al.: Limitations of human 3D force discrimination. Human-Centered Robotics Systems (2006)
14. Uddin, R., Ryu, J.: Predictive control approaches for bilateral teleoperation. Ann. Rev. Control **42**, 82–99 (2016)
15. Wichmann, F.A., Hill, N.J.: The psychometric function: I. fitting, sampling, and goodness of fit. Percept. Psychophys. **63**(8), 1293–1313 (2001)

16

Can Stiffness Sensations be Rendered in Virtual Reality using Mid-Air Ultrasound Haptic Technologies?

M. Marchal[1,2(✉)], G. Gallagher[3], A. Lécuyer[3], and C. Pacchierotti[4]

[1] Univ. Rennes, INSA, IRISA, Inria, CNRS, Rennes, France
maud.marchal@irisa.fr
[2] IUF, Paris, France
[3] Inria, Univ. Rennes, IRISA, Rennes, France
[4] CNRS, Univ. Rennes, Inria, IRISA, Rennes, France

Abstract. Mid-air haptics technologies convey haptic sensations without any direct contact between the user and the interface. A popular example of this technology is focused ultrasound. It works by modulating the phase of an array of ultrasound emitters so as to generate focused points of oscillating high pressure, which in turn elicit haptic sensations on the user's skin. Whilst using focused ultrasound to convey haptic sensations is becoming increasingly popular in Virtual Reality (VR), few studies have been conducted into understanding how to render virtual object properties. In this paper, we evaluate the capability of focused ultrasound arrays to simulate varying stiffness sensations in VR. We carry out a user study enrolling 20 participants, showing that focused ultrasound haptics can well provide the sensation of interacting with objects of different stiffnesses. Finally, we propose four representative VR use cases to show the potential of rendering stiffness sensations using this mid-air haptics.

1 Introduction

Focused airborne ultrasound is nowadays the most mature and popular technology able to provide mid-air haptics. Arrays of ultrasonic transducers can produce phase-shifted acoustic waves which constructively interfere at points in space called focal points and destructively interfere elsewhere, conveying haptic sensations by varying acoustic radiation pressure on the skin. Focused ultrasounds have been already employed in several applications of Virtual Reality (VR) [4,5,9,10]. However, despite the recent popularity of mid-air ultrasound technologies, to the best of our knowledge, no study has analyzed if and to what extent ultrasound haptic arrays can provide effective stiffness sensations. Most work using this technology in VR has been in fact dedicated to the rendering of shapes [6,9] and textures [1].

This work studies the capability of mid-air ultrasound haptics of rendering stiffness sensations when interacting with virtual objects. More specifically, we aim at identifying the differential threshold for stiffness perception when using a focused ultrasound array to render objects in VR. Of course, it is important to highlight that we are not rendering force feedback as if the user was interacting with a real piston. Our objective is to understand whether we can elicit/simulate stiffness sensations using focused ultrasound arrays. Our paper comprises a perceptual evaluation as well as four VR use cases (see Fig. 3), where we show the potential of our approach as an alternative to contact haptic feedback [2,11] in VR scenarios.

2 Perceptual Evaluation

2.1 Experimental Setup

To validate focused ultrasound as a tool to provide stiffness sensations in VR, we prepared an experimental setup enabling participants to interact with 1-D stiffnesses. The setup is shown in Fig. 1. The virtual environment was composed of a virtual piston placed on a black table. The real environment was composed of an Ultrahaptics STRATOS platform, which is a commercial focused ultrasound array. It comprises a 16×16 planar array of transducers emitting 40 kHz ultrasound in an upward direction. The virtual environment was shown to the participant through an HTC Vive VR headset. A HTC Vive Tracker was attached to the dominant wrist of the participants to track the motion of their hands, and a virtual hand avatar mimicked this motion in the virtual environment. Finally, an HTC Vive controller was held by the participant in their non-dominant hand to answer the in-screen perceptual questions, and a pair of noise-canceling headphones avoided potential effects due to auditory cues arising from the device operation.

2.2 Haptic Rendering

The task consisted in comparing the stiffness of two virtual pistons. Each virtual piston was modeled as a 1-D spring following Hooke's law. Whenever a user enters in contact with the piston, the system simulates a spring-like feedback, where the pressure commanded by the Ultrahaptics device is defined by $p = k(z_0 - z) + p_0$ if the user contacts the piston, 0 otherwise. k is the simulated stiffness of the piston (in Pa/m, sound pressure over displacement), z the current altitude of the piston, $z_0 = 30\,\text{cm}$ its resting position, $\Delta z = z_0 - z$ its current compression, and p_0 = 146.87 dB SPL (441 Pa) the absolute detection threshold we registered at 30 cm (when $\Delta z = 0$). The piston is fully compressed

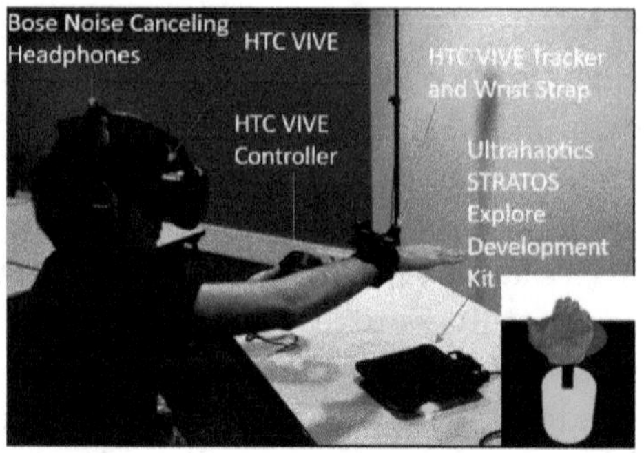

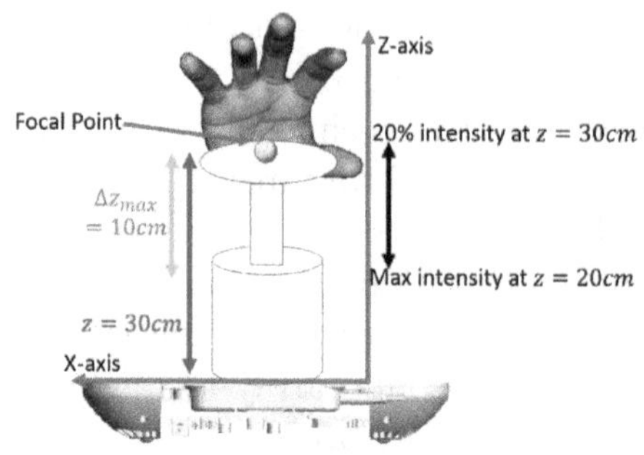

Fig. 1. (Left) Setup: subjects interact with the Ultrahaptics interface while wearing a HTC Vive display. The dominant hand is tracked using a Vive Tracker while the other hand holds a Vive Controller to answer the questions. The virtual scene with the piston is shown as an inset. (Right) Visual representation of the focal point and its relation with the displacement of the piston.

at $z = 20$ cm ($\Delta z_{\max} = 10$ cm). The Ultrahaptics device generates localized pressure at a designated focal point. We rendered this point at the centroid of the upper plate of the piston (see Fig. 1). When the user interacts with the piston, this point results at the center of the user's palm as well as the center of the ultrasound array. As soon as the user contacts the piston at its resting position ($z = 30$ cm, $\Delta z = 0$ cm), the device starts generating a pressure on the palm. This pressure increases as the user presses the piston down, reaching its maximum when the piston is fully compressed ($z = 20$ cm, $\Delta z_{\max} = 10$ cm). The STRATOS platform can provide a maximum of 163.35 dB SPL at $z = 20$ cm and p_0 thus represents 15% of the maximum power. We rendered the focal point with the Ultrahaptics device using spatiotemporal modulation (STM), introduced by Kappus and Long [8]. In STM, focal points are generated with a fixed frequency (usually the maximum achievable by the device, i.e., 40 kHz). Since this frequency is very high, it poses significantly fewer constraints on the temporal evolution of the peak intensity and focal point position. Frier et al. [3] have investigated the trade-off between pattern repetition rate in STM and perceived intensity. A study on human's detection of focal points and basic shapes rendered via focused ultrasound stimuli can be found in [4].

2.3 Experimental Procedure

Participants were first required to fill out a pre-experiment questionnaire. Then, they were asked to wear the HTC Vive headset, tracker, controller (see Fig. 1). Participants had to compare two pistons with different rendered stiffness, modeled by a 1D spring law, as detailed in Sect. 2.2. At the beginning of each interaction, the virtual environment only showed a transparent hand, marking the target hand position for starting the task. Before the start of the first interaction, the virtual hand of the participant was calibrated to ensure it matched the transparent hand along the three different axes. Once participants placed their hand at the starting position, the piston appeared right below it. This calibration phase prevents from too many wrist motions of the user's hand since the motion between the starting position and the piston is straightforward along the vertical axis. Participants were then requested to touch the top of the piston and press it down. As soon as the hand contacted the upper plate of the piston, the latter became green. Participants were asked to press onto the piston until it was fully compressed, which was indicated by the piston becoming red. At this point, participants moved the hand up, releasing the piston. After that, they were asked to interact in a similar way with a second piston. After this second interaction, participants were finally asked to judge *which* of the two pistons felt *stiffer*. One piston served as a reference, displaying a reference stiffness k_{ref}, while the other piston displayed a variable stiffness k_{test}. After preliminary testings, we considered 6 values of test stiffness k_{test} to be compared with 3 values of reference stiffness k_{ref}.

The three stiffness values of the reference piston were:

- $k_{ref,1} = 7358$ Pa/m (155.39 dB SPL when $\Delta z = z_{\max}$, which is 40% of the device power range).
- $k_{ref,2} = 13242$ Pa/m (158.91 dB SPL when $\Delta z = z_{\max}$, 60% of the range),
- $k_{ref,3} = 19126$ Pa/m (161.41 dB SPL when $\Delta z = z_{\max}$, 80% of the range),

The six values of the test piston were: +5884 Pa/m (20% of the device power range when $\Delta z = z_{\max}$), +2942 Pa/m (10%), +1471 Pa/m (5%), −5884 Pa/m, −2942 Pa/m, −1471 Pa/m with respect to the reference stiffness.

2.4 Conditions and Experimental Design

Two conditions are considered in our experimental design:

- **C1** is the difference of stiffness between the reference piston and the test piston, $|k_{ref} - k_{test}|$.
- **C2** corresponds to a binary variable, which is true if the piston perceived as the stiffest is indeed the one rendered with a higher stiffness constant.

The order of presentation of the two pistons was counterbalanced to avoid any order effect: every couple of pistons was presented in all orders. The starting reference was also alternated to ensure that fatigue did not influence the last block. Thus, participants were presented with 90 trials per reference stiffness (270 in total), divided in 5 blocks of 6 trials in a randomized order for each block. The experiment lasted approximately 40 min, with breaks between the blocks.

2.5 Participants and Collected Data

Twenty participants (16 males, 4 females) took part to the experiment, all of whom were self-identified right-handed. 18 of them had previous experience with haptic interfaces. All were naive with respect to the study objectives. The age range of the participants was between 21 and 29 years (M = 24).

For each couple of pistons, we collected as an objective measure the participant's answer. This answer corresponds to the piston (first or second) which was reported by the participant as the stiffest. The measure was then collected as a true discovery rate if the answer corresponds to the stiffest value rendered. Participants also completed a subjective questionnaire. The first set of questions was asked three times, after the 5 blocks dedicated to one reference stiffness, using a 7-item Likert scale: (Q1): I felt confident when choosing the response after each interaction; (Q2): After the experiment, I felt tired; (Q3): The task was easy; (Q4): It felt like pressing a real piston. Then, at the end of the experiment, we asked them to answer two open questions: (Q5): Would you describe what you felt as stiffness? If not, please attempt to describe it; (Q6): Do you any have any further comment or suggestion?

3 Results

Reference stiffness: $k_{ref,1}$. Answers to the questionnaire regarding confidence (Q1) ranged from 2 (nearly very unconfident) to 7 (very confident) out of 7, with a mean of 4.75 and standard deviation (SD) 1.2. Regarding fatigue (Q2), answers ranged from 1 (not fatigued) to 6 (moderately fatigued) out of 7, with a mean of 4.1 (SD = 1.3). When the user was asked how easy the task was (Q3), answers ranged from 4 (slightly easy) to 7 (very easy) out of 7, with a mean of 5.45 (SD = 0.9). The reported realness of the piston (Q4) ranged from 1 (not real at all) to 6 (moderately real) out of 7, with a mean of 3.6 (SD = 1.5). Figure 2a shows the psychometric curve as well as the mean and standard deviation for each comparison piston. We obtained a JND value of 20% using a 75% threshold, along with a Point of Subjective Equality (PSE) of 2.16%.

Reference stiffness: $k_{ref,2}$. Answers to the questionnaire regarding confidence (Q1) ranged from 2 to 6 out of 7, with a mean of 4 and SD 1.5. Regarding fatigue (Q2), answers ranged from 1 to 6 out of 7, with a mean of 4.25 and SD 1.5. When the user was asked how easy the task was (Q3), answers ranged from 3 to 7 out of 7, with a mean of 5.05 and SD 1.3. The reported realness of the piston (Q4) ranged from 1 to 6 out of 7, with a mean of 4 and SD 1.6. Figure 2b shows the psychometric curve as well as the mean and standard deviation for each comparison piston. Under this reference, a 75% differential threshold of 32% was obtained with a PSE of 3.65%.

Reference stiffness: $k_{ref,3}$. Answers to the questionnaire regarding confidence (Q1) ranged from 2 to 7 out of 7, with a mean of 4.1 and SD 1.3. Regarding fatigue (Q2), answers ranged from 2 to 6 out of 7, with a mean of 4.3 and SD 1.4. When the user was asked how easy the task was (Q3), answers ranged from 2 to 7 out of 7, with a mean of 5.25 and SD 1.4. The reported realness of the piston (Q4) ranged from 2 to 6 out of 7, with a mean of 3.94 and SD 1.5. Figure 2c shows the psychometric curve as well as the mean and standard deviation for each comparison piston. Differently from the other curves, this time we were not

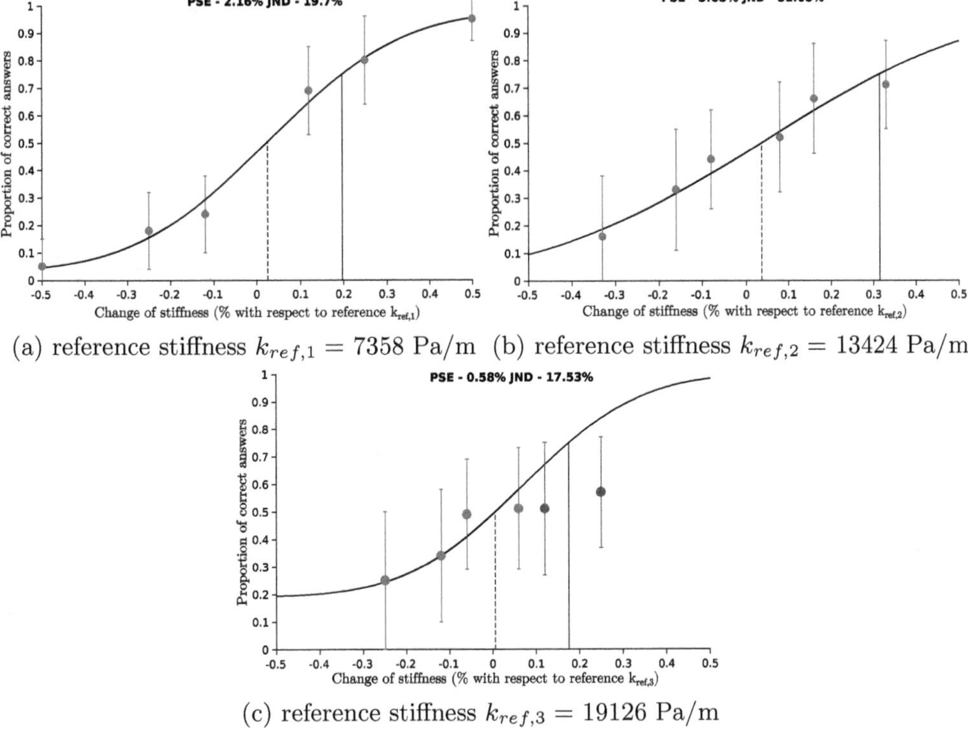

(a) reference stiffness $k_{ref,1} = 7358$ Pa/m (b) reference stiffness $k_{ref,2} = 13424$ Pa/m

(c) reference stiffness $k_{ref,3} = 19126$ Pa/m

Fig. 2. Psychometric curves for the three reference stiffness values, fitting a cumulative Gaussian to the data. We plot the proportion of correct answers in function of the percentage increase in stiffness with respect to the reference one $k_{ref,1}$. The vertical dashed and solid lines represent the PSE and the 75% differential threshold. Error bars represent standard deviation. (Color figure online)

able to reach proportions of correct answers close to 1 on the right-hand side of the curve. This result could be due to the fact that the considered reference stiffness $k_{ref,3}$ requires pressures close to the device maximum, i.e., 161.41 dB SPL when $\Delta z = z_{\max}$, which is the 80% of the device power range. For this reason, it was not possible to test large increments. Another explanation for this behavior could be the presence of refractions and artifacts generated by the acoustic waves, which become more intense as the peak pressure increases and interfere with the overall perception of stiffness. This latter point is supported by how users described the haptic sensation over the three reference conditions. In fact, while during experiments on reference stiffness $k_{ref,1}$ and $k_{ref,2}$ users most often reported to feel a "circular shape", during experiments on $k_{ref,3}$ users started to report feeling "lines" or "bars". The focal point generated by the device should remain circular at all intensity levels. For this reason, we evaluated the psychometric curve only taking into account the stiffness intensities for which users reported feeling a circular shape (blue points in Fig. 2c). Under this reference, a 75% differential threshold of 18% was obtained with a PSE of 0.58%.

Post-experiment Questionnaire. All users were able to detect that the force increased over the displacement. However, only 48% of the participants were able to feel that the minimum pressure they felt when they first interacted with the piston was always the same (146.86 dB SPL, 15% of the full range). When asked if the sensation they felt reassembled stiffness (Q5), 80% of users said that it did. The remaining 20% could not express what they felt, but still recognized an increase in force. When asked to describe the sensations they felt over the duration of all 60 pistons, answers ranged from "feeling a real piston" to feeling a "stream", "circular air flows", and "some kind of resistance".

4 Use Cases in Virtual Reality

We demonstrate the viability of rendering stiffness sensations using ultrasound focused arrays through four use cases in Virtual Reality, shown in Fig. 3[1].

The first use case (see Fig. 3a) represents a scene at a carnival fair. It is composed of a stand at a carnival fair, featuring a pump, a release button, and a balloon to be inflated. Users are asked to inflate a balloon by repeatedly pressing on the pump. Every time the pump is pressed, it becomes a little stiffer to render the increased pressure inside the balloon. The second use case (see Fig. 3b) is composed of a small piano placed on a table. Piano keys are generally weighted having a higher stiffness for the lower register and a lower stiffness for the higher register. We render four different octaves, each having variable degrees of stiffness. Users are able to select a different set of octaves by pressing a button next to the piano. The third use case (see Fig. 3c) is composed of a hospital room with a virtual patient lying upon a bed. A 2-cm-wide area on the patient's stomach was rendered stiffer than the rest. Users are instructed to palpate the users stomach and indicate where they feel the stiffer region. The fourth use case (see Fig. 3d) is composed of four blocks that need to be pressed in a certain sequence to open a door containing a treasure chest. Each block has a different stiffness. To access the treasure, users must press the blocks in order of stiffness, from the lowest to the highest. On top of the door, there are four lights, that indicate the progress of the task.

5 Discussion and Conclusions

Ultrasound haptics is considered a very promising technology, as it is able to convey compelling haptic sensations without any direct contact between the user and the interface. However, as only recently ultrasound arrays have become available, very few works have studied the type of haptic sensations we can render with this technology. This work evaluates whether it is possible to render stiffness sensations in Virtual Reality using haptic feedback generated by ultrasound focused arrays. To calculate the JND and the PSE for this type of stiffness sensation, we carried out a human subject study enrolling 20 participants. Subjects

[1] A video is available at https://youtu.be/sJKYV1nI_IY.

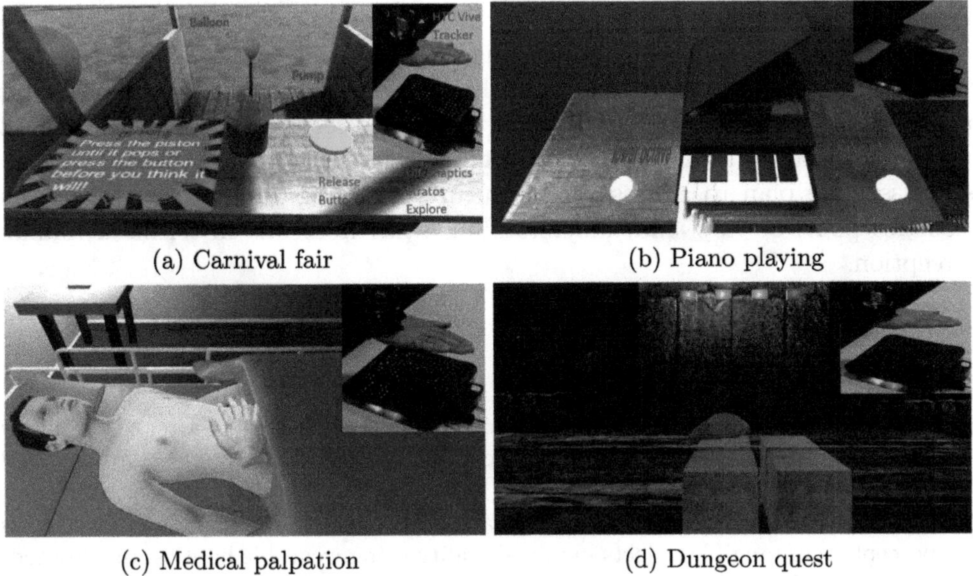

(a) Carnival fair

(b) Piano playing

(c) Medical palpation

(d) Dungeon quest

Fig. 3. We implemented four use cases in Virtual Reality. We render different stiffness sensations using the ultrasound stimuli generated by our Ultrahaptics interface. (Color figure online)

were asked to compare the perceived stiffness of multiple virtual pistons, whose stiffness was rendered by an Ultrahaptics device via ultrasound haptic stimuli. In the literature, researchers have shown that the JND for stiffness discrimination can range from 8 to 23% [7,12]. Jones and Hunter [7] have reported an average JND of 23% for participants comparing the stiffness of springs simulated using two servo-controlled electromagnetic linear motors. Each motor was coupled to one wrist of the subject. Tan et al. [12] calculated the JND of stiffness for a task which required grasping two plates with the thumb and index fingers and squeezing them along a linear track. A force which resisted the squeeze, simulating different levels of stiffness, was generated by an electromechanical system. When subjects had to squeeze the plates always for a fixed displacement, the JND registered was of 8%; on the other hand, when the displacement was randomized from trial to trial, the JND was of 22%. Of course, all these works rendered stiffness by providing kinesthetic feedback.

In our study, we found JND of 17%, 31%, and 19% for the three reference stiffness values 7358 Pa/m, 13242 Pa/m, 19126 Pa/m (sound pressure over displacement), respectively. The subjective questionnaires show that most subjects indeed identified the provided haptic sensations as stiffness. These results prove that it is indeed possible to simulate stiffness sensations using ultrasound haptic feedback in VR. Four use cases showed the potential and viability of our approach in immersive VR applications. Despite these promising results, our study has some limitations. First, it is important to stress that the haptic sensations rendered by ultrasound arrays is of course different than the haptic sensations usually felt when pressing a piston. For this reason, our objective is to *simulate* stiffness sensations. Another drawback is that the behavior we registered when commanding pressures higher than 162.43 dB SPL (90% of the maximum power of the device). The circular focal point started to feel like something different (a "line", a "bar") and the stiffness recognition rate significantly degraded. This is an issue we plan to address in the future, studying what happens from an acoustics point of view and understanding what it means in terms of human perception.

References

1. Beattie, D., Georgiou, O., Harwood, A., Clark, R., Long, B., Carter, T.: Mid-air haptic textures from graphics. In: Proceedings of the IEEE World Haptics (WiP Paper) (2019)
2. De Tinguy, X., Pacchierotti, C., Marchal, M., Lécuyer, A.: Enhancing the stiffness perception of tangible objects in mixed reality using wearable haptics. In: Proceedings of the IEEE Conference on Virtual Reality and 3D User Interfaces (VR), pp. 81–90 (2018)
3. Frier, W., et al.: Using spatiotemporal modulation to draw tactile patterns in mid-air. In: Prattichizzo, D., Shinoda, H., Tan, H.Z., Ruffaldi, E., Frisoli, A. (eds.) EuroHaptics 2018. LNCS, vol. 10893, pp. 270–281. Springer, Cham (2018). https://doi.org/10.1007/978-3-319-93445-7_24
4. Howard, T., Gallagher, G., Lécuyer, A., Pacchierotti, C., Marchal, M.: Investigating the recognition of local shapes using mid-air ultrasound haptics. In: Proceedings of IEEE World Haptics, pp. 503–508 (2019)
5. Howard, T., Marchal, M., Lécuyer, A., Pacchierotti, C.: Pumah: pan-tilt ultrasound mid-air haptics for larger interaction workspace in virtual reality. IEEE Trans. Haptics **13**, 38–44 (2020)
6. Inoue, S., Makino, Y., Shinoda, H.: Designing stationary airborne ultrasonic 3D tactile object. In: Proceedings of the IEEE/SICE International Symposium System Integration, pp. 159–162 (2014)
7. Jones, L.A., Hunter, I.W.: A perceptual analysis of stiffness. Exp. Brain Res. **79**(1), 150–156 (1990)
8. Kappus, B., Long, B.: Spatiotemporal modulation for mid-air haptic feedback from an ultrasonic phased array. J. Acoust. Soc. Am. **143**(3), 1836–1836 (2018)
9. Long, B., Seah, S.A., Carter, T., Subramanian, S.: Rendering volumetric haptic shapes in mid-air using ultrasound. ACM Trans. Graph. **33**(6), 181 (2014)
10. Makino, Y., Furuyama, Y., Inoue, S., Shinoda, H.: Haptoclone (haptic-optical clone) for mutual tele-environment by real-time 3D image transfer with midair force feedback. In: Proceedings of the ACM CHI, pp. 1980–1990 (2016)
11. Salazar, D.S.V., Pacchierotti, C., De Tinguy, X., Maciel, A., Marchal, M.: Altering the stiffness, friction, and shape perception of tangible objects in virtual reality using wearable haptics. IEEE Trans. Haptics **13**, 167–174 (2020)
12. Tan, H., Durlach, N., Beauregard, G., Srinivasan, M.: Manual discrimination of compliance using active pinch grasp: the roles of force and work cues. Percept. Psychophys. **57**, 495–510 (1995)

17

Rendering Ultrasound Pressure Distribution on Hand Surface in Real-Time

Atsushi Matsubayashi(✉), Yasutoshi Makino, and Hiroyuki Shinoda

The University of Tokyo, Tokyo, Japan
Matsubayashi@hapis.k.u-tokyo.ac.jp

Abstract. In this paper, we propose a method for rendering the pressure distribution on the skin surface of a hand in real-time using an ultrasonic phased array. Our method generates a polygon mesh model representing the hand shape by fitting a rigid template to the point cloud captured by depth sensors. Obtaining the entire hand shape as a mesh model enables to solve scattering problem to generate a precise distribution on the hand surface. Therefor, for example, our method can control the width of the distribution on the fingertip according to the size of the contact area with the virtual object. We have experimentally verified that considering the scattering on the mesh model contributes to accurate pressure pattern reproduction.

Keywords: Mid-air haptics · Scattering problem · Airborne ultrasound

1 Introduction

Ultrasound haptics is a technology to generate a tactile sensation on a human skin by creating a point with high sound pressure using an ultrasound phased array. Since a tactile presentation by airborne ultrasound was first demonstrated in 2008 [9], many attempts have been made to create haptic images in the air using this technology. In order to create a pressure distribution with the desired shape in the air, many methods solve the inverse problem using the relationship between the sound pressure of control points and the complex amplitudes of the transducers [4,6,10]. Since the intensity of a stimulus felt on the skin depends only on the amplitude of the sound pressure, the phase of the target sound pressure distribution can be set arbitrarily in the inverse problem. Properly setting this phase by solving eigenproblem [10] or phase retrieval problem [6] widens the range of reproducible haptic image. Some method, furthermore, present a stronger stimulus by tracking the hand and generating a pressure distribution only on the contact area of the hand touching the image, allowing the user to identify the shape of the haptic image more clearly [10,11]. However, since these above methods do not consider scattering on the hand surface, the pressure

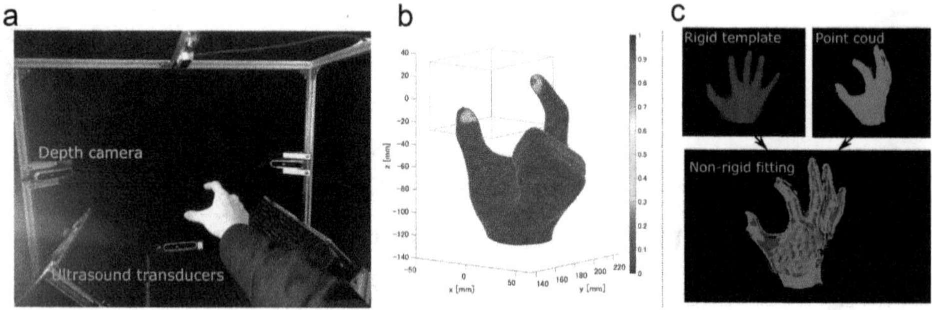

Fig. 1. a, b) The phase of the ultrasound transducers is determined according to the hand mesh model generated from the depth information acquired by depth cameras, and the desired pressure distribution is generated at the fingertip. c) By fitting the template rigid model to the point cloud, a non-rigid mesh model is dynamically generated in real-time.

distribution actually generated on the skin surface differs from target pressure distribution to be reproduced. Solving the scattering problem will enable more accurate reconstruction of the pressure pattern. Inoue et al. have proposed a method for generating a stronger focal point by considering the scattering on a polygon mesh model of a finger [7]. They demonstrated that a stronger ultrasound focus could be created by solving a scattering problem using a static mesh model, but it has not been possible to control the pressure distribution on the mesh model dynamically generated in real-time.

In this paper, we propose a method to render the pressure distribution in real-time on the polygon mesh model deforming according to the hand shape. In this method, the shape of the hand placed above a transducer array is aquired with multiple cameras as shown in Fig. 1 (a), and the hand polygon mesh model deforms non-rigidly to fit this shape. The scattering model formulates the relationship between a sound pressure pattern on the mesh model and phases of the ultrasound transducers in the style of the boundary element method. Based on this relationship, our method optimize both phases of transducers and phases of target pressure distribution to generate the desired pattern at any position on the hand surface. For example, as shown in Fig. 1 (b) our method can generate a distribution according to the size of the contacting region with a virtual object.

2 Method

2.1 Generation of Mesh Model

In order to dynamically generate a polygon mesh model of the hand, we used a mesh reconstruction technique similar to that proposed by Zollhöfer et al. [12]. Mesh reconstruction process consists of two phases. First, a rigid template is created by scanning the hand with a fixed form using multiple depth cameras. Then, as shown in Fig. 1 (c), a non-rigid mesh model is generated by fitting the rigid template to the point cloud obtained from the depth cameras. We used the fitting method proposed by Dou et al. [5]. which has the advantage of being able to generate a mesh model that closely matches the skin surface of the actual hand compared to skeletal hand tracking methods used, for instance, in Leap Motion [2]. This is an important property for controlling the pressure distribution on the hand surface.

2.2 Scattering Model of Hand Surface

The relationship between the sound pressure on the faces of the mesh model and the phases of the ultrasound transducers is formulated in style of the boundary element method, similar to Inoue's adaptive focusing method [7]. The sound pressure $p(\boldsymbol{r}) \in \mathbb{C}$ scattered on the smooth surface Ω of a sound-hard rigid body is given by the following boundary integral Eq. [3].

$$\frac{1}{2}p(\boldsymbol{r}) = p_{inc}(\boldsymbol{r}) - \int_{\Omega} p(\boldsymbol{r})\frac{\partial g(\boldsymbol{r},\boldsymbol{s})}{\partial \boldsymbol{n}} dS, \tag{1}$$

where g is the Helmholtz green function, and p_{inc} is the incident wave from the transducers. In our method, this is simplified by a spherical wave with directivity D_n as

$$p_{inc}(\boldsymbol{r}) = \sum_n D_n(\boldsymbol{r})\frac{e^{-jk\|\boldsymbol{r}-\boldsymbol{x}_n\|}}{\|\boldsymbol{r}-\boldsymbol{x}_n\|}a_n e^{\phi_n}, \tag{2}$$

where $a_n \in \mathbb{R}, \phi_n \in \mathbb{R}$ and $\boldsymbol{x}_n \in \mathbb{R}^3$ are the amplitude, phase and position of a transducer $n \in \{1, \cdots N\}$ respectively. To reduce computational cost of the optimization, we set the amplitude constant, i.e. $a_n = a$.

When the boundary surface is represented by a polygon mesh and the sound pressure and the gradient of the Green's function are approximated to be constant on each face of the mesh, the boundary integral equation (1) is discretized as follows:

$$B\left(p_1, \cdots, p_M\right)^{\mathrm{T}} = G\left(e^{\phi_1}, \cdots, e^{\phi_N}\right)^{\mathrm{T}}, \tag{3}$$

where

$$B = \begin{pmatrix} \frac{\partial g}{\partial n}(\boldsymbol{y}_1,\boldsymbol{y}_1)A_1 + \frac{1}{2} & \cdots & \frac{\partial g}{\partial n}(\boldsymbol{y}_1,\boldsymbol{y}_M)A_M \\ \vdots & \ddots & \vdots \\ \frac{\partial g}{\partial n}(\boldsymbol{y}_M,\boldsymbol{y}_1)A_1 & \cdots & \frac{\partial g}{\partial n}(\boldsymbol{y}_M,\boldsymbol{y}_M)A_M + \frac{1}{2} \end{pmatrix}, \tag{4}$$

$$G = \begin{pmatrix} D_1(\boldsymbol{y}_1)\frac{ae^{-jk\|\boldsymbol{y}_1-\boldsymbol{x}_1\|}}{\|\boldsymbol{y}_1-\boldsymbol{x}_1\|} & \cdots & D_N(\boldsymbol{y}_1)\frac{ae^{-jk\|\boldsymbol{y}_1-\boldsymbol{x}_N\|}}{\|\boldsymbol{y}_1-\boldsymbol{x}_N\|} \\ \vdots & \ddots & \vdots \\ D_1(\boldsymbol{y}_M)\frac{ae^{-jk\|\boldsymbol{y}_M-\boldsymbol{x}_1\|}}{\|\boldsymbol{y}_M-\boldsymbol{x}_1\|} & \cdots & D_N(\boldsymbol{y}_M)\frac{ae^{-jk\|\boldsymbol{y}_M-\boldsymbol{x}_N\|}}{\|\boldsymbol{y}_M-\boldsymbol{x}_N\|} \end{pmatrix}, \tag{5}$$

and $p_m \in \mathbb{C}, \boldsymbol{y}_m \in \mathbb{R}^3$ and $A_m \in \mathbb{R}$ is the sound pressure, position, and area of a face $m \in \{1, \cdots, M\}$ of the mesh model respectively.

2.3 Optimizing Phases of Ultrasound Transducers

Given the target sound pressure amplitude $\boldsymbol{p}' = (p'_1, \cdots, p'_M)^{\mathrm{T}} \in \mathbb{R}^M$, we want to determine the phases of the transducers $\boldsymbol{\phi} = (\phi_1, \cdots, \phi_N)^{\mathrm{T}} \in \mathbb{R}^N$ and phases of the sound pressure $\boldsymbol{\theta} = (\theta_1, \cdots, \theta_M)^{\mathrm{T}} \in \mathbb{R}^M$ that minimize the least square error $\| \left(p'_1 e^{\theta_1}, \cdots, p'_M e^{\theta_M}\right)^{\mathrm{T}} - B^{-1} G \left(e^{\phi_1}, \cdots, e^{\phi_N}\right)^{\mathrm{T}} \|_2^2$. However, calculating the inverse of B is very computationally expensive, so we solve the following optimization problem instead (Fig. 2).

$$\min_{\boldsymbol{\phi}, \boldsymbol{\theta}} \|B \left(p'_1 e^{\theta_1}, \cdots, p'_M e^{\theta_M}\right)^{\mathrm{T}} - G \left(e^{\phi_1}, \cdots, e^{\phi_N}\right)^{\mathrm{T}} \|_2^2. \tag{6}$$

We solve this problem iteratively using the Levenberg-Marquardt method. At each iteration, parameters $\boldsymbol{t} = (\phi_1, \cdots, \phi_N, \theta_1, \cdots, \theta_M)^{\mathrm{T}}$ is updated as follows:

$$\boldsymbol{t} \leftarrow \boldsymbol{t} - (J^{\mathrm{T}} J + \lambda I)^{-1} J^{\mathrm{T}} \boldsymbol{f}, \tag{7}$$

where the residual vector $\boldsymbol{f} = B \left(p'_1 e^{\theta_1}, \cdots, p'_M e^{\theta_M}\right)^{\mathrm{T}} - G \left(e^{\phi_1}, \cdots, e^{\phi_N}\right)^{\mathrm{T}}$, and J is the Jacobian of $\boldsymbol{f}$. If the number of parameters $M + N$ is large, the time taken for an iteration will be very long, but when pressure is generated only in a local part such as a fingertip, excluding zero pressure faces can save computation time.

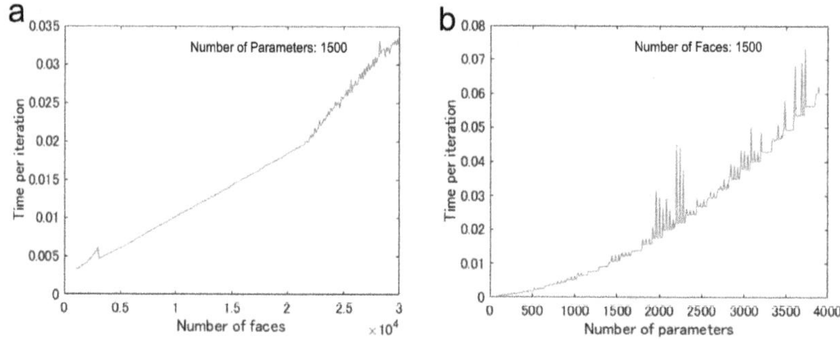

Fig. 2. a) The time per iteration against the number of faces. b) the time per iteration against the number of parameters

3 Implementation

The above algorithms were implemented with CUDA on two GeForce RTX 2080 Ti GPUs. One is used for mesh generation algorithm and the other is used for phase optimization. We measured the time taken for one iteration of the phase optimization in this environment. Figure 3 shows the time per iteration against the number of faces and parameters. The number of parameters is the sum of the number of transducers and the number of faces with non-zero pressure. In consideration of this result, possible resolution of the pressure distribution and

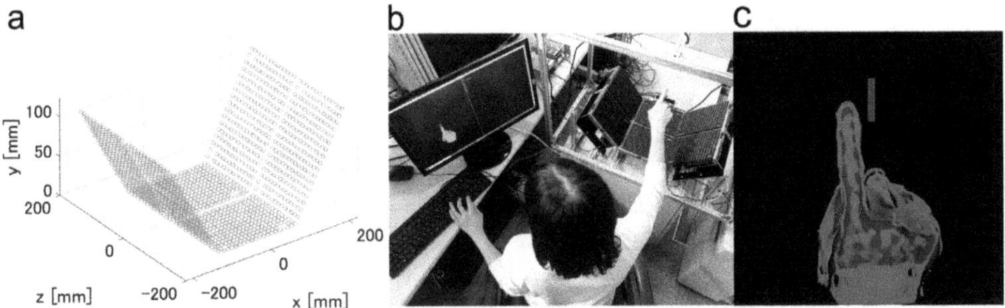

Fig. 3. a) The coordinate system and the arrangement of the ultrasound transducers in the experimental setup. b,c) The participants sat in front of the system and touched the box checking the position of the hand and box displayed on a LCD.

the limitations of the devices used, we set the number of faces to about 10,000 and the number of transducers to 1496. Therefore the time per iteration is about 10 ms, so we set the update frequency of the phase to 20 Hz with five iteration.

We constructed an experimental setup as shown in Fig. 1 (a). We installed Intel RealSense Depth Camera D415 [1] to measure the hand. The resolution of the depth image captured by each camera is 640 $\times$ 360, and the refresh rate as well as the update frequency of the mesh generation is 30 Hz. The architecture of the ultrasound transducer array unit is that proposed by Inoue et al [8]. The resonant frequency of the transducer is 40 kHz, and 200 Hz amplitude modulation is applied to make the tactile stimulus easier to perceive. Figure 3 (a) shows the coordinate system and arrangement of the ultrasound transducers in our setup.

4 Numerical Analysis

We performed numerical simulation to verify how close the distribution could be to the target in the experimental setup.

Figure 4 shows the simulation results of our method. In the target distribution (a1-a3), a constant pressure is applied to faces inside a box-shaped region. The width of the box is 5 mm, 8 mm and 11 mm in a1, a2 and a3 respectively. It can be seen that the distribution generated by our method (b1-b3) is close to the target and changes according to the width of the box. Figure 4 (c1-c3) shows the simulation result of the phase optimization performed without consideration of the scattering, which means replacing matrix B in our algorithm with the identity matrix. The result suggest an appropriate distribution cannot be generated without considering scattering. Our method can be applied to the case of touching with multiple fingers as well. The Fig. 4 (a4, b4 and c4) shows the simulation result of the case where a virtual box is grasped.

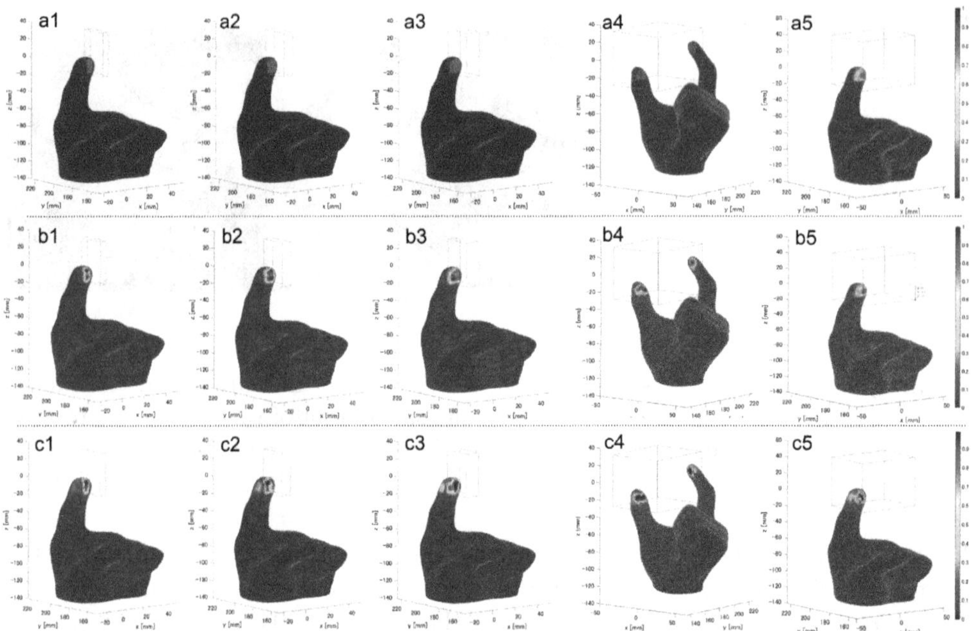

Fig. 4. Simulation results. a1-a5) Target pressure distribution. b1-b5) Distribution reproduced by our method. c1–c5) Distribution reproduced without scattering model.

When actually touching an object, the pressure on the contact area is not uniform, but greater toward the center. Figure 4 (a5, b5 and c5) shows the simulation result of a simplified model that a strong pressure is presented proportional to the penetration distance into the box. Although the shape is somewhat deformed, target distribution is reproduced. In these simulations, 30 iterations were performed in the phase optimization with the initial value as the zero vector. However, it has been empirically known that by setting the phases of the previous frame to the initial value, convergence can be sufficiently achieved in 5 to 10 iterations.

5 User Study

To verify if our method can generate a discernible difference in the pressure distribution, we conducted a user study. In this study, participants performed tasks of touching and identifying three types of distribution. We compared the accuracy of identification between the two methods. One is our method using the scattering model, and the other is the method without considering scattering.

Procedure. The participants sat in front of the system and placed his hand above the transducer array. For the stability of mesh generation, form of the hand was limited to only the index finger up throughout the experiment as shown in Fig. 3 (b). Then, the participant's hand was scanned and a rigid template was

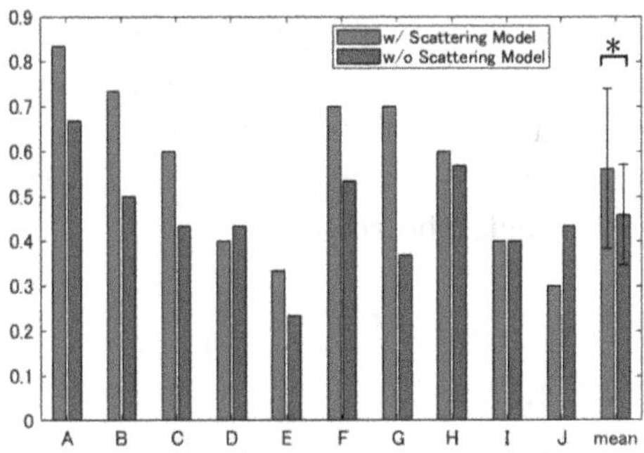

Fig. 5. Accuracy rates of the participants and the corresponding mean value.

created, which takes about 20 sec. After confirming that the mesh generation was working properly, the participants were asked to experience three different widths of pressure pattern for 15 sec each. As in the simulation, a uniform pressure is applied to the part that enters a box-shaped region. See the Fig. 4 (b1-b3) for the size of the region. The participants were not allowed to move their fingers horizontally to feel the width, but only to move vertically checking their hand and the box-shaped region displayed on a LCD as shown in the Fig. 3 (c). Then, the participants were asked to repeatedly perform the tasks to identify the width. After 15 s of touching, the tactile presentation was stopped, and participants answered one of three widths. Participants performed three task as a practice and then performed 10 tasks for each width (total 30 tasks). In either case, no answer was taught to the participants. The order of the tasks is randomized. The above process was done separately under two methods to avoid confusion between methods. Five of the ten participants performed the experiment with scattering model and the other five performed the experiment without scattering model.

Result and Discussion. Ten participants (eight males and two females), aged between 23 to 24, took part in the experiment. Figure 5 shows the accuracy rate of the participants. The participant A to E performed the experiment with scattering model first and the participant F to J performed the experiment without scattering model first. The mean value of the accuracy rates among participants was 0.56 with scattering model and 0.47 without scattering model, and the Wilcoxon signed-rank test yielded a significant difference ($p < 0.05$) between the two methods. The mean accuracy indicates that the differences in the distributions generated by our method are discernable to some extent, but not perfect. One of the reasons for this may be that an accurate mesh model could not be generated due to the error of the depth camera. However, the difference in accuracy between the two methods suggests that it is effective to consider scattering even in such a case. Also, in this experiment, we did not give instructions on the appropriate speed of touching. Since there is a delay between capturing the hand and presenting the tactile sensation, an appropriate distribution cannot be presented for a fast movement of the finger. This may have led to a large differences among accuracy rates of participants. In particular, it is considered that participant E and J were greatly affected by the delay because their fingers shook during the experiment. We are required to verify how much delay there is and how it affects the result.

6 Conclusion

In this paper, we proposed and examined a method for rendering an ultrasound pressure distribution by solving the scattering problem. Although in the experiment, the pressure presentation was limited to the fingertip, our method can produce a pressure pattern on the entire hand surface, so there is still room for verification as to what kind of and how high the pressure distribution can be generated. At present, there is limitations on the temporal and spatial resolutions of the distribution due to computational cost, sensing accuracy, and transducer's resonant frequency. However, these problems will be solved with the advancement of the devices. One of our future work is the complete reproduction of the pressure distribution when touching a soft object using the presented approach.

References

1. Intel corporation (2018). https://www.intel.com/
2. Ultraleap ltd. (2020). https://www.ultraleap.com/
3. Bai, M.R., Ih, J.G., Benesty, J.: Acoustic Array Systems: Theory,implementation, and Application. Wiley, Hoboken (2013)
4. Carter, T., Seah, S.A., Long, B., Drinkwater, B., Subramanian, S.: UltraHaptics: multi-point mid-air haptic feedback for touch surfaces. In: Proceedings of the 26th Annual ACM Symposium on User Interface Software and Technology, pp. 505–514. ACM (2013)
5. Dou, M., et al.: Fusion4D: real-time performance capture of challenging scenes. ACM Trans. Graph. (TOG) **35**(4), 1–13 (2016)
6. Inoue, S., Makino, Y., Shinoda, H.: Active touch perception produced by airborne ultrasonic haptic hologram. In: Proceedings of the World Haptics Conference, pp. 362–367. IEEE (2015)
7. Inoue, S., Makino, Y., Shinoda, H.: Mid-air ultrasonic pressure control on skin by adaptive focusing. In: Bello, F., Kajimoto, H., Visell, Y. (eds.) EuroHaptics 2016. LNCS, vol. 9774, pp. 68–77. Springer, Cham (2016). https://doi.org/10.1007/978-3-319-42321-0_7
8. Inoue, S., Makino, Y., Shinoda, H.: Scalable architecture for airborne ultrasound tactile display. In: Hasegawa, S., Konyo, M., Kyung, K.-U., Nojima, T., Kajimoto, H. (eds.) AsiaHaptics 2016. LNEE, vol. 432, pp. 99–103. Springer, Singapore (2018). https://doi.org/10.1007/978-981-10-4157-0_17
9. Iwamoto, T., Tatezono, M., Shinoda, H.: Non-contact method for producing tactile sensation using airborne ultrasound. In: Ferre, M. (ed.) EuroHaptics 2008. LNCS, vol. 5024, pp. 504–513. Springer, Heidelberg (2008). https://doi.org/10.1007/978-3-540-69057-3_64

10. Long, B., Seah, S.A., Carter, T., Subramanian, S.: Rendering volumetric haptic shapes in mid-air using ultrasound. ACM Trans. Graph. **33**(6), 181:1–181:10 (2014)
11. Matsubayashi, A., Oikawa, H., Mizutani, S., Makino, Y., Shinoda, H.: Display of haptic shape using ultrasound pressure distribution forming cross-sectional shape. In: 2019 IEEE World Haptics Conference (WHC), pp. 419–424. IEEE (2019)
12. Zollhöfer, M., et al.: Real-time non-rigid reconstruction using an RGB-D camera. ACM Trans. Graph. (ToG) **33**(4), 1–12 (2014)

18

Soft-Wearable Device for the Estimation of Shoulder Orientation and Gesture

Aldo F. Contreras-González(✉), José Luis Samper-Escudero, David Pont-Esteban, Francisco Javier Sáez-Sáez, Miguel Ángel Sánchez-Urán, and Manuel Ferre

Centre for Automation and Robotics (CAR) UPM-CSIC, Universidad Politécnica de Madrid, 28006 Madrid, Spain
af.contreras@alumnos.upm.es
https://www.car.upm-csic.es/?portfolio=exoflex-flexible-exoskeleton

Abstract. This study presents the development of a wearable device that merges capacitive soft-flexion and surface electromyography (sEMG) sensors for the estimation of shoulder orientation and movement, evaluating five natural movement gestures of the human arm. The use of Time Series Networks (TSN) to estimate the arm orientation, and a pattern recognition method for the estimation of the classification of the gesture are proposed. It is demonstrated that it is possible to know the orientation of the shoulder, and that the algorithm is capable of recognising the five gestures proposed with two different configurations. The study is performed on people who reported healthy upper limbs.

Keywords: Soft robotics · Wearable sensors · UpperLimb · sEMG.

1 Introduction

There have been many attempts to identify the movement of the human body in a virtual way by monitoring the behaviour of the extremities for haptic interfaces [7], teleoperation tasks [1] and assistive and rehabilitation devices [4,16]. Robots increase the number of repetitions performed in a rehabilitation session, thus improving patient morale and motivation [24]. In recent years, rehabilitation devices use sEMG as main source of feedback [15] for control [8].

Several sEMG techniques are used for the identification and classification of movements [3], some of the most relevant being the Detrended Fluctuation Analysis (DFA) for the identification of low-level muscle activation [19], the sEMG signal decomposition into Motor Unit Action Potential Trains (MUAPTs) [18], the Tunable-Q factor Wavelet Transform (TQWT) based algorithm proposed for the classification of physical actions [2], and Convolutional Neural Network (CNN), recently confirmed as as a powerful tool for the classification of operator movements [25]. These methods, combined with appropriate signal filtering techniques [5], are useful for estimating the movement of the human body.

Data fusion [13] using sEMG sensors is widely used in rehabilitation. Movement recognition algorithms generally combine sEMG signals with the Inertial Measurement Unit (IMU) [11], or with force sensors [10]. There are particular cases where flexion sensors [22] are used to avoid the accumulated error on the measurement.

This paper focuses on the development of a soft-compressive jacket with a network of soft-flexion sensors, merged with sEMG sensors attached to it for movement detection of the upper limbs. This device allows the user to quickly start estimating shoulder orientation without the need for prior calibration.

2 Materials and Methods

Using a configuration of seven one-axis sensors, as in previous work [21], it is possible to obtain 95% of the variance of the principal components for the shoulder gestures. The configuration proposed in this paper places only an array of four flexion sensors in the intermediate positions due to the fact that they provide flexion measurements in two axes.

The array of four flexion sensors Sx (being 'x' the sensor number) was placed over a compression jacket (see Fig. 1). The capacitive flexion sensors are the *Two Axis Sensor of Bendlabs* [12] and its operation is explained and well detailed in [20]. The sensors have been attached to a compression jacket by sewing two small rigid pieces which hold and guide the sensor in the arm movement direction and to neglect properties such as wrinkles and stretching. The first support (FxA) (see Fig. 1b) holds the sensor in a fixed position while the second one (FxB) allows it to slide inside it and guides it over the arm (see Fig. 1c).

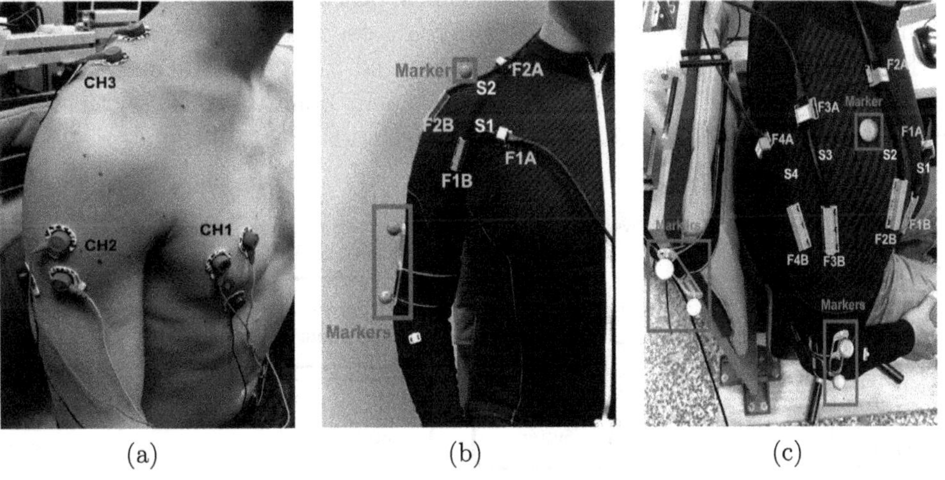

(a) (b) (c)

Fig. 1. Soft Sensor Device. sEMG location (1a): Trapezius Descendens (CH3), Deltoideus Medius (CH2) and Pectoralis major (CH1). Markers location: one over the shoulder Acromion bone, two on the arm (1b) and two vertically over the base (1c).

The sensor arrangement allows shoulder movement to be measured in a six-degree-of-freedom (DoF) work-space where arm rotation around its longitudinal axis is not included, this measurement is converted into two angle XY and YZ given by the conversion of the position of the ground truth. sEMG sensors [23], are allocated following the recommendations of Surface Electromyography for the Non-Invasive Assessment of Muscles (SENIAM) [9]. The electrodes are placed on the user (as shown on Fig. 1); then, the user puts on the compression jacket over the electrodes (not shown on Fig. 1b nor Fig. 1c). The design of this device allows the deformation and stretching of the fabric to be disregarded due to the small rigid pieces, in addition to not limiting the user's mobility on daily tasks.

The gestures performed were simplified to cover the natural range of arm movement [14] for daily tasks, and were assigned a number for further identification: **1**. Abduction/Adduction of the shoulder until the arm reaches 120° inclination; **2**. Flexion/Extension of the shoulder from 0° to 120°; **3**. Horizontal adduction/displacement of the arm at 90° flexion, hand crosses sagittal plane till arm reaches a 30° displacement; **4**. Closing/Swing drill movement of the arm inwards from 0° to 120°; and, **5**. Opening/Swing drill movement, starting with a flexion of 120° to 0°. The method developed in this study was evaluated in four healthy subjects; tests were spread over three different days to avoid exhaustion of the muscles. Each subject performed a total of five repetitions of each of the five gestures, continuously and without interruptions. Participants' ages ranged from 24 to 30 years old. All the gestures made by the subjects were performed in a chair facing a screen.

2.1 Data Acquisition

To start data collection, the sEMG sensors and the flex sensor compression jacket are placed on the subject's right arm. Then, OptiTrack [17] markers are located as shown in Fig. 1, in order to obtain the real pose of the subject's arm.

Both flexion and sEMG sensors are connected to a custom acquisition board based on the LAUNCHXL-F28379D development board. On the one hand, the sEMG sensors provide an amplified, rectified and integrated analogical signal

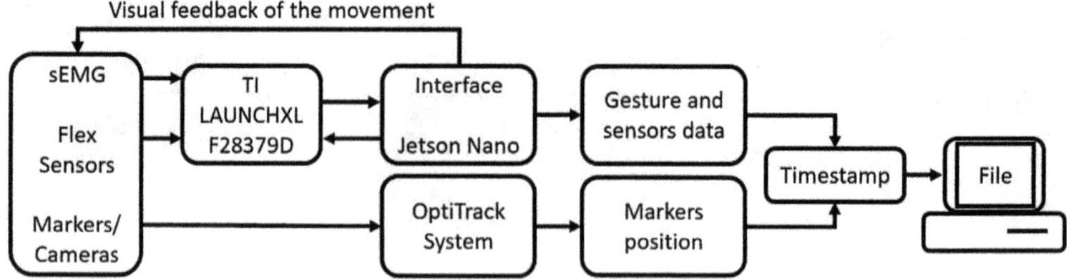

Fig. 2. The EMG signals and angles of the user's movements (first box on the left) were acquired using visual feedback generated by the interface on the Jetson Nano, which also stores this data. The OptiTrack system stores the position of the markers. In the end, both files are merged into one.

(AKA the EMG's envelope), which is obtained by the micro-controller at a rate of 1kHz. On the other hand, the flexion sensors communicate with the micro-controller via I2C protocol at a frequency of 200 Hz.

A graphical user interface has been developed to guide the speed and kind of movement of the participants while performing the gestures and to log all obtained data. This software has been implemented on an NVIDIA Jetson Nano. This device communicates with the acquisition board via SPI at 500 Hz and stores the data contained in every received message along with the timestamp and the gesture that is being performed in a plain text document. Simultaneously to the start of the sensors' data acquisition, Optitrack data acquiring is initiated at 240fps. In the end, a file with the positions of the markers belonging to the OptiTrack system is exported. The interaction of all elements is shown in Fig. 2.

2.2 Data Processing

The sessions for each subject are condensed into a single file. Given that the Optitrack system captures are made at 240 fps, an interpolation is performed to reach a frequency of 500 Hz in the data. The interpolation method consists on taking the Optitrack file which is the shortest and matching it with the number of samples with the Jetson Nano file by adding with a quadratic splines method the missing data. The signal from the sEMG sensors is filtered offline. To Smooth this data a Savitzky-Golay smoothing local regression using weighted linear least squares and a 2nd degree polynomial filter is used with an span of 0.7% of the total number of data points. The angle between the markers of the Optitrack system is obtained by calculating the angle generated between the line generated from the arm markers on the shoulder Acromion bone, and the vertical from the markers of the backrest of the rehabilitation system.

A Time series Network [6] with Levenberg-Marquardt algorithm is used to calculate the orientation of the arm using the angles given by the flexion sensors as input data, and the OptiTrack markers reference as target. With the use of Matlab's Machine Learning and Deep Learning Toolbox, it was possible to estimate that the best parameters for this task were 10 hidden neurons and consecutive samples. For the training of the neural network, 70% of the data was used for training, 15% for validation and 15% for testing, in order to find the lower MSE and the best Regression value (R).

For the classification of the gestures, dummy variables of the numbers assigned to each movement (as listed on Sect. 2) are used to recognise each pattern from the fusion of the signals of the filtered sEMG sensors and the data from the flexion sensors; a two-layer feed-forward network, with sigmoid hidden and softmax output neurons tool was used as pattern recognition. Ten, fifteen, twenty and twenty five hidden neurons where evaluated by testing the computation time and the number of iterations in order to get the best cross-entropy value; fifteen hidden neurons where the most appropriate for this task. The networks were trained with scaled conjugate gradient back-propagation (trainscg) using again, 70% of data for training, 15% for validation and 15% for testing.

3 Results and Discussion

For the estimation of the orientation, two Time series Network configurations were designed, one for dummy variables and one for the gestures as numbered in Sect. 2, resulting in a MSE of $1.49E-05$ with a Regression value of $9.99E-01$ and a MSE of $1.50E-04$ and R of $9.99E-01$, respectively. It can be concluded that the selection of either of the two target variables does not have a significant influence on the results, given that both have a regression value (R) of 0.99%, and the difference on the MSE is minimum.

In order to evaluate the trained networks for both orientation and gesture, a new single session is performed by one of the original subjects. It is observed that the proposed device is valid to find the orientation of an arm when the network is calibrated with a sub-millimeter system. This can be noted in the box on Fig. 3, corresponding to one portion of the whole closing drill movement; the data comes from flexion sensors only and is processed offline with the trained network and later compared with the ground truth data of that new session. It can be seen that the estimation is close to the calibration system, with an MSE of $1.32E-05$.

For gesture classification, the condensed data from the flex sensors is taken along with the sEMG data in order to train a pattern recognition neural network. To verify that the fusion of the data is feasible, three different networks are trained, one network only with the EMG data, another only with the flex sensors, and the third with the two of them. The resulting performance values are displayed in Table 1.

In order to compare the models, F-score is used. Given by: $Fscore = (2*Recall*Precision)/(Recall+Precision)$, where $Recall = TP/(TP+\sum FN)$ (being TP the true positive value and FN the false negative values); and

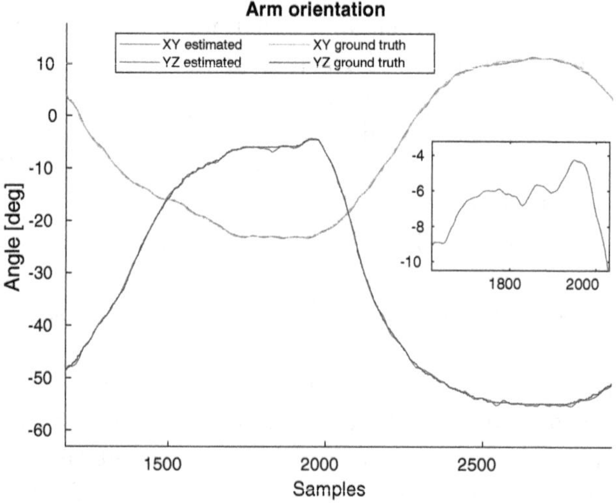

Fig. 3. Signal of the angle generated by the arm with the data of the ground truth together with the signal estimated by the network.

Table 1. Performance in percentage of the classification for sEMG (50.6%) and Soft-Flexion sensors (89.8%) and combined sEMG with Flexion (95.4%).

		sEMG		Flexion			sEMG + Flexion		
#	Gesture	Recall	Precision	Recall	Precision	**F-score**	Recall	Precision	**F-score**
1	Abduction	40.4	49.5	91.3	91.1	**91.2**	96.1	98.0	**97.5**
2	Flexion	66.8	56.8	90.5	87.1	**88.7**	97.2	94.3	**95.7**
3	Horizontal add	54.4	41.4	89.5	90.6	**90.0**	93.1	93.1	**93.1**
4	Closing drill	41.6	53.7	85.8	87.5	**86.6**	93.7	95.5	**94.6**
5	Opening drill	43.8	52.0	92.0	92.8	**92.4**	95.7	95.9	**95.8**

$Precision = TP/(TP + \sum FP)$, (being FP the false positive values for each of the Confusion Matrices).

The network using only the sEMGs shows poor results for this application, whilst the Flexion network and the combination of sEMG and Flexion sensors both have promising results. It could be said that flexion sensors are sufficient for the classification of movements for a certain type of application that does not require great sensitivity, while the fusion of both sensors denotes a great performance with minimum error. The overall performance of the network with the fusion of the two type of sensors is 95.4%; the best results were obtained by the Abduction gesture with 98% of precision, which could be a result of it being the only gesture generated in a different space and different muscle activation with respect to the other four gestures. On the other hand, Horizontal Adduction (93.1%) shares estimations with the Closing Drill and Opening Drill gestures; this can be given to the fact that they share movement space on certain spots. Using the data acquired for the new session and tested offline, it can be noted that the gestures, that coincide in the Flexion movement space such as the drilling gestures, cause an error in the estimation of the pattern. Table 2 depicts the response to the estimation in percentage for each gesture made during the new data collection. Horizontal Adduction presents the least exact estimation, contrary to Abduction, which presents a minor magnitude of error which coincides in a way with the training performance for the two sensors network.

3.1 Discussion

Since the objective of this study is to control flexible exoskeletons used in rehabilitation and assistive devices for the upper limbs, the feedback of the shoulder

Table 2. Trained network estimation: Ranking results for each gesture performed

	Abduction	Flexion	Horizontal Add	Closing Drill	Opening Drill
Recall	98.0	94.3	93.1	95.5	95.9
Precision	97.1	97.2	93.1	93.7	95.7

position and the gesture performed are extremely important for Control. This device, in its prototype mode, was created in a single compression shirt size, always being able to adapt in different sizes. This document does not present a study of the comparison of undefined gestures. It is estimated that the developed algorithm could be functional for new gestures as long as the data is processed and is not within the range of movement of the other gestures.

4 Conclusions

In this document, the signals of three electromyography sensors and an array of four flexion sensors are used to compose a flexible device to estimate five predefined gestures and the orientation of the shoulder. Two different algorithms are used to perform each characteristic, one for the identification of patterns to estimate the gesture being performed, and a recurrent neural network to estimate the orientation of the arm. The results show that the device consisting of an array of four flexion sensors is capable of estimating the gestures with a performance of 89.8%, with results showing improvement by adding the sEMG signal to the algorithm with a performance of 95.4%, there being an area of improvement in this last characteristic, such as filtering the sEMG signal online. Depending on the desired performance for the application, different arrangements can be used.

References

1. Artemiadis, P.K., Kyriakopoulos, K.J.: EMG-based teleoperation of a robot arm in planar catching movements using ARMAX model and trajectory monitoring techniques. In: Proceedings 2006 IEEE International Conference on Robotics and Automation. ICRA 2006, pp. 3244–3249. IEEE (2006)
2. Chada, S., Taran, S., Bajaj, V.: An efficient approach for physical actions classification using surface EMG signals. Health Inf. Sci. Syst. **8**(1), 3 (2020)
3. Chowdhury, R.H., Reaz, M.B., Ali, M.A.B.M., Bakar, A.A., Chellappan, K., Chang, T.G.: Surface electromyography signal processing and classification techniques. Sensors **13**(9), 12431–12466 (2013)
4. Cogollor, J.M., et al.: Handmade task tracking applied to cognitive rehabilitation. Sensors **12**(10), 14214–14231 (2012)
5. De Luca, C.J., Gilmore, L.D., Kuznetsov, M., Roy, S.H.: Filtering the surface EMG signal: movement artifact and baseline noise contamination. J. Biomech. **43**(8), 1573–1579 (2010)
6. Faust, O., Hagiwara, Y., Hong, T.J., Lih, O.S., Acharya, U.R.: Deep learning for healthcare applications based on physiological signals: a review. Comput. Methods Programs Biomed. **161**, 1–13 (2018)
7. Frisoli, A., Rocchi, F., Marcheschi, S., Dettori, A., Salsedo, F., Bergamasco, M.: A new force-feedback arm exoskeleton for haptic interaction in virtual environments. In: First Joint Eurohaptics Conference and Symposium on Haptic Interfaces for Virtual Environment and Teleoperator Systems. World Haptics Conference, pp. 195–201. IEEE (2005)
8. Gunasekara, J., Gopura, R., Jayawardane, T., Lalitharathne, S.: Control methodologies for upper limb exoskeleton robots. In: 2012 IEEE/SICE International Symposium on System Integration (SII), pp. 19–24. IEEE (2012)

9. Hermens, H.J., et al.: European recommendations for surface electromyography. Roessingh Res. Dev. **8**(2), 13–54 (1999)
10. Jimenez-Fabian, R., Verlinden, O.: Review of control algorithms for robotic ankle systems in lower-limb orthoses, prostheses, and exoskeletons. Med. Eng. Phys. **34**(4), 397–408 (2012)
11. Krasoulis, A., Vijayakumar, S., Nazarpour, K.: Multi-grip classification-based prosthesis control with two EMG-IMU sensor. IEEE Trans. Neural Syst. Rehabil. Eng. (2020)
12. Labs, B.: Bend labs. Internet draft (2018). https://www.bendlabs.com/products/2-axis-soft-flex-sensor/
13. López, N.M., di Sciascio, F., Soria, C.M., Valentinuzzi, M.E.: Robust EMG sensing system based on data fusion for myoelectric control of a robotic arm. Biomed. Eng. online **8**(1), 5 (2009)
14. Magermans, D., Chadwick, E., Veeger, H., Van Der Helm, F.: Requirements for upper extremity motions during activities of daily living. Clin. Biomech. **20**(6), 591–599 (2005)
15. McCabe, J.P., Henniger, D., Perkins, J., Skelly, M., Tatsuoka, C., Pundik, S.: Feasibility and clinical experience of implementing a myoelectric upper limb orthosis in the rehabilitation of chronic stroke patients: a clinical case series report. PloS One **14**(4) (2019)
16. Monroy, M., Ferre, M., Barrio, J., Eslava, V., Galiana, I.: Sensorized thimble for haptics applications. In: 2009 IEEE International Conference on Mechatronics, pp. 1–6. IEEE (2009)
17. NaturalPoint, I.: Optitrack. Internet draft (2019). https://optitrack.com
18. Nawab, S.H., Chang, S.S., De Luca, C.J.: High-yield decomposition of surface EMG signals. Clin. Neurophysiol. **121**(10), 1602–1615 (2010)
19. Phinyomark, A., Phukpattaranont, P., Limsakul, C.: Fractal analysis features for weak and single-channel upper-limb EMG signals. Expert Syst. Appl. **39**(12), 11156–11163 (2012)
20. Reese, S.P.: Angular displacement sensor of compliant material (Jan 27 2015), uS Patent 8,941,392
21. Samper-Escudero, J.L., Contreras-González, A.F., Ferre, M., Sánchez-Urán, M.A., Pont-Esteban, D.: Efficient multiaxial shoulder-motion tracking based on flexible resistive sensors applied to exosuits. Soft Robot. (2020)
22. Sankaran, S.: Robotic arm for the easy mobility of amputees. Int. J. Innov. Technol. Exploring Eng. 9 (2020). https://doi.org/10.35940/ijitee.B1151.1292S219
23. Technologies, A.: Myoware. Internet draft (2016). https://cdn.sparkfun.com/assets/a/3/a/f/a/AT-04-001.pdf
24. Washabaugh, E.P., Treadway, E., Gillespie, R.B., Remy, C.D., Krishnan, C.: Self-powered robots to reduce motor slacking during upper-extremity rehabilitation: a proof of concept study. Restorative Neurol. Neurosci. **36**(6), 693–708 (2018)
25. Yamanoi, Y., Ogiri, Y., Kato, R.: Emg-based posture classification using a convolutional neural network for a myoelectric hand. Biomed. Sig. Process. Control **55**, 101574 (2020)

19

A Parallel Elastic Haptic Thimble for Wide Bandwidth Cutaneous Feedback

Daniele Leonardis(✉), Massimiliano Gabardi, Massimiliano Solazzi, and Antonio Frisoli

Percro Laboratory, Scuola Superiore Sant'Anna of Pisa, Pisa, Italy
d.leonardis@santannapisa.it
https://www.santannapisa.it/it

Abstract. Design of wearable fingertip haptic devices is often a compromise between conflicting features: lightness and compactness, against rich and neat haptic feedback. On one side direct drive actuators (i.e. voice coils) provide a clean haptic feedback with high dynamics, with limited maximum output forces. On the other side mechanical transmissions with reduction can increase output force of micro sized motors, at the cost of slower and often noisy output signals. In this work we present a compact fingertip haptic device based on a parallel elastic mechanism: it merges the output of two differently designed actuators in a single, wide bandwidth haptic feedback. Each actuator is designed with a different role: one for rendering fast, high frequency force components, the other for rendering constant to low frequency components. In the work we present design and implementation of the device, followed by experimental characterization of its performance in terms of frequency response and rendering capabilities.

Keywords: Cutaneous feedback · Haptics · Bandwidth · Fingertip · Wearable · Parallel elastic

1 Introduction

In recent years, rendering of the sense ot touch in teleoperated or virtual reality has become a rich field of research, especially concerning highly wearable haptic devices. In particular the scientific literature shows the development of different devices able to provide the user with a specific cutaneous feedback, such as thermal [5], vibratory [14], contact orientation [2], contact force [7], or a combination of the mentioned feedback [4,16]. In [12], a complete review of portable and wearable haptic devices for the fingertips can be found.

Rendering the correct physical interaction is a challenging objective [1], and concerning portable and wearable haptic devices, practical requirements such as wearability and portability of the devices determine limits to features of the rendered feedback. Limitations can be, for instance, in terms of bandwidth and

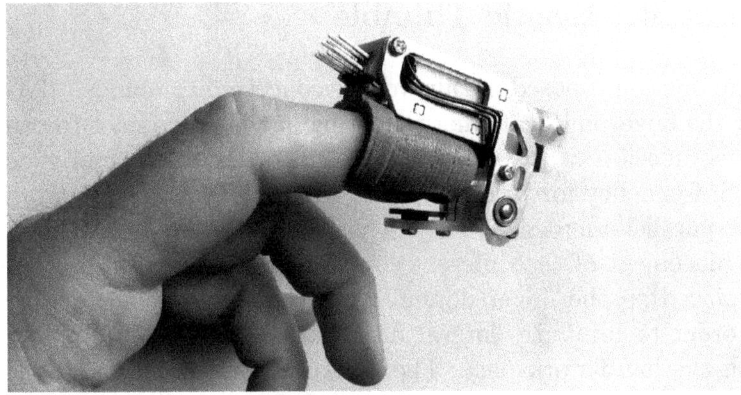

Fig. 1. The presented Parallel Elastic Thimble, featuring two actuators coupled by an elastic element to render from static to high frequency cutaneous feedback

force amplitude for force rendering devices, range of motion for shape rendering thimbles or heat flux for thermal devices. The choice of the actuation system is a trade-off between feedback performance (max. force, bandwidth, max. stroke, noise) and device requirements (mass, dimensions, wearability). In fact, the actuation system is usually the heaviest part of a portable fingertip haptic interface. Typical electromagnetic actuators (DC motors or voice coils) used in haptic devices allow for high quality haptic rendering, ranging from constant to high frequency force components, with the drawback of a limited maximum output force. Small actuators provided with mechanical reduction can be used to amplify the output force, yet at the cost of reduced output bandwidth and degraded quality of the haptic feedback in terms of noise and backlash. A different solution to increase the feedback bandwidth while keeping a reasonable constant force is obtained by coupling in a serial manner a macro-actuator (or a small reduced actuator) featuring low bandwidth and high output force, with a micro-actuator, with wide bandwidth but low output force. Such a solution has been explored in grounded haptic devices in a series configuration, i.e. a very compact "micro" actuator is placed at the end-effector of a desktop or grounded haptic device [9,11,15] to enhance its dynamic response. Concept of parallel micro-macro configuration via elastic parallel transmission was proposed in [10] and then developed for robotic arm manipulators in [13] and [17]. To the knowledge of authors, micro-macro solutions have never been applied to a fully wearable and compact fingertip haptic display. In this paper, the proposed novel fingertip device features a parallel elastic actuation system, obtained by combining the output of two micro DC motors of the same size: one with high mechanical reduction and considerable continuous force, the second with low reduction and high dynamics of the output force (Fig. 1).

2 The Parallel Elastic Thimble

The fingertip device proposed in this work is conceived to render 1 dof cutaneous feedback at the fingerpad, featuring rendering of the no-contact to contact transition and modulation of the contact force. In order to efficiently render from static to high-frequency force components, a parallel elastic configuration implementing two parallel micro-sized motors has been experimented. Overview of the design and placement of the different components is shown in Fig. 2. Actuators have been placed on the finger dorsum, and the whole device design has been studied in order to minimize lateral interference with other fingers and interference with the hand workspace. The device is 16 mm wide and weights 21 g. Importantly, the slim design at the sides of the device allow for easy switching between thimbles of different sizes. Different thimble sizes were fabricated by 3D printing in TPU (Thermoplastic Polyurethane) soft polymer, resulting in a compliant and precise fit of the device to the specific finger shape, not requiring additional fastening elements (velcro or clips). A slider mechanism allows easy and rapid switch between different thimbles (Fig. 3).

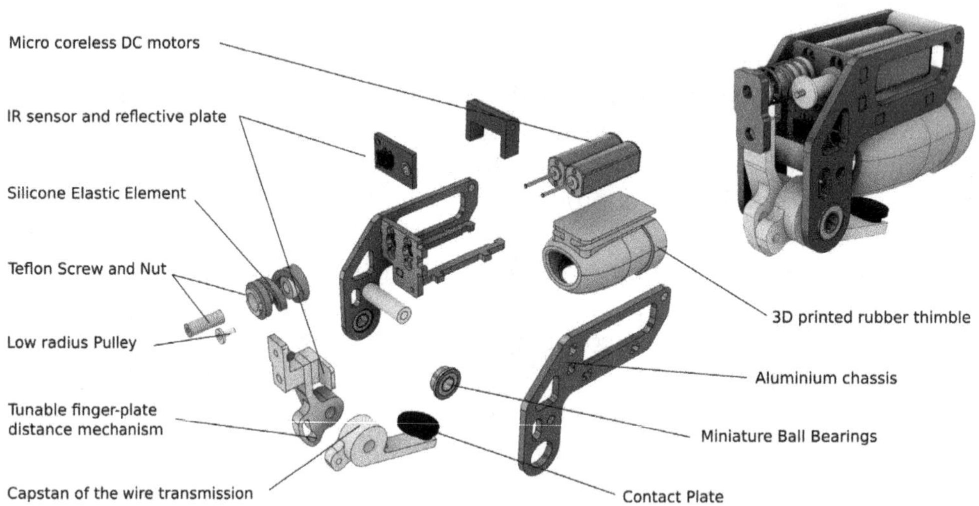

Fig. 2. Mechanical components of the Parallel Elastic Haptic Thimble

The moving plate in contact with the fingerpad has been implemented through a 1 dof link with a revolute joint. A slot mechanism with a fastening screw has been designed in order to tune distance of the plate with respect of the finger surface, thus minimizing the required displacement of the plate. Considering that a displacement of few millimeters of the contact plate is a sufficient range in cutaneous haptic devices [6,8], the consequent angular displacement, due to the revolute joint, can be negligible (18 mm radius). Also, the revolute joint with miniaturized ball bearings allow to minimize friction with respect to a linear slider mechanism.

Fig. 3. The slim lateral profile of the device (left) allows easy switch of rubber thimbles with different finger sizes through a slider mechanism (right)

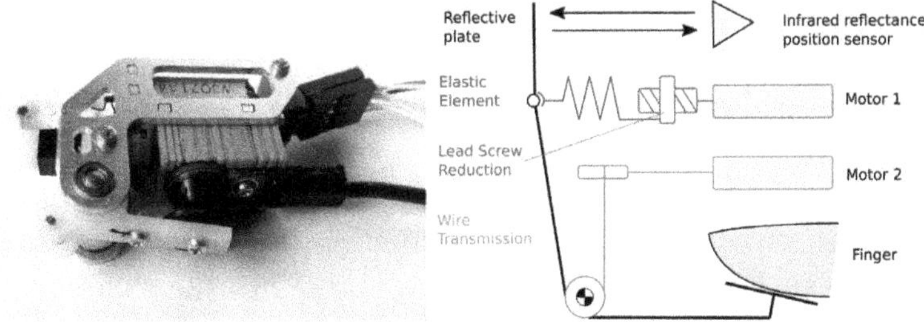

Fig. 4. Scheme of the transmission mechanism (left) and detail of the force sensor mounted in place of the fingertip for characterization of the device

2.1 Actuation Scheme

The parallel elastic actuation scheme is shown in Fig. 4 (left). As a first prototype of the parallel elastic concept design, we decided to implement two identical actuators of the same size, varying only the mechanical reduction between each of them and the moving plate. Actuators were two Minebea K30 micro DC motors, diameter 8 mm, 5 V nominal voltage. The output of the first actuator is connected through a lead-screw mechanism and an elastic element to the moving link. The lead-screw obtains a high mechanical reduction, although with no-backdrivability. Importantly, the use of the lead-screw has been chosen in order to avoid introduction of sources of noise, as it would happen, in example, for a more conventional gear reduction. The second actuator is coupled to the moving link by means of a one branch wire transmission: a capstan (radius 8 mm at the moving link is connected by the actuation wire to a pulley (radius 1 mm) at the output shaft of the motor. It results in a low reduction, highly reversible mechanical transmission. The elastic element has been fabricated from a silicon tube: after preliminary experiments it was preferred with respect to a steel spring due to the inherent presence of a damping factor. A position sensor has been embedded into the device, measuring displacement of the moving link with the contact plate. We used a reflectance infrared sensor, due to its very compact size, to the measurement range particularly suitable for the device and to the sensitivity of the sensor to small displacement (measured noise of 0.01 mm in the middle point of the measuring range).

3 Experimental Characterization

The experimental activity was conducted to characterize the novel (for the size of a fingertip mechanism) compact parallel elastic structure in terms of frequency response and output forces and displacement. A holder for a compact force sensor (Optoforce 10N with resolution of 1 mN) was fabricated to be mounted in place of the rubber thimble (Fig. 4 left). A microcontroller board (Teensy 3.6) was used to implement the low level control of the device, to acquire the analog infrared position sensor, and to drive motors through a dual H-bridge (Texas Instruments DRV8835). Sample time of the low-level control loop was 1 KHz. Communication with a host PC was implemented through a Wiz5500 Ethernet module and UDP communication. A Matlab Simulink Desktop-Real Time model, executed on the host PC, implemented the high level control interface and data recording.

The first experimental activity consisted in measuring the force output of the two actuators. The contact plate was positioned at the contact threshold with the force sensor. Then, a slow voltage reference ramp was commanded to each motor separately for ten repetitions. The obtained current intensity to force characteristics are shown in Fig. 5 (left). The graph highlights the different mechanical reduction of the two identical actuators: the first obtains a higher output force, presenting non-linearity due to friction of the lead-screw mechanism. The second actuator shows a lower output force and a more linear characteristic. A position control loop was then tuned for the first actuator, in order to control displacement of the moving plate. Step response of the position control loop is shown in Fig. 5 (middle). Bandwidth of the two actuators was then measured. The first actuator was controlled in closed loop with a chirp reference position signal, ranging from 0.5 to 40 Hz. The obtained frequency response shows a limit of the first actuator bandwidth at 15 Hz (Fig. 5, right). The second actuator was commanded in open loop with a chirp voltage reference ranging from 5 to 250 Hz. The second actuator response shows a cutoff frequency of 120 Hz, which is about

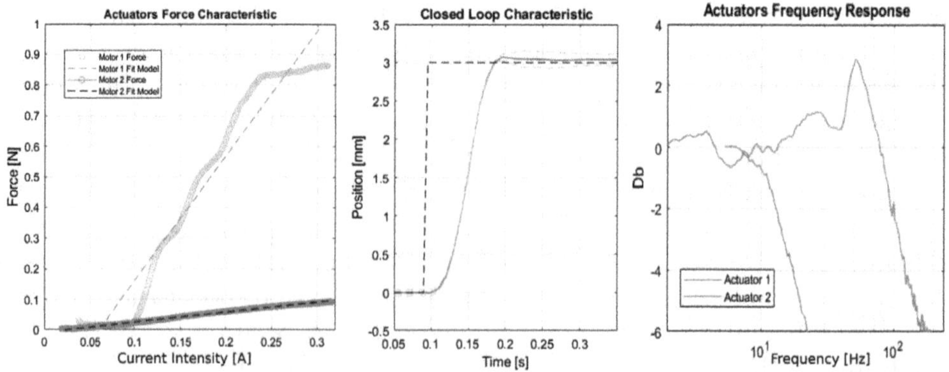

Fig. 5. Force characterization of the two actuators (left), closed loop step response of the first actuator (middle) and frequency response of the two actuators (right)

one order of magnitude greater than the first actuator. Also, a peak appears at 55 Hz, possibly due to a resonant frequency introduced by the elastic element of the system.

3.1 Experimental Evaluation of Sample Texture Rendering

Overall device performance was finally evaluated using a pre-recorded signal involving contact with a texturized surface. The device was evaluated by wearing it onto the experimenter's index finger. Displacement measurements of the contact plate were recorded through the embedded infrared position sensor. The texture pattern was taken from the "Sandpaper 100" object of the texture library of the Penn Haptic Texture Toolkit [3].

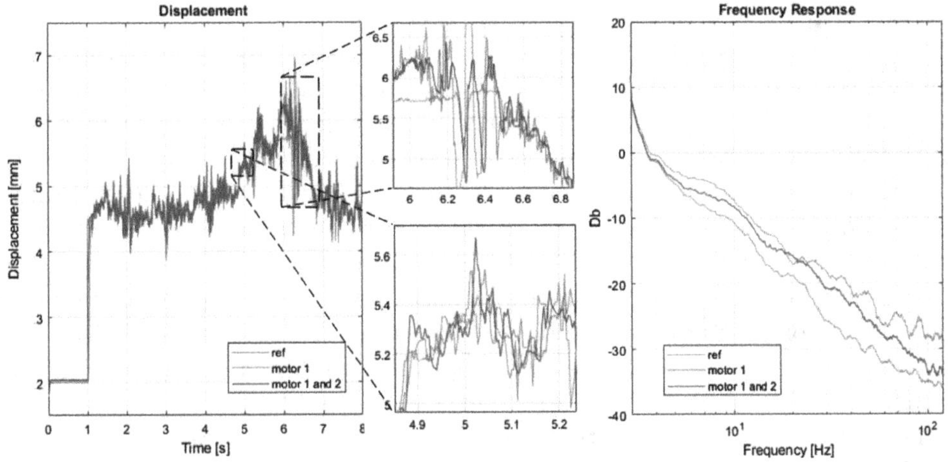

Fig. 6. Bench test of the device rendering a sample texture (sandpaper) with contact transition and non-zero constant component of the normal force

For the position-controlled actuator, normal force was converted to displacement, approximating stiffness of the fingerpad to a constant value of 0.5 N/mm. In order to gain full advantage of the parallel configuration, force reference for the second actuator was high-pass filtered at the cutoff frequency of the first actuator. With this method, the second actuator was not in charge of rendering the constant to low frequency components of the normal force, which in the simulated signal had a noticeably high value. Two data acquisition were performed: with both actuators enabled, and with the first actuator only enabled. Results are shown in Fig. 6. The benefit of both the actuators can be noticed from the frequency response (Fig. 6 (right)), closer to the reference, and from details of Fig. 6 (middle). The output of second actuator produces more crisp and reactive dynamics of the plate, whereas the first actuator alone, especially at the higher indentation levels (top detail), tends to a more flat response.

4 Conclusions

The novel design of a wearable fingertip device implementing a parallel elastic mechanism was proposed. The idea was originated from the contrasting requirements of fingertip haptic devices, involving compactness and wearability of the device and rendering of relatively high constant forces together with wide bandwidth tactile cues. The parallel structure allows to optimize each actuator for different purposes: the first, with high mechanical reduction, for rendering static to low frequency cues, which in typical applications can be noticeably high (i.e. when grasping a virtual object or exploring a surface). The second actuator, with low reduction and high transparency, was designed to render high frequency tactile cues, which typically have a reduced amplitude with respect to the static and slow force components.

The obtained prototype included two miniaturized motors with noiseless mechanical reduction (a lead-screw and a capstan wire transmission) and an elastic element to couple the two actuators. Mechanical design of the prototype was focused on enhancing wearability by minimizing mass and dimensions (16 mm total width, 21 g mass), by optimizing arrangement of actuators, and by implementing a user's tailored and switchable soft thimble design.

Force characterization and frequency response confirmed the desired different behavior of the two actuators (same motors with different reduction) in complementary frequency ranges. A resonant peak was noticeable, and further investigation is required in order to obtain a more flat frequency response. A deeper study of the mechanical model of the system can guide the choice of the elastic element stiffness, with the aim of optimizing interaction between the two actuators.

The final evaluation with the sample texture evidenced how the reference signal can be conveniently split between the two actuators. Although more investigation is required to obtain proper optimization of the developed device, the proposed method can result in more compact wearable devices with better energy efficiency and better capabilities, in terms of quality of the output signal and hi-fidelity rendering.

References

1. Caldwell, D.G., Tsagarakis, N., Wardle, A.: Mechano thermo and proprioceptor feedback for integrated haptic feedback. In: 1997 Proceedings of the IEEE International Conference on Robotics and Automation, vol. 3, pp. 2491–2496. IEEE (1997)
2. Chinello, F., Malvezzi, M., Pacchierotti, C., Prattichizzo, D.: Design and development of a 3RRS wearable fingertip cutaneous device. In: 2015 IEEE International Conference on Advanced Intelligent Mechatronics (AIM), pp. 293–298. IEEE (2015)
3. Culbertson, H., Lopez Delgado, J.J., Kuchenbecker, K.J.: The Penn haptic texture toolkit for modeling, rendering, and evaluating haptic virtual textures (2014)

4. Gabardi, M., Leonardis, D., Solazzi, M., Frisoli, A.: Development of a miniaturized thermal module designed for integration in a wearable haptic device. In: 2018 IEEE Haptics Symposium (HAPTICS), pp. 100–105. IEEE (2018)
5. Gallo, S., Rognini, G., Santos-Carreras, L., Vouga, T., Blanke, O., Bleuler, H.: Encoded and crossmodal thermal stimulation through a fingertip-sized haptic display. Front. Robot. AI **2**, 25 (2015)
6. Gleeson, B.T., Horschel, S.K., Provancher, W.R.: Design of a fingertip-mounted tactile display with tangential skin displacement feedback. IEEE Trans. Haptics **3**(4), 297–301 (2010)
7. Leonardis, D., Solazzi, M., Bortone, I., Frisoli, A.: A wearable fingertip haptic device with 3 DoF asymmetric 3-RSR kinematics. In: 2015 IEEE World Haptics Conference (WHC), pp. 388–393. IEEE (2015)
8. Leonardis, D., Solazzi, M., Bortone, I., Frisoli, A.: A 3-RSR haptic wearable device for rendering fingertip contact forces. IEEE Trans. Haptics **10**(3), 305–316 (2016)
9. Lu, T., Pacoret, C., Hériban, D., Mohand-Ousaid, A., Regnier, S., Hayward, V.: Kilohertz bandwidth, dual-stage haptic device lets you touch brownian motion. IEEE Trans. Haptics **10**(3), 382–390 (2016)
10. Morrell, J.B., Salisbury, J.K.: Parallel-coupled micro-macro actuators. Int. J. Robot. Res. **17**(7), 773–791 (1998)
11. Pacchierotti, C., Prattichizzo, D., Kuchenbecker, K.J.: Cutaneous feedback of fingertip deformation and vibration for palpation in robotic surgery. IEEE Trans. Biomed. Eng. **63**(2), 278–287 (2015)
12. Pacchierotti, C., Sinclair, S., Solazzi, M., Frisoli, A., Hayward, V., Prattichizzo, D.: Wearable haptic systems for the fingertip and the hand: taxonomy, review, and perspectives. IEEE Trans. Haptics **10**(4), 580–600 (2017)
13. Shin, D., Sardellitti, I., Khatib, O.: A hybrid actuation approach for human-friendly robot design. In: 2008 IEEE International Conference on Robotics and Automation, pp. 1747–1752. IEEE (2008)
14. Solazzi, M., Frisoli, A., Bergamasco, M.: Design of a novel finger haptic interface for contact and orientation display. In: 2010 IEEE Haptics Symposium, pp. 129–132. IEEE (2010)
15. Wall, S.A., Harwin, W.: A high bandwidth interface for haptic human computer interaction. Mechatronics **11**(4), 371–387 (2001)
16. Wang, D., Ohnishi, K., Xu, W.: Multimodal haptic display for virtual reality: a survey. IEEE Trans. Ind. Electron. **67**(1), 610–623 (2019)
17. Zinn, M., Khatib, O., Roth, B., Salisbury, J.K.: Large workspace haptic devices-a new actuation approach. In: 2008 Symposium on Haptic Interfaces for Virtual Environment and Teleoperator Systems, pp. 185–192. IEEE (2008)

20

Sound-Image Icon with Aerial Haptic Feedback

Seunggoo Rim, Shun Suzuki(✉), Yutaro Toide(✉), Masahiro Fujiwara(✉), Yasutoshi Makino(✉), and Hiroyuki Shinoda(✉)

The University of Tokyo,
5-1-5 Kashiwanoha, Kashiwa-shi, Chiba-ken 277-8561, Japan
{rim,suzuki,toide}@hapis.k.u-tokyo.ac.jp,
Masahiro_Fujiwara@ipc.i.u-tokyo.ac.jp,
yasutoshi_makino@k.u-tokyo.ac.jp,
hiroyuki_shinoda@k.u-tokyo.ac.jp

Abstract. In this study, we attempt to define a novel invisible mid-air three-dimensional (3D) object, which informs users of its existence and location via sound and haptic feedback. The correlation between the senses of hearing and touch creates the feeling of touching a sound source, which the user recognizes as a virtual object: sound-image icon. The sound from the icon instantaneously notifies the user about its position without requiring vision. In addition, aerial tactile sensation enables users to freely interact with and manipulate these icons with no need to wear any devices. Therefore, this approach exhibits enormous potential in various situations, such as surgical operations, works in factories, driving cars, and button/switch operations in daily life. In this study, we prototyped the sound-image icon and experimentally examined their feasibility. We confirmed that users could estimate the location of the icons and measured the time required to access these icons. The results indicate that the sound-image icon is feasible as a novel 3D interface.

Keywords: Mid-air haptics · Haptic display · Sound-source localization

1 Introduction

In this study, we propose a sound-image icon, which is an invisible 3D object that integrates sound-source localization and mid-air tactile sensation. This sound and haptic feedback creates a virtual object with no visual appearance, without requiring the user to wear any devices.

A typical method of reproducing tactile sensation in mid-air [2,3,6,8] is installing an airborne ultrasound tactile display (AUTD) that presents the moving stimulus on a skin by remotely producing the radiation pressure of focused aerial ultrasound. Such mid-air haptic feedback has been integrated with visual floating images in previously conducted studies [9,11]. From the viewpoint of interface design, vision is the most efficient channel to transmit the spatial

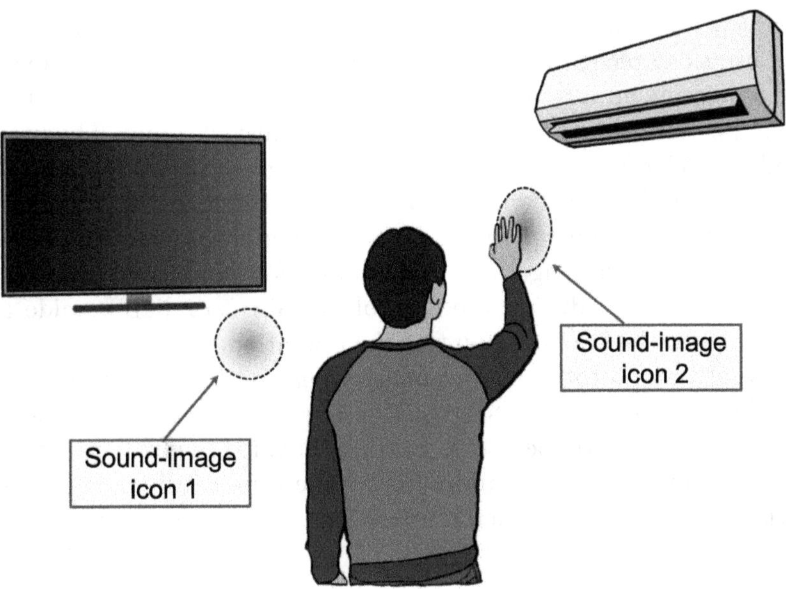

Fig. 1. Concept of a sound-image icon. The person selects the sound-image icon of the air conditioner to control the temperature. The sound from the icon informs the user about the position of itself. The icon provides tactile feedback without any visual image.

arrangement of an object to a user, while haptics facilitates the transmission of the will of a user to a computer system. Therefore, a 3D visual interface with mid-air haptics is a reasonable integration as an efficient interface. However, the eyes are sometimes occupied by a specific task such as in-car driving or a surgical operation. In addition, glassless 3D vision is still immature, where it is difficult to secure a wide view angle, while a head-mounted display sometimes causes fatigue and VR sickness. Instead of vision, the use of sound is another option to display the object position, as humans can instantaneously identify the direction of the sound when they are in an environment where sound can be clearly heard [1]. In addition, the sound can transmit words and tones that express various attributes.

Many studies have been performed to create virtual sound sources at specific locations under various conditions and environments. Recent studies have focused on virtual sound source positioning for acoustic navigation in unknown spaces [14] or vector base amplitude panning for creating 2D or 3D sound fields without considering the placements of any number of loudspeakers [13]. Although the aforementioned technologies form a wide research domain, we could not find studies that integrated virtual sound sources and mid-air haptics technologies. It would be intriguing to investigate whether auditory and haptic perceptions effectively complement each other.

The concept of a sound-image icon is depicted in Fig. 1. The user hears a binaural sound and identifies the direction of the sound-source. We refer to this sound source as a "sound image." The sound image can represent various functions, and users can recognize the role of the object by its sound. For example, an icon that represents an air-conditioner generates a sound to explain it in words, while an audio-volume icon produces a pleasant musical sound. The users utilize this sound as a clue to reach for the icons. Using tactile cues, they can recognize the exact positions of the icons and then perform fine tasks; for example, a user who accepts the objects of the air-conditioner can control the temperature by operating the sound-image icon. The haptic feedback is critical not only to improve the operability during the control but also to reliably guide and hold the user's hand to the starting point of the operation.

In this study, we prototype sound-image icons and experimentally verify their feasibility. We aim to realize a system where a user can select the desired icon among multiple icons and operate it. In this study, for the first step, we examine whether users can find an icon and measure the time required to access it. The combination of auditory and tactile sensations enables users to accurately and effectively locate the icons.

2 Proposed Method

A sound-image icon is realized using a sound source with the sense of touch provided via acoustic radiation pressure. In this section, we describe the method used to create the sound-image icon.

2.1 Producing a Sound Image

The user specifies the direction of the sound source using a binaural sound. We plan to provide binaural sounds using ultrasound beams to reach the ears. However, in this experimental system, the binaural sound was provided to the users by an in-ear binaural headset (CS-10EM, Roland). The binaural sound was recorded using the microphone in the headset that was fixed to the ears of one of the authors, keeping the sound source at the icon position. By reproducing the recorded sound in both the ears, the listener perceived the same 3D sound image as the real sound, under the assumption that the head related transfer functions are common [10].

2.2 Aerial Haptic Feedback

The aerial tactile sensation is presented at the icon location by using AUTD. The users actively search for the ultrasound focus, where the acoustic radiation pressure produces a tactile sensation of the virtual icon.

AUTD is a phased array that generates an ultrasonic focal point at an arbitrary position in the air [5,6]. The acoustic radiation pressure is proportional to the sound energy density on the skin surface [3]. Though an AUTD can produce various pressure patterns by controlling the amplitude and phase of each transducer at the frame-rate of 1 kHz [4], a single focus is created in this prototype. The users can perceive a certain stimulus around the focal point, where the tactile feel becomes vivid when the ultrasound amplitude is modulated in the amplitude or the focus position is laterally vibrated on the skin [15].

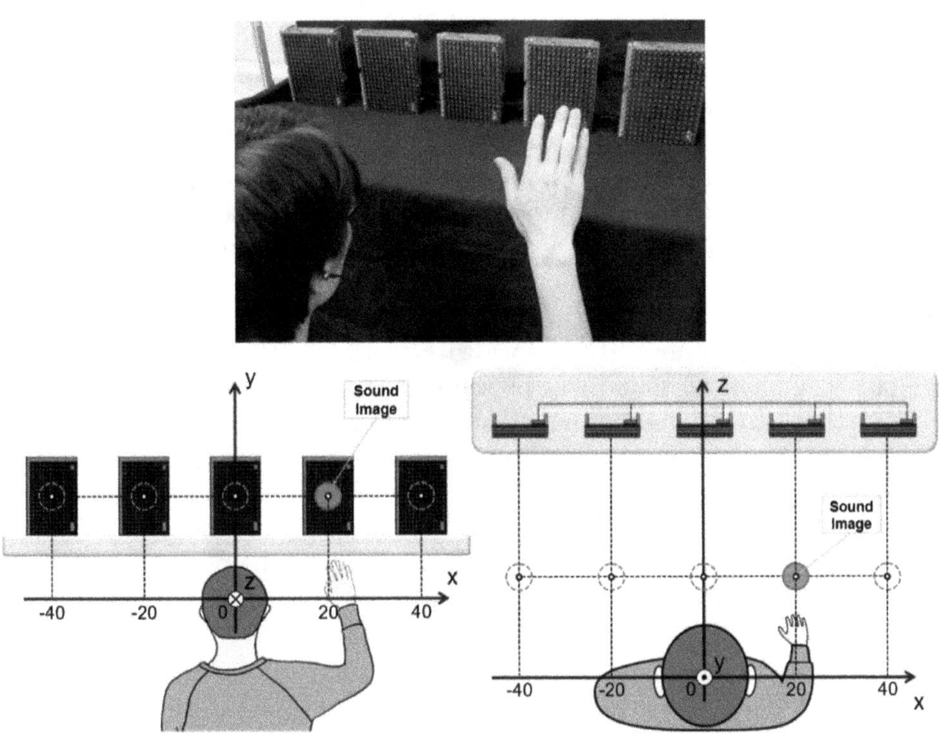

Fig. 2. Experimental setup. Five AUTDs were deployed 30 cm behind the five spots where the sound-image icon must be placed. The units of the numbers are in cm.

3 Experiment

We experimentally verified that humans could haptically identify the location of a particular icon by following the perception of sound. We measured the accuracy and time for haptic identification.

3.1 Procedure

The experimental setup is depicted in Fig. 2. In this experiment, we displayed five icons and examined whether the participants could identify them, and then we measured the time required for the identification. The icons were placed at $(-40, 20, 20)$, $(-20, 20, 20)$, $(0, 20, 20)$, $(20, 20, 20)$, and $(40, 20, 20)$ cm, where the origin was the center of the head, z-axis was parallel to the front direction, y-axis was parallel to the vertical direction, and x-axis is set as forming a right-handed system. The five AUTDs were placed 30 cm behind the sound image. A single corresponding AUTD emitted a focused ultrasound with 200 Hz sinusoidal amplitude modulation. The unit of the AUTD is an ultrasound phased array (SSC-HCT1, Shinko Shoji Co., Ltd.) with 14×18 elements. The maximum force displayed by a single unit is 10 mN.

As sound sources, we recorded the solos of the following five kinds of musical instruments: drum, bass, acoustic guitar, piano, and flute. We defined the drum sound as the target sound, as it was the easiest one to locate the position. We instructed the participants that the drum was the sound of the target sound-image icon to locate. Several sound sources (five at maximum), which included the target sound, were randomly selected and played at random positions in the five locations. As tactile feedback, a single ultrasound focus of the target icon was created at the target position.

The finding-target experiment was conducted considering the following two conditions: auditory-only and auditory-with-tactile. In the auditory-only condition, only the binaural sound was presented, while in the auditory-with-tactile condition, both sound and tactile stimulation were simultaneously presented.

We asked the participants to estimate the location of the target sound-image icon as soon as possible after they recognized the start cue, i.e., the moment the audio was played. In addition, we instructed them to close their eyes during fumble to prevent the visual effect. After determining the position of the icon, the participants indicated the position number among the five options from 1 to 5 with the keyboard. We applied white noise to eliminate the effects of AUTD driving noise.

The participants in this experiment were twelve men in their twenties who had no problems with hearing or health.

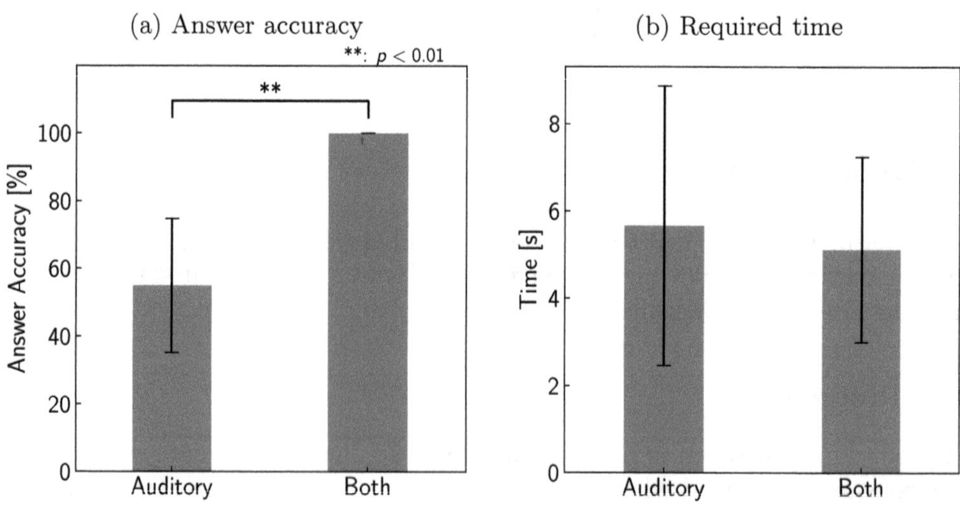

Fig. 3. Average of participants' (a) answer accuracy and (b) required time.

3.2 Results and Evaluations

The results are depicted in Figs. 3 (a) and (b). According to Fig. 3 (a), the answer accuracy was 55% when only the sound was informed of the location to the participants. Despite the high error rate of the "auditory-only condition," the accuracy rate of the "auditory+tactile condition" was almost 100%. Using the t-test, we examined whether the correct answer rate could be significantly improved by adding a tactile sensation to the sound cue. As a result of the test, the p-value between "auditory" and "auditory+tactile" was smaller than 0.01. This result means that the participants could exactly pinpoint the location of the sound image when they were able to search using tactile sensations.

In addition, Fig. 3 (b) shows that the average required times of each case were almost the same. Accordingly, the average time for "auditory" was 5.67 s, and that for "auditory+tactile" was 5.12 s. The standard deviation for "auditory+tactile" was less than that for "auditory." The standard deviation for "auditory+tactile" was approximately 2.12 s, and that for "auditory" was 3.20 s. This indicates that presenting both the stimuli reduced their standard deviations. For clarification, we used Levene's test for the standard deviations and Welch's t-test for the averages. As a result of Levene's test, the p-value between "auditory" and "auditory+tactile" was smaller than 0.01. According to the test, a significant difference was observed between the variances of required time for the two conditions. Additionally, the significance between the average amounts was not noticed, as the p-value from the Welch's t-test was 0.121.

4 Discussion

As depicted in Fig. 3 (a), in the case of sound alone, the exact position of the icon could not be estimated, and mistakes occurred. On the other hand, the correct answer rate became 100% by adding tactile feedback. This result indicates that sound localization was instantaneous, but it was inaccurate and unreliable. This drawback was compensated via haptic feedback, which offers reasonable cooperation between auditory and haptic perceptions. That is, the participants grasped the approximate position by hearing the sound and determined the exact position by touching the sound-image icon [7].

As additional information, it was possible to localize the position of the icon only by tactile sensation. To clarify this, we also conducted an additional experiment for the tactile-only condition. The participants and procedures were the same as those described in the Experiment section, and the start cue was an extra monaural audio. In this case, the time to perform localization was 5.30 ± 3.39 s. Although the average of the required time was comparable to that for the "auditory+tactile" condition, the variance was significantly longer.

Before this additional experiment, the time cost was expected to be the shortest in the case of "auditory+tactile." However, this hypothesis was not observed in this experiment. Searching the entire space without prior information was not a time-consuming task, as it only took approximately 2 s for the participants to fumble around the area with their hands. Nevertheless, considering that the standard deviation for the "auditory+tactile" condition is the smallest, it was confirmed that the combination of sound and haptic feedback facilitated the search of the icon.

To avoid confusion, we reconfirm the purpose of the combination of auditory and tactile sensations as follows. The role of the sound is to notify the user of the existence and attributes of the icon around the user. Tactile sensation is necessary to determine the exact location and operate the icon. Therefore, even if the localization time for the tactile-only condition is short, it does not mean that the auditory cue is unnecessary.

5 Conclusion and Future Works

In this study, we proposed a sound-image icon and examined the basic feasibility of icon localization. The sound-image icon represents the virtual existence of sound and haptics without visual presentation. Through the research, we confirmed that the participants could search and estimate the location of a single icon in an efficient manner using their tactile and auditory senses. For future work, we will investigate the possibility of efficiently displaying multiple icons.

We used a headset as a sound display device, as this was a feasibility study to examine the effectiveness of the auditory–haptic integration. However, it is also possible to produce binaural sounds in a non-contact manner using airborne ultrasound [12]. Performing a detailed operation using the sound-image icon was beyond the scope of this paper, and it would be the next important challenge of the sound-image icon.

References

1. Blauert, J.: Spatial Hearing: The Psychophysics of Human Sound Localization. MIT Press, Cambridge (1997)
2. Carter, T., Seah, S.A., Long, B., Drinkwater, B., Subramanian, S.: UltraHaptics: multi-point mid-air haptic feedback for touch surfaces. In: Proceedings of the 26th Annual ACM Symposium on User Interface Software and Technology, pp. 505–514 (2013)
3. Hoshi, T., Takahashi, M., Iwamoto, T., Shinoda, H.: Noncontact tactile display based on radiation pressure of airborne ultrasound. IEEE Trans. Haptics **3**(3), 155–165 (2010)
4. Inoue, S., Makino, Y., Shinoda, H.: Scalable architecture for airborne ultrasound tactile display. In: Hasegawa, S., Konyo, M., Kyung, K.-U., Nojima, T., Kajimoto, H. (eds.) AsiaHaptics 2016. LNEE, vol. 432, pp. 99–103. Springer, Singapore (2018). https://doi.org/10.1007/978-981-10-4157-0_17
5. Iwamoto, T., Shinoda, H.: Two-dimensional scanning tactile display using ultrasound radiation pressure. In: 2006 14th Symposium on Haptic Interfaces for Virtual Environment and Teleoperator Systems, pp. 57–61. IEEE (2005)
6. Iwamoto, T., Tatezono, M., Shinoda, H.: Non-contact method for producing tactile sensation using airborne ultrasound. In: Ferre, M. (ed.) EuroHaptics 2008. LNCS, vol. 5024, pp. 504–513. Springer, Heidelberg (2008). https://doi.org/10.1007/978-3-540-69057-3_64

7. Kaul, O.B., Rohs, M.: Haptichead: a spherical vibrotactile grid around the head for 3D guidance in virtual and augmented reality. In: Proceedings of the 2017 CHI Conference on Human Factors in Computing Systems, pp. 3729–3740 (2017)
8. Korres, G., Eid, M.: Haptogram: ultrasonic point-cloud tactile stimulation. IEEE Access **4**, 7758–7769 (2016)
9. Makino, Y., Furuyama, Y., Inoue, S., Shinoda, H.: Haptoclone (haptic-optical clone) for mutual tele-environment by real-time 3D image transfer with midair force feedback. In: Proceedings of the 2016 CHI Conference on Human Factors in Computing Systems, pp. 1980–1990 (2016)
10. Møller, H.: Fundamentals of binaural technology. Appl. Acoust. **36**(3–4), 171–218 (1992)
11. Monnai, Y., Hasegawa, K., Fujiwara, M., Yoshino, K., Inoue, S., Shinoda, H.: HaptoMime: mid-air haptic interaction with a floating virtual screen. In: Proceedings of the 27th Annual ACM Symposium on User Interface Software and Technology, pp. 663–667 (2014)
12. Ochiai, Y., Hoshi, T., Suzuki, I.: Holographic whisper: rendering audible sound spots in three-dimensional space by focusing ultrasonic waves. In: Proceedings of the 2017 CHI Conference on Human Factors in Computing Systems, pp. 4314–4325 (2017)
13. Pulkki, V.: Virtual sound source positioning using vector base amplitude panning. J. Audio Eng. Soc. **45**(6), 456–466 (1997)
14. Storek, D., Rund, F., Suchan, R.: Virtual auditory space for the visually impaired-experimental background. In: 2011 International Conference on Applied Electronics, pp. 1–4. IEEE (2011)
15. Takahashi, R., Hasegawa, K., Shinoda, H.: Tactile stimulation by repetitive lateral movement of midair ultrasound focus. IEEE Trans. Haptics **13**, 334–342 (2019)

21

Shared Haptic Perception for Human-Robot Collaboration

Kazuki Katayama[1(✉)], Maria Pozzi[2,3], Yoshihiro Tanaka[1], Kouta Minamizawa[4], and Domenico Prattichizzo[2,3]

[1] Nagoya Institute of Technology, Nagoya, Japan
k.katayama.806@nitech.jp, tanaka.yoshihiro@nitech.ac.jp
[2] University of Siena, Siena, Italy
[3] Istituto Italiano di Tecnologia, Genoa, Italy
[4] Keio University, Tokyo, Japan

Abstract. To obtain a fluent human-robot collaboration, reciprocal awareness is fundamental. In this paper, we propose to achieve it by creating a haptic connection between the human operator and the collaborative robot. Data coming from a wearable skin vibration sensor are used by the robot to recognize human actions, and vibrotactile signals are used to inform the human about the correct recognition of her/his actions. It is shown that the proposed communication paradigm, based on *shared haptic perception*, allows to improve cycle time performance in a complex human-robot collaborative task.

Keywords: Shared perception · Human-Robot Collaboration · Wearable haptics

1 Introduction

Human-Robot Collaboration (HRC) is expected to significantly advance manufacturing by introducing high flexibility in assembly cells [1], but also promises to enhance human capabilities in other fields, including domestic welfare and assistance to medical doctors [2,3]. To achieve a smooth collaboration between a human operator and a collaborative robot, *reciprocal awareness* is fundamental: the robot has to be aware of the human actions and the human has to know the robot state to fluently proceed with the collaborative task. This need was underlined by Drury *et al.*, in a review on awareness in Human-Robot Interaction [4].

Recent advances in interfaces for improved human and robot perception in HRC were surveyed in [5]. On the one hand, human sensorimotor information can be used to monitor human behaviour and plan appropriate robot responses in different phases of a collaborative task [6–8]. Peternel *et al.*, for example, used a vision system and EMG electrodes to detect human motion and muscular activity [6], whereas Ishida *et al.*, used a wearable vibration sensor to discriminate human actions [7]. On the other hand, visual, auditory, and tactile feedback can be employed to improve human situation awareness in HRC [1,9]. In [9], for instance, human intention was inferred based on visual monitoring, and mutual understanding was achieved by alerting the human through haptic cues when the robot understood human intention with a certain level of confidence.

In this paper, we present a human-robot collaborative set-up where the human sensorimotor system is virtually connected to the system of sensors and actuators of the robot through wearable devices. Human actions are recognized thanks to a wearable skin vibration sensor, and successful recognition is communicated to the human through the activation of a vibrotactile ring. The proposed collaboration paradigm is sketched in Fig. 1. The idea is to integrate the benefits of shared human perception [7] with those of operator awareness [9], creating a bilateral haptic connection between humans and robots, that we call *shared haptic perception*. The effectiveness of the proposed communication paradigm was demonstrated through an experimental validation involving 8 trained volunteers performing a complex collaborative task with a robot arm.

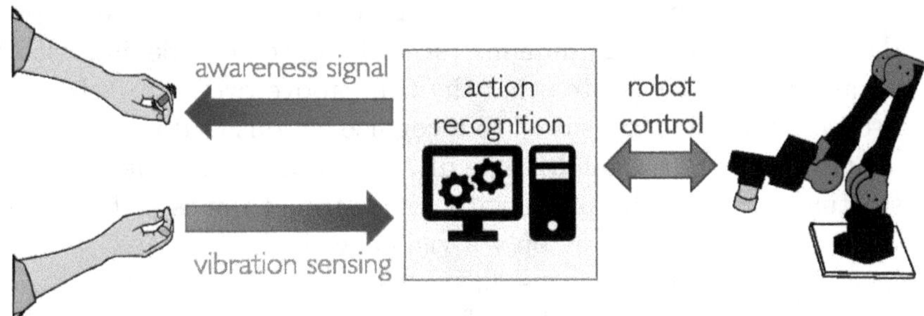

Fig. 1. Shared haptic perception between humans and robots: general idea. Human perception is shared because the same vibrations that are sensed by human touch receptors during the collaborative task are also detected by the wearable sensor and, thus, by the robot. Robot perception (enhanced by an action recognition algorithm) is shared with the human thanks to the tactile signal sent by the robot through the haptic device.

2 Methodology

The proposed collaboration paradigm is based on the use of two wearable devices, a vibration sensor and a vibrotactile ring, and on an action recognition algorithm.

Wearable Devices. In this study, the wearable skin vibration sensor developed by Tanaka *et al.* [10] is used for sending tactile information from the human to the robot. The sensor uses polyvinylidene difluoride (PVDF) film and detects vibrations propagating on the human skin surface. The acquired data are used to detect the current human action. The PVDF sensor does not hinder the natural movements of the human hand and allows to directly touch objects, because it is light (about 20 g) and can be worn by wrapping it around one of the fingers, as a ring. In [7], authors showed the advantages of putting the sensor on the human finger, with respect to applying it on the manipulated object. Not only the sensor output "directly represents operator's perception" [7], but instrumenting the human makes it possible to apply the proposed framework in different situations, without having to modify the environment around the user.

To send tactile information from the robot to the human, a wearable vibrotactile ring embedding a HAPTIC^{TM} Reactor (ALPS ALPINE CO., LTD.), is used. Two vibration bursts separated by an interval of 20 ms were sent to the participant to alert her/him that her/his action was recognized. We chose a frequency of 200 Hz for the vibration, as in [9] this kind of feedback was found to be easily recognizable and helpful to proceed smoothly with a HRC task.

Action Recognition. A paradigmatic task in which the human closes an envelope and the robot applies a stamp over it was chosen to show the effectiveness of the proposed tactile communication strategy. A Support Vector Machine (SVM) was used to recognize, based on the PVDF sensor output, the three different human actions involved in the task (see Fig. 2-(left)): gluing (human applies the glue on the envelope), tracing (human traces the envelope opening with index fingernail), and no contact (state other than the above two states). Note that a vibration sensor is particularly suited to recognize actions that imply interaction with the environment. It might be difficult, for example, to infer whether the human is actually tracing the paper with some strength or is just moving over it without even touching it, using only a vision system.

Similarly to [7], to distinguish the different states with the SVM, we used two features: vibration intensity (i_{RMS}) and frequency ratio (r). They were computed based on the power spectral density (PSD) of the sensor output calculated in the range between $f_1 = 100$ Hz and $f_2 = 1000$ Hz[1]: $i_{RMS} = log\sqrt{\int_{f_1}^{f_2} PSD(f)df}$, $r = \frac{A}{B}$. The value i_{RMS} indicates the root mean square (RMS) of the PSD of each sample, A is the log(RMS) of the PSD in the range [850–1000 Hz] and B is the log(RMS) of the PSD in the range [$F_{peak} \pm 75$ Hz]. F_{peak} is the frequency at which the PSD reaches its maximum value. Before each experiment, participants were asked to wear the vibration sensor and perform the three different actions, five times each. The collected data were used to create a linear SVM model based on the values of the two indices defined above. Figure 2-(right) presents

[1] Data below 100 Hz were not considered as they could easily be affected by minimal body motions and heart beat. For frequencies above 1000 Hz, the sensor output hardly changes based on user body motions [7].

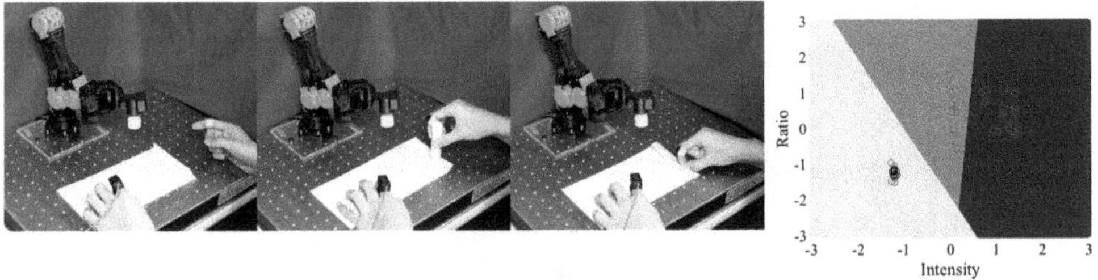

Fig. 2. (Left) Human states recognized by the SVM: no contact, gluing, tracing. (Right) Example of SVM model where data are well separated considering the intensity and ratio parameters (black: no contact, blue: gluing, red: tracing). (Color figure online)

an example of obtained SVM model. The top panel of the graphs in Fig. 3 show examples of complete acquisitions from the sensor for the gluing and the tracing state. From a total of 2 s, a central interval lasting 1 s was selected and divided into 5 samples of 0.2 s each (middle panel). For each sample, i_{RMS} and r were computed from the PSD (lower panel). The gluing action generates vibrations with a lower amplitude than those related to tracing.

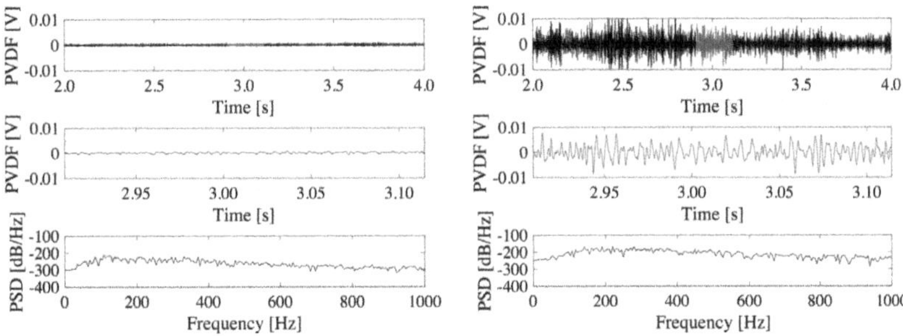

Fig. 3. Examples of PVDF sensor output and power spectral density (PSD) for gluing state (left) and tracing state (right). Top panel: complete acquisitions, middle and lower panels: sensor output and PSD for a sample of 0.2 s.

3 Experiments

3.1 Experimental Procedure

To design our experimental set-up (Fig. 4) we took inspiration from the previously described prototypical task of closing and stamping an envelope (Fig. 2), and made it more complex, so to better study the effectiveness of the proposed communication paradigm. In particular, we wanted to investigate how awareness vibrotactile signals affect the performance of well trained participants. This is an advancement with respect to [9], where participants only underwent a brief training, but were not expert in the performed task.

Fig. 4. Experimental set-up for the chosen HRC task.

Participants wore the haptic ring on the left hand and the PVDF sensor on the right, and listened to white noise while conducting the experiments. They sat in front of a collaborative robot arm, the open source manipulator Mikata arm (ROBOTIS Co., Ltd.), having four actuators and a stamp attached at the end-effector. In each experimental trial, the human operator had to trace with the right index finger a long piece of paper (size: 60×1000 mm), and the robot had to put a stamp in a predefined position upon recognition of the tracing state. In particular, the current PVDF sensor output was classified according to the found SVM model every 0.02 s. If the result of the classification was "tracing state" for 50 consecutive times (*i.e.*, for 1 s), the robot started its stamping task.

Trials were conducted under two conditions, one including vibrotactile feedback from the robot after tracing action recognition (awareness signal), and one without it. To make participants aware of the fact that the collaboration was mediated by an action recognition algorithm, they were instructed to trace slowly until the robot recognized the tracing motion, and then to complete the task as soon as possible. In other words, the goal was to finish the job as quickly as possible, but participants had to take into account the communication with the robot to be sure to get the paper stamped and thus successfully accomplish the task. Coordination between human and robot was important for two main reasons: *i*) the robot could put a stamp only after the human traced the part of the paper where the stamp had to be applied, and *ii*) the human had to be sure that the robot recognized the tracing action before it was actually completed. Note that when haptic feedback was not active, the user could infer robot state only by looking at it and waiting to see it moving towards the stamping position.

A within-subjects experimental design with complete counterbalancing was adopted. Each participant tested both conditions, with randomly assigned orderings. In particular, half of the participants initially conducted the experiment with feedback and then without, the other half did the opposite. Eight volunteers (6 males, 2 females, average age 26.5) participated in the study. They all had previous experience with wearable haptics. Informed consent was obtained from all of them and the experimental evaluation protocol followed the Declaration of Helsinki. Participants did not perceive any payment and were able to leave the experiment at any moment. Firstly, they were asked to record data to create the

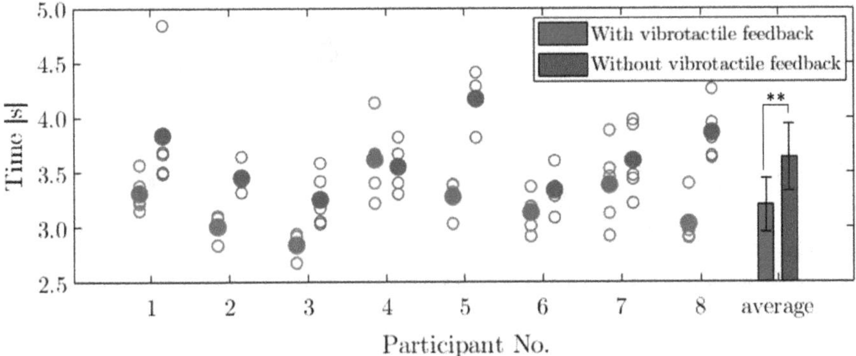

Fig. 5. Task execution time in two conditions (with/without feedback): single trial (empty circle) and average (filled circle) for each participant, and bar plot of mean and std of the averages. ** indicates $p < 0.01$ with the paired t-test.

SVM model, as described in Sect. 2. Then, each of them performed 15 trials per condition as *training phase* and, lastly, 5 trials for each condition as *test phase*. In the test phase, users' performance in terms of execution time was recorded. At the end of each trial, users had to press a button on the keyboard of a laptop placed on their right and then wait for a fixed amount of time (showed through a countdown on the screen), before starting the new trial.

In the first part of the training phase (10 trials), we were more interested in making the users learn the task, and thus we kept the robot stationary until the recognition of the tracing state. However, in real applications, the robot is never left idle and usually executes other actions while waiting for human operations. This is why, in the second part of the training phase (5 trials) and in the test phase, the arm was programmed to randomly reach four different poses, emulating other possible tasks, while waiting for the action recognition.

3.2 Experimental Results

The execution time of the 5 trials of the test phase, in the two conditions, is displayed for all participants in Fig. 5. The empty circles show the execution time of each trial, and the filled ones indicate the average execution time for each participant over five trials. The mean and standard deviation (3.20 ± 0.25 s with vibrotactile feedback, and 3.64 ± 0.31 s without vibrotactile feedback) of these average data are used to plot the bar plots on the right labeled as "average". Regarding these data, the Shapiro-Wilk test showed normal distribution and the paired t-test for each condition showed that there was a significant difference between the average execution times for the two conditions ($t_7 = 3.8$, $p = 7.0 \times 10^{-3}$). In other words, when haptic feedback was active, participants took significantly less time for completing their task, than when there was no haptic feedback.

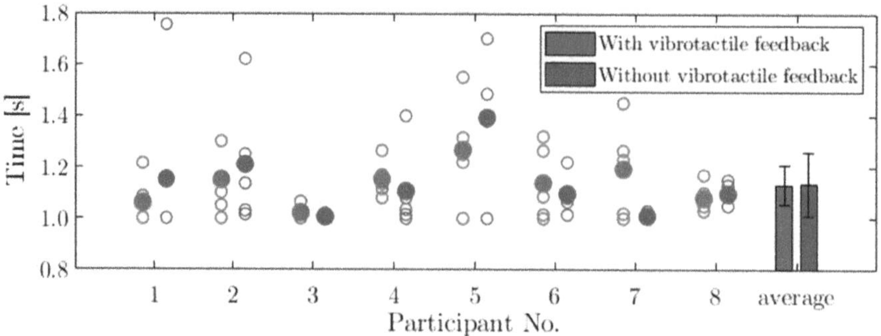

Fig. 6. Recognition time in two conditions (with/without feedback): single trial (empty circle) and average (filled circle) for each participant, and bar plot of mean and std of the averages.

In both conditions, the PVDF sensor worn by participants was active and was used to recognize user actions. The recognition was successful in all the trials. To ensure the validity of this result, we analysed the *recognition time* of the robot, *i.e.*, the time that it took to recognize that the human was tracing, in the two conditions. Figure 6 shows the recognition time for each participant for each trial (empty circles) and on average (filled circles). As before, the bar plots are built by considering mean and standard deviation (1.13 ± 0.08 s with vibrotactile feedback, and 1.13 ± 0.12 s without vibrotactile feedback) of the average values for all participants. In this case, no significant difference was found between the two conditions at a significance level of 5% for all participants. Thus, the recognition time did not significantly vary between the two conditions.

4 Discussion

Results presented in Sect. 3.2 show that not only the proposed communication paradigm offers a viable solution for implementing human-robot collaborative tasks, but also, and more importantly, that the vibrotactile feedback significantly improves human performance. The vibrotactile awareness signal allows operators to understand whether their action was successfully recognized, without having to wait to see the robot moving towards the stamping position. Besides, the fact that the robot performs other actions before the recognition, makes it even more difficult for users to understand robot next movements just from sight.

The advantages of enhancing operator awareness were initially observed in [9], and in this paper we show that awareness is important also in a completely different scenario, where human actions are not predicted but recognized, using skin vibration sensing and not visual monitoring, and, above all, where participants are not novice, but are well trained to perform the task.

5 Conclusions

This work presents a new human-robot communication paradigm based on the concept of *shared haptic perception*: the user sends to the robot haptic cues that allow the robot to recognize human actions, and the robot informs the human through symbolic vibrotactile signals (awareness signals) about the successful interpretation of the received data. This bilateral communication, achieved through the use of unobtrusive wearable sensing and actuation devices, allows to reach reciprocal awareness and mutual understanding between the two partners.

An experimental validation with 8 participants was conducted and showed that awareness signals allow well trained users to complete their task in significantly less time than without haptic feedback. Future work will focus on investigating other tactile feedback modalities (*e.g.*, continuous exchange of tactile information), on finding other collaborative tasks that can benefit from the proposed communication strategy, and on studying whether shared haptic perception can improve also the learning process of a task for untrained operators.

References

1. Valeria, V., Fabio, P., Francesco, L., Cristian, S.: Survey on human-robot collaboration in industrial settings: safety, intuitive interfaces and applications. Mechatronics **55**, 248–266 (2018)
2. Canal, G., Alenyà, G., Torras, C.: Adapting robot task planning to user preferences: an assistive shoe dressing example. Auton. Robots **43**(6), 1343–1356 (2018). https://doi.org/10.1007/s10514-018-9737-2
3. Grischke, J., Johannsmeier, L., Eich, L., Haddadin, S.: Dentronics: Review, first concepts and pilot study of a new application domain for collaborative robots in dental assistance. In: 2019 International Conference on Robotics and Automation (ICRA), pp. 6525–6532 (2019)
4. Drury, J.L., Scholtz, J., Yanco, H.A.: Awareness in human-robot interactions. In: 2003 IEEE International Conference on Systems, Man and Cybernetics. Conference Theme-System Security and Assurance, vol. 1, pp. 912–918. IEEE (2003)
5. Ajoudani, A., Zanchettin, A.M., Ivaldi, S., Albu-Schäffer, A., Kosuge, K., Khatib, O.: Progress and prospects of the human-robot collaboration. Auton. Robots **42**(5), 957–975 (2018)
6. Peternel, L., Tsagarakis, N., Ajoudani, A.: A human-robot co-manipulation approach based on human sensorimotor information. IEEE Trans. Neural Syst. Rehabil. Eng. **25**(7), 811–822 (2017)
7. Ishida, R., Meli, L., Tanaka, Y., Minamizawa, K., Prattichizzo, D.: Sensory-motor augmentation of the robot with shared human perception. In: Proceedings of IEEE/RSJ International Conference Intelligent Robots and Systems, Madrid, Spain, pp. 2596–2603 (2018)
8. DelPreto, J., Rus, D.: Sharing the load: human-robot team lifting using muscle activity. In: 2019 International Conference on Robotics and Automation (ICRA), pp. 7906–7912 (2019)

9. Casalino, A., Messeri, C., Pozzi, M., Zanchettin, A.M., Rocco, P., Prattichizzo, D.: Operator awareness in human-robot collaboration through wearable vibrotactile feedback. IEEE Robot. Autom. Lett. **3**(4), 4289–4296 (2018)
10. Tanaka, Y., Nguyen, D.P., Fukuda, T., Sano, A.: Wearable skin vibration sensor using a PVDF film. In: 2015 IEEE World Haptics Conference (WHC), pp. 146–151 (2015)

22

Adaptive Fuzzy Sliding Mode Controller Design for a New Hand Rehabilitation Robot

Alireza Abbasimoshaei[1], Majid Mohammadimoghaddam[2], and Thorsten A. Kern[1](✉)

[1] University of Technology Hamburg Harburg, Eissendorferstr. 38, 21073 Hamburg, Germany
{al.abbasimoshaei,t.a.kern}@tuhh.de
[2] Tarbiatmodares University, Amirabad, 14115 Tehran, Iran
m.moghadam@modares.ac.ir
https://www.tuhh.de/imek

Abstract. Hand rehabilitation is one of the most important rehabilitation procedures. Due to the repetitive nature of rehabilitation training, a full robotic system could help the physiotherapists to gain time for creating new training schemes for a larger number of patients. Such a system can be based on live or recorded data and consists of the operator-device, patient-device, and control mechanism. This paper focuses on the design of the patient-device and its control-system in a decoupled training scenario. It presents a robot for hand rehabilitation training fingers and wrist independently based on only two actuators. These two actuators are configurable to allow consecutive training on the wrist and all joints of the fingers. To overcome uncertainties and disturbances, a sliding mode controller has been designed and an adaptive fuzzy sliding mode controller is used to reduce the chattering effects and compensate the varying forces of the patients. The experimental results show an approximate 80% improvement in tracking the desired trajectory by the adaptation.

Keywords: Adaptive fuzzy control · Rehabilitation robot · Haptics

1 Introduction

The need for rehabilitation of hand-fractures origins from two sources. One is hand-fractures, in general occurring among all ages including boys and girls, among which one third face fractures before the age of 17 [1,2]. The second source is rehabilitation after surgery or plastering to regain mobility. The traditional method usually requires the active involvement of a physiotherapist and requires a lot of time with repetitive training. Due to a lack of resources for therapy, new methods and equipment such as rehabilitation robots and actuated home-rehabilitation [3,4] are under strong development.

Acceptance of such active systems is usually good if the patient feels to be in charge due to understandable and expectable motions and the possibility for an emergency stop. An additional benefit is always the opportunity to record and collect data about the progress of therapy. Combining robotic therapy with other methods, such as motor learning, control or bio-signal processing, helps to develop the potentiality of rehabilitation [5]. Although some items such as device-accuracy in the medical robots need to be considered, a large number of clinical studies confirmed the efficiency of robotic rehabilitation robots [6].

Coming into technical details, a lot of different systems for hand and finger-rehabilitation were proposed by researchers and commercial vendors for therapeutic systems. A device-taxonomy can be given by the number of actuated DOFs, the physiological joints in therapeutic focus, whether they are grounded or wearable, mode of rehabilitation exercises and in general the complexity of the device according to Table 1.

The scope of this paper is about a combined wrist and finger rehabilitation robot with the capability to exercise each phalanx individually, with a maximum of multi DOFs combined in one device at an affordable price-point. Despite all systems from Table 1 have their benefits, nearest to the scope of this paper is [16], [12], and [19] from different points of view. [16] shows a reconfigurable system but it was not for fingers. [12] is for the rehabilitation of wrist and fingers and it differs from our system because it was not for each finger individually. [19] is for each finger but it was not for each phalanges.

Concerning the underlying control algorithm especially [20] shows an interesting approach by force control and [19] due to using impedance control, in this system an adaptive fuzzy sliding mode controller is used which will be described in the following.

2 Design and Prototyping

Figure 1a shows the schematic view of the designed wrist and finger rehabilitation robot, which moves finger joints and wrist with two motors. As can be seen in Fig. 1a, the hand is located in the upper section that includes the green finger part and two ball bearings. Because during the rotation, the joints center of motion changes, a flexible system is used for the finger part. In this system, the first motor (motor 1) moves the cable and rotates the finger. The wrist is rotated by the second motor (motor 2) while the ball bearings and a shaft transfer the rotation of the motor to the wrist [21,22].

A detailed view of the finger part is shown in Fig. 1b. There is a bar at the backside of the system to lock or unlock the joints. The configuration of the bar shown in Fig. 1b is for DIP training of the index finger. The finger part is adjusted by changing the engaged track (Fig. 1b) and the circular end of the bar is for making the movement of the bar easier. By changing the unlocked joint, the rehabilitation can be applied to each phalanx. As it is shown in Fig. 1c, DIP sits at the tip of the finger part and according to the size of the finger, the tracks will be fixed. The cable connected to the tip of the system moves the finger to the palm and the spring moves it in the reverse direction.

Table 1. Main features of some of the most common previous devices for wrist and finger rehabilitation

Name	DOF	Joints	Fixation	Mode of Rehabilitation	Source
Rutgers Master II	4	Four fingers (without little finger)	Wearable	Active	[7]
Wristbot	3	Wrist	Grounded	Active and Passive	[8]
Gloreha	5	Fingers	Wearable	Active	[9]
CR2-Haptic	1	Forearm and Wrist	Grounded	Active	[10]
Hand of Hope	5	Fingers	Wearable	Active	[11]
HWARD	3	Wrist and Fingers	Wearable	Active	[12]
Reha-Digit	4	Four Fingers (without thumb)	Grounded	Passive	[9]
CyberGrasp	5	Fingers	Wearable	Active	[13]
ARMin	2	Forearm and Wrist	Wearable	Additional hand module	[14]
GENTLE/G	3	Fingers	Wearable	Additional hand module	[15]
WReD	1	Forearm and Wrist	Grounded	Active	[16]
Amadeo	5	Fingers	Grounded	Passive	[17]
BiManu Track	1	Forearm and Wrist	Grounded	Active and Passive	[18]
Hand Robot Alpha-Prototype II	1	Fingers	Grounded	Additional hand module	[19]
HandCARE	5	Five fingers	Grounded	Active	[20]

In Fig. 2 the manufactured robot and rehabilitation procedure of the wrist and finger are shown. The system includes two actuators, rotating and fixed plates. Furthermore, an emergency key is designed to stop the system in an emergency condition. Due to the decoupled degrees of freedom, the actuation system moves the fingers and wrist separately. For rehabilitation, the patient's hand should be placed at the hand holder and according to the desired movement, finger or wrist will be trained.

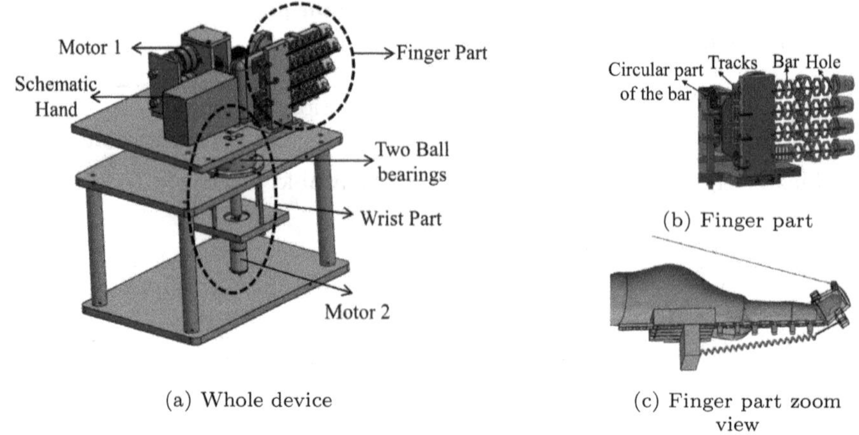

(a) Whole device

(b) Finger part

(c) Finger part zoom view

Fig. 1. Schematic design of the system.

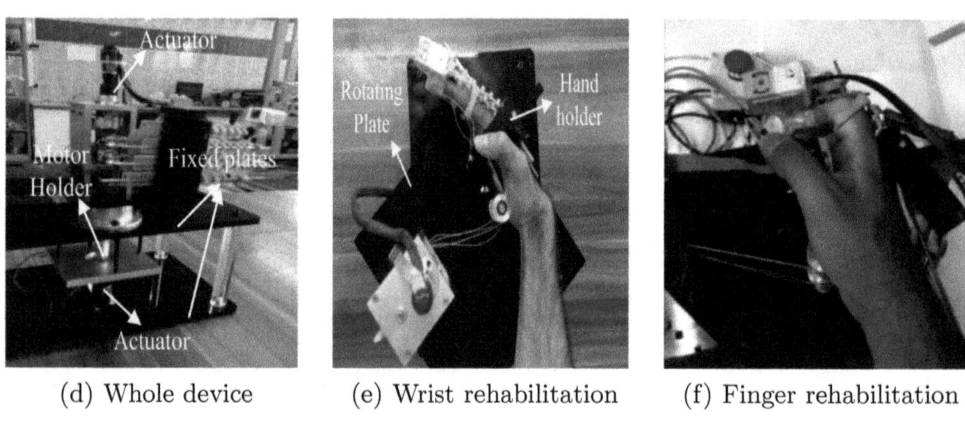

(d) Whole device (e) Wrist rehabilitation (f) Finger rehabilitation

Fig. 2. Prototype of the rehabilitation robot

3 Mathematical Model of the Device and SMC Design

The dynamic equation of the rehabilitation robot is the result of Newton's law applied to the fingertip. The overall equation of the system is obtained as follows:

$$I\ddot{\theta} = T \times \sin(\alpha) \times l_3 + T \times \cos(\alpha) \times E - K \times ((\sqrt{A} - \sqrt{B}) \times \cos(\beta) \times l_3 + (\sqrt{A} - \sqrt{B}) \times \sin(\beta) \times G) - C\dot{\theta} - K_1\theta \tag{1}$$

$$A = (H + l_3 \sin(\theta))^2 + (l_1 + l_2 + l_3 \cos(\theta))^2 \tag{2}$$

$$B = H^2 + (l_1 + l_2 + l_3)^2 \tag{3}$$

$$I\ddot{\theta} = T \times R. \tag{4}$$

Figure 3a shows the simplified kinematic model of the robot for Fig. 1 and E, G, and H are the distances shown in the picture. In Eq. 1, l_1, l_2, and l_3 are the length of the phalanges, I is the inertia of the rotating part, R is the motor shaft, and θ is the rotation angle of the finger. C, K_1, and K represent the damping and stiffness of the robot and stiffness of the spring. I is the system's moment of inertia and T shows the force of the cable. α and β have the following relations and the distance between the finger part and the connection point of the cable with the system is shown by D in Fig. 3b.

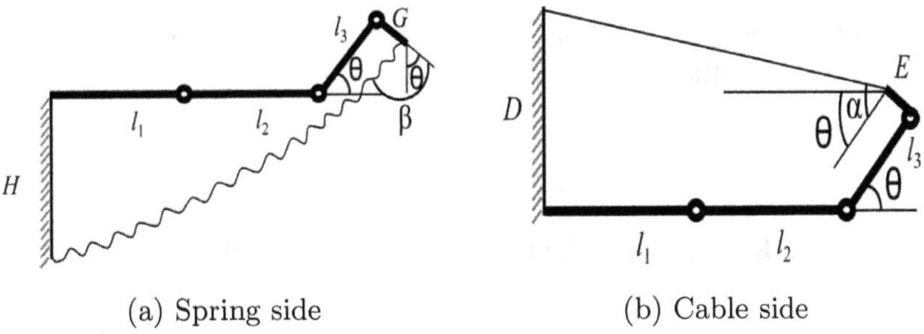

(a) Spring side (b) Cable side

Fig. 3. Simplified kinematic model of the robot

$$\alpha = \theta + \text{atan}(\frac{D - l_3 \sin(\theta) - E\cos(\theta)}{l_1 + l_2 + l_3\cos(\theta) - E\sin(\theta)}) \tag{5}$$

$$\beta = \theta + \text{atan}(\frac{l_1 + l_2 + l_3\cos(\theta) + G\sin(\theta)}{H + l_3\sin(\theta) - G\cos(\theta)}) \tag{6}$$

In Eq. 1, θ is the finger rotation angle, l is the cable length, x and y are the horizontal and vertical axes of the cable length respectively. Because of unknown parameters and uncertainties in the mechanical model identification of the system, a sliding mode controller (SMC) has been used. This controller can reduce the effects of parameter variations, uncertainties, and disturbances.

For designing the SMC, it should be considered that the sliding mode controller could guarantee the stability of the system and it consists of two subcontrollers u_{eq} and u_{rb}. To make the system stable in the Lyapunov sense, $S\dot{S}$ should be less than zero. u_{eq} is the equivalent controller and u_{rb} is used to control the uncertainties and disturbances. In this system, u_{eq} and u_{rb} are considered as Eq. 8 and Eq. 9. The final design of the SMC found as follows [23].

$$u = u_{eq} + u_{rb} \tag{7}$$

$$u_{eq} = g^{-1}(\ddot{x}_d - f - k(\dot{x} - \dot{x}_d) - \eta s) \tag{8}$$

$$u_{rb} = -g^{-1}\rho.\text{sgn}(s) \tag{9}$$

In which, η is a positive constant. If we consider the general equation of the system as Eq. 10 and Eq. 11, g and f formula for this system would be obtained as Eq. 12 and Eq. 13.

$$\ddot{x} = f(x,t) + g(x,t)u + \lambda \tag{10}$$

$$y = x \tag{11}$$

$$g = (\frac{1}{I})(\sin(\alpha)l_3 + \cos(\alpha)E) \tag{12}$$

$$\begin{aligned} f = (\frac{1}{I})(-K \times ((\sqrt{A} - \sqrt{B}) \times \cos(\beta) \times l_3 \\ + (\sqrt{A} - \sqrt{B}) \times \sin(\beta) \times G) - C\dot{\theta} - K_1\theta) \end{aligned} \tag{13}$$

Where $g(x,t)$ and $f(x,t)$ are unknown functions of the system dynamic equation. Moreover, λ is unknown disturbances satisfying Eq. 14.

$$|\lambda| < \rho \tag{14}$$

4 Adaptive Fuzzy Sliding Mode Controller Design

The sliding mode controller reduces the error of the system. But it has a sign function which leads to an undesired chattering phenomenon. To overcome this error, fuzzy controller design is proposed. In the previous work [23], a fuzzy sliding mode controller (FSMC) is designed for the rehabilitation robot by integrating a fuzzy controller into an SMC. $S(t)$ and $\dot{S}(t)$ are the inputs of the fuzzy system and the output of the system is u_{fa} [23].

In this configuration, undesired chattering is overcome. However, during the experiments, it is shown that due to the different stiffness of the patients' hands, various interactive forces are entered into the hand and robot. To overcome this, the robot needs an adaptive controller according to Fig. 4.

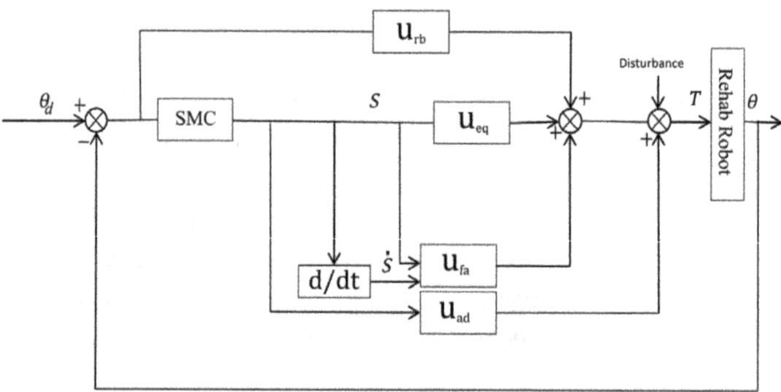

Fig. 4. The overall block diagram of the system containing adaptive controller

The adaptive controller tuning law is derived based on the Lyapunov theory to guaranty the system stability. This adaptive law is designed to approximate the indeterminacy and the interaction force and drives the trajectory tracking error to zero. After considering disturbances, unknown parameters, and patients' interaction force, the mathematical model of the system can be expressed as follows.

$$x_1 = \theta \tag{15}$$

$$\dot{x_1} = x_2 \tag{16}$$

$$\ddot{x} = (\frac{1}{I})(T \times \sin(\alpha) \times l_3 + T \times \cos(\alpha) \times E - K \times ((\sqrt{A} - \sqrt{B}) \times \cos(\beta) \times l_3 + (\sqrt{A} - \sqrt{B}) \times \sin(\beta) \times G) - C\dot{\theta} - K_1\theta + F_{int} + \lambda) \tag{17}$$

$$y = x_1 \tag{18}$$

Where x_1,x_2, and y are the state vectors and F_{int} is the interaction force of the robot and the hand. We also suppose that the interaction force changes slowly.

$$\dot{F}_{int} = 0 \tag{19}$$

The proposed Lyapunov function is defined as follow.

$$v = (\frac{1}{2})(s^2) + (\frac{1}{2})(\tilde{F}^2) \tag{20}$$

$$\tilde{F} = F_{int} - \hat{F} \tag{21}$$

In which $\hat{F}$ is the estimation of the interaction force(F_{int}), and $\tilde{F}$ is the error of this estimation. Thus,

$$\dot{\tilde{F}} = \dot{F}_{int} - \dot{\hat{F}} = -\dot{\hat{F}} \tag{22}$$

$$\dot{V} = S \times \dot{S} + \tilde{F} \times \dot{\tilde{F}} = S \times \dot{S} - \tilde{F} \times \dot{\hat{F}} \tag{23}$$

$$\dot{V} = S \times ((\ddot{x}_1 - \ddot{x}_d) + K(\dot{x}_1 - \dot{x}_d)) - \tilde{F} \times \dot{\hat{F}} \tag{24}$$

$$\ddot{x}_1 = f(x,t) + g(x,t)u + \lambda + \frac{F_{int}}{I}. \tag{25}$$

Taking Eq. 25 into Eq. 24, then

$$\dot{V} = s \times gu_{ad} + \frac{(\tilde{F} + \hat{F})}{I}s - \tilde{F} \times \dot{\hat{F}} + [-\eta s^2 - \rho|s| + \lambda s]. \tag{26}$$

The Eq. 27 was reached in the sliding mode section.

$$-\eta s^2 - \rho|s| + \lambda s < 0 \tag{27}$$

So,

$$\dot{V} < s \times g \times u_{ad} + \frac{(\tilde{F} + \hat{F})}{I}s - \tilde{F} \times \dot{\hat{F}} \tag{28}$$

$$u_{ad} = -\frac{\hat{F}}{I \times g} \tag{29}$$

$$\hat{F} = \int \frac{s}{I} \tag{30}$$

$$u_{ad} = -\frac{1}{l_3 \sin(\alpha) + E\cos(\alpha)} \int \frac{s}{I} \tag{31}$$

Thus, with this adaptive signal which is added to the other signals, $\dot{V}$ is always negative and the system stability is guaranteed.

5 Experiments and Results

Our robot design was developed with the focus on easy application in daily professional life and by advice from physiotherapists. Two trajectory tracking experiments were done to validate the controlling system and robot. The first one was for wrist and the second one was for fingers. In the first experiment, ten subjects (seven males and three females) did the tracking training three times and every training session takes time between 2 to 4 min. Each volunteer was encouraged to keep relaxed for training. In this experiment, a cosine wave function is defined as the desired trajectory for the wrist. Figure 5 shows the average error of the experiments and depicts that the error of the system for wrist trajectory tracking is reduced and the movement of the system became smooth and near to the desired. As shown in this figure, the fuzzy sliding mode controller reduced the error and the measured trajectory follows the desired trajectory better. But adaptive fuzzy SMC can reduce the errors resulting from the differences between patients. Therefore, this controller is used to reduce the effects of the different patients' interactions with the robot.

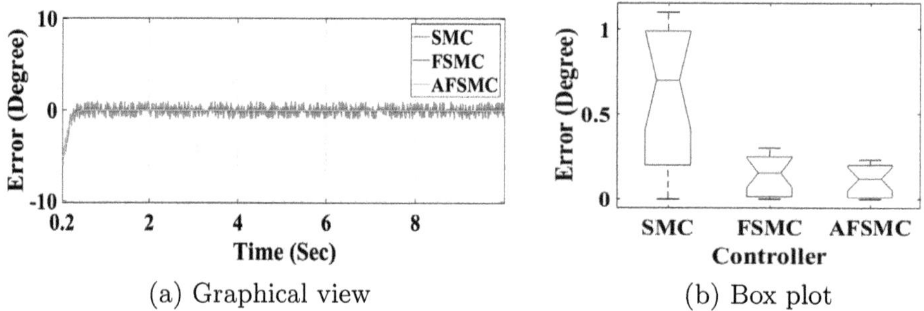

(a) Graphical view (b) Box plot

Fig. 5. Different controllers error

In the other experiment, the slow movement of each phalanx was explored. To find the desired trajectory of phalanges, the movements kinematic of all of them were analyzed during their tasks. Ten healthy subjects, seven males and three females, with different finger sizes, performed finger trials under the supervision of a physician [24]. They moved their phalanges (without robot) according to the physician instructions and an attached gyro sensor measured angle of rotation. The average of the collected data was found and fitted with a polynomial. Then, the experiments were done with the robot and different control algorithms. Figure 6 shows the results of the experiments with sliding mode controller and adaptive fuzzy SMC.

It can be understood from these experiments that the sliding mode controller improves the tracking performance, but there are some errors because of the chattering effects. The fuzzy controller reduces the chattering effects and makes the performance of the system better because it adjusts the output of the system according to the errors and disturbances. Adaptive fuzzy SMC decreases the error because this controller adapts the robot with different patients. According to the average data of the experiments, it is computed that using an adaptive fuzzy sliding mode controller (AFSMC) reduces the average errors in the wrist and phalanges about 80%.

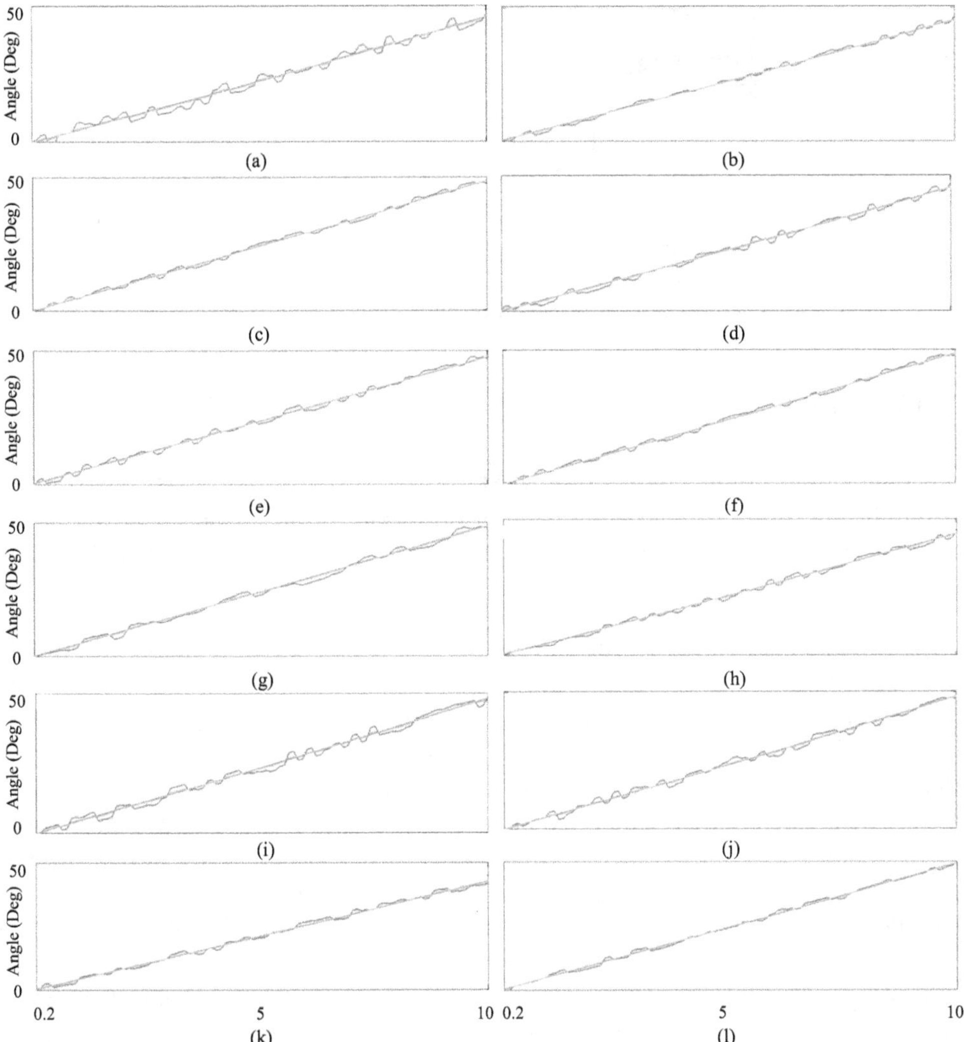

Fig. 6. Trajectory (blue line), output of the system with SMC (red line), and adaptive fuzzy SMC (green line) for each phalanx: a) DIP phalanx of index b) DIP phalanx of middle c) DIP phalanx of ring d) DIP phalanx of little e) PIP phalanx of index f) PIP phalanx of middle g) PIP phalanx of ring h) PIP phalanx of little I) MCP phalanx of index j) MCP phalanx of middle k) MCP phalanx of ring l) MCP phalanx of little finger (Color figure online)

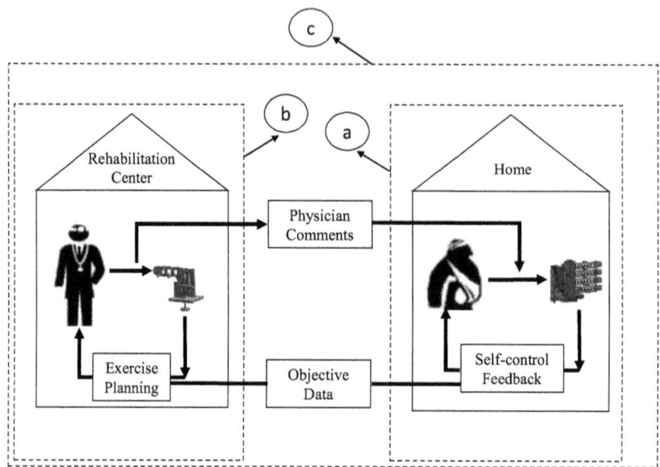

Fig. 7. Full telemanipulation system

6 Conclusion

In this paper, a novel mechanism for wrist and fingers is presented. In this system, the number of motors is reduced and the robot can rehabilitate all of the joints and wrist with only two motors. Still, each phalanx can be rehabilitated by this robot that makes rehabilitation very cost-efficient.

Furthermore, an AFSMC design method is proposed to control this robot. This controller can deal with unknown parameters and uncertainties and it enhances the system robustness. In this controller, the output of the fuzzy controller is calculated based on the error. Thus, the controller is more robust and independent of the system model. On the other hand, with different patients, there are different interaction forces between hand and robot and it is an important parameter that should be considered in the dynamic equation of the system. Therefore, there is a requirement for adapting the parameters, thus an adaptive controller beside the fuzzy SMC is designed to eliminate the effects of these forces. The effectiveness of the control system is examined with some trajectory tracking experiments. The experiments results show that the proposed AFSMC has much less error and as an average, the system performance improves by 80%.

For the future, following previous works like [4], a haptic system will be designed to make communication between the physician and the patient. This system can improve the efficiency of the rehabilitation procedure and has the potential not only to make the expert involvement more efficient but also to reduce the total duration of the rehabilitation due to only partially supervised offline-training capabilities (Fig. 7).

References

1. Feehan, L.M., Sheps, S.B.: Incidence and demographics of hand fractures in British Columbia, Canada: a population-based study. J. Hand Surg. **31**(7), 1068–e1 (2006)
2. Cooper, C., Dennison, E.M., Leufkens, H.G., Bishop, N., van Staa, T.P.: Epidemiology of childhood fractures in Britain: a study using the general practice research database. J. Bone Miner. Res. **19**(12), 1976–1981 (2004)
3. Heo, P., Gu, G.M., Lee, S.-J., Rhee, K., Kim, J.: Current hand exoskeleton technologies for rehabilitation and assistive engineering. Int. J. Precis. Eng. Manuf. **13**(5), 807–824 (2012)
4. Prange, G.B., et al.: Script: tele-robotics at home; functional architecture and clinical application. In: Proceedings of the Sixth International Symposium on e-Health Services and Technologies and the Third International Conference on Green IT Solutions, pp. 58–63. SciTePress (2012)
5. Iandolo, R., et al.: Perspectives and challenges in robotic neurorehabilitation. Appl. Sci. **9**(15), 3183 (2019)
6. Bogue, R.: Rehabilitation robots. Ind. Robot Int. J. **45**(3), 301–306 (2018)
7. Bouzit, M., Burdea, G., Popescu, G., Boian, R.: The Rutgers Master II-new design force-feedback glove. IEEE/ASME Trans. Mechatron. **7**(2), 256–263 (2002)
8. Masia, L., Casadio, M., Giannoni, P., Sandini, G., Morasso, P.: Performance adaptive training control strategy for recovering wrist movements in stroke patients: a preliminary, feasibility study. J. Neuroeng. Rehabil. **6**(1), 44 (2009)
9. Bos, R.A., et al.: A structured overview of trends and technologies used in dynamic hand orthoses. J. Neuroeng. Rehabil. **13**(1), 62 (2016)
10. Khor, K., Chin, P., Hisyam, A., Yeong, C., Narayanan, A., Su, E.: Development of CR2-haptic: a compact and portable rehabilitation robot for wrist and forearm training. In: 2014 IEEE Conference on Biomedical Engineering and Sciences (IECBES), pp. 424–429. IEEE (2014)
11. Balasubramanian, S., Klein, J., Burdet, E.: Robot-assisted rehabilitation of hand function. Curr. Opin. Neurol. **23**(6), 661–670 (2010)
12. Takahashi, C.D., Der-Yeghiaian, L., Le, V., Cramer, S.C.: A robotic device for hand motor therapy after stroke. In: 9th International Conference on Rehabilitation Robotics, ICORR 2005, pp. 17–20. IEEE (2005)
13. Nikolakis, G., Tzovaras, D., Moustakidis, S., Strintzis, M.G.: Cybergrasp and phantom integration: enhanced haptic access for visually impaired users. In: 9th Conference Speech and Computer (2004)
14. Nef, T., Mihelj, M., Colombo, G., Riener, R.: Armin-robot for rehabilitation of the upper extremities. In: Proceedings 2006 IEEE International Conference on Robotics and Automation, ICRA 2006, pp. 3152–3157. IEEE (2006)
15. Loureiro, R.C., Harwin, W.S.: Reach & grasp therapy: design and control of a 9-DOF robotic neuro-rehabilitation system. In: 2007 IEEE 10th International Conference on Rehabilitation Robotics, pp. 757–763. IEEE (2007)
16. Xu, D., et al.: Development of a reconfigurable wrist rehabilitation device with an adaptive forearm holder. In: 2018 IEEE/ASME International Conference on Advanced Intelligent Mechatronics (AIM), pp. 454–459. IEEE (2018)
17. Helbok, R., Schoenherr, G., Spiegel, M., Sojer, M., Brenneis, C.: Robot-assisted hand training (Amadeo) compared with conventional physiotherapy techniques in chronic ischemic stroke patients: a pilot study. DGNR Bremen, November 2010

18. Hesse, S., Schulte-Tigges, G., Konrad, M., Bardeleben, A., Werner, C.: Robot-assisted arm trainer for the passive and active practice of bilateral forearm and wrist movements in hemiparetic subjects. Arch. Phys. Med. Rehabil. **84**(6), 915–920 (2003)
19. Masia, L., Krebs, H.I., Cappa, P., Hogan, N.: Design and characterization of hand module for whole-arm rehabilitation following stroke. IEEE/ASME Trans. Mechatron. **12**(4), 399–407 (2007)
20. Dovat, L., et al.: Handcare: a cable-actuated rehabilitation system to train hand function after stroke. IEEE Trans. Neural Syst. Rehabil. Eng. **16**(6), 582–591 (2008)
21. Dehghan Neistanak, V., Moghaddam, M.M., Abbasi Moshaei, A.: Design of a hand tendon injury rehabilitation system using a DOF constrainer mechanism. Modares Mech. Eng. **20**(1), 1–12 (2019)
22. Niestanak, V.D., Moshaii, A.A., Moghaddam, M.M.: A new underactuated mechanism of hand tendon injury rehabilitation. In: 2017 5th RSI International Conference on Robotics and Mechatronics (ICRoM), pp. 400–405. IEEE (2017)
23. Abbasi Moshaii, A., Mohammadi Moghaddam, M., Dehghan Niestanak, V.: Fuzzy sliding mode control of a wearable rehabilitation robot for wrist and finger. Ind. Robot **46**(6), 839–850 (2019). https://www.emerald.com/insight/content/doi/10.1108/IR-05-2019-0110/full/html
24. Moshaii, A.A., Moghaddam, M.M., Niestanak, V.D.: Analytical model of hand phalanges desired trajectory for rehabilitation and design a sliding mode controller based on this model. Modares Mech. Eng. **20**(1), 129–137 (2020)

23

Wearable Vibrotactile Interface Using Phantom Tactile Sensation for Human-Robot Interaction

Julian Seiler[1], Niklas Schäfer[1(✉)], Bastian Latsch[1], Romol Chadda[1], Markus Hessinger[1], Philipp Beckerle[2,3], and Mario Kupnik[1]

[1] Technische Universität Darmstadt, Measurement and Sensor Technology, Merckstraße 25, 64283 Darmstadt, Germany
schaefer@must.tu-darmstadt.de

[2] Technische Universität Dortmund, Robotics Research Institute, Otto-Hahn-Straße 8, 44227 Dortmund, Germany

[3] Technische Universität Darmstadt, Institute for Mechatronic Systems, Otto-Berndt-Straße 2, 64287 Darmstadt, Germany

Abstract. We present a wearable vibrotactile feedback device consisting of four linear resonant actuators (LRAs) that are able to generate virtual stimuli, known as phantom tactile sensation, for human-robot interaction. Using an energy model, we can control the location and intensity of the virtual stimuli independently. The device consists of mostly 3D-printed rigid and flexible components and uses commercially available haptic drivers for actuation. The actuators have a rated frequency of 175 Hz which is close to the highest skin sensitivity regarding vibrations (150 to 300 Hz). Our experiment was conducted with a prototype consisting of two bracelets applied to the forearm and upper arm of six participants. Eight possible circumferential angles were stimulated, of which four originated from real actuators and four were generated by virtual stimuli. The responses given by the participants showed a nearly linear relationship within $\pm 10^\circ$ for the responded angle against the presented stimulus angle. These results show that phantom tactile sensation allows for an increase of spatial resolution to design vibrotactile interfaces for human-robot interaction with fewer actuators.

Keywords: Vibrotactile feedback · Phantom tactile sensation · Human-robot interface

1 Introduction

Human-robot interaction (HRI) becomes more and more common due to progress in fields like robotics and artificial intelligence but also psychology. In particular, when a human and a robot are working on a common task, a bidirectional transfer of information is required [1,2].

Usually, the visual channel is already in use. Therefore, vibrotactile feedback can be helpful when added to provide additional information [3], especially when multiple tasks are being performed and the workload is high [4]. Vibrotactile feedback devices can be used to present physical information, e.g., contact location, as well as abstract information, e.g., direction. They have been investigated in various applications such as robotic teleoperation [5], spatial awareness in virtual reality [6], navigation [7], and motion guidance [8].

Most collaborative tasks in the context of HRI, e.g., handling a tool or carrying an object, are performed by the human using hands and arms. Thus, vibrotactile feedback to the human arm offers a possibility to provide intuitively understandable information. In particular, circumferential feedback, i.e., feedback at different locations around the arm, enables providing information from different directions.

There are many vibrotactile feedback devices in research [9], including some for feedback around the arm [10–12]. Most of them use eccentric rotating mass motors (ERMs) due to the simplicity of control, small form factor, and low cost. However, the inherent coupling of amplitude and frequency of an ERM can be a limitation because the perceived intensity of a vibrotactile stimulus depends not only on its amplitude but also on its frequency [13].

A commercially available vibrotactile feedback device using ERMs is VibroTac (SENSODRIVE, Weßling, Germany). It was originally developed at the German Aerospace Center for the application on the human arm [12]. Due to the ergonomic design, it can be worn on a wide range of arm circumferences. It provides vibrotactile stimuli at six circumferential locations.

The spatial resolution of a vibrotactile feedback device can be increased by utilizing tactile illusions [14]. In [15] an illusion known as phantom tactile sensation was used to induce vibrotactile cues at any circumferential location around the wrist with six ERMs. Phantom tactile sensations can be classified regarding the perceived stimulus either being stationary or moving across the skin [16].

In this paper, we present a wearable vibrotactile feedback device for the human arm consisting of two bracelets. We investigate the feasibility of generating vibrotactile cues at eight circumferential locations around the arm with only four actuators by using stationary phantom tactile sensation. The application of linear resonant actuators (LRAs) ensures a constant frequency for all vibration amplitudes. The modular feedback device is evaluated experimentally on the forearm and the upper arm.

2 Fundamentals

The occurrence of phantom tactile sensations in haptics, not to be confused with phantom limb illusions, was first described by von Békésy in 1957 [17]. It terms the phenomenon that two simultaneous vibrotactile stimuli produced by two closely spaced actuators are perceived as one single vibration in between (Fig. 1a). This effect is based on sensory funneling [18]. Location and intensity of the phantom tactile sensation can be controlled by the intensities of the actuators. The location results from the actuators' relative magnitudes, whereas the intensity can be controlled by the actuators' absolute magnitudes. Two

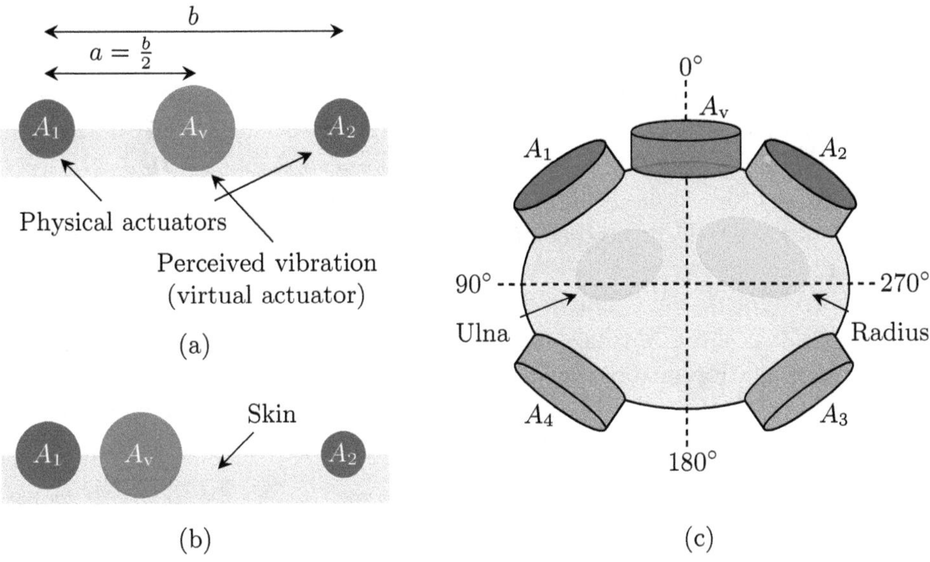

Fig. 1. Basic principle of phantom tactile sensation and placement of the actuators. The phantom tactile sensation is based on sensory funneling. Two simultaneous vibrotactile stimuli produced by two closely spaced actuators are perceived as one single vibration in between (a). Adjusting the actuators' vibration intensities allows shifting the perception closer to the actuator with higher magnitude (b). In order to provide directional cues, four LRAs are arranged equidistant around the left human forearm (c). A phantom tactile sensation is created by activating two adjacent actuators. Location and intensity of the virtual actuator are controlled based on an energy model [19].

vibrations with equal intensities result in a centered phantom tactile sensation. Adjusting the magnitudes equally leads to a sensation with the same location but different intensity. If the intensities are different, the phantom tactile sensation is located closer to the actuator with the higher magnitude (Fig. 1b).

The energy model proposed in [19] allows controlling the relative location $\beta = \frac{a}{b}$ and the intensity A_v of a virtual actuator induced by phantom tactile sensation independently. The required intensities of the two physical actuators are

$$A_1 = \sqrt{1-\beta} \cdot A_v, \quad A_2 = \sqrt{\beta} \cdot A_v. \tag{1}$$

This energy model is based on two assumptions. First, the vibration frequencies of both actuators are equal. Second, the skin sensitivity thresholds at the locations of the physical actuators are identical.

3 Design and Construction

In order to provide directional vibrotactile feedback, four LRAs (G1036002D, Jinlong Machinery & Electronics, Wenzhou, China) are arranged equidistant around the arm (Fig. 1c). Unlike ERMs, the vibration amplitude of an LRA can be adjusted without changing the vibration frequency. This satisfies the energy model's first assumption of equal vibration frequencies. With 175 Hz, the rated frequency of the LRAs is close to the highest sensitivity of the Pacinian corpuscles, which is usually found between 150 and 300 Hz [20,21].

The feedback device is designed to be wearable as a bracelet on the arm. It consists of multiple 3D-printed segments, which are mounted on an elastic cord (Fig. 2). There are two types of segments. The actuator segments consist of a rigid basis (polylactic acid) and a comparatively flexible mounting (thermoplastic polyurethane, shore hardness 98 A) for an LRA which aims at reduction of vibration propagation into the mechanical structure. The intermediate segments carry the electronics as well as the control unit and are used for cable routing. The alternating arrangement of the segments creates a zigzag pattern, which increases the overall elasticity and an equidistant actuator arrangement [12].

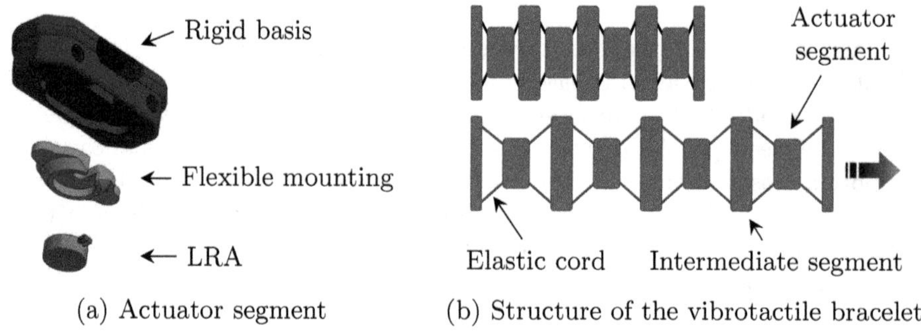

(a) Actuator segment (b) Structure of the vibrotactile bracelet

Fig. 2. Each actuator segment consists of a rigid basis, a flexible mounting, and an LRA (a). Actuator segments and intermediate segments are arranged alternating on an elastic cord (b). The zigzag pattern of the elastic cord ensures equal distances between the actuators in relaxed and stretched state [12].

The LRAs require a sinusoidal driving voltage at their resonance frequency. We use commercially available haptic drivers (DRV2605L, Texas Instruments, Dallas, Texas, U.S.) in combination with an ESP32-WROOM-32 module (Espressif Systems, Shanghai, China) controlling the amplitudes. The control unit receives commands containing direction and magnitude from a PC via Bluetooth. The desired vibrotactile cues between two physical actuators are generated by a control algorithm that applies the energy model (Eq. 1).

4 System Evaluation

The goal of our evaluation experiment was to investigate the perceived direction of vibrotactile cues generated by the developed prototype (Fig. 3a). The locations of the vibrotactile cues resulted either from one real actuator at its own location or from two actuators by inducing phantom tactile sensation in between. Both, forearm and upper arm, were stimulated with vibrotactile cues. In our first test, six participants (1 female, 5 male, 22.7 ± 1.6 years) gave prior informed consent and took part in the experiment. They were informed that their vibrotactile perception is investigated in the experiment but no information about phantom tactile sensation and placement of the actuators was given.

After measuring the circumferences of the forearm (25.8 ± 3.3 cm) and the upper arm (30.8 ± 2.3 cm), the participants were requested to wear the system on the left arm. The vibrotactile bracelets were placed in the middle of the respective arm segment, ensuring an equidistant arrangement of actuators. The origin of the reference frame for each arm segment was defined to be collocated with the driver electronics. The bracelet with the control unit and the battery was always worn on the upper arm. The elastic cord was adjusted to the individual arm circumference of each participant in order to ensure that the vibrotactile bracelets could be worn comfortably.

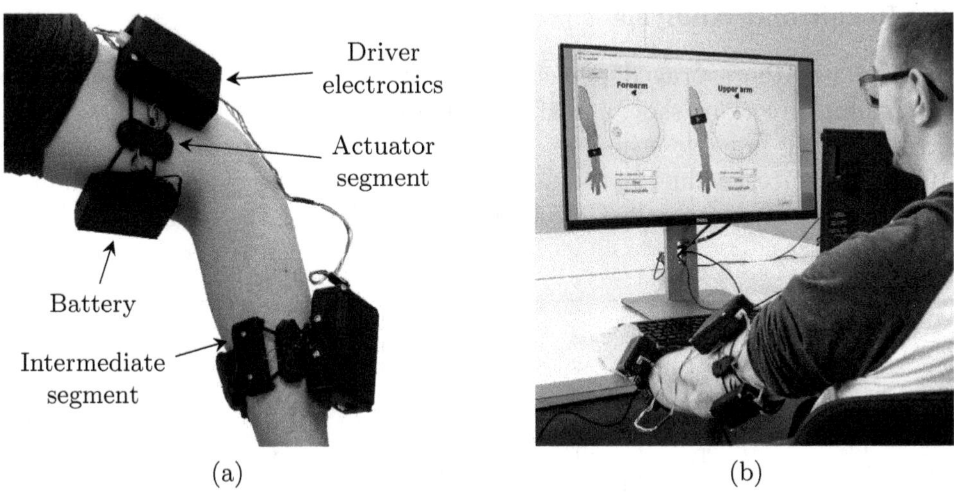

Fig. 3. Prototype of the vibrotactile feedback device consisting of two bracelets worn on the forearm and the upper arm (a). The bracelet on the upper arm contains the control unit (hidden behind the upper arm), the driver electronics, and the power supply. Due to the modular system architecture, up to eight devices with up to eight actuators each can be connected. During the evaluation experiment, the subjects were asked to adjust the rotary knob to the perceived stimulus angle (b).

4.1 Experimental Procedure

The participants were seated in front of a computer screen with a graphical user interface (GUI) consisting of two rotary knobs for an intuitive selection of the vibrotactile cue direction at the forearm and the upper arm, respectively (Fig. 3b). Each arm segment was stimulated with 32 vibrotactile cues. These vibrotactile cues pointed in one of eight possible directions [0°, 45°, 90°, 135°,

180°, 225°, 270°, and 315° (Fig. 1c)], which were tested four times each in random order. Each vibrotactile cue lasted until a response was given by the participant. The LRAs were driven by a sinusoidal voltage with a frequency of 175 Hz. When stimulating at the location of a real actuator, the rated amplitude of 2.0 V_{RMS} was used. In the case of phantom tactile sensation, the amplitudes of the two actuators in use were set such that the intensity of the resulting virtual actuator corresponded to the intensity of one real actuator at rated amplitude (Eq. 1). The participant indicated the direction perceived after each stimulus using the rotary knobs in the GUI (resolution of 1°). In addition to the perceived direction, the time for locating the vibrotactile cues was measured as well. After finishing one arm segment, a short break was taken and the participant was requested to rate the difficulty of locating the vibrotactile cues on a scale from 1 to 10 (1 meaning very easy and 10 meaning very hard). The experiment lasted approximately 25 min for each participant.

4.2 Result and Analysis

The results of the averaged perceived directions of the vibrotactile cues over the stimulus directions show a nearly linear relationship for both arm segments (Fig. 4). For all but two stimulus angles, the mean response deviates less than ±10° from the real value. It should be noted though that visual and auditory modalities were not controlled, which may have affected the results.

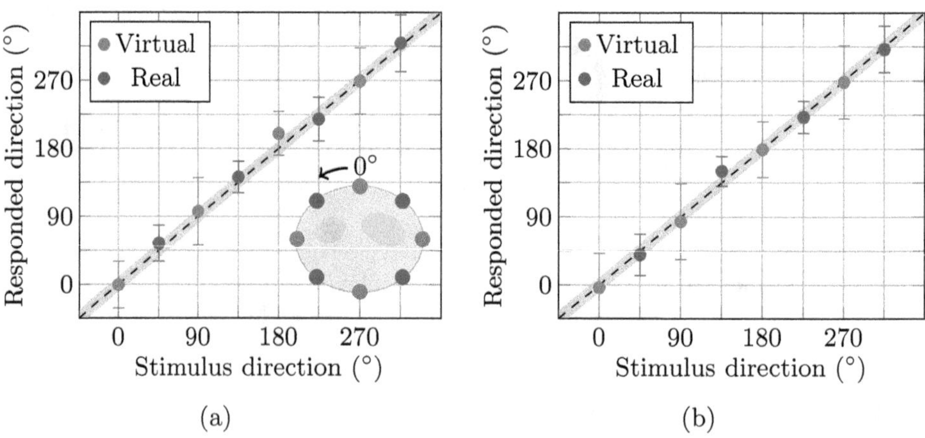

Fig. 4. Mean values of the responded angles against the presented stimulus angles for the forearm (a) and the upper arm (b). The standard deviations, achieved with the virtual actuators, are higher compared to those observed with the real actuators. For all but two angles, the mean response deviates less than ±10° (gray band) from the real value. The experiment was always conducted on the left arm (Fig. 1c).

It is noticeable that the perceived vibrotactile cues of the real actuators (forearm $R^2 = 91.81\,\%$, upper arm $R^2 = 93.45\,\%$) deviate less than those induced by virtual actuators (forearm $R^2 = 87.20\,\%$, upper arm $R^2 = 83.72\,\%$) with respect to the ideal linear response. Comparing the results of both arm segments shows that the scattering of the perceived virtually-generated stimuli on the upper arm is stronger than on the forearm. Furthermore, a Wilcoxon signed-rank test ($W = 0$, $p = 0.0156$) indicated that the difficulty of locating the vibrotactile cues was rated significantly higher for the upper arm (mean 4.67) in contrast to the forearm (mean 3.17). One possible reason for the latter two observations is the lower innervation density of the mechanoreceptors on the upper arm [22].

In addition to the quantitative results, some of the participants expressed their subjective opinions. They reported that it was difficult to assign the vibrotactile cues using the rotary knobs in the GUI, in particular for the upper arm. This impression is consistent with the higher rating of difficulty for the upper arm. Furthermore, the participants estimated their accuracy of locating the vibrotactile cues between 20 to 30°.

5 Conclusion and Outlook

The wearable feedback device developed is capable of generating vibrotactile cues across all circumferential locations around the human arm. This is achieved with only four actuators. In our evaluation experiment the spatial resolution of the vibrotactile feedback can be doubled from four to eight by inducing phantom tactile sensations midway between two actuators. Therefore, we conclude that LRAs with a rated frequency of 175 Hz are suitable for this type of application although our evaluation experiment satisfies the first assumption of the energy model only.

In future work we will include a determination of skin sensitivity thresholds to check if the second assumption of the energy model is satisfied. At the same time, we plan to apply acoustic and visual shielding to the actuators to gain focus on the vibrotactile cues. For a detailed analysis, further experiments with more participants will be conducted to reinforce the already promising results for applications in HRI, e.g., collision avoidance in teleoperation.

Acknowledgements. This research received support from the Deutsche Forschungsgemeinschaft (DFG) under grants KU 3498/3-1 and KA 417/32-1 within the priority program *The Active Self* (SPP 2134).

References

1. Beckerle, P., et al.: A human-robot interaction perspective on assistive and rehabilitation robotics. Front. Neurorobot. **11**, 24 (2017)
2. Ajoudani, A., et al.: Progress and prospects of the human-robot collaboration. Auton. Robot. **42**, 957–975 (2018)
3. Elliott, L.R., Coovert, M.D., Redden, E.S.: Overview of meta-analyses investigating vibrotactile versus visual display options. In: Jacko, J.A. (ed.) HCI 2009. LNCS, vol. 5611, pp. 435–443. Springer, Heidelberg (2009)

4. Burke, J.L., et al.: Comparing the effects of visual-auditory and visual-tactile feedback on user performance: a meta-analysis. In: Proceedings of the 8th International Conference on Multimodal Interfaces - ICMI 2006, Banff, Alberta, Canada, p. 108. ACM Press (2006)
5. Bimbo, J., et al.: Teleoperation in cluttered environments using wearable haptic feedback. In: 2017 IEEE/RSJ International Conference on Intelligent Robots and Systems (IROS), Vancouver, BC, pp. 3401–3408. IEEE, September 2017
6. Louison, C., Ferlay, F., Mestre, D.R.: Spatialized vibrotactile feedback improves goal-directed movements in cluttered virtual environments. Int. J. Hum.-Comput. Interact. **34**, 1015–1031 (2018)
7. Erp, J.B.F.V., et al.: Waypoint navigation with a vibrotactile waist belt. ACM Trans. Appl. Percept. **2**, 106–117 (2005)
8. Bark, K., et al.: Effects of vibrotactile feedback on human learning of arm motions. IEEE Trans. Neural Syst. Rehabil. Eng. **23**, 51–63 (2015)
9. Pacchierotti, C., Sinclair, S., Solazzi, M., Frisoli, A., Hayward, V., Prattichizzo, D.: Wearable Haptic Systems for the Fingertip and the Hand: taxonomy, review, and perspectives. IEEE Trans. Haptics **10**, 580–600 (2017)
10. Pezent, E., et al.: Tasbi: multisensory squeeze and vibrotactile wrist haptics for augmented and virtual reality. In: 2019 IEEE World Haptics Conference (WHC), Tokyo, Japan, pp. 1–6. IEEE, July 2019
11. Tsetserukou, D., Tachi, S.: Efficient object exploration and object presentation in TeleTA, Teleoperation system with Tactile feedback. In: World Haptics 2009 - Third Joint EuroHaptics conference and Symposium on Haptic Interfaces for Virtual Environment and Teleoperator Systems, Salt Lake City, UT, USA, pp. 97–102. IEEE (2009)
12. Schaetzle, S., et al.: VibroTac: an ergonomic and versatile usable vibrotactile feedback device. In: 19th International Symposium in Robot and Human Interactive Communication, Viareggio, Italy, pp. 670–675. IEEE, September 2010
13. Verrillo, R.T., Fraioli, A.J., Smith, R.L.: Sensation magnitude of vibrotactile stimuli. Percept. Psychophysics **6**, 366–372 (1969)
14. Barghout, A., Cha, J., El Saddik, A., Kammerl, J., Steinbach, E.: Spatial resolution of vibrotactile perception on the human forearm when exploiting funneling illusion. In: 2009 IEEE International Workshop on Haptic Audio visual Environments and Games, Lecco, Italy, pp. 19–23. IEEE, November 2009
15. Salazar Luces, J.V., Okabe, K., Murao, Y., Hirata, Y.: A phantom-sensation based paradigm for continuous vibrotactile wrist guidance in two-dimensional space. IEEE Robot. Autom. Lett. **3**, 163–170 (2018)
16. Park, G., Choi, S.: Tactile information transmission by 2D stationary phantom sensations. In: Proceedings of the 2018 CHI Conference on Human Factors in Computing Systems - CHI 2018, Montreal QC, Canada, pp. 1–12. ACM Press (2018)
17. Békésy, G.V.: Sensations on the skin similar to directional hearing, beats, and harmonics of the ear. J. Acoust. Soc. Am. **29**, 489–501 (1957)
18. Békésy, G.V.: Funneling in the nervous system and its role in loudness and sensation intensity on the skin. J. Acoust. Soc. Am. **30**, 399–412 (1958)
19. Israr, A., Poupyrev, I.: Tactile brush: drawing on skin with a tactile grid display. In: Proceedings of the 2011 Annual Conference on Human Factors in Computing Systems - CHI 2011, Vancouver, BC, Canada, p. 2019. ACM Press (2011)
20. Choi, S., Kuchenbecker, K.J.: Vibrotactile display: Perception, technology, and applications. Proc. IEEE **101**, 2093–2104 (2013)

21. Bolanowski, S.J., Gescheider, G.A., Verrillo, R.T.: Hairy skin: psychophysical channels and their physiological substrates. Somatosens. Mot. Res. **11**, 279–290 (1994)
22. Békésy, G.V., Wever, E.G.: Experiments in Hearing. McGraw-Hill, New York City (1960)

24

Visuo-Haptic Display by Embedding Imperceptible Spatial Haptic Information into Projected Images

Yamato Miyatake[1], Takefumi Hiraki[1], Tomosuke Maeda[2], Daisuke Iwai[1(✉)], and Kosuke Sato[1]

[1] Osaka University, Toyonaka, Osaka, Japan
{miyatake,hiraki,iwai,sato}@sens.sys.es.osaka-u.ac.jp
[2] Toyota Central R&D Labs., Inc., Nagakute, Aichi, Japan
tmaeda@mosk.tytlabs.co.jp

Abstract. Visuo-haptic augmented reality (AR) systems that represent visual and haptic sensations in a spatially and temporally consistent manner are used to improve the reality in AR applications. However, existing visual displays either cover the user's field-of-view or are limited to flat panels. In the present paper, we propose a novel projection-based AR system that can present consistent visuo-haptic sensations on a non-planar physical surface without inserting any visual display devices between a user and the surface. The core technical contribution is controlling wearable haptic displays using a pixel-level visible light communication projector. The projection system can embed spatial haptic information into each pixel, and the haptic displays vibrate according to the detected pixel information. We confirm that the proposed system can display visuo-haptic information with pixel-precise alignment with a delay of 85 ms. We can also employ the proposed system as a novel experimental platform to clarify the spatio-temporal perceptual characteristics of visual and haptic sensations. As a result of the conducted user studies, we revealed that the noticeable thresholds of visual-haptic asynchrony were about 100 ms (temporal) and 10 mm (spatial), respectively.

Keywords: Visuo-haptic display · High-speed projection

1 Introduction

Visuo-haptic displays that are used to provide visual and tactile sensations to users and maintain these two sensations consistent, both spatially and temporally, can promote natural and efficient user interaction in augmented reality

(AR) applications. To facilitate effective visuo-haptic AR experiences, it is essential to ensure the spatial and temporal consistency of the visual and haptic sensations. Conventional systems allowed achieving the consistency by using optical combiners such as a half-mirror [10] or video see-through systems including a head-mounted display [2] to overlay visual information onto a haptic device. However, these systems require inserting visual display devices between a user and the haptic device, which constrains the field-of-view (FOV) and interaction space, and potentially deteriorates the user experiences. They also prevent multi-user interactions. A possible solution to this problem is to integrate a tactile panel into a flat panel display [1]. This enables a spatiotemporally consistent visuo-haptic display to facilitate multi-user interactions without covering their FOVs. However, such displays are limited to flat surfaces at the moment.

Another promising approach of visuo-haptic AR display to overcome the above-mentioned limitations is to combine a projection-based AR system for displaying visual information and a haptic display attached on a user's finger which is controlled by the luminance of each projected pixel [6,9]. This approach can be used to maintain the temporal and spatial consistency between the visual and haptic sensations while not being limited to flat surfaces owing to the projection mapping technology. However, potentially, the displayed image quality may be significantly degraded, as the luminance of the original image needs to be spatially modulated depending on the desired haptic information.

In this paper, we propose a visuo-haptic display based on the projection-based AR approach to provide both visual image and haptic control information. The proposed system controls a haptic display attached to a user's finger using temporal brightness information imperceptibly embedded in projected images using pixel-level visible light communication (PVLC) [4]. The embedded information varies with each pixel. We embed the temporal brightness pattern in a short period of each projector frame so that the modulation does not significantly affect the perceived luminance of the original projection image. Owing to the short and simple temporal pattern, the haptic feedback is presented with an unnoticeably short latency. We can design a visuo-haptic display with various surface shapes as the projection mapping technique can overlay images onto a non-planar physical surface. Multiple users can experience the system in which no visual display device needs to be inserted between the users and the surface.

We develop a prototype system comprising a high-speed projector that embeds spatially-varying haptic information into visual images based on VLC principle and a haptic display device that changes vibrations according to the obtained information. Through a system evaluation, we confirm if the proposed system can consistently represent visuo-haptic sensations. We can also use the system as a novel experimental platform to clarify the spatio-temporal perceptual characteristics of visual-haptic sensations. A user study is conducted to investigate whether the delay time and misalignment of visual-haptic asynchrony are within an acceptable range for user experiences.

2 Methods and Implementation

The proposed visuo-haptic AR display can represent haptic sensations corresponding to projected images when users touch and move the haptic display device on a projection surface. The system keeps the consistency of time and position between the visual and haptic sensations at a pixel level. Figure 1 shows the concept of the proposed system. The system comprises a projection system that can embed imperceptible information in each pixel of images and a haptic display device that can control a vibration.

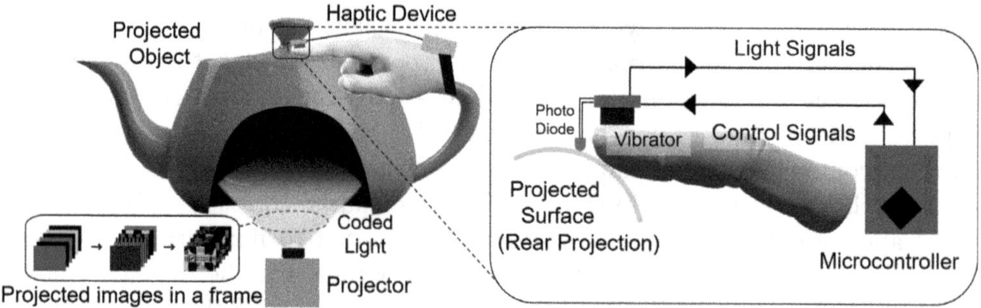

Fig. 1. Concept of the proposed system

2.1 Projection System

We utilize PVLC [4] for embedding haptic information into projected images using a DLP projector. When a projector projects an original image and its complement alternately at a high frequency, human eyes see only a uniform gray image owing to the perception characteristics of vision. Although human eyes cannot distinguish this imperceptible flicker, a photosensor can detect it and use it as signal information.

We employed a high-speed DLP projector development kit (DLP LightCrafter 4500, Texas Instruments) to project images using PVLC. We can control the projection of binary images using the specified software of the development kit. Each video frame consists of two segments. The first segment consists of 36 binary images that correspond to each bit of synchronization information and data for controlling haptic displays and takes 8.5 ms for projection. The second segment displays a full-color image for humans, which also compensates for the luminance nonuniformity caused in the first segment and takes 12 ms for projection. Thus, the time for projection in a frame is 20.5 ms, which means the frame-rate is 49 Hz. We embedded the 26 bits data on x and y coordinates ($x = 10$ bits, $y = 11$ bits) and the index number of the vibration information (5 bits) corresponding to a projected texture image using PVLC.

2.2 Haptic Display Device Controlled by PVLC

We developed a wearable haptic display controlled by PVLC. It comprises a receiver circuit with a photodiode (S2506-02, Hamamatsu Photonics), a controller circuit, a vibration actuator, and a Li-Po battery. The controller circuit has a microcontroller (Nucleo STM32F303K8, STMicroelectronics) and an audio module (DFR0534, DFRobot) for playing the audio corresponding to the vibration. The microcontroller is used to acquire the position and spatial haptic information by decoding the received signals to determine a type of vibration, and send it to the audio module that drives the vibration actuator. We use the linear resonant actuator (HAPTIC™ Reactor, ALPS ALPINE) as a vibration actuator. This actuator responds fast and has good frequency characteristics over the usable frequency band for haptic sensation. Therefore, the proposed haptic display device (hereinafter referred to as "Device HR") can present various haptic sensations.

Figure 2 provides an overview of the proposed system and the appearance of its user interface. We employed the data obtained from the LMT haptic texture database [8] as a source of projected images and the spatial haptic information. This database provides image files with textures and audio files with corresponding vibrations. We stored the vibration information in the audio module of Device HR in advance, and the device presents haptic feedback by playing the received index number of vibration information.

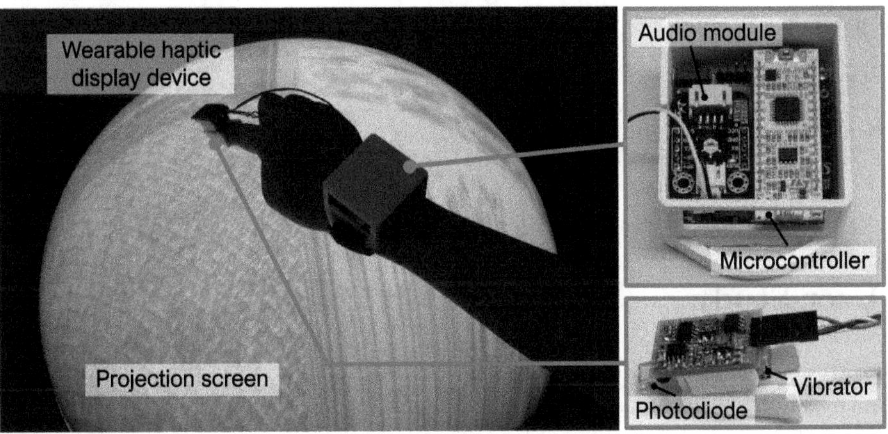

Fig. 2. Overview of the proposed system—the system comprises a projection system with a screen and a haptic display device controlled by the obtained light information

2.3 Latency Evaluation

The latency of the proposed system is defined as the duration from the time when the haptic display device is placed inside an area to the time when the device performs vibration. This latency (T_{late}) can be calculated as follows:

$$T_{late} = T_{wait} + T_{recv} + T_{vib} \tag{1}$$

where T_{wait} is the waiting time for synchronization, T_{recv} is the time to receive the data, and T_{vib} is the time to perform vibration using the actuator. According to the estimation of the previous work [3] and settings of the proposed system, we calculate T_{recv} equal to 8.5 ms and T_{wait} equal to 10.2 ms.

We measure T_{vib} by calculating the time from the moment when the microcontroller sends a control signal to the actuator of the two devices to the moment when the actuator is enabled. We project the sample image with the control information embedded for turning on the actuator in the left half of a projected image and that for turning off in the right half. We attach an acceleration sensor (KXR94-2050, Kionix) to the devices to detect vibration. We place the device at each on and off areas on the screen and conduct the measurement a 100 times using the microcontroller at each boundary of the area. As a result, the averaged values of T_{vib} are 66.5 ms for the Device HR.

Table 1 shows the values of T_{wait}, T_{recv}, T_{vib}, and T_{late} corresponding to each device. T_{vib} of the Device HR is a sum of latency values of the audio module and that of the actuator (HAPTIC™ Reactor) itself. We measure the latency of the audio module 100 times and the average value was 48.8 ms. Therefore, we can estimate that the latency of the HAPTIC™ Reactor is about 66.5 − 48.8 = 17.7 ms.

Table 1. Delay time between providing the haptic information and visual information when using the proposed system—the evaluation was performed for Device HR

	T_{wait} [ms]	T_{recv} [ms]	T_{vib} [ms]	T_{late} [ms]
Device HR (with an audio module)	10.2	8.5	66.5	85.2

3 User Study

We conducted a user study to investigate the human perception characteristics of the threshold time of perception of the visual-haptic asynchrony and the misalignment tolerance of the visual-haptic registration accuracy of the proposed system. According to the previous studies, this threshold time was approximately 100 ms [7], and this misalignment tolerance was approximately 2 mm [5]. However, we could not simply apply these values to the proposed system. The visuo-haptic displays of the previous studies covered the user's view by visual displays from the user's fingers to which the haptic feedback was provided, while our system allows the user to see the finger directly. In the present user study, we performed the two experiments using the proposed system. The first experiment was focused on the evaluation of the threshold time of perception of a visual-haptic asynchrony, and the second was aimed to estimate the misalignment tolerance of the visual-haptic registration accuracy.

3.1 Setup for User Study

Figure 3 represents the experimental situation of the user study. We employed a tabletop display in which the proposed projection system was built-in. The screen size of the tabletop display was 0.77 m × 0.48 m, and its height was 0.92 m. We embedded the data of vibration control and the delay time into a projected image in each of the green and red areas separated by numbers. The haptic device turned on the vibration in the green area after the set delay time and turned off in the red area. We set the width of the moving area equal to 182 pixels in the projected image, and the resolution of the projected image was 1.22 pixels/mm in this setup; therefore, the actual width of the moving area was approximately 150 mm.

We implemented an alternative haptic display device for this study, which can present vibrations faster than Device HR by function limitation; this means it focuses on on/off of a constant vibration without the audio module. We used another actuator (LD14-002, Nidec Copal) in the device (hereinafter denoted as "Device LD"), and revealed the latency of Device LD is 34.6 ms by the same latency evaluation. Given that we could set the waiting time for sending a control signal to an actuator using the embedded data, the system was able to provide haptic feedback in the specific delay time ($\geq$34.6 ms).

Fig. 3. Experimental situations considered in the user study, (a) appearance of the experiment related to the threshold time of perception of visual-haptic asynchrony, (b) appearance of the experiment related to the visual-haptic registration accuracy (Color figure online)

3.2 Participants and Experimental Methods

Ten participants (seven males and three females, aged from 21 to 24, all right-handed) volunteered to participate in the present user study. They were equipped with a haptic device on the index finger of their dominant hand. In the first experiment, we prepared 12 variations of the delay time from 50 to 160 ms at intervals of 10 ms (these delay times included the device-dependent delay time). The participants were instructed to move their index fingers from a red to a green area and answer whether they noticed the delay corresponding to the haptic sensation with respect to the moment when they visually identified the finger entering the green area. In the second experiment, we prepared 12 variations of misalignments from 0 (0 mm) to 26 px (21.32 mm). The participants were instructed to move their index fingers between the white boundary lines within each of the red and green areas as many times as they wanted. Then, they answered whether the timing of haptic feedback matched with crossing the red and green boundaries of the projected image. To influence the moving speed of the user's fingers, we displayed a reference movie in which a user was moving his/her finger at the speed of 150 mm/s during the experiment. The participants performed each procedure 12 times as the projected image had 12 areas in both the experiments. We defined the 10 different patterns of interconnections between providing haptic sensations with a delay time or a misalignment and the areas to cancel the order effects. The participants experienced these patterns in each experiment, thereby repeated each procedure 120 times in total.

3.3 Results and Discussion

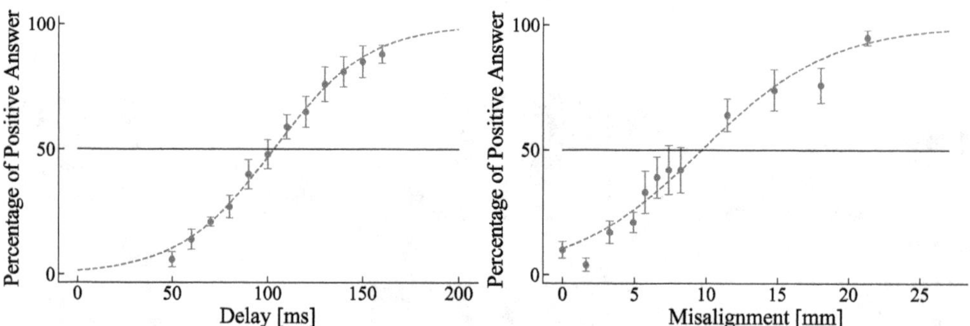

Fig. 4. Percentages of positive answers in the experiment for a threshold time of a visual-haptic asynchrony (left) and that for a visual-haptic regisration accuracy (right).

Figure 4 represents the averaged percentage of positive answers obtained in the first experiment. Herein, error bars represent the standard error of the means, and the curve is fitted using a sigmoid function defined as below:

$$y = \frac{1}{1 + \exp(-k(x - x_0))} \times 100 \tag{2}$$

In Figure 4 (left), we obtained the following values of parameters: $k = 0.04$ and $x_0 = 103$, as a result of the fitting and used these values in calculations. We identified the threshold time of perception of the visual-haptic asynchrony (T_{th}); It was set as the time at which users perceive the delay with a 50% possibility. The results indicated $T_{th} \approx 100$ ms, as presented in the fitted sigmoid curve. Similar results of T_{th} were reported in the previous research [7], that supported the result of this experiment. As the latency of Device HR is 85.2 ms, the proposed haptic displays meet the requirement of having the delay time such that users cannot perceive visual-haptic asynchrony with their eyes.

In Fig. 4 (right), we obtained the values of parameters: $k = 0.22$ and $x_0 = 9.7$, as a result of the fitting and used these values as parameters of the sigmoid function. We identified the misalignment tolerance of the visual-haptic registration accuracy (denoted as L_{th}) equal to the length perceived as a misalignment by half of the users. The results indicated $L_{th} \approx 10$ mm, as presented in the fitted sigmoid curve. The result indicates that the proposed system can provide haptic feedback to users without a perception of misalignment if it is kept within 10 mm, which can be considered as design criteria for visuo-haptic displays. Additionally, L_{th} (10 mm) is larger than the value (2 mm) reported in the previous research [5]. We can also conclude that the proposed system can extend the misalignment tolerance of the visual-haptic registration accuracy as the users can visually observe their finger with the haptic display in the system.

4 Conclusion

In the present paper, we proposed a novel visuo-haptic AR display that allowed eliminating visual-haptic asynchrony of the time and position perceived by the users. We implemented the projection system that could embed information into each pixel of images and the haptic display device that could control vibrations based on the obtained information. We conducted the user studies and revealed that the threshold of visual-haptic asynchrony obtained using the proposed visual-haptic display was about 100 ms for the time delay and about 10 mm for the position. From this result, we can conclude that the proposed display device can represent visual and haptic sensations in a synchronized manner as the system can represent them with the pixel-precise alignment at the delay of 85 ms. As future work, we will conduct similar user studies with various directions of the hand moving and with more participants to investigate the systematic thresholds. Furthermore, we will design a model to determine the vibration intensity and frequency of the haptic display based on haptic information corresponding to the texture image and the user's movements on a display.

References

1. Bau, O., et al.: TeslaTouch: electrovibration for touch surfaces. In: Proceedings of the UIST 2010, pp. 283–292 (2010)
2. Harders, M., et al.: Calibration, registration, and synchronization for high precision augmented reality haptics. IEEE TVCG **15**(1), 138–149 (2009)
3. Hiraki, T., et al.: Sensible Shadow: tactile feedback from your own shadow. In: Proceedings of the AH 2016, pp. 23:1–23:4 (2016)
4. Kimura, S., et al.: PVLC projector: image projection with imperceptible pixel-level metadata. In: Proceedings of the ACM SIGGRAPH 2008 Posters, p. 135:1, August 2008

5. Lee, C.-G., Oakley, I., Ryu, J.: Exploring the impact of visual-haptic registration accuracy in augmented reality. In: Isokoski, P., Springare, J. (eds.) EuroHaptics 2012. LNCS, vol. 7283, pp. 85–90. Springer, Heidelberg (2012). https://doi.org/10.1007/978-3-642-31404-9_15
6. Rekimoto, J.: SenseableRays: opto-haptic substitution for touch-enhanced interactive spaces. In: Proceedings of the CHI EA 2009, pp. 2519–2528, April 2009
7. Silva, J.M., et al.: Human perception of haptic-to-video and haptic-to-audio skew in multimedia applications. ACM TOMM **9**(2), 9:1–9:16 (2013)
8. Strese, M., et al.: A haptic texture database for tool-mediated texture recognition and classification. In: Proceedings of the HAVE 2014, pp. 118–123, November 2014
9. Uematsu, H., et al.: HALUX: projection-based interactive skin for digital sports. In: Proceedings of the ACM SIGGRAPH 2016 Emerging Technologies, pp. 10:1–10:2 (2016)
10. Wang, D., et al.: Analysis of registration accuracy for collocated haptic-visual display system. In: Proceedings of the HAPTICS 2008, pp. 303–310 (2008)

25

Confinement of Vibrotactile Stimuli in Periodically Supported Plates

Ayoub Ben Dhiab(✉) and Charles Hudin

CEA, LIST, 91191 Gif-sur-Yvette, France
{ayoub.ben-dhiab,charles.hudin}@cea.fr

Abstract. For multitouch and multiuser interactions on a touch surface, providing a local vibrotactile feedback is essential. Usually, vibration propagation impedes this localization. Previous work showed that narrow strip-shaped plates could allow the confinement of vibrotactile stimuli to the actuated area. Adding to this principle, periodically supported plates also provide a non-propagative effect at low frequencies. Using both geometrical properties, we provide a device allowing a multitouch interaction through an array of piezoelectric actuator. Experimental validation show that vibrations are well confined on top of actuated areas with vibration amplitude over 2 μm.

Keywords: Surface haptics · Confinement · Vibrotactile stimuli · Narrow plate · Ribbed plate · Non-propagating · Evanescent wave · Vibrations

1 Introduction

Wave propagation in today's surface haptic interfaces limits the user to a single point of interaction whereas most exploratory procedures benefit from the use of multiple fingers to properly process surface information [7]. Solving this problem requires to localize vibrations. There are several methods related to technologies that allow localized haptic feedback on continuous surfaces. For spatial localization of vibrations, i.e., the creation of local deformation at a point or area of the plate, there are two techniques: *Time-Reversal* [5] and *Modal Superimposition* [4]. For these two techniques, the wavelength of the vibrations to obtain a local deformation at the centimeter or millimeter scale necessarily involves high frequencies. The *Time-Reversal Wave Focusing* technique uses the propagation of elastic waves to generate constructive interference at a given time and position on the plate. The acceleration peak created by the focusing of the waves causes the ejection of a static or moving fingerpulp, giving a haptic feedback smaller than the fingertip. However, this approach needs a calibration procedure and is subjected to external parameters (e.g. temperature, finger interaction), which can impede the tactile stimulation. As for *Modal Superimposition*, it uses a truncated modal decomposition to focus a deformation shape and control its position. The high frequencies produced by an array of piezoelectric actuators allow for the appearance of a tactile lubrication phenomenon, i.e. a variation in friction that is only felt when the finger is moved [10]. Both techniques rely on propagation of high frequency waves. During user interaction, the non-linear behavior of the finger significantly modifies the vibrational behavior of the plate. Such modifications are particularly striking for high frequencies thus leading to many complications (incl. flexural waves scattering, mode damping, mode translation). In order to avoid these limitations and provide a haptic feedback both to static and moving fingers, the *Inverse-Filter* approach [8] proposes to dynamically control low-frequency waves, which are less impacted by finger interaction, to provide the user with the desired stimuli only at the contact points. Nonetheless, this technique is based on (consequent) computation, signal processing and calibration procedures. As this technique uses waves within the tactile frequency range (0–1 kHz), it induces a global movement of the plate and therefore limits the interaction to five control points. Generally, all the previously mentioned methods depend on wave propagation and thus, are in need of calculations and signal processing in order to achieve localization. Therefore, we have investigated in our previous work [1] another method that overcomes such requirements by relying on geometry features and wave evanescence instead. We have shown that it is possible to obtain localized deformations above the actuators for low frequency signals in narrow thin plates (1D). A particularity of this technique is that it allows the spatial localization of low-frequency stimuli i.e. a local deformation of the plate even if we use low-frequencies with long wavelength. In addition, finger interaction does not attenuate low-frequency evanescent waves. No matter the surface in contact, i.e. finger, hand, arm, foot... the behavior of the vibrating plate is not impacted and a localized stimuli can be provided. Although interesting, this approach is limited to narrow plates. However, for a rich multitouch interaction, extending this approach to an arbitrary 2D plate becomes necessary and is the focus of this paper. Because waves tend to directly propagate in 2D plates, the confinement i.e. the suppression of propagative waves in favor of evanescence, was not easily achieved. In order to do so, we used a theoretical result raised by Mead [6]. He states that a periodically supported beam exhibits a non-propagating low-frequency band up to the first resonant mode of isolated segments. Meaning in our case that if we have a periodically bounded plate and if each formed areas have each a waveguide geometry, a cut-off frequency exists and we can have the spatial localization of low frequency stimuli. Therefore, in this paper, we verify this assumption experimentally with a novel setup and discuss the various possibilities it opens up.

2 Principle

2.1 Confinement by the Ribs

In this section we explain how vibrations can be confined along both axis of a ribbed plate depicted in Fig. 1. On the x-axis, we find ourselves solving a problem of an infinite beam supported periodically (Fig. 1). Regularly supported beams can be seen as a set of individual supported beam portions applying

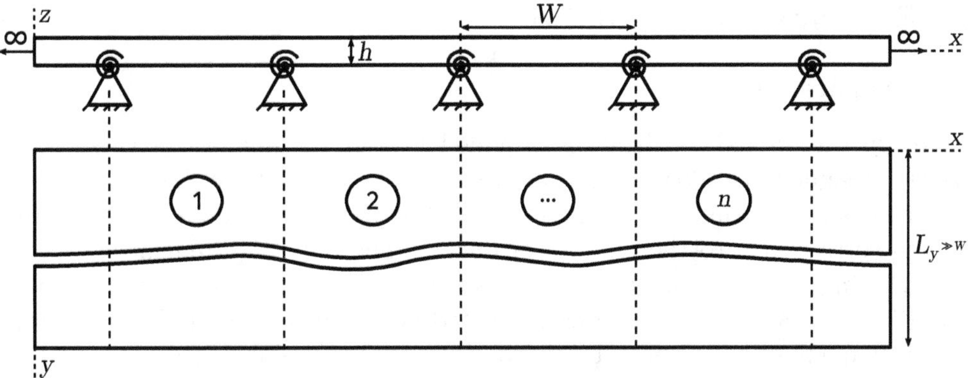

Fig. 1. Plate bounded by a set of equidistant ribs forming n areas which theoretically behaves like narrow-plate bounded on their longer edges to a rigid frame.

bending moments (represented by rotation spring in Fig. 1) to their neighboring beam portions. In such systems, vibrations propagate from one portion to another through bending moments produced at the junction between two portions. Mead [6] has shown that for frequencies bellow the first resonance of an individual portion, the propagation from one portion to another attenuates exponentially. This means that in our system, the cut off frequency f_1 that marks the transition between propagative and evanescent waves along the waveguide dimension, also corresponds to the transition from propagative to evanescent wave in the transverse dimension. This enables the extension of the waveguide approach describes in [1] to 2D surfaces regularly supported by thin ribs.

2.2 Evanescence and Waveguide Geometry

The localization along the y-axis of low frequencies is implied by the waveguide geometry of the propagation medium. In such medium, it was shown that bending waves cannot propagate below the cut-off frequency of the first propagation mode. This non-propagation effect allows the confinement of vibrotactile stimuli and thus can be used for multitouch haptic interactions. If we suppose a perfect bounding of the ribs to a rigid frame, each of the n areas possesses their first cut-off frequency equal to [1]:

$$f_1 = \frac{\pi}{4\sqrt{3}} \frac{h}{W^2} \sqrt{\frac{E}{\rho(1-\nu^2)}} \tag{1}$$

with ρ the mass density, E the Young's modulus, ν the Poisson's ratio, h the plate thickness, W the distance between ribs. When an area is submitted to a vibration of frequency $f < f_1$, waves propagating along the y-axis and the x-axis are evanescent and dies exponentially with the distance.

3 Experimental Validation

3.1 Apparatus

To verify the spatial localization provided by our method, we have set up a system designed to allow a user to freely explore a surface. The size of the device thus corresponds to the size of an adult hand, and the number of areas formed corresponds to the number of fingers. The only requirement associated with the implementation of this method is having a plate correctly bounded periodically to a rigid frame. If each created area have a waveguide geometry, a cut-off frequency exists and a localized vibration can be obtained.

Mechanical Components. The apparatus consists in a glass plate, measuring $150 \times 130 \times 0.5\,\text{mm}^3$, bounded on a set of 6 equidistant ribs of width 4 mm forming 5 areas. In order to provide haptic feedbacks, piezoelectric actuators (muRata 7BB-20-3) of circular geometry, composed of two part: a plate of diameter 20 mm, thickness of 0.1 mm; and a piezoelectric transducer of diameter 12.8 mm, thickness of 0.11 mm, were glued on the bottom side of the plate between each ribs. The out of plane displacement of the surface is measured by a laser vibrometer (Polytec MLV-100/OFV-5000) mounted on a motorized 3 axis platform. This setup is illustrated on Fig. 2.

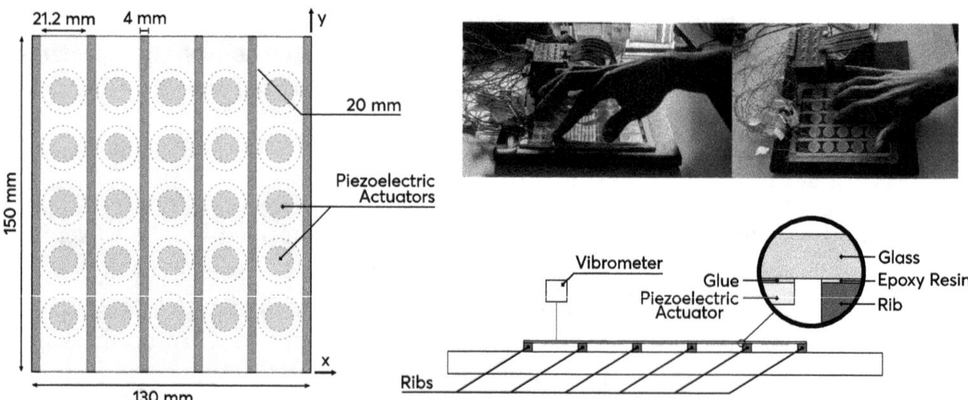

Fig. 2. Experimental setup. A glass plate is bounded onto a set of 6 equidistant ribs with epoxy resin. The actuators are glued to the bottom of the plate, 5 per area between each rib, for a total of 25 actuators.

Driving Components. Because vibration localization is induced by the propagation medium geometry, no specific calculation nor wave control implementation are needed. Signal amplification for each actuators was assured by a Piezo Haptics Driver DRV8862 from Texas Instrument. A voltage output module NI-9264 was used to send requested analog signals to each driver for amplification.

Communication with the NI-9264 voltage output module and signal design was made with Python using the PyDAQmx package.

3.2 System Frequency Response Function (FRF)

The frequency response function or FRF (ratio of the displacement at a given point to the voltage applied to an actuator in the frequency domain) for the actuator was measured by sending a linear sweep signal of 40 V amplitude going from 0 Hz to 5 kHz sampled at 10 kHz and is represented on Fig. 3. We search with this FRF frequencies where the amplitude at the center of the actuator (in light gold) presents noticeable differences with the amplitude outside the actuator area (in dark blue). We can notice that, from 0 to 1.2 kHz, vibration amplitudes inside the actuator area are 30 dB higher in average than outside the actuator area which shows that elastic waves do not propagate throughout the plate for vibration frequency in this range. The FRFs at other points were also measured and show the same behavior, though with some differences. We supposed in Sect. 2 that clamping conditions were perfect thus having the same cut-off frequency for every area. But the FRF in other areas actually present different cut-off frequencies meaning that the clamping quality of each rib was not assured. The boundary condition being made with epoxy resin we can assume that eventual air bubbles or gaps could have been left during the mounting process thus giving slight behavior differences between each area and locally within each area.

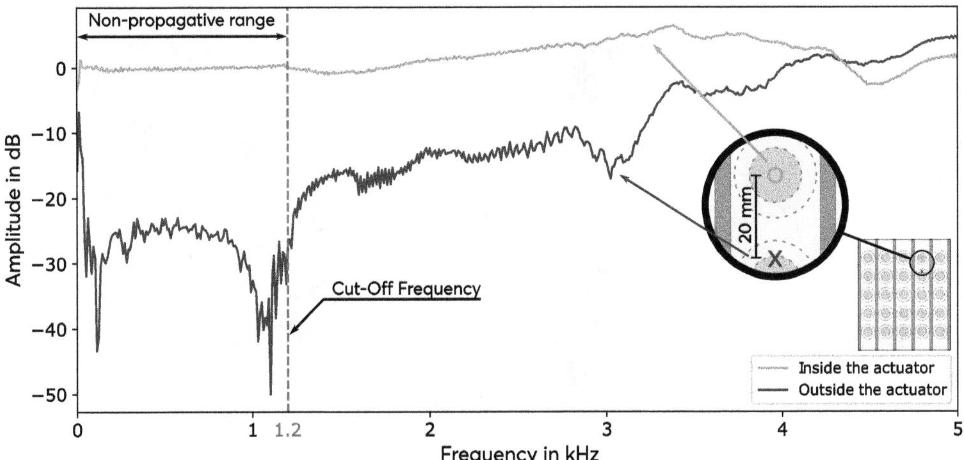

Fig. 3. System Frequency Response Function (FRF) $H_{dB} = 20\log_{10}|H|$ at the center of the activated actuator (in light gold) and 20 mm away outside the actuator inside the same area (in dark blue). (Color figure online)

3.3 Stimuli Confinement

To illustrate the multitouch capability of our device we mapped plate amplitudes when submitted to signals sent with multiple piezoelectric actuators. We chose a 250 Hz (tactile sensitivity peak) 5 cycles burst excitation and a driving voltage amplitude of a 100 V for every actuator used. Figure 4 shows the maximum displacement throughout the plate when using 1, 2, 3, 5, 6 and 7 actuators at the same time. We can notice that waves are confined above activated actuators with amplitudes reaching 3 μm inside the actuator area. Outside the actuated area, waves propagating along the y-axis are evanescent and die exponentially. Along the x-axis, vibration propagation is impeded by the clamped ribs surrounding the actuator. The energy representation with a logarithmic scale of Fig. 5 shows certain areas of interest. Apart from localized energy area above each actuator, we can note leaks with a 15 dB amplitude difference between vibrations inside actuator areas and leaked vibrations while other areas present a 30 dB difference. This leak is actually due to clamping imperfection caused during the prototype assembly. Another area which is less visible (squared in green in Fig. 5), asses the evanescent behavior along the x-axis due to the set of supports. This important loss of energy (around 25 dB loss) comes from the evanescence behavior and the width of the ribs which, by providing strong bending moments, reduce the transmitted energy. Thinner ribs would still provide a localized effect but with a reduced energy loss.

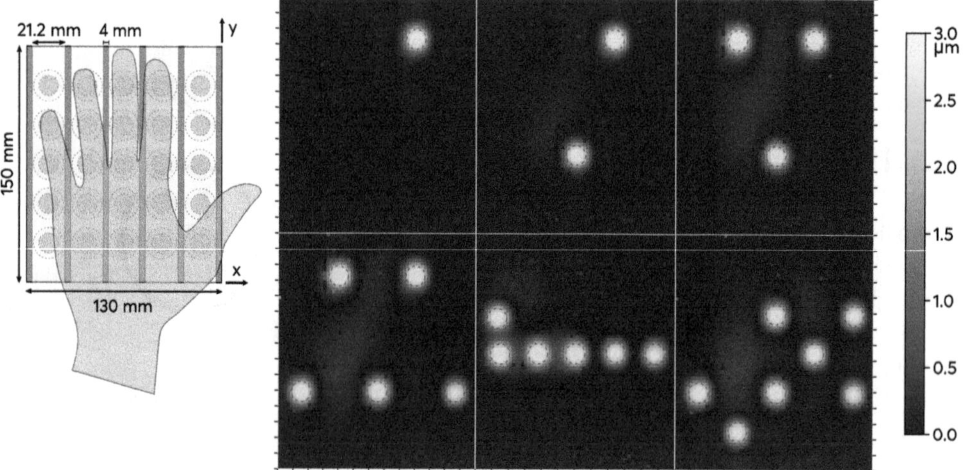

Fig. 4. Maximum out of plane displacement in μm of the plate for 1, 2, 3, 5, 6 and 7 actuators activated at same time. Vibration sources are localized and reach a vibration amplitude above 3 μm while the rest of the plate stays at rest.

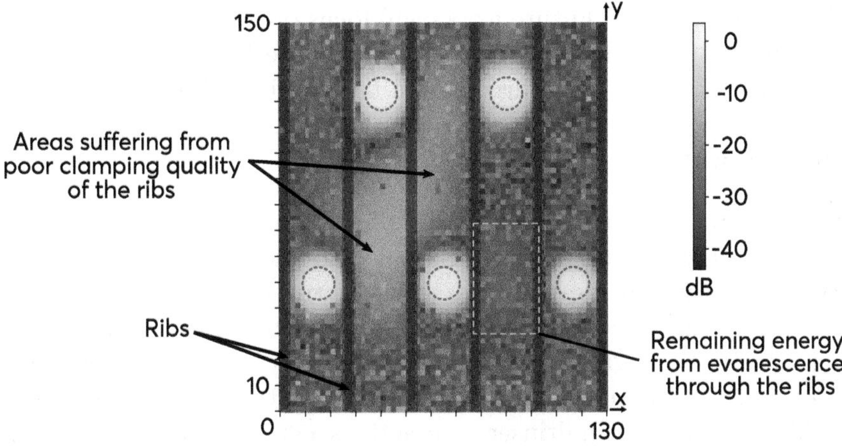

Fig. 5. Energy representation with a logarithmic scale of the plate submitted to 5 activated actuators. Most of the energy is localized above each piezoelectric actuator.

4 Discussion and Perspective

The device shown here can provide localized vibrotactile feedback in several areas of a continuous plate. The confinement is achieved along both axis by low frequency evanescence phenomenon: one based on the geometry of the propagation medium; the other based on the periodically placed supports. This system is particularly unique and there is to our knowledge no setup with such capabilities and we believe that our device offers new possibilities for studying the tactile perception and to develop new interactions. The interface is simple and robust, i.e. it does not require any special signal processing or computation to work and is not impacted by user interaction. However, since evanescent waves are used, the localization of stimuli is only done in the area of each actuator. In order to increase the resolution of such a device, the number of actuators must be multiplied as well as the number of ribs. It raises questions about the control electronics, the power consumption and the available amplitude (sufficient amplitudes cannot be guaranteed with small actuators). Another point that can also be addressed is concerning possible use case of such device. The authors believe that the method in question is easily applicable to medium to large surfaces such as car dashboards. Breitschaft and al. [2] indicates that in the automotive domain four tasks must be performed by tactile interiors: exploration, detection, identification and usage. These tasks are already achievable as is if the method is applied to a thin touch screen (<2 mm). The user can explore the surface freely with one or more fingers or by sliding or tapping or even by placing his hand entirely on the surface without changing its behavior. The detection of the localized stimulus and its identification is ensured by the shape and frequency content of the signal used, which can also be varied according to the position of the fingers if one wants to create areas with different vibratory behaviors. Finally the confirmation action is done by the selected zone by sending a signal with a strong frequency dynamic to simulate a button (this function can be improved by adding a force sensor). Future works will focus on two axes, one dealing with the possibility of thinner ribs and the other on an interface use case, in particular the localization of a vibratory targets on a flat continuous surface.

5 Conclusion

At low frequency, bounded ribbed-plates allow for the localization of vibrotactile stimuli. A piezoelectric actuator bounded to such medium mostly produce evanescent waves which are confined to the actuator covered area as long as the driving frequency is lower than the first cut-off frequency of our system. No control strategies nor signal processing are needed, directly sending the desired signal to the desired actuator suffice in order to obtain a localized vibrotactile stimuli. Multitouch and multiuser interactions can therefore be implemented with ease. Application such as tactile fingerspelling [3], tactile keyboard, tactile memory games and applications using exploratory procedures on a plates can be implemented here. Although the presence of actuators underneath the plate limits applications to surfaces where transparency is not necessary, recent breakthroughs shows that transparent piezoelectric actuators are at hand [9] making our technology compatible with screen surfaces.

Acknowledgment. The revised version of this article benefited from insightful comments from Dr. Sabrina Panëels.

References

1. Ben Dhiab, A., Hudin, C.: Confinement of vibrotactile stimuli in narrow plates: principle and effect of finger loading. IEEE Trans. Haptics (2020)
2. Breitschaft, S.J., Clarke, S., Carbon, C.C.: A theoretical framework of haptic processing in automotive user interfaces and its implications on design and engineering. Front. Psychol. **10**, 1470 (2019)
3. Duvernoy, B., Topp, S., Hayward, V.: "HaptiComm", a haptic communicator device for deafblind communication. In: Kajimoto, H., Lee, D., Kim, S.-Y., Konyo, M., Kyung, K.-U. (eds.) AsiaHaptics 2018. LNEE, vol. 535, pp. 112–115. Springer, Singapore (2019). https://doi.org/10.1007/978-981-13-3194-7_26
4. Enferad, E., Giraud-Audine, C., Giraud, F., Amberg, M., Semail, B.L.: Generating controlled localized stimulations on haptic displays by modal superimposition. J. Sound Vibr. **449**, 196–213 (2019)
5. Hudin, C., Lozada, J., Hayward, V.: Localized tactile feedback on a transparent surface through time-reversal wave focusing. IEEE Tran. Haptics **8**, 188–198 (2015)
6. Mead, D.J.: Free wave propagation in periodically supported, infinite beams. J. Sound Vibr. **11**, 181–197 (1970)
7. Morash, V.S., Pensky, A.E.C., Miele, J.A.: Effects of using multiple hands and fingers on haptic performance. Perception **42**, 759–777 (2013)
8. Pantera, L., Hudin, C.: Multitouch vibrotactile feedback on a tactile screen by the inverse filter technique. IEEE Trans. Haptics (2020)
9. Qiu, C., et al.: Transparent ferroelectric crystals with ultrahigh piezoelectricity. Nature **577**, 350–354 (2020)
10. Wiertlewski, M., Fenton Friesen, R., Colgate, J.E.: Partial squeeze film levitation modulates fingertip friction. PNAS **113**, 9210–9215 (2016)

26

2MoTac: Simulation of Button Click by Superposition of Two Ultrasonic Plate Waves

Pierre Garcia[1,2(✉)], Frédéric Giraud[1], Betty Lemaire-Semail[1], Matthieu Rupin[2], and Michel Amberg[1]

[1] Univ. Lille, Centrale Lille, Arts Et Metiers Institute of Technology, Yncrea Hauts-de France, ULR 2697 L2EP, 59000 Lille, France
{pierre.garcia,frederic.giraud, betty.lemaire-semail,michel.amberg}@univ-lille.fr

[2] Hap2u, 20 Rue du Tour de l'Eau, 38400 Saint-Martin-d'Hères, France
{pierre.garcia,matthieu.rupin}@hap2u.net

Abstract. Recent studies have shown that a button click sensation could be simulated thanks to ultrasonic vibrations. In this context, a travelling wave may enhance the simulation because it creates internal lateral stresses that are released during the stimulation. However, this solution is difficult to integrate on plates. We present 2MoTac, a method which superpose a longitudinal and a bending mode simultaneously on a plate, in order to create a pseudo-travelling wave. We present the design, and a psychophysical study to deduce the optimal ratio between the bending and longitudinal mode amplitudes, in terms of detection threshold and robustness.

Keywords: Haptic display · Tactile perception · Ultrasonic vibration · Vibration mode · Keyclick · Button click

1 Introduction

Most of new human-machine interaction devices now rely on touch screens. They have become so cost effective that physical buttons and knobs are removed and replaced by virtual buttons displayed on the flat and hard surface of the display panel in vending machines, car dashboards, and so on. However, touch screens do not involve the sense of touch in the interaction with the machine: they do not provide information through this channel, unlike physical buttons for instance. Therefore, sight is predominant for whom wants to interact with the aforementioned machines, leading to many disadvantages: elderly and visually-impaired individuals struggle to use touch screens, and drivers must look away from the road, which is a major safety issue in automobile. Therefore, technological improvements to touch screens are needed, in order to involve touch when interacting with a machine through its touch screen.

To create the illusion of touching a button on a panel, lateral displacement [1] or vibrotactile stimulation [11] can be used. The low frequency vibration of the touch screen directly stimulates the skin mechanoreceptors; because this vibration is difficult to contain, [3] identifies the frequency response of the touch screen (FRF) and then uses the frequency that maximises the vibration displacement at a specific point. In [7], the authors invert the FRF and can control the vibration at three different positions where actuators are located. However, using vibrotactile stimulation to create the simulation of a button click has the disadvantage to produce audible noise. To cope with this issue, [10] uses the rapid vibration of a standing wave at ultrasonic frequency, to reduce the internal stresses inside the finger pulp due to the friction that appears when pressing the touchscreen. More robust results are obtained if a net tangential force is produced, by using electroadhesion force synchronized on ultrasonic lateral displacement [15] or by using a travelling wave [6]. These solutions however seem difficult to be integrated on plates, without obstructing the view by actuators.

This paper introduces a new concept of tactile stimulation that uses two orthogonal modes to simulate a button click. The elliptical motion of the particles in contact with the fingertip creates a lateral force as if a travelling wave was used. After presenting the technological principle that derives from [2], a study has been conducted in order to define the ratio between the two modes that optimizes the feeling of a single click when reversing the lateral force direction.

2 Presentation of the Two Modes Stimulation

2.1 Theoretical Background

We consider a plate, which length is L, thickness b and height H. Its vibration can result in the superposition of different types of modes: the longitudinal modes are characterized by the out-of plane translation of the plate's cross-sections while bending modes are characterized by an in-plane translation and an out-of plane rotation of the cross-section, as described in Fig. 1.

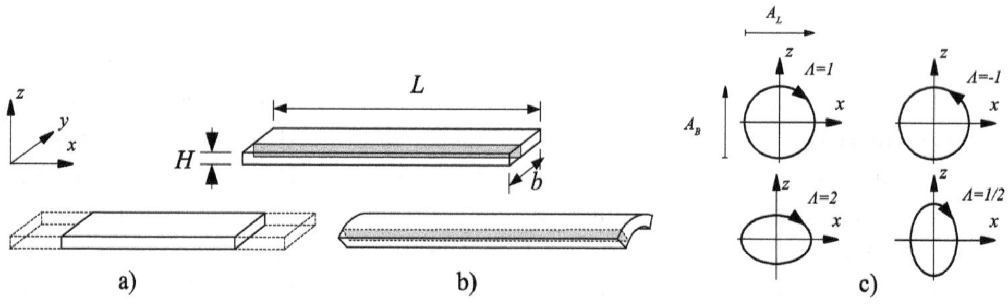

Fig. 1. Vibration mode a) Longitudinal, b) bending and c) Elliptical motion in the middle of the top surface for several values of Λ

When the two modes are produced at the same vibrating frequency, then the point in the middle of the top surface undergoes a displacement which has two components:

- along x, due to the longitudinal mode, denoted $a_L(t)$,
- along z, due to the bending mode, denoted $a_B(t)$.

In this paper, the two modes are energized at the same frequency f, with a phase shift of $\pm\pi/2$. We then write:

$$a_L(t) = \frac{A_L}{2}\sin(2\pi f t) \qquad a_B(t) = \frac{A_B}{2}\cos(2\pi f t) \tag{1}$$

with A_L and A_B the vibration amplitude of each mode (peak-peak); if $A_B < 0$, the phase shift is $\pi/2$. Hence, by combining the two vibration modes, the points at the top surface follow an elliptical motion, which is able to create a net lateral force, as described in [4]. By changing the ratio $\Lambda = \frac{A_L}{A_B}$, the shape of the elliptical trajectory is modified, as described in Fig. 1c), promoting the normal displacement over the longitudinal one for $\Lambda < 1$ and vice versa for $\Lambda > 1$. In the remaining of this paper, we introduce the maximum vibration speed $U_L = 2\pi f A_L$ and $U_B = 2\pi f A_B$ because they combine frequency and displacement.

2.2 Related Work

To produce a button click sensation, [10] uses a rapid change in friction between the fingertip and a plate by increasing or decreasing ultrasonic vibration. The detection threshold of the click is found to be lower if the friction is decreased compared with a friction increased. A fraction of the elastic energy stored in the finger pulp is due to some tangential contact forces that appear during touch. When it is suddenly released, it creates a stimulus that is detectable by the skin's mechanoreceptors. However, the detection thresholds of this click are higher compared with those measured to detect a friction change in presence of a lateral motion of the fingertip [12]. Therefore, [6] suggests to use a travelling wave instead of a standing wave. Indeed, the results show a lower perceptual threshold for travelling waves, and participants press less times per trial and exert smaller normal force on the surface in order to perceive click effect.

Travelling wave can increase the tangential contact forces due to the elliptical motion of the particles that are in contact with the fingertip, thus increasing the stimulus when they are released. Two theories can explain this phenomenon. In [14], the tangential force derives from the contact conditions between a vibrating plate and an elastic medium. In [9], the authors introduce the lateral viscous forces that are generated by a travelling wave, a phenomenon which is compatible with the existence of the squeeze-film. For both theories, the lateral force is a complex function of the normal and tangential displacements of the particles.

In a travelling wave, the ratio Λ between the normal and lateral vibration amplitude is fixed by the geometry of the vibrating plate. To cope for this issue,

[2] presents a prototype that can produce a longitudinal and a bending mode which resonant frequencies are equal. However, the actuator for the longitudinal mode is bulky, while the vibration amplitude of each mode are not controlled. With 2MoTact, the two components U_B and U_L can be independently set, offering the possibility to optimize the tuning of Λ in order to improve the lateral contact forces produced to enhance the click sensation. A study is then conducted in order to determine which ratio is optimal in terms of psychophysical threshold. To compare the thresholds between each other, the stimulation level is defined as $U = \sqrt{U_L^2 + U_B^2}$, which combines the vibration speed for the longitudinal and the bending mode. We include in the study the case of a pure bending mode displacement ($U_L = 0$, $\Lambda = 0$).

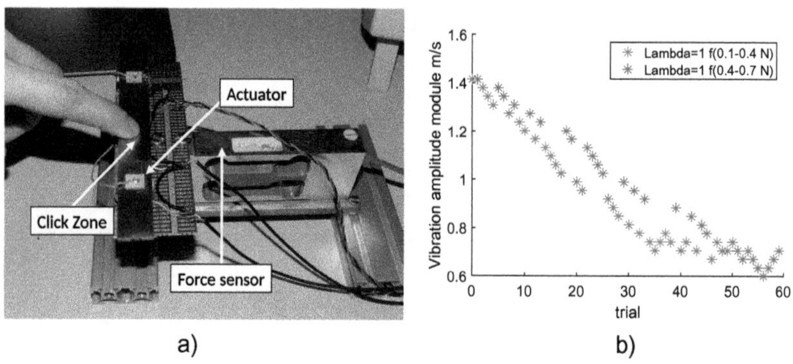

Fig. 2. The Experimental setup a) and typical example of 2 interlaced psychophysical staircases, which targets the 50% perceptual threshold by a one-up one-down test. At each trial, the implemented staircase is chosen at random with a probability of 1/2.

2.3 Design of the Plate

Our prototype consists of a $148 \times 18 \times 2$ mm^3 aluminium plate, actuated by nine piezoelectric ceramic actuators (5 mm $\times$ 7 mm $\times$ 0.5 mm from Noliac, Denmark) as presented Fig. 3c). The plate was designed such that both modes (longitudinal and bending) can be excited at the same frequency (f = 34 kHz). To energize the longitudinal mode, eight actuators placed on the upper and lower side of the plate are used. For the bending mode, only one ceramic placed in the middle of the plate on the lower side is used. Two other ceramic plates (14 mm $\times$ 2 mm $\times$ 0.3 mm, Noliac Denmark) are added as sensors. Two voltage amplifiers (WMA-300 from Falco, The Netherlands) can apply a voltage up to 300 V peak to peak to the actuators' terminals.

The deformation shape for each mode is presented in Fig. 3. Due to the deformation shape for each mode, the ratio Λ is not constant over the top surface, and its value is specified in the middle of the plate. The speed and phase of the vibration of each mode are controlled independently, using the vector control method [4,5]. From the vector control method we can define:

$$U_L = \sqrt{U_{Ld}^2 + U_{Lq}^2} \qquad U_B = \sqrt{U_{Bd}^2 + U_{Bq}^2} \tag{2}$$

For instance, an elliptical motion of the particle with the same vibration speed along x and y of 0.3 m/s is simply obtained by setting the references $U_{Ld} = U_{Bq} = 0.3$ and $U_{Lq} = U_{Bd} = 0$. The closed loop control is embedded into a DSP (STM32F405 from ST Microelectronics). The response time of the vibration speed for both modes is set to about 2 ms as presented in Fig. 3b).

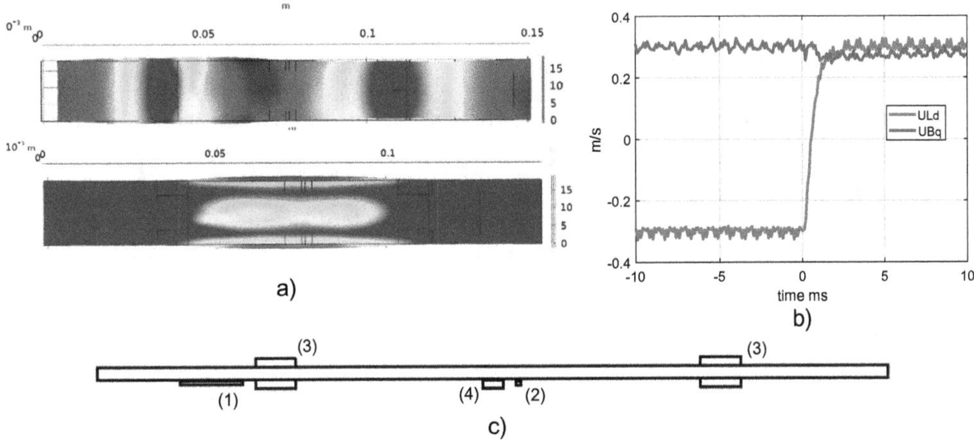

Fig. 3. Measurements on the device; a) deformation mode shape for the longitudinal mode (up) and the bending mode and b) transitory response of the vibration when Λ is switched from -1 to 1 at $U_B = U_L = 0.3$ m/s. c) Side view of the aluminium plate. (1) longitudinal sensor, (2) bending sensor, (3) longitudinal actuator (4) bending actuator

3 Materials and Methods

3.1 Participants

Data were collected from seven healthy volunteers aged between 18 and 40 (3 females). Participants were wearing noise-cancelling headphones in order to prevent noise disturbance. All participants gave written informed consent. The investigation conformed to the principles of the Declaration of Helsinki and experiments were performed in accordance with relevant guidelines and regulations.

3.2 Experimental Set-Up

The plate is mounted on a force sensor that measures the normal force at which a participant presses on the plate as shown in Fig. 2a). The keyclick rendering was performed as in [6]; two normal force thresholds were defined f_1 and $f_2 = f_1 + 0.3N$. When the user reaches f_1, we turn on the two modes, with specific vibration speeds U_L and U_B leading to a value for Λ. When f_2 is reached, the direction of the elliptical motion is reversed simply by inverting U_B. At the end, when the user releases his finger from the surface, we turn off the device. The force is sampled at 10 kHz by the DSP, and a Laptop PC is used to send the threshold value f_1 and the amplitude set points U_B and U_L to the DSP through USB.

3.3 Experimental Procedure

Before starting the experiment we ask the participants to wash their hands and we clean the plate to standardize the surface.

After a training period during when participants could discover the haptic feedback by testing the device at maximum intensity, at different Λ and at two different activation force levels, they had to press once on the middle of the plate with their index finger as shown in Fig. 2. They were asked to say whether they could feel the virtual click or not. The estimation of the psycho-physical threshold was performed with a simple one-up one-down staircase procedure, which targets the 50% performance level on a psychometric function, corresponding to the level at which the probability of a detectable click equals the probability of an undetectable one [8].

As in [6], two force levels $f_1 = [0.1N, 0.4N]$ are interleaved in order to avoid the prediction of the next stimulation intensity. Five different values for $\Lambda = [0.5\ 2/3\ 1\ 1.5\ 2\ \infty]$ were tested. The order of the conditions was pseudo-randomized across participants to avoid learning curve effects. The experiment ended when 6 turnovers or 60 trials were achieved.

4 Results

For all force criteria ($f_1 = [0.1N, 0.4N]$) and vibration ratio $\Lambda = [0\ 0.5\ 2/3\ 1\ 1.5\ 2\ \infty]$ we have computed the median level thresholds which are presented Fig. 4 and in Table 1.

The result shows very different threshold levels, depending on the value of Λ: for $\Lambda \in [1/2\ 2/3\ 1]$, the threshold is close to 0.7 m/s, and doesn't change much with the force level. For $\Lambda \in [1.5\ 2\ \infty]$, the threshold level is higher (around 0.9) and decreases when the force level f_1 increases. Overall, the averaged threshold level is minimal for $\Lambda = 1/2$ if $f_1 = 0.1N$ and for $\Lambda = 1$ when $f_1 = 0.4N$.

Table 1. Experimental results: 50% module threshold for different Λ and different activation pressure levels

		Λ					
f_1		0.5	2/3	1	1.5	2	∞
0.1N	Threshold (m.s-1)	0.73	0.72	0.70	0.98	0.95	0.97
	IQR	0.62–0.77	0.62–0.80	0.65–0.73	0.91–1.06	0.62–0.97	0.94–0.98
	var	0.017	0.027	0.003	0.020	0.033	0.00092
0.4N	Threshold (m.s-1)	0.70	0.75	0.76	0.91	0.87	0.97
	IQR	0.56–0.84	0.64–0.95	0.68–0.77	0.87–1.01	0.68–1.02	0.94–1
	var	0.024	0.023	0.002	0.010	0.019	0.00071

Interestingly, we also compare in Fig. 4c) and d) the variance for each condition. A F-Test ($\alpha = 0.05$, $F_{crit} = 4.28$) have been performed on the variance of threshold level for $\Lambda = 1$ against the others. The results are: for $f_1 = 0.1N$ $\{\Lambda = 0.5$, F = 4.68; $\Lambda = 2/3$, F = 7.34; $\Lambda = 1.5$, F = 5.5; $\Lambda = 2$, F = 8.83$\}$ and for $f_1 = 0.4N$ $\{\Lambda = 0.5$, F = 9.73; $\Lambda = 2/3$, F = 9.42; $\Lambda = 1.5$, F = 4.08; $\Lambda = 2$, F = 7.69$\}$. We observe that for both force conditions, the condition $\Lambda = 1$ produces less variance than other values.

5 Discussion

Our study shows that the elliptical motion of particles can indeed decrease the amount of vibration amplitude that is needed to give the illusion of a button click. Therefore, we can suggest that lateral displacement helps to increase the internal lateral stresses that are first stored when participants touch the plate, before they are released by inverting the direction of the particles' motion. Moreover, we have not seen many differences between the values for $\Lambda \leq 1$ on the detection threshold, and this threshold doesn't change with the force level; the condition $\Lambda = 0$ has been tested but the averaged detection threshold has been found to be higher than the capability of the device. Therefore, we hypothesize that the value of Λ does not change the lateral stresses when in the range $0.5 \leq \Lambda \leq 2/3$. We also show that the variance is minimal for $\Lambda = 1$. Therefore, this gives rise to the optimal value at which the plate should operate. However, for now we do not give an explanation for this specific behaviour; a modelling that takes into account the intermittent contact could be used for that aim [13].

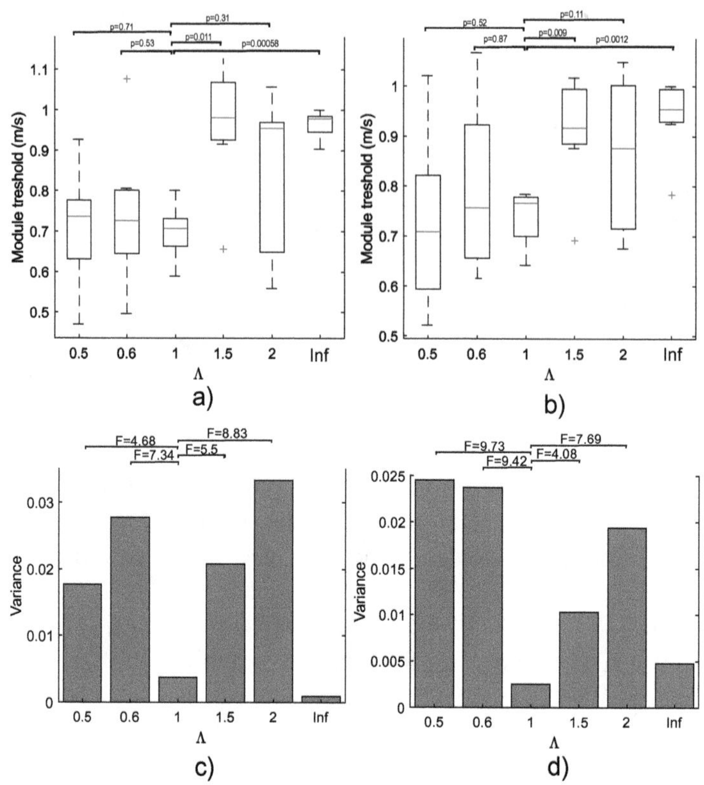

Fig. 4. Experimental results: 50% module threshold, compute for different Λ and different activation pressure levels : a) $f_1 = 0.4N$, b) $f_1 = 0.1$. The error bars, the whisker boxes and the horizontal bars show respectively the min. and max. values, their interquartile range and the median value and corresponding variance c) and d) respectively.

6 Conclusion

In this paper we used two modes simultaneously to produce the simulation of a click on a static finger. To create a simulation with the lowest detection threshold as well as the lowest variance between participants, an equal amount of normal and lateral displacement should be set. This finding will be useful to design and control new tactile interfaces.

Acknowledgement. This work is supported by IRCICA (Research Institute on software and hardware devices for information and Advanced communication, USR CNRS 3380).

References

1. Banter, B.: Touch screens and touch surfaces are enriched by haptic force-feedback. Inf. Display **26**(3), 26–30 (2010)
2. Dai, X., Colgate, J.E., Peshkin, M.A.: Lateralpad: a surface-haptic device that produces lateral forces on a bare finger. In: 2012 IEEE Haptics Symposium (HAPTICS), pp. 7–4, March 2012
3. Emgin, S.E., Aghakhani, A., Sezgin, T.M., Basdogan, C.: Haptable: An interactive tabletop providing online haptic feedback for touch gestures. IEEE Trans. Vis. Comput. Graph. **25**(9), 2749–2762 (2019)
4. Ghenna, S., Vezzoli, E., Giraud-Audine, C., Giraud, F., Amberg, M., Lemaire-Semail, B.: Enhancing variable friction tactile display using an ultrasonic travelling wave. IEEE Trans. Haptics **10**(2), 296–301 (2017)
5. Giraud, F., Giraud-Audine, C.: Piezoelectric Actuators: Vector Control Method. Butterworth-Heinemann, Oxford (2019)
6. Gueorguiev, D., Kaci, A., Amberg, M., Giraud, F., Lemaire-Semail, B.: Travelling ultrasonic wave enhances keyclick sensation. In: Prattichizzo, D., Shinoda, H., Tan, H.Z., Ruffaldi, E., Frisoli, A. (eds.) EuroHaptics 2018. LNCS, vol. 10894, pp. 302–312. Springer, Cham (2018). https://doi.org/10.1007/978-3-319-93399-3_27
7. Hudin, C., Panëels, S.: Localisation of vibrotactile stimuli with spatio-temporal inverse filtering. In: Prattichizzo, D., Shinoda, H., Tan, H.Z., Ruffaldi, E., Frisoli, A. (eds.) EuroHaptics 2018. LNCS, vol. 10894, pp. 338–350. Springer, Cham (2018). https://doi.org/10.1007/978-3-319-93399-3_30
8. Lekk, M.R.: Adaptive procedures in psychophysical research. Percept. Psychophys. **63**, 1279–1292 (2001). https://doi.org/10.3758/BF03194543
9. Minikes, A., Bucher, I.: Noncontacting lateral transportation using gas squeeze film generated by flexural traveling waves–numerical analysis. J. Acoust. Soci. Am. **113**(5), 2464–2473 (2003)
10. Monnoyer, J., Diaz, E., Bourdin, C., Wiertlewski, M.: Ultrasonic friction modulation while pressing induces a tactile feedback. In: Bello, F., Kajimoto, H., Visell, Y. (eds.) EuroHaptics 2016. LNCS, vol. 9774, pp. 171–179. Springer, Cham (2016). https://doi.org/10.1007/978-3-319-42321-0_16
11. Park, G., Choi, S., Hwang, K., Kim, S., Sa, J., Joung, M.: Tactile effect design and evaluation for virtual buttons on a mobile device touchscreen. In: Proceedings of the 13th MobileHCI conference, pp. 11–20 (2011)
12. Saleem, M.K., Yilmaz, C., Basdogan, C.: Psychophysical evaluation of change in friction on an ultrasonically-actuated touchscreen. IEEE Trans. Haptics **11**(4), 599–610 (2018)
13. Torres Guzman, D.A., Lemaire-Semail, B., Kaci, A., Giraud, F., Amberg, M.: Comparison between normal and lateral vibration on surface haptic devices. In: 2019 IEEE World Haptics Conference (WHC), pp. 199–204, July 2019
14. Wallaschek, J.: Contact mechanics of piezoelectric ultrasonic motors. Smart Mater. Struct. **7**(3), 369–381 (1998)
15. Xu, H., Klatzky, R.L., Peshkin, M.A., Colgate, J.E.: Localized rendering of button click sensation via active lateral force feedback. In: 2019 IEEE World Haptics Conference (WHC), pp. 509–514, July 2019

27

Investigating the Influence of Haptic Feedback in Rover Navigation with Communication Delay

Marek Sierotowicz(✉), Bernhard Weber, Rico Belder, Kristin Bussmann, Harsimran Singh, and Michael Panzirsch

Institute of Robotics and Mechatronics, German Aerospace Center, Muenchener Street 20, 82234 Wessling, Germany
marek.sierotowicz@dlr.de

Abstract. Safe navigation on rough terrain in the presence of unforeseen obstacles is an indispensable element of many robotic applications. In such conditions, autonomous navigation is often not a viable option within certain safety margins. Yet, a human-in-the-loop can also be arduous to include in the system, especially in scenarios where a communication delay is present. Haptic force feedback has been shown to provide benefits in rover navigation, also when confronted with higher communication delays. Therefore, in this paper we present the results of a user study comparing various performance metrics when controlling a rover with a car-like interface with and without fictitious force feedback, both with no communication delay and with a delay of 800 ms. The results indicate that with force feedback the navigation is slower, but task performance in the proximity of obstacles is improved.

Keywords: Teleoperation · Rover navigation · Wheeled mobile robot · Haptic feedback · TDPA

1 Introduction

With the renewed interest in manned exploration of celestial bodies, first and foremost the Moon, robot-assisted surface exploration is going to play a major role in the near future in many space programs. In various cases, however, full robot autonomy is not a viable option within certain margins of safety, and higher level commands designed for high communication delays may be overly time consuming and complex. Some form of teleoperation has been shown to be possible in scenarios where the operator has to control the robotic platform from orbit with communication delays in the order of magnitude of a second or more. Therefore, teleoperation is deemed preferable whenever possible in space related tasks involving remote functionalities [1,2]. Different space missions, such as ESA Haptics-1 [3], Kontur-2 [4] and Analog-1 [5], have investigated the feasibility of telemanipulation and telenavigation in microgravity conditions. In [6], a fictitious force feedback principle for high communication delays was developed for the Kontur-2 mission. A space qualified DLR force feedback joystick with two degrees of freedom (DoF) along with a car-like curvature and longitudinal velocity interface was used to access the three planar DoFs of the omni-directional rover. A comparable 2-DoF interface without force feedback was used in the Analog-1 mission in 2019 [7], which involved telenavigation as well as sample picking and placing with an earth-based rover from the ISS at >800 ms round-trip delay. The rover was navigated through relatively obstacle-free environment, such that force-feedback is of minor importance during telenavigation. To name an example in the foreseeable future, a similar interface to the one proposed in [7] is planned to be used in the upcoming *Arches* experiment [8] on mount Etna, albeit with both the pilot and the rover being based on the ground, and with no force feedback. However, some form of corrective feedback is necessary for telenavigation tasks in non-deterministic environments in the presence of communication delays, which otherwise may lead to performance deterioration. Previous studies [9], show the benefits of haptic force feedback in rover navigation in such conditions in terms of collision avoidance. However, introducing a closed loop force feedback can lead to instability at high delays. Different control principles as Routh-Hurwitz [10], Llewellyn approach [11] and Time Domain Passivity Control (TDPA, [12]) have been proposed to guarantee stability in delayed telenavigation with haptic feedback. In [13] and [6], the TDPA was extended for telemanipulation and different types of force feedbacks.

In consideration of these previous studies, we propose that a force feedback setup with a fitting TDPA control can bring more sensible benefits in a complex to navigate physical environment. Therefore, in this paper, we present a user study involving the DLR Joystick [14] and the DLR Lightweight Rover Unit (LRU, [15]) with the goal to evaluate the advantages of telenavigation with fictitious force feedback against telenavigation without force feedback. The TDPA is applied in this work due to its robustness to varying delay, packet loss and jitter. The main goal of this study is to investigate the effects of our force feedback setup on rover navigation in close proximity to physical obstacles.

2 Materials and Methods

2.1 Sample

The user study was conducted with 16 subjects (3 females, 13 males) with an average age of $M = 25.2$ yrs. ($SD = 2.9$ yrs.; range of 21 to 32 yrs.). All of them signed an informed consent form prior to the experimental session.

2.2 Apparatus

Rover. Subjects controlled the LRU wheeled mobile robot (WMR) [15], a prototypical rover system specifically designed for rough terrain. The LRU has 12 DoF, with four wheel actuators, four steering actuators, two series-elastic joints and two joints in the pan-tilt unit (which is equipped with a black-and-white stereo and a colour camera). The total weight is 30 kg with a maximal payload of 5 kg. Two battery packs allow for more than 120 min operation time. The maximal speed is 1.11 m/s. The stereo camera images are processed by performing a dense stereo matching using an FPGA implementation of the so-called Semi-Global Matching (SGM) algorithm [16]. Additionally, the colour camera images are mapped onto the resulting depth image for object detection. The resulting estimates are used for generating a danger map indicating insurmountable obstacles.

Joystick. The DLR's Kontur-2 force feedback joystick [14] was used to drive the rover. The joystick has a 2-DoF, $\pm 20°$ workspace, a maximum force of 15 N and an update rate of 1 kHz. A car-like mapping of the 2 DoFs was implemented, i.e. longitudinal velocity was commanded by moving the joystick forwards and backwards, whereas curvature (steering the LRU's front and back wheels) was commanded by lateral movements of the joystick. In order to navigate, the user has to press the dead-man button on the joystick. In order to switch the current movement direction of the LRU between forward and backward, the user has to press the lower side of the switch on top of the handle.

2.3 Force Feedback Controller

Figure 1 shows the signal flow diagram of a delayed bilateral teleoperator (BT), where T_1 and T_2 are the forward and backward delays, respectively. The coupling controller *Ctrl* ensures that the LRU (slave robot) follows the delayed master reference v_m^{del} and in turn generates a fictitious force F_f, which is felt by the operator through the master haptic-device (DLR's force feedback joystick) after a communication delay.

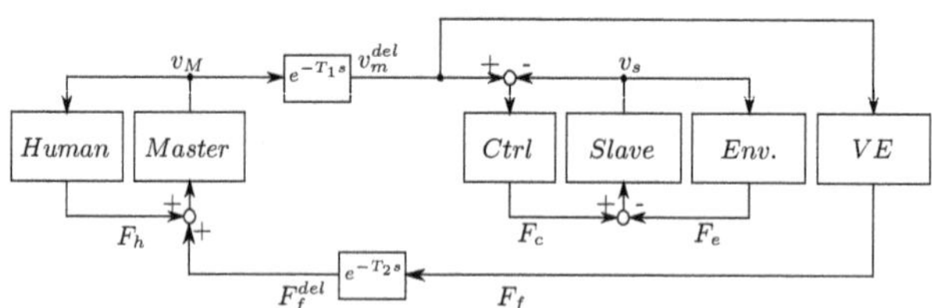

Fig. 1. Signal flow diagram of a bilateral teleoperator with fictitious force feedback

Persuasive force-feedback from the virtual environment VE is produced via the direction dependent curvature polygons P_L and P_R (Fig. 2) overlapping with the danger map (Fig. 3) which is generated using stereo vision. The danger map associates to any pixel (x, y) in the vicinity of the rover a binary danger index $D(x, y)$ (0 if there is no obstacle, 1 if an obstacle is present). The force components are computed according to:

$$F_d \propto \Sigma_{(x,y) \in P_d} D(x, y) \quad \text{for} \quad d = R, L \tag{1}$$

$$F_B \propto \Sigma_{(x,y)\in P_R \cup P_L} D(x,y) = F_L + F_R \quad (2)$$

An equally valid way of describing the calculation of the fictitious force feedback component is considering the obstacles and curvature polygons as sets containing the corresponding pixels on the danger map as elements. This way, the force feedback components can be computed using set operators. Figure 2 uses this notation to show a particular example with the calculation of force components for a specific obstacle and curvature polygon configuration. Notice that the curvature polygons are placed in a manner such that the subscripts of the variables F, P and O are consistent in the shown formulas, rather than respecting the actual right and left side in the rover coordinate frame. Such a system is prone to instability due to the energy generation by the delayed communication channel. In order to passivate the communication channel, Time-Domain-Passivity-Approach (TDPA) was implemented [6]. TDPA introduces adaptive virtual damping elements, both in a series and parallel fashion, at the master and slave side, to dissipate the exact amount of energy necessary to stabilize the overall system.

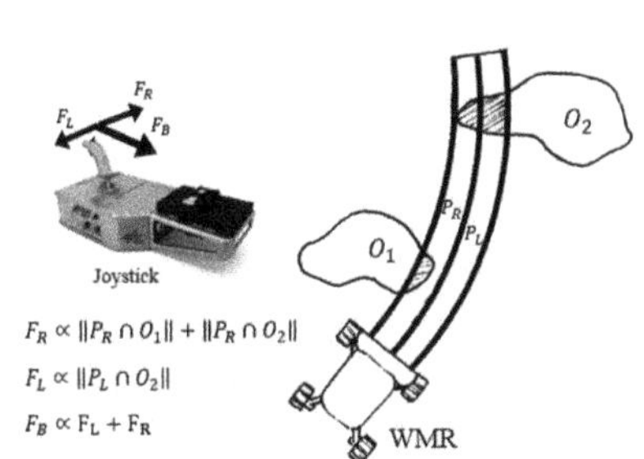

Fig. 2. An example of fictitious force component computation [6]

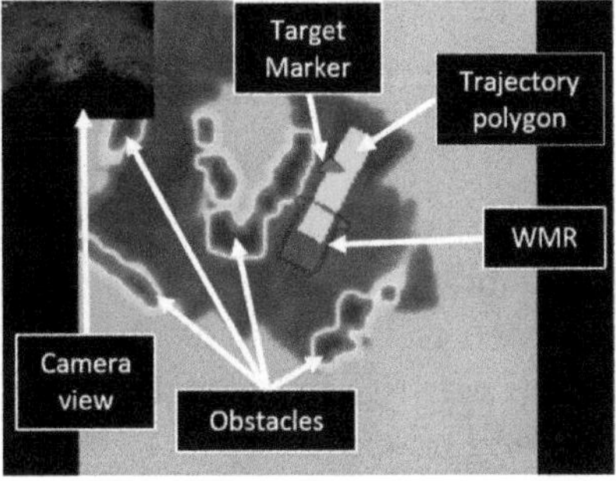

Fig. 3. Screenshot of the user interface showcasing the danger map

2.4 Experimental Task and Design

Participants had to drive the rover along or through different rock formations avoiding collisions (see Fig. 4). One complete experimental trial consisted of three subtasks: 1) navigating the rover through a narrow passage, 2) navigating along a curved rock formation as close as possible to the concave side, 3) navigating as close as possible along a convex boulder (see Fig. 5). Each trial was started from the same, predefined starting position and after having completed subtask 2, the rover was re-positioned by the experimenters to have an optimal starting position for the final subtask.

The two experimental factors Force Feedback (FF vs. noFF) and Delay (0 ms vs. 800 ms) resulted in four experimental conditions. For each condition, there

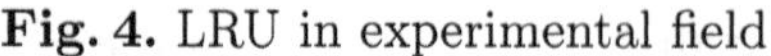

Fig. 4. LRU in experimental field

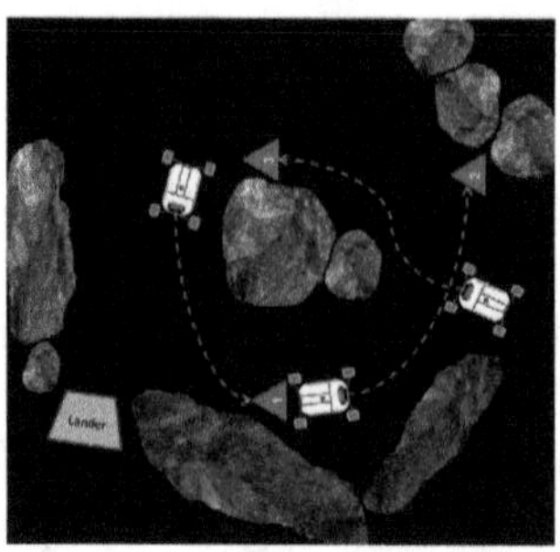

Fig. 5. Schematic subtask representation

were two subsequent experimental trials, for a total of eight trials per subject. While the order of the two force feedback conditions was counterbalanced across subjects, these always started with the no delay condition and then proceeded with the 800 ms delay condition, as pre-tests showed that navigation with 800 ms delay was too demanding for inexperienced users.

2.5 Procedure

First, subjects were given instructions on the experimental task and procedure. They conducted the experiment at a table, sitting on a chair. The joystick was positioned to the right of the subject. Subjects were asked to adjust chair height so that their right arm rested comfortably on the padded arm rest of the joystick module. The experimental GUI (see Fig. 3) was displayed on a 23" monitor in front of the subjects. Since the participants controlled the rover remotely (i.e. from a separated room), the rover's position and a danger map were displayed in the GUI together with a video stream shown in the upper left corner of the window. After having finished two training trials (with force feedback and without delay), the eight trials of the main experiment were started. In the room where the LRU was located, a technician and a supervisor managed the experiment parameters, and provided feedback about collisions and successful reaching of the intermediate milestones for each subtask.

2.6 Measures and Data Analysis

The metrics chosen to assess user performance are the number of actual collisions between rover and obstacles, task completion times, mean rover speed, mean and standard deviation of lateral forces on the master side of the control loop. Additionally, the centroid of all the odometry-measured path points followed by the LRU was used as a reference point in order to obtain the mean radius of curvature at which the subjects drove for subtask 2. For this subtask specifically, this metric can be used to estimate task fulfillment in terms of mean proximity of the followed path to the concave rock formation. For subtask 3, an analogous metric was computed based on the mean minimal distance for each path point from the line connecting the LRU's average starting position for subtask 3 to the centroid of all recorded path points. Data was analysed using a repeated measures ANOVA (rmANOVA) with Force Feedback (FF vs. noFF), Delay (0 ms vs. 800 ms) and Subtask as within factors. See Table 1 for a result overview.

Table 1. Result overview; means, standard deviations (in parentheses) for all experimental conditions and significant ANOVA main effects.

Measure [Unit]		No force feedback		Force feedback		Significant ANOVA effects
		No delay	800 ms	No delay	800 ms	
Collisions [#]		0.19 (0.54)	0.44 (0.81)	0.50 (0.89)	0.13 (0.34)	None
Compl. time [s]	All tasks	75.9 (16.6)	72.9 (34.1)	81.6 (28.6)	82.9 (30.2)	Force feedback:
	Task 1	70.5 (21.4)	82.3 (16.1)	84.5 (60.4)	83.7 (46.2)	$F(1,14) = 3.3$; $p<.10$
	Task 2	74.4 (32.3)	63.0 (34.3)	68.5 (26.8)	63.0 (18.6)	Task:
	Task 3	82.7 (16.1)	73.5 (14.4)	91.6 (25.0)	102 (36.1)	$F(2,28) = 3.7$; $p < .10$
Mean Speed [m/s]		0.13 (0.02)	0.14 (0.03)	0.12 (0.03)	0.12 (0.03)	Force feedback: $F(1,14) = 23.7$; $p < .001$
Mean Force [N]		3.29 (2.32)	3.16 (3.28)	2.67 (1.43)	2.08 (1.59)	Force feedback: $F(1,14) = 7.4$; $p < .05$
SD Force [N]		6.02 (3.13)	5.26 (3.21)	5.36 (2.12)	4.11 (2.47)	Force feedback: $F(1,14) = 8.0$; $p < .05$
Mean radius for subtask 2 [m]		4.62(0.16)	4.68 (0.12)	4.73 (0.15)	4.72 (0.10)	Force feedback: $F(1,14) = 7.1$; $p < .05$
Mean deviation for subtask 3 [m]		2.72 (0.34)	2.75 (0.25)	2.68 (0.33)	2.67 (0.36)	None

3 Results

While no significant effects were evident for the actual collisions, completion times tended to be longer when force feedback (FF) was activated compared to the noFF baseline, although the conventional level significance was not reached ($p < .10$). Similarly, there was a trend for the Subtask factor ($p < .10$). Specifically, completion times were longer for Subtask 1 (80.3 s) and Subtask 3 (87.4 s) compared to subtask 2 (67.2 s). A post-hoc contrast analysis, comparing the effect of FF on vs. off on completion times in each subtask revealed a (marginally) significant effect for subtask 3 only ($t(15) = 2.09$; $p = .05$), i.e. times were longer with FF compared to noFF. No significant differences were found for subtask 1 and 2. The mean speed of the rover was significantly reduced when FF was activated compared to the noFF condition ($p < .001$). The mean as well as the standard deviation (SD) of the lateral mean force was reduced when FF was provided at the joystick (both ps $< .05$). The task number has no observable effect on this metric, i.e. the positive effect of decreased mean and SD of force in the presence of FF was evident for all three subtasks. Finally, we checked the statistical power of the current study design since sample size was comparably small. Post-hoc statistical power analysis showed a power $1 - \beta = .99$ (well above .80 which is the desired probability) for the utilized design, sample and determined effect size.

4 Discussion

The fact that lateral force consistently decreases in the presence of FF for all subtasks indicates less overlap between the control polygon and obstacles on the danger map and therefore a safer navigation. This is to be expected, as the FF would exert forces on the input device inducing the subject to adjust the commanded trajectory in such a way that the overlap with obstacles is minimized. Despite the force feedback, the position drift of the TDPA brings a positive effect which was also found for measured force feedback in the telemanipulation setup of [17]. Since forces only appear in case of overlaps of the polygon with the obstacles, the position drift appears specifically in the presence thereof and prevents the overlap from increasing. In the absence of this feedback, the subjects are unhindered in commanding trajectories which intersect with obstacles.

The mean average velocity is consistently lower in the presence of FF. This indicates that the subjects tended to drive the rover more cautiously in this case. In fact, FF prevents the user to drive at higher velocities. The fact that the radius of curvature for subtask 2 tends to be higher in the presence of FF (ANOVA yields effect significance with $p < .05$), while the number of collision remains constant, shows that FF does provide the driver with information allowing for safe navigation even if closer to the outer rock formation. Interestingly, ANOVA shows no significant effect of the FF/noFF condition on completion time for subtask 1 and 2. When looking at this result, together with the reduced velocity in the presence of FF, this indicates that a more efficient path was followed using FF. Specifically, considering that the mean radius of curvature increases and mean velocity decreases in the presence of FF, the only way of explaining the absence of a significant difference in completion time is to infer that the subjects tended to change the commanded path curvature more often in the absence of FF, thus leading to a less efficient overall trajectory. In subtask 3, no significant effects of the FF condition were observed on the mean distance from the central rock formation. It would therefore seem that the FF/noFF condition has less bearing on navigation performance when confronted with convex structures, such as the one present in subtask 3. However, the lower incidence of lateral force in this subtask with FF, even though task completion was equivalent with or without FF, could be considered an index of safer navigation. These results show that some sensible benefits on rover navigation of using a force feedback setup with a fitting TDPA controller are measurable in a hard to navigate physical environment, even with sensible communication delays.

Acknowledgements. We want to thank Carina Schweiger, Karin Brüch and Margit Kanter for their support while conducting the experiments.

References

1. ISECG. The global exploration roadmap (2018). www.nasa.gov/sites/default/files/atoms/files/ger_2018_small_mobile.pdf. Accessed 20 May 2020

2. ISECG. Telerobotic control of systems with time delay gap assessment report (2018). https://www.globalspaceexploration.org/wordpress/docs/Telerobotic%20Control%20of%20Systems%20with%20Time%20Delay%20Gap%20Assessment%20Report.pdf. Accessed 20 May 2020
3. Schiele, A., et al.: Haptics-1: preliminary results from the first stiffness JND identification experiment in space. In: Bello, F., Kajimoto, H., Visell, Y. (eds.) EuroHaptics 2016. LNCS, vol. 9774, pp. 13–22. Springer, Cham (2016). https://doi.org/10.1007/978-3-319-42321-0_2
4. Artigas, J., et al.: Kontur-2: force-feedback teleoperation from the international space station. In: ICRA, pp. 1166–1173. IEEE (2016)
5. DLR. An astronaut controls a rover on earth (2019). https://www.dlr.de/content/en/articles/news/2019/04/20191125_astronaut-controls-rover-on-earth.html. Accessed 31 January 2020
6. Panzirsch, M., Singh, H., Stelzer, M., Schuster, M.J., Ott, C., Ferre, M.: Extended predictive model-mediated teleoperation of mobile robots through multilateral control. In: IEEE IV, pp. 1723–1730. IEEE (2018)
7. Krueger, T., et al.: How to design a rover cockpit for operation onboard the ISS. In: ASTRA, ESA (2019)
8. Wedler, A., et al.: Analogue research from robex etna campaign and prospects for arches project: advanced robotics for next lunar missions. In: EPSC-DPS Joint Meeting, EPSC (2019)
9. Ma, L., Xu, Z., Schilling, K.: Robust bilateral teleoperation of a car-like rover with communication delay. In: 2009 ECC, pp. 2337–2342. IEEE (2009)
10. Farkhatdinov, I., Ryu, J.-H.: Improving mobile robot bilateral teleoperation by introducing variable force feedback gain. In: International Conference on Intelligent Robots and Systems, pp. 5812–5817. IEEE (2010)
11. Li, W., Liu, Z., Gao, H., Zhang, X., Tavakoli, M.: Stable kinematic teleoperation of wheeled mobile robots with slippage using time-domain passivity control. Mechatronics **39**, 196–203 (2016)
12. Ryu, J.-H., Artigas, J., Preusche, C.: A passive bilateral control scheme for a teleoperator with time-varying communication delay. Mechatronics **20**(7), 812–823 (2010)
13. Van Quang, H., Farkhatdinov, I., Ryu, J.-H.: Passivity of delayed bilateral teleoperation of mobile robots with ambiguous causalities: time domain passivity approach. In: IROS, pp. 2635–2640. IEEE (2012)
14. Riecke, C., et al.: Kontur-2 mission: The DLR force feedback joystick for space telemanipulation from the ISS. In: i-SAIRAS, December 2016
15. Wedler, A., et al.: LRU-lightweight rover unit. In: 2009 ASTRA (2015)
16. Ernst, I., Hirschmüller, H.: Mutual information based semi-global stereo matching on the GPU. In: Bebis, G., et al. (eds.) ISVC 2008. LNCS, vol. 5358, pp. 228–239. Springer, Heidelberg (2008). https://doi.org/10.1007/978-3-540-89639-5_22
17. Panzirsch, M., Singh, H., Krüger, T., Ott, C., Albu-Schäffer, A.: Safe interactions and kinesthetic feedback in high performance earth-to-moon teleoperation. In: IEEE Aerospace Conference (2020)

28

A 6-DoF Zero-Order Dynamic Deformable Tool for Haptic Interactions of Deformable and Dynamic Objects

Haiyang Ding[1(✉)] and Shoichi Hasegawa[2,3,4]

[1] Department of Computational Intelligence and Systems Science, Tokyo Institute of Technology, Tokyo, Japan
haiyang.d.aa@m.titech.ac.jp

[2] Precision and Intelligence Laboratory, Tokyo Institute of Technology, Tokyo, Japan
hase@pi.titech.ac.jp

[3] Independent Administrative Corporation, Tokyo, Japan

[4] Japan Science and Technology Agency (JST), Kawaguchi, Japan

Abstract. Continuous collision detetion is required for haptic interactions with thin and fast-moving objects. However, previous studies failed to eliminate the force artifacts caused by the tool's inertia. In this paper, we propose a multi-sphere proxy method for a 6-DoF deformable virtual tool with continuous collision detection. We use Zero-order Dynamics to avoid force artifacts caused by the tool's inertia. In addition, we eliminate the "tunneling" problem introduced by the use of Zero-order Dynamics. As a result, we support fast motions of both the tool and the virtual object with sphere-mesh-level contacts and real-time simulation. Stability is guaranteed via a position-based dynamics simulator and an optional multi-rate architecture.

Keywords: Haptic rendering · Continuous collision detection · Deformable objects

1 Introduction

Haptic interaction requires accurate collision detection in order to render the contact force between the virtual tool and the virtual environment. The "tunneling" problem, also called the pop-through effect, caused by using discrete collision detection can be avoided by using continuous collision detection (CCD).

Garre et al. [3] presented a deformable 6-DoF tool which was able to interact with deformable objects using CCD. However, they used bidirectional viscoelastic coupling between the device and the tool, which introduced force artifacts caused by the force of the tool's inertia. These artificial forces reduce rendering transparency, and fast motion input from the device may trigger stability problems when interacting with heavy objects.

To the contrary, the traditional proxy method [11] can directly manipulate the proxy position without force artifacts. This simulation method is called Zero-order Dynamics (ZoD) [6].

In this paper, we propose a multi-sphere proxy (MSP) model to achieve 6-DoF haptic interactions with ZoD. In addition, this method is also able to perform CCD by using the method from [2] to handle collisions between the proxy sphere and triangle meshes.

However, ZoD may induce the "tunneling" problem if the collisions are not identified during the constraint computation. In this paper, we perform an additional CCD to solve this problem. Therefore, constraints, such as deformation, can be performed correctly without causing the "tunneling" problem. We list our contributions below:

- An MSP model which enables 6-DoF haptic interactions with dynamic and deformable objects through sphere-mesh-level CCD contacts;
- A ZoD simulation of a deformable 6-DoF haptic tool which eliminates the force artifacts caused by the tool's inertia as well as the "tunneling" problem.

2 Background and Related Works

2.1 Haptic Rendering with Zero-Order Dynamics

ZoD [6] was proposed to describe the simulation of the traditional virtual proxy method [11]. This method uses a virtual finite-radius sphere, i.e., the proxy, to represent a 3-DoF virtual tool. When the device moves, the proxy tries to follow its path via iterative collision detections. If contact occurs, the proxy finds the closest position to the device constrained by contacts. If there is no contact, the proxy tracks the device perfectly. The time integration has no mass or velocity involved.

When considering the dynamics of the 6-DoF haptic tool, many studies use second-order dynamics [3,4] with virtual coupling [10], thus producing force artifacts. Meanwhile, the constraint-based [9] and configuration-based optimization [12] methods can be used to remove force artifacts. However, these methods are limited to rigid tools. Mitra et al. [6,7] used first-order dynamics but position constraints must be transferred into velocity constraints making contact forces difficult to compute.

2.2 Haptic Rendering with Continuous Collision Detection

The traditional virtual proxy method [11] checks just the collisions between the moving proxy and static virtual objects. Therefore, if a dynamic thin virtual object is moving quickly or deforming greatly during one time step and pass through the proxy position, the collision will not be detected.

Ding et al. [2] proposed a method utilizing triangle-proxy CCD and Proxy Pop-out processes to solve this problem. Triangle-proxy CCD computes the CCD between the triangle and the proxy by solving the coplanar condition between the moving triangle and the proxy center. After that, the Proxy Pop-out carries our iterative discrete collision detections between multiple triangular meshes and the proxy sphere. These processes are used to secure the start of the proxy to avoid the "tunneling" problem.

For the CCD used in 6-DoF haptic rendering, Ortega et al. [9] used a constraint-based god-object method for rigid-rigid haptic interactions. Garre et al. [3,4] can simulate deformation on both the tool and the object. Other haptic rendering approaches can be found in the survey [10].

3 Proposal

3.1 Multi-sphere Proxy Model for a Virtual Tool

As described in Sect. 2.2, CCD between the proxy and dynamic triangular models can be computed using a sphere proxy[2]. Here, we extend the method used in [2] via the MSP model.

The Oriented Particles (OP) [8] method uses ellipsoid particles to simulate solid deformations. We directly use the particles of the OP model as our MSP model. The particle of the virtual tool is called the tool particle, and the particle representing the device is called the device particle. Since we apply CCD and proxy method described in [2] for each tool particle, we use spherical particles instead of ellipsoids for better performance. However, since ellipsoids can be used to represent a more precise contact model compared to spheres, it will be interesting to conduct further research using ellipsoids.

Since the number of tool particles is related directly to both collision accuracy and simulation speed, collision accuracy and system efficiency should be balanced. In this paper, we use the same method as [8] to create the OP model. An example is shown in Fig. 3.

This method is similar to that employed in [1] and [12], which also utilize spheres. However, their methods cannot handle CCD contact between the sphere and the triangular mesh, and method in [1] cannot avoid force artifacts caused by the tool's inertia.

3.2 Six Degree-of-Freedom Haptic Rendering

Force and Torque Feedback. We calculate the force and torque feedback from the discrepancy between the virtual tool and the device. As shown in Fig. 1, we first calculate force and torque of each pair of tool and device particles. Only the particles that have collided are considered in the calculation. Next, we sum all the forces and all the torques, respectively. Finally, we divide each of these sums by the total number of tool particles. We use translational and rotational springs to adjust the feedback magnitude.

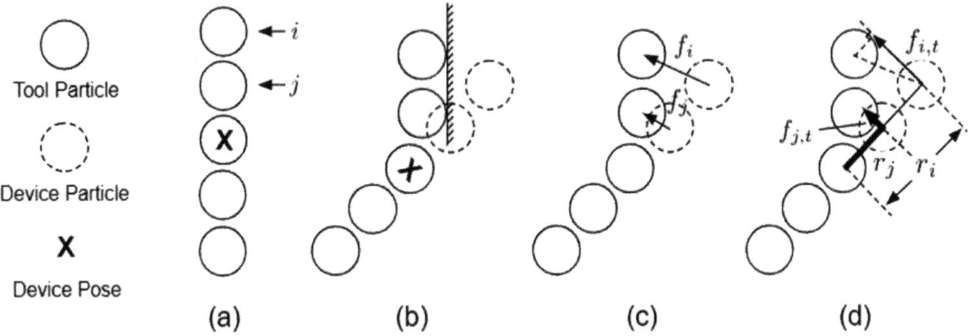

Fig. 1. Force and torque calculation of the multi-sphere Proxy model. (a) The start. (b) The deformable tool encounters a contact. (c) The force $\mathbf{f}_i$ and $\mathbf{f}_j$ and, (d) the torque $\mathbf{r}_i \times \mathbf{f}_{i,t}$ and $\mathbf{r}_j \times \mathbf{f}_{j,t}$ of tool particle i and j, respectively.

Haptic Contact Force Computation. The contact force applied to the virtual object is computed using the method in [2], which uses a distributed point-like contact force applied as an external force of PBD to the corresponding OP particle of the virtual object.

Multi-rate Architecture. To improve interaction stability, we use a multi-rate architecture. First, we simply synchronize all the tool particle positions from the physics thread to the haptic thread. The feedback force and torque are calculated in the haptic thread. However, the delay caused by synchronization may induce "dragging" forces. Therefore, we also synchronize the collision information (collision occurs or not) to eliminate the force artifacts when no contact occurs.

3.3 Zero-Order Dynamic Deformable Haptic Tool

As introduced in Sect. 2.2, the traditional proxy method [11] uses ZoD to avoid force artifacts. We achieve ZoD by manipulating the position of the tool particle directly with a position-based haptic constraint.

Haptic Constraint. The haptic constraint helps us to apply the haptic device input to the virtual tool by computing current position of the device particle as the goal position. The computation is as follows:

$$\mathbf{g}_i = Q_{dev}\mathbf{o}_i + \mathbf{d}_{dev}. \tag{1}$$

Here, $\mathbf{o}_i$ represents the tool particle's original barycentric coordinates before deformation, while Q_{dev} and $\mathbf{d}_{dev}$ represent for the device's orientation matrix (3×3) and position, respectively. The variable with a bold font refers to a 3×1 vector.

After the goal position is computed, we perform the traditional proxy method [11] to update tool particles to the goal positions, i.e., the positions of device particles (shown in Fig. 2(b)).

The "Tunneling" Problem Caused by Constraints. Since we use a stiff haptic constraint in PBD, it cancels the effect of the other constraints. To solve this problem, we apply the haptic constraint only once before the other constraints. Therefore, the other constraints, e.g., the deformation constraint, can be performed correctly.

However, if we perform the constraint calculation, the result may violate the collision constraints and cause the "tunneling" problem (shown in Fig. 2(c)). Unfortunately, it is impossible to identify all of the collision constraints ahead in the proxy method collision detection we executed when applying the haptic constraint since they have different starts and goals.

Solving the "Tunneling" Problem. To solve the "tunneling" problem caused by the constraint calculation, our proposal is to run an additional CCD, which is the same as the proxy method, for the constraint calculation (shown in Fig. 2(d)) to revise the particle positions. In order to do so, we record the tool particle positions before and after the PBD constraint calculation. After that, we perform the proxy method between the recorded start and end. The whole progress is shown in Fig. 2.

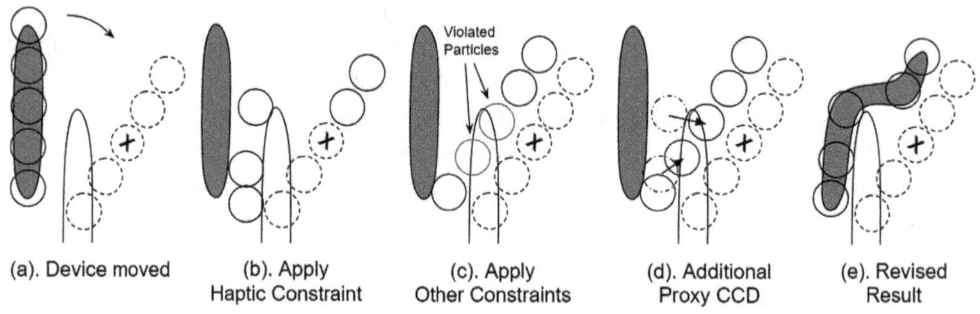

Fig. 2. Simulation of a zero-order dynamic deformable haptic tool

3.4 Simulation of a Zero-Order Dynamic Deformable Haptic Tool

Our simulation loop of the physics thread is executed as follows:

1. Physics thread start:
2. Simulate the virtual tool:
   (a) Perform triangle-CCD and Proxy Pop-out for tool particles; (Sect. 2.2)
   (b) Calculate and apply haptic constraint; (Sect. 3.3)
   (c) Perform the traditional proxy method for each tool particle;
   (d) Record current tool particle positions;
   (e) Perform and recored the result of other PBD constraint iterations;
   (f) Perform proxy CCD with the recorded start and end; (Sect. 3.3)

   (g) Update the tool particle position;
   (h) Calculate haptic contact forces; (Sect. 3.2)
3. Apply haptic contact forces as external forces to the contact object;
4. Simulate the other virtual objects.

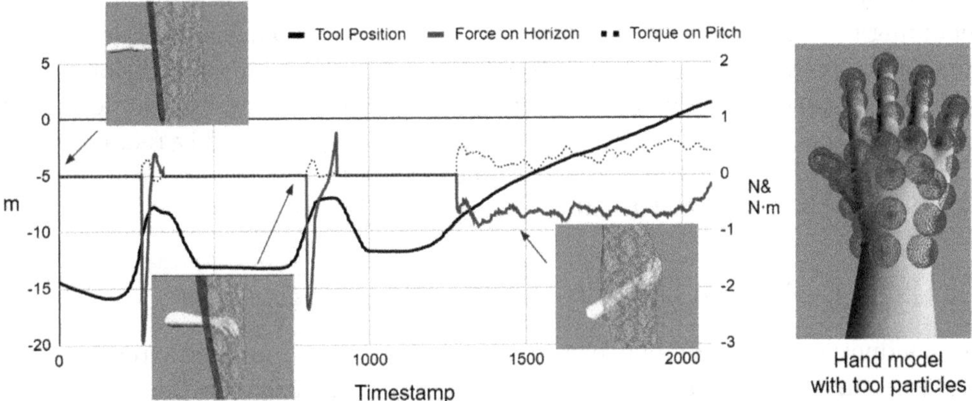

Fig. 3. Evaluation of interactions. Left: the recorded tool position, feedback force, and torque are presented with screenshots of a deformable hand interacting with a yellow curtain. Right: the hand model and its tool particles with the proxy radius. (Color figure online)

4 Evaluations

In this section, we will introduce two evaluations of our method. The evaluations were performed on an Intel i5-7300 4-core CPU PC without GPU. A Spidar-G6 was used as the haptic device. We also provide a supplementary video.

4.1 The Evaluation of Interactions and Efficiency

In this evaluation, we used a deformable 1 kg hand model [5] as the tool to interact with a double-faced, 8-m, 200 g curtain model. The curtain model contained 1089 vertices and 4096 triangles, while each vertex was modeled with one OP particle and connected with another eight nearby particles. The hand model had 3919 vertices and 3906 triangles with 37 OP particles (the placement of the tool particles can be further optimized). Only shape-matching and distance constraints were simulated for the two models. The PBD iteration counts were two and four for the curtain and the hand models, respectively. The feedback springs were both set to 20 N/m. No damping of virtual coupling was used.

The result is displayed in Fig. 3. A series of interactions were performed, including tapping and pressing, on the curtain model. From Fig. 3, we can see that the tool moved freely in the air without the force caused by the inertia. The system was stable even fast motions were inputted with strong impacts while the tool and the device deformation were performed correctly. The whole simulation took 2.5 s. The data was collected from the haptic thread which was running at 1kHz, while one time-stamp indicated one loop of the calculation.

The simulation ran at an average rate from 45 to 59 FPS, depended on the collision number. The calculation of the PBD constraints took 4 ms. The CCD, including triangle-proxy CCD and Proxy Pop-out, required 3 ms, while the two runs of the proxy method required 8 to 12 ms depending on the collision count. We used a basic pruning method which ignored far-off meshes (at least 1 m from every tool particle). The computational efficiency was highly related to the number of tool particles; therefore, we also ran a test of this scene using tool particles numbering from 1 to 50 (illustrated in Fig. 4(a)).

4.2 The Evaluation of Multi-rate Haptic Rendering

We conduct a comparison between multi-rate and single-rate haptic rendering to evaluate the force artifacts caused by multi-rate simulation. In this evaluation, the device slid along a virtual horizontal plane using the same hand model of the first evaluation. The results in Fig. 4(b) and (c) show that the horizontal "dragging" forces (forces on X and Z axis) arise only in the multi-rate case as the device moves. During our tests, the magnitude of the force artifacts was proportional to the computation time of the physics simulation.

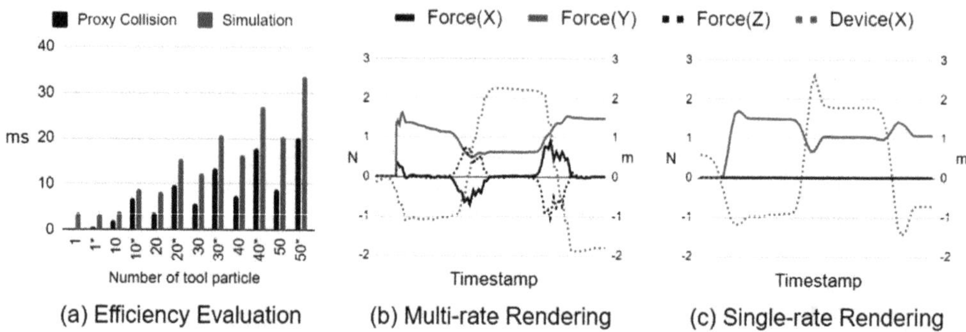

Fig. 4. Evaluation of efficiency (a) and Comparison Between Multi-Rate (b) and Single-Rate (c) Haptic Rendering. The efficiency evaluation utilized the average computation time for the simulation and proxy method using 1 to 50 tool particles. The label with "*" indicates collisions are occurred in the simulaiton while others are not.

5 Conclusion, Limitations, and Future Works

We propose a 6-DoF deformable tool that can interact with another deformable virtual object. The contact is handled between spherical proxies and triangular meshes. The force artifacts caused by the tool's inertia were eliminated, and tool deformation was performed without the "tunneling" problem. Our simulation is stable even with fast motion input using a large feedback spring. We also provide a multi-rate haptic rendering option which improves the stability but induces other force artifacts.

Compared to other studies, our system uses a less accurate contact tool model compared to the one in [3], in which the tool has 1441 triangular meshes for collision detection (not sure about the deformable object). The hand model we used in the evaluations does not have a rigid-body or joint constraint; therefore, the physics behavior of the hand model is less accurate than that used in [3]. Also, as we represent the tool with spherical particles, objects that are thinner than the gap between particles may result in penetrations. In the future, we plan to find solutions to cover this gap and use ellipsoids to handle accurate contacts.

Acknowledgment. This work was support by JSPS KAKENHI Grant Number 17H01774. Here, we are also grateful to the support of Springhead physical engine and the developers.

References

1. Cirio, G., Marchal, M., Otaduy, M.A., Lécuyer, A.: Six-oof haptic interaction with fluids, solids, and their transitions. In: 2013 World Haptics Conference (WHC), pp. 157–162. IEEE (2013)
2. Ding, H., Mitake, H., Hasegawa, S.: Continuous collision detection for virtual proxy haptic rendering of deformable triangular mesh models. IEEE Trans. Haptics **12**(4), 624–634 (2019)
3. Garre, C., Hernández, F., Gracia, A., Otaduy, M.A.: Interactive simulation of a deformable hand for haptic rendering. In: 2011 IEEE World Haptics Conference, pp. 239–244. IEEE (2011)
4. Garre, C., Otaduy, M.A.: Haptic rendering of objects with rigid and deformable parts. Comput. Graph. **34**(6), 689–697 (2010)
5. gotferdom: Free hand 3D model (2018). https://www.turbosquid.com/3d-models/hand-hdri-shader-3d-model-1311775. Accessed 25 Jan 2020
6. Mitra, P., Niemeyer, G.: Dynamic proxy objects in haptic simulations. In: 2004 IEEE Conference on Robotics, Automation and Mechatronics, vol. 2, pp. 1054–1059. IEEE (2004)
7. Mitra, P., Niemeyer, G.: Haptic simulation of manipulator collisions using dynamic proxies. Presence Teleoperators Virtual Environ. **16**(4), 367–384 (2007)
8. Müller, M., Chentanez, N.: Solid simulation with oriented particles. ACM Trans. Graph. **30**, 92 (2011)
9. Ortega, M., Redon, S., Coquillart, S.: A six degree-of-freedom god-object method for haptic display of rigid bodies. In: IEEE Virtual Reality Conference (VR 2006), pp. 191–198. IEEE (2006)
10. Otaduy, M.A., Garre, C., Lin, M.C.: Representations and algorithms for force-feedback display. Proc. IEEE **101**(9), 2068–2080 (2013)
11. Ruspini, D.C., Kolarov, K., Khatib, O.: The haptic display of complex graphical environments. In: Proceedings of the 24th Annual Conference on Computer Graphics and Interactive Techniques, pp. 345–352 (1997)

Permissions

All chapters in this book were first published by Springer; hereby published with permission under the Creative Commons Attribution License or equivalent. Every chapter published in this book has been scrutinized by our experts. Their significance has been extensively debated. The topics covered herein carry significant findings which will fuel the growth of the discipline. They may even be implemented as practical applications or may be referred to as a beginning point for another development.

The contributors of this book come from diverse backgrounds, making this book a truly international effort. This book will bring forth new frontiers with its revolutionizing research information and detailed analysis of the nascent developments around the world.

We would like to thank all the contributing authors for lending their expertise to make the book truly unique. They have played a crucial role in the development of this book. Without their invaluable contributions this book wouldn't have been possible. They have made vital efforts to compile up to date information on the varied aspects of this subject to make this book a valuable addition to the collection of many professionals and students.

This book was conceptualized with the vision of imparting up-to-date information and advanced data in this field. To ensure the same, a matchless editorial board was set up. Every individual on the board went through rigorous rounds of assessment to prove their worth. After which they invested a large part of their time researching and compiling the most relevant data for our readers.

The editorial board has been involved in producing this book since its inception. They have spent rigorous hours researching and exploring the diverse topics which have resulted in the successful publishing of this book. They have passed on their knowledge of decades through this book. To expedite this challenging task, the publisher supported the team at every step. A small team of assistant editors was also appointed to further simplify the editing procedure and attain best results for the readers.

Apart from the editorial board, the designing team has also invested a significant amount of their time in understanding the subject and creating the most relevant covers. They scrutinized every image to scout for the most suitable representation of the subject and create an appropriate cover for the book.

The publishing team has been an ardent support to the editorial, designing and production team. Their endless efforts to recruit the best for this project, has resulted in the accomplishment of this book. They are a veteran in the field of academics and their pool of knowledge is as vast as their experience in printing. Their expertise and guidance has proved useful at every step. Their uncompromising quality standards have made this book an exceptional effort. Their encouragement from time to time has been an inspiration for everyone.

The publisher and the editorial board hope that this book will prove to be a valuable piece of knowledge for researchers, students, practitioners and scholars across the globe.

List of Contributors

Hirobumi Tomita and Shin Takahashi
University of Tsukuba, 1-1-1 Tennodai, Tsukuba, Ibaraki, Japan

Satoshi Saga
Kumamoto University, 2-39-1, Kurokami, Chuo-ku, Kumamoto, Japan

Emiri Sakiyama and Atsushi Matsubayashi
The University of Tokyo, 7-3-1 Hongo, Bunkyo-ku, Tokyo, Japan

Aysien Ivanov, Daria Trinitatova and Dzmitry Tsetserukou
Skolkovo Institute of Science and Technology (Skoltech), Moscow 121205, Russia

Jonathan Tirado, Vladislav Panov and Dzmitry Tsetserukou
Skolkovo Institute of Science and Technology (Skoltech), Moscow 121205, Russia

Vibol Yem
Tokyo Metropolitan University, Tokyo, Japan

Georgios Korres and Mohamad Eid
Engineering Division, New York University Abu Dhabi, Abu Dhabi, United Arab Emirates

Satoshi Tanaka, Keigo Ushiyama, Akifumi Takahashi and Hiroyuki Kajimoto
The University of Electro-Communications, 1-5-1 Chofugaoka, Chofu, Tokyo, Japan

Takeshi Tanabe, Hiroshi Endo and Shuichi Ino
Human Informatics Research Institute, National Institute of Advanced Industrial Science and Technology (AIST), Central 6, 1-1-1 Higashi, Tsukuba, Ibaraki 305-8566, Japan

Hiroaki Yano and Hiroo Iwata
Faculty of Engineering, Information and Systems, University of Tsukuba, 1-1-1 Tennodai, Tsukuba, Ibaraki 305-8577, Japan

Suhas Kakade and Subhasis Chaudhuri
Department of Electrical Engineering, Indian Institute of Technology Bombay, Mumbai, India

M. Marchal
Univ. Rennes, INSA, IRISA, Inria, CNRS, Rennes, France
IUF, Paris, France

G. Gallagher and A. Lécuyer
Inria, Univ. Rennes, IRISA, Rennes, France

C. Pacchierotti
CNRS, Univ. Rennes, Inria, IRISA, Rennes, France

Aldo F. Contreras-González, José Luis Samper-Escudero, David Pont-Esteban, Francisco Javier Sáez-Sáez, Miguel Ángel Sanchez-Urán and Manuel Ferre
Centre for Automation and Robotics (CAR) UPM-CSIC, Universidad Politécnica de Madrid, 28006 Madrid, Spain

Seunggoo Rim, Shun Suzuki, Yutaro Toide, Masahiro Fujiwara, Yasutoshi Makino, Hiroyuki Shinoda and Daichi Matsumoto
The University of Tokyo, 5-1-5 Kashiwanoha, Kashiwa-shi, Chiba-ken 277-8561, Japan

Kentaro Arig
Graduate School of Information Science and Technology, The University of Tokyo, Tokyo, Japan

Masahiro Fujiwara, Yasutoshi Makino and Hiroyuki Shinoda
Graduate School of Information Science and Technology, The University of Tokyo, Tokyo, Japan
Graduate School of Frontier Sciences, The University of Tokyo, Chiba, Japan

William Frier and Orestis Georgiou
Ultraleap Ltd., Bristol, UK

Noor Alakhawand, Kipp McAdam Freud and Nathan F. Lepora
Department of Engineering Mathematics, University of Bristol, Bristol, UK
Bristol Robotics Laboratory, Bristol, UK

Komi Chamnongthai, Takahiro Endo, Shohei Ikemura and Fumitoshi Matsuno
Kyoto University, Kyoto 615-8540, Japan

Atsushi Matsubayashi
The University of Tokyo, Tokyo, Japan

Alireza Abbasimoshaei and Thorsten A. Kern
University of Technology, Harburg Hamburg Eissendorferstr. 38, 21073 Hamburg, Germany

Majid Mohammadimoghaddam
Tarbiatmodares University, Amirabad, 14115 Tehran, Iran

Julian Seiler, Niklas Schäfer, Bastian Latsch, Romol Chadda, Markus Hessinger and Mario Kupnik
Technische Universität Darmstadt, Measurement and Sensor Technology, Merckstraße 25, 64283 Darmstadt, Germany

Philipp Beckerle
Technische Universität Dortmund, Robotics Research Institute, Otto-Hahn-Straße 8, 44227 Dortmund, Germany
Technische Universität Darmstadt, Institute for Mechatronic Systems, Otto-Berndt-Straße 2, 64287 Darmstadt, Germany

Kouta Minamizawa
Keio University, Tokyo, Japan

Charles Hudin
CEA, LIST, 91191 Gif-sur-Yvette, France
CEA, LIST, Sensory and Ambient Interfaces Laboratory, Palaiseau, France

Marek Sierotowicz, Bernhard Weber, Rico Belder, Kristin Bussmann, Harsimran Singh and Michael Panzirsch
Institute of Robotics and Mechatronics, German Aerospace Center, Muenchener Street 20, 82234 Wessling, Germany

Ayoub Ben Dhiab
CEA, LIST, 91191 Gif-sur-Yvette, France

Kazuki Katayama and Yoshihiro Tanaka
Nagoya Institute of Technology, Nagoya, Japan

Maria Pozzi and Domenico Prattichizzo
University of Siena, Siena, Italy
Istituto Italiano di Tecnologia, Genoa, Italy

Daniele Leonardis, Massimiliano Gabardi, Massimiliano Solazzi and Antonio Frisoli
Percro Laboratory, Scuola Superiore Sant'Anna of Pisa, Pisa, Italy

Lucie Pantera and Sabrina Panëels
CEA, LIST, Sensory and Ambient Interfaces Laboratory, Palaiseau, France

Frédéric Giraud and Betty Lemaire-Semail and Michel Amberg
Univ. Lille, Centrale Lille, Arts Et Metiers Institute of Technology, Yncrea Hauts-de France, ULR 2697 L2EP, 59000 Lille, France

Pierre Garcia
Univ. Lille, Centrale Lille, Arts Et Metiers Institute of Technology, Yncrea Hauts-de France, ULR 2697 L2EP, 59000 Lille, France
Hap2u, 20 Rue du Tour de l'Eau, 38400 Saint-Martin-d'Hères, France

Matthieu Rupin
Hap2u, 20 Rue du Tour de l'Eau, 38400 Saint-Martin-d'Hères, France

Chiara Gaudeni and Tommaso Lisini Baldi
Department of Information Engineering and Mathematics, University of Siena, Siena, Italy

Gabriele M. Achilli
Department of Engineering, University of Perugia, Perugia, Italy

Marco Mandalà
Department of Medicine, Surgery and Neuroscience, University of Siena, Siena, Italy

Anna Metzger and Knut Drewing
Justus-Liebig University of Giessen, Giessen, Germany

Domenico Prattichizzo
Department of Information Engineering and Mathematics, University of Siena, Siena, Italy
Department of Advanced Robotics, Istituto Italiano di Tecnologia, Genoa, Italy

Yamato Miyatake, Takefumi Hiraki, Daisuke Iwai and Kosuke Sato
Osaka University, Toyonaka, Osaka, Japan

Tomosuke Maeda
Toyota Central R&D Labs., Inc., Nagakute, Aichi, Japan

Kenichi Ito, Yuki Ban and Shin'ichi Warisawa
Graduate School of Frontier Sciences, The University of Tokyo, Chiba 2770882, Japan

Haiyang Ding
Department of Computational Intelligence and Systems Science, Tokyo Institute of Technology, Tokyo, Japan

Shoichi Hasegawa
Precision and Intelligence Laboratory, Tokyo Institute of Technology, Tokyo, Japan
Independent Administrative Corporation, Tokyo, Japan
Japan Science and Technology Agency (JST), Kawaguchi, Japan

Index